insistence of rapid transport, and the new appeal of entertainment spirituality. How will the aesthetic traditions of the old temples fare as Vrindavan becomes a virtual theme park? As a seventy-story temple is planned to bring world attention to the pastoral land of Krishna? Hawley tackles these discouraging developments with zest and scholarly authority. He brings into his narrative the voices of ambitious developers and of women, the widows of Vrindavan, for whom the new dispensation is not so bad. And with his own narrative he tracks the profound and singular voice of Shrivatsa Goswami, a traditional yet modern religious leader and friend whose biography spans these crucial decades from the old world to the new, from the horse-cart to the iPhone. Hawley and Goswami, in their different ways, make clear that Vrindavan is not alone in finding its cultural heritage submerged by the very hunger that draws pilgrims to it. This beloved place is a particularly poignant test of whether a global future can find a spiritual homeland without making it into a spiritual Disneyland.

—**Diana L. Eck, Professor of Comparative Religion and Hindu Studies, Director, The Pluralism Project, Harvard University**

A model study of the transformation of a sacred space during these—what to call it?— virtual or anthropocene or obscene times. It is a very readable and highly accessible book that will certainly interest general readers ... as well as those who have fallen in love with Vrindavan, both Indians and foreigners.

—**David L. Haberman, Professor, Department of Religious Studies, Indiana University**

This ambitious work addresses most brilliantly the sea-change that is being visited upon Vrindavan, both as a place and as a religious idea. The book is based on the deepest and widest erudition relating to the history of bhakti in India. In an almost painful sense the book constitutes a necessary complement to that work, for as the author's canary-in-the-cage metaphor suggests, what happens in this center of devotionalism betokens likely change all over the religious map of South Asia. ... Such changes extend far beyond India herself; for Hinduism is not alone in deriving its semblance of 'good taste' from a certain kind of safe antiquity, only to see this threatened by the impact of modernity in its many forms. ... Each of the chapters adds a radically new perspective to the whole. ... Throughout, one gains a sense of the dynamism of the situation: the very function and design of the skyscraper temple mutates as we read, and the reader is implicitly invited to watch news or internet headlines for further developments. *Krishna's Playground* will be required reading for anyone interested in religious history, in bhakti, and in development writ large.

—**Rupert Snell, Professor Emeritus, Department of Asian Studies, The University of Texas at Austin**

KRISHNA'S
PLAYGROUND

KRISHNA'S PLAYGROUND

Vrindavan in the 21st Century

JOHN STRATTON HAWLEY

OXFORD
UNIVERSITY PRESS

OXFORD
UNIVERSITY PRESS

Oxford University Press is a department of the University of Oxford.
It furthers the University's objective of excellence in research, scholarship,
and education by publishing worldwide. Oxford is a registered trademark of
Oxford University Press in the UK and in certain other countries.

Published in India by
Oxford University Press
22 Workspace, 2nd Floor, 1/22 Asaf Ali Road, New Delhi 110002, India

© Oxford University Press 2020

The moral rights of the author have been asserted.

First Edition published in 2020

ISBN-13 (print edition): 978-0-19-012398-7
ISBN-10 (print edition): 0-19-012398-2

ISBN-13 (eBook): 978-0-19-099134-0
ISBN-10 (eBook): 0-19-099134-8

Typeset in ScalaPro 10/13
by Tranistics Data Technologies, Kolkata 700 091
Printed in India by Replika Press Pvt. Ltd

In memory of Robyn Beeche

Contents

Acknowledgments

No book writes itself and none really has a single author, but this book is even more interactive than most. It is almost wholly built on observation and conversation; it's a part of the world it describes. This means I am deeply indebted not just to colleagues, mentors, and helpers, but to the world of Vrindavan at large, including a whole set of people whose names I do not even know. Take for instance the woman whose folded hands and beautifully age-inflected face beckoned me to take her picture as she sat along one of Vrindavan's main roads. You can see her in the last image accompanying Chapter 3. Wares spread out on the table beside her, she was watching the scene as I was, and though we did not talk to each other—never "met", as people say—she was in that silent moment a fellow traveler, someone whose perspective informed mine. I am grateful.

Hundreds of others join her at levels of more specific engagement. You will see many of their names in the notes, but let me mention some without whom the book simply could have not come into being. First of all, there's Shrivatsa Goswami, my wise and gentle guide for more than four decades, the person who brought me to Vrindavan in the first place. There's also the entire Goswami family to which he belongs, including those who serve them. As this book took shape, the members of this distinguished, outward-looking family ranged in age from 94 to 2½. Among them I am particularly indebted to Abhinav and Suvarna Goswami, for expert help with beautiful photographs and timely information on the ground. Vishnupriya Goswami, in the next generation down, makes a cameo appearance in Chapter 4.

There are many, many more—priests, patrons, and interpreters in Vrindavan's temples and ashrams; workers like Chandrakant Gupta, who welcomed me to the town's principal sewage treatment plant one day when I dropped in out of the blue; Mohini Giri, Meera Khanna, and their associates at the Ma Dham Ashram and Guild for Service; Chandi Heffner, my improbable countrywoman; and religious leaders such as Swami Vishwananda, Paramadvaiti Swami, and Satyanarayan Das. No less important were people such as Revatikaant, Vishwamohini (I use shorthand in each case), Usha Garg, and Robert Lindsey, who taught me what it meant to be active in their communities and shared their reflections on what it meant. Jan "Jagat" Brzezinski was an unfailing source of historical and contemporary perspective, both in his personal capacity and as the editor of *Vrindavan Today*. Manpreet Kaur gave the project an invaluable kick-start in a brief but extremely productive trip to Vrindavan in 2015. Throughout the project I have benefited from the thoughtful generosity of people connected with the Vrindavan Chandrodaya Mandir. From Chanchalapati Das, Madhu Pandit Das, and Usha Gururaj at the top leadership levels, down through the ranks to local Vrindavan representatives such as Lakhan Dube, I am truly grateful. Sarvanand Gaurang Das and the architect Rimpesh Sharma, both in Gurgaon, deserve special, affectionate mention. Chapter 3 circles around these cheerful, dedicated souls.

Starting in 2016 Sadhu Maharaj and his family, both biological and spiritual, welcomed me to the Munger Mandir in Vrindavan time and again. There Elida Jacobsen and Samrat Kumar offered a deep and perceptive knowledge of the town from a set of angles that were initially quite new to me—and gave me the chance to interact with their vibrant kids. As I envision the scene in their sitting room I see Samrat's cell phone ringing, Elida's computer open on the table, Radhika engrossed in a video, Mohan careening around the room on ever more stable legs, and Sunita coming in from the kitchen with coffee and a great big smile. How many times did Samrat release me from some intractable digital knot or make sure I knew about an event that was just about to happen?

While Vrindavan is the epicenter of this book, it also connects to places far and near. I am grateful to Priya Chopra for meeting me at the World Bank in Washington, to Swami Revatikaant for showing me around the Bhakti Marga center in Germany, and to Radhanath Das and his tech-savvy associates at the Govardhan Eco Village not far from Mumbai. Kavita Singh and Kunal and Shubhra Chakrabarty provided precious occasions to learn from their students and colleagues at Jawaharlal Nehru University—and from themselves. No one could have been a more gracious, stimulating host and interlocutor than Rajeev Bhargava at the Center for the Study of Developing Societies, and Awadhendra Sharan, also at the CSDS, was a source of wisdom about ecological matters. Crispin Branfoot was wise, wide-ranging, and bibliographically very helpful in regard to "heritage". From his unusual perspective as technological entrepreneur and Vrindavan bhakta, Varun Aggarwal shared his thoughts about a series of issues that arise in the last chapter. To the entire staff at Fulbright House in Delhi, especially Adam Grotsky, Priyanjana Ghosh, Anupam Anand, Neelam Pradhan, Kalden Shringla, Meena Tyagi, and that excellent Brajbasi Neeraj Goswami, I owe a debt of gratitude that goes well beyond logistical and financial support. Theirs is a kingdom of friendship and fun, and it extends all the way out to the Gatehouse Gang, night and day. Talks at JNU, the Fulbright conference, the University of North Carolina at Charlotte, the Wisconsin Conference on South Asia, and Columbia's University Seminar on South Asia gave me the chance to formulate some of my ideas as they developed and to benefit from others' reactions to them. A year's research leave from Barnard College in 2016–17, coupled with my Fulbright-Nehru Fellowship, was crucial for launching the project, and Barnard also helped with some of the production costs for the book. To the Leonard Hastings Schoff Publication Fund of the Columbia University Seminars I am grateful for a grant that was crucial in allowing the book to include so many images, many in color. I am also grateful to several individuals and institutions for photographs that appear among these images, as indicated in the captions that accompany them. If no such citation appears, the photograph is one that I have taken myself.

Oxford University Press (OUP) India has been an utter joy to work with. Its editorial staff believed in the book from the very first moments we began to talk about it and have translated that belief into the best possible outcome on the page. I appreciate their willingness to let me be so actively involved. Seetha Natesh has been peerless as a copy-editor—all-seeing, and with a degree of involvement that far outruns surface concerns—and her successor at the Press, hardly less so. Meanwhile, at OUP New York, I have benefited once again from Cynthia Read's comprehensive and inevitably quick-witted knowledge of what publishing involves.

I particularly want to thank Shrivatsa Goswami, David Haberman, Samrat Kumar, Joel Lee, and Rupert Snell, who read all or most of the manuscript, providing counsel and encouragement and saving me from numerous errors great and small. Let me draw attention to the "small" ones. In the aggregate they are hardly small, and small is often the measure of large. What would one do without such friends—and scholars? And trumpets, please, to herald the signal contribution of Laura Shapiro, my wife. Consummate stylist and editor, she has stood behind, beside, and sometimes creatively athwart everything I have ever written, and never more so than with this book. If you find yourself smiling at the way a particular thought was shaped or phrased, you can be sure that Laura was the actual author, not I.

I dedicate the book with reverence and affection to the great photographer, archivist, and documentarian Robyn Beeche. Robyn lost her life to cancer a year before this book began, living with remarkable energy to the end. Shrivatsa Goswami offered me the chance to live in her apartment in Jaisingh Ghera as I learned and worked; it had lain empty in the intervening year. Nothing could have been more inspirational than to enter Robyn's world—the example of her dedication to Radharamanji, the warmth she spread through friends even in her physical absence, and the humble utensils and fridge-affixed photos that continued to mediate her presence. I developed a special relationship with the toaster. No one loved Vrindavan more than Robyn, and no one hoped more ardently for its future.

Note on the Text

On the whole I have tried to avoid the technicalities of proper transliteration in this book, hoping that familiar ways of representing Indic terms will carry the day. Where I quote a portion of text from Hindi or Sanskrit, however, I do use diacritics, so that readers can reconstruct exactly what is being said in the source language. The same is true when I gloss an individual term or phrase with respect to its Hindi or Sanskrit original. Transliteration of this sort is rare in the main text but much more common in the endnotes. If questions remain, readers are urged to consult the index, where anglicized words appear alongside their transliterated Indic forms—first the simple "clean" one we see typically in the main text, then the more ornate "technical" one that contains diacritical markings.

What do these diacritics mean? Macrons—the bars that appear above vowels—show that the vowel in question is long. The first syllable in the name of the black snake Kāliya, for instance, is pronounced not like the English "uh" but "aah." Other vowels are made "heavy," as Sanskrit and Hindi put it, in similar ways. If you see a word like bhramar, meaning a certain sort of black bee, you know the vowels are short—two "uh"s. As for nasalization, I usually indicate it as Hindi would, by simply positioning a superscript dot just after the vowel in question. If a consonant or sibilant is retroflex, it has a dot beneath it.

Ś indicates a dental aspirate, as in "Shame on you!" Properly speaking one should distinguish between aspirate and non-aspirate consonants, as Hindi and Sanskrit do, but I have allowed *ch* to transliterate both forms. This avoids the more "correct" unaspirated *c*, which often causes English speakers to mispronounce the word in question. If the word chār, meaning four, were transliterated by the book, it would be cār, but the word itself should remind one of a charwoman, not an automobile.

Where the last consonant in a word requires that it be pronounced with a following schwa, as in the case of the snake Kaliya (i.e., Kāliya), I have written in that final *a*. In other cases, however, there is no audible final vowel in Hindi and I have omitted it in transliteration (dhām). Unfortunately this runs contrary to standard ISKCON practice, which prefers to suggest the Sanskrit pronunciation where the implicit final *a* would be heard. I have instead followed Hindi usage. Thus the gentleman known as Sarvananda Gauranga Dasa on his business card becomes Sarvanand Gaurang Das in my telling. Not the tiniest loss of gravitas is intended. I make an exception to this rule in the case of several names that have become so well established in the final -*a* form that it seems best not to try to alter them even if in Hindi the final *a* is rarely heard—Rupa, Sanatana, and Jiva Gosvami, eminences of Vrindavan's Gaudiya (i.e., Gauḍīya) tradition. Similarly, the title of a Sanskrit document will retain the final *a* while the Hindi analogue may not. Bhagavata Purana refers to a Sanskrit text; Bhagavat Katha or Bhagavat Saptah refers to its week-long exposition in Hindi. As for Tamil, whose appearance here is rare, I adopt the "heard" transliteration system in the main text (for instance, the poet Andal), but the proper transliteration in the notes (Āṇṭāḷ). Both will show up in the index.

If all this sounds a little messy, indeed it is, but I hope that the spirit of the whole will emerge in its telling. Native speakers of English have to remember that their language is notoriously unsystematic when it comes to representing heard sounds in a single, consistent way. This sometimes makes it helpful to include a diacritical mark to distinguish between two distinct Hindi/Sanskrit words whose Roman spellings would otherwise be identical—nāgara (a "citified" or "urbane" temple style) as against nagara (a city); or rās (a dance form) as against ras (mood or flavor).

As you will have observed in the paragraphs just above, I prefer to avoid italics. This gets tricky in the case of a composition such as the Bhagavata Purana (Bhāgavata Purāṇa)—undoubtedly the title of a printed book, hence deserving both italics and diacritics, yet so important among Hindus that it often has a Bible-like status. To honor that, I drop both italics and diacritical marks in the main text, while retaining both in the notes. The same is true for the Bhagavad Gita and the Ramayana and Mahabharata epics (Bhagavad Gītā, Rāmāyaṇa, Mahābhārata). I extend this populist courtesy to the Bhagavata Mahatmya (Bhāgavata Māhātmya), since it is closely related to the Bhagavata Purana and plays a significant role in our story, but I retain diacritics for less frequently seen actors such as the Harivaṃśa.

Finally there is the matter of capitalization and place names. Throughout the book I refer to "the new Vrindavan" when I want to designate the dramatically new parts of Vrindavan in a collective way, hoping to avoid the impression that such a term can be found on any census record. I also speak of "the Chatikara Road" and "the Parikrama Marg." These terms designate two of Vrindavan's thoroughfares, both of which have changed enormously in recent years so as to accommodate vast increases in vehicular traffic. In local usage, however, both names retain their lower-case meanings—the road leading to Chatikara, a nearby village, and the road (mārg) that permits a circumambulation (parikramā) of Vrindavan itself. Not long ago the latter was mostly an unpaved footpath. Chatikara Road and Parikrama Marg are only beginning to be fully analogous to Kasturba Gandhi Marg in Delhi or Fifth Avenue in New York, hence I retain the definite article *the* in speaking of them.

In all that I have said above, I refer to parts of the book that I myself have written. When I am quoting another's prose, I retain the spellings that person has chosen to adopt. In this regard, especially, the notes sometimes look a bit different from the main text. One final matter—changes in the standard spelling of place names—and it relates to what I have just said. Vrindavan people typically accept the new spelling of Kolkata (as against Calcutta) and the pronunciation it reflects when referring to the capital city of West Bengal. I follow suit. With Bangalore, however, it is different. The word's pronunciation in Vrindavan is generally rather distant from the now-standard Bengaluru, and the older spelling Bangalore is what

ISKCON Bangalore has chosen to designate itself. I stick to that spelling, therefore, when discussing ISKCON Bangalore, switching over to the currently standard Bengaluru only in more neutral contexts. In the notes and bibliography I adhere to the spelling used by the publication to which I am referring. Hence, for example, if a book was published before Calcutta became Kolkata in its anglicized spelling, I retain that. Language should try to remember, but it's not always easy when the present is changing so fast.

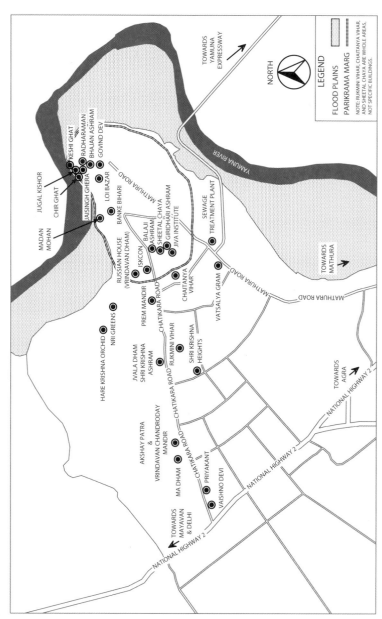

Map of Vrindavan, drawn by A.R. Sushant Bharti (not to scale).

1

Paradise—Lost?

I grew up in a world where work was worship, or so it seemed. My father always brought his briefcase home—there was too much work to fit into a workday—and I was always a little shocked on those Sunday mornings when he said he was going to skip church and get his religion on the golf course. Golf? Religion was no game. It was work, real work—the ritual, the morality, even the music. As I grew older, the ruts deepened. In high school and beyond, there was all this talk of what God was *doing* in the world. The whole point of life was to discern what it was and join the cause. One of my favorite hymns put it succinctly:

> Come, labor on.
> Who dares stand idle on the harvest plain,
> while all around him waves the golden grain?
> And to each servant does the Master say,
> "Go work today".[1]

With verses like that running through my head, I understood Max Weber's "Protestant ethic" long before I read the book.[2]

Imagine what it was like, then, to meet Krishna—the god who plays, the god who would have understood my father perfectly (Fig. 1.1). I had started graduate school at Harvard expecting to study religion and psychology, but I enrolled in Wilfred Cantwell Smith's "Introduction to World Religion" and there went that. Suddenly I was in comparative religion, and I was there to stay. Smith began with India; soon we were reading the Bhagavad Gita in translation. Now the Sanskrit word Gita means "song", but this was a very serious kind of song indeed. Revealed by Krishna to the warrior prince Arjuna, it was intended to provide the philosophical and emotional basis that would enable Arjuna, that sensitive Everyman, to take on the most difficult aspects of the battle of life—in his case, releasing the arrows that would usher in the end of the human race as he knew it. Later Krishna would turn wily, as he urged Arjuna to fight dirty in the cause

Figure 1.1.   Krishna interrupting a gopī as she churns butter. Page from an illustrated mid-eighteenth-century Sūrsāgar in the collection of Bharat Kala Bhavan, Banaras.

of winning a righteous war. He was God, in other words, doing what God does, working out his will in the world.

But not always. The more I read about Krishna, the more I realized I had never known a god like this—a god with a childhood that practically overshadowed his adulthood. All over India people worship the baby Krishna, the toddler Krishna, the naughty boy Krishna, the amorous Krishna. They sing about him, read about him, write poems about him; painters have for centuries gloried in his vivid blue face. The warrior Krishna of the Gita commands allegiance, but devotees cherish his growing-up years with a special delight. The day I discovered the Hindi poet Surdas, whose savvy, rapturous songs to the child Krishna can still be heard in the streets of India five hundred years after his lifetime, I knew I had a dissertation topic. Off I went to India, settling down in Banaras the way my Harvard advisors had suggested, but gradually it became clear that the Krishna I was looking for actually lived somewhere else. I followed him to Vrindavan.

Vrindavan is celebrated as the place where Krishna spent his childhood, and Krishna is celebrated as the divine force that calls us human beings away from our deadly self-involvements—away from the world's entanglements—to the persons we really are. Vrindavan projects a timeless youth, a paradise where we all should be living some essential part of our lives. Luckily, I had help getting there. In Banaras I had met Shrivatsa Goswami, the scion of an important Vrindavan Brahmin family; he was studying for a PhD, just like me. Shrivatsa became my special host in Vrindavan, opening many doors and showing me many ropes. His wife Sandhya did the same for my wife Laura. We arrived in the fall of 1974.

Vrindavan did seem a kind of paradise back then. It was gentle, reflective, off the beaten track. And it was deeply playful. I mean this literally: it was home to a genre of plays that served as a theater for every aspect of Krishna's playfulness, and they did so in the language Krishna had adopted as his own speech. This was Brajbhasha, the speech (bhāṣā) of the Braj region, a branch of Hindi with a rustic flavor and an elaborate literary history that included the poetry of Surdas. Far from the mood of the Bhagavad Gita with its formal Sanskrit cadences, Krishna's days in Braj and Vrindavan were filled with singing, dancing, and playing the flute. The name Vrindavan means "the basil forest" (vṛndā is the tulsi plant), and it's meant to evoke a vast expanse of low-lying trees, a wilderness in which could be found, as Thoreau said, the preservation of the world.[3]

I've gone back to Vrindavan many times in the course of the last forty years, mostly for short visits occasioned by a conference nearby, or the need to talk with Shrivatsa about some particularly recalcitrant Surdas poems. Those poems, which I've been thinking and writing about since my graduate school years, always kept me focused on the Vrindavan of myth and story. In the last ten or fifteen years, though, it's become harder and harder to visit paradise when I visit Vrindavan. It may still be an intricate warren of gardens, trees, and temples, but another wilderness has been growing on top of the mythic one—a wilderness of real estate development, plastic bags and containers tossed everywhere, pollution of all sorts, billboards crowding the roads, multi-colored fountains lighting up the night sky, and temples designed like theme parks. The last time I was there, the world's tallest religious business was soon scheduled to rise, story by story, in the basil forest. This is the new Vrindavan.

At Play with Krishna

When Laura and I settled into Vrindavan in the mid-1970s we lived in the upstairs flat that had been Shrivatsa Goswami's home as a child (Fig. 1.2). Organized around a courtyard, it offered a view of another courtyard below—Shrivatsa says they used to perform ras lilas there, the musical plays on the life of Krishna. There was a kitchen, a little storeroom, and a well with a bucket in case the electricity went off and doused the pump. Asim Krishna Das, wearing a big smile and a threadbare dhoti, lived his simple charismatic life down the hall (Fig. 1.3). Born Alan Shapiro in Far Rockaway, New York, he had backpacked across Asia from Europe, reaching Vrindavan by land. Those were the days when you could still do a thing like that: the Iranian revolution of 1979 was yet to happen.

Our apartment formed part of the interlocking compound of dwellings that had grown up around the temple of Radharamanji (Radha's Lover), a deity who is said to have manifested out of a bunch of black shalagram stones in 1542. By revealing himself in material form this way, Radharaman (another name for Krishna) was responding to the desire of one of his most devoted worshipers, a man called Gopal

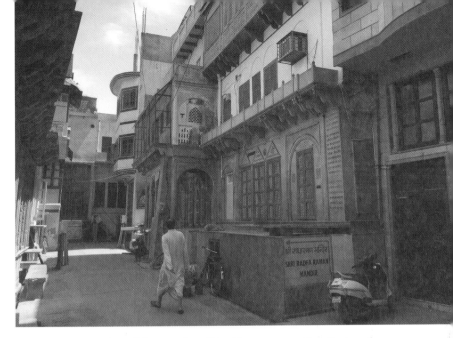

Figure 1.2.   A portion of the complex of dwellings surrounding the temple of Radharaman, in which the temple's priestly families live. March 23, 2017.

Figure 1.3.   Asim Krishna Das fanning the fire on his little stove. Radharaman Ghera, 1975.

Bhatt who had taken on great travels of his own. Gopal Bhatt walked all the way to Vrindavan from Shrirangam in Tamil-speaking south India, but still had no personal image he could serve. One day, as he expressed his longing for such a deity yet again, Krishna fulfilled his wish, emerging as a beautiful 11-inch-tall image bent at the ankles, waist, and neck in his traditional flute-playing pose. This was Radharaman. He poked at the lid of the basket where Gopal Bhatt kept his holy shalagram stones—a playful act if ever there was one. One of the stones had come to life in him. Gopal Bhatt built a temple for Radharaman in the sixteenth century, and it was replaced by another, bigger one in the nineteenth. There the faithful can still share Gopal Bhatt's vision, responding to temple bells that begin to ring before dawn each morning (Fig. 1.4).

Step into the temple, and if Radharaman is visible—he emerges from his private quarters behind a curtain nine times a day—you'll see that big welcoming eyes have been affixed to his face. His elbows are poised in such a way as to allow both hands to appear alongside his right cheek. They seem ready to hold Krishna's cowherd flute, its call so irresistible to the cowherd girls (gopīs) who fill the Braj countryside, but the flute itself often isn't there. His outer hand, the right, grasps a cowherd's stick instead. Radharaman's name, which means "the one who brings enjoyment to Radha", evokes his beautiful consort, Krishna's favorite sweetheart among the gopis. Radha is considered, by members of the community to which Shrivatsa belongs, who are spiritual successors of Gopal Bhatt, to be in some way Krishna himself, his own intrinsic feminine aspect. So intimate is their connection that even the flute might seem to interrupt it. It is as if to Radha that bamboo flute, which in Braj is always imagined as female, would seem to present some sort of competition, like a co-wife. Hence except on two special occasions in the course of the ritual year, Radharaman keeps his flute elsewhere than at his lips—perhaps the priests tuck it into his waistband. In a similar gesture Radha, rather than looking outward toward the worshippers as Krishna does, is seen by them only in profile. Decorated with silks, jewels, and a crown that echoes Radharaman's own, she trains her gaze solely on her beloved. When worshippers see them together, then, they enact a relationship of mysterious difference and nondifference, what the Gaudiya theologians call achintyabhedabheda.

Figure 1.4. Radharamanji. Photograph by Abhinav Goswami, courtesy of the archives of the Sri Chaitanya Prem Sansthan.

In all this we're a long way from the hard, righteous world of the Gita—so distant, in fact, that the ras lilas, the signature Krishna dramas of the Braj region, are forbidden to show the encounter between Krishna and Arjuna on the battlefield at Kurukshetra, or any other aspect of Krishna's adult life. The stories told in these ras lilas, whose central roles have traditionally been reserved for prepubescent boys, belong entirely to Krishna's childhood and adolescence—to the charmed precincts of Braj itself. Let the rest of the world go its own way! I found myself so entranced by these ras lilas, that, working with Shrivatsa and using a transcription prepared by Murari Lal Varma, I translated several of them in my first book, *At Play with Krishna*.

Before we go farther, let me say a word about names and places. In the ancient texts Vrindavan is not systematically distinguished from the region called Braj (the Sanskrit word vraja, from which it is derived, refers to a nomadic encampment) or Gokul (literally "herd of cows"). Each of these terms can be used to designate the pastoral domain in which Krishna grew up, and they are often used interchangeably. Apparently it was only in the course of the sixteenth century, when Vrindavan was marked out as a specific physical place, that these words came to designate separate entities—Vrindavan for the temple town we have been discussing, Gokul for a similar town located on the east back of River Yamuna, and Braj for the region as a whole. Yet there was a division of the house as to what should properly be called Vrindavan. The majority view, which was ratified by the Mughal state, sided with followers of the Bengali ecstatic Chaitanya, who located Vrindavan on the shores of the Yamuna five miles north of Mathura. This is the Vrindavan about which we have been speaking so far, and this is the broad community to which Shrivatsa's family and lineage, traced from Gopal Bhatt, belong. The minority opinion, by contrast, belonged to the followers of Chaitanya's contemporary Vallabhacharya, who insisted that the real Vrindavan was to be found twenty miles farther west in the vicinity of Mount Govardhan. We will be accepting common usage and speaking of Vrindavan as the town that has such an important Gaudiya—that is, Bengali—historical presence, but it is important to remember that in the classic Sanskrit texts the usage is far more fluid. There the terms Vrindavan, Gokul, and Braj all refer generally to the rustic environment where Krishna played and spent his youth; the borders between them are indistinct.

Indeed, there is something indistinct about his own person. In a sense, Krishna was only on loan to his own idyllic childhood. As the story goes, he had actually been born in Mathura, and was a member of the royal Vrishni family—a prince. The very night he was born, however, he was spirited out of town to rural Braj by his father, since the imposter who had deposed the rightful ruler of Mathura was out for the little boy's blood. This was Kamsa, a king in the mold of the biblical Herod, and in fact many times worse. As with Herod, it had been foretold that the baby, once grown to maturity, would remove the king from his ill-gotten throne, and both kings are said to have sponsored a massacre of innocents to make sure the divine child died among the rest. Historically this can't be true for Herod, and to Kamsa we have no historically reliable access at all, but myths have a life of their own. Hindu myths say that the evil Kamsa sent an unending stream of demons against the baby Krishna—a poison-wielding wet nurse, a donkey, a cyclone, a big black snake, and many more. Nothing worked, for Krishna fended off each of these attackers with insouciant ease. Every victory forms a much-loved tale in the huge corpus of his childhood exploits.

In adolescence, though, things begin to change. Krishna leaves Vrindavan and suddenly his mortal side is exposed. His victories become more tenuous, and he even suffers defeat, though the texts remain confident of his divine powers. Now he is at work in the realm of dharma, fighting to restore the world to its proper balance, and the struggle is arduous. Adulthood is a complicated and bloody business. He and his older brother Balaram manage to kill Kamsa, but this earns him the hatred of the tyrant's far-flung kin, and prompts many more battles. At length he ascends his own throne, in Dvaraka, far to the west on the banks of the Arabian Sea. After a period of happy rule, he returns to north-central India to take up more struggles against the wicked. This time he's not a combatant, only the mastermind behind the action, but the results are brutal even so. Upon returning to Dvaraka, he dies like Achilles—an arrow piercing his foot.

How different from his effortless childhood! Life in Vrindavan was everything that his adult life was not. If there were battles, they were battles of love. He could herd cattle, feast on milk and butter, and feast, too, on the milk of love that flowed from the breasts of his foster mother Yashoda. Suppose she or one of the other cowherd women had stored some freshly churned butter, soft and sweet, in pots they had hung from the ceiling so that it would be out of the reach of any animal that might happen to come into the room. That was no obstacle for this animal! Somehow or other, he could always manage to reach it. Later, a myriad of cowherd girls, entranced by his exploits, would coyly or freely offer Krishna a more adult version of this "butter"—their own unstinting love—thereby providing him with a seamless transition from home to village and from son to lover. And if they did not, he was apt to claim it all the same. Gossip and jealousies sometimes keep the plot going, but these realities touch him very little; they merely show what a prize he is to all. Krishna's job is just to be the beguiling flute-player he is—or in a different mood, an irresistible prankster. Once he raised the stakes of his childhood thieving episodes and stole the gopis' clothes while they were bathing. He demanded that they parade themselves naked on the bank before he would return his loot. From an amorous point of view he seemed to be the only man in town, even if he was only a boy or scarcely more. The moods of parental and erotic love often blurred together when they focused on him, and they were often joined by emotions of friendship and devotion, as well. It was a paradise of lila—play in all its meanings—and the serious struggles of dharma were far away.

Such a realm lent itself naturally, even necessarily, to poetry and song. Evocations of Vrindavan's magical landscape became frequent in Brajbhasha, and in the course of the sixteenth century Krishna's language became the most important literary register of Hindi, across a surprisingly wide swath of the subcontinent. Here is an example from the poetry of Surdas, who is usually regarded as pre-eminent among Brajbhasha poets. The poet reveals his identity with an oral signature that appears toward the end of the poem, but in the meantime he takes on the more generic voice of one of Krishna's companions—perhaps a fellow cowherd (gopāl) but more likely one of the cowherd women:

> Behold Vrindavan's splendor,
>   lotus-eyed one,
> Where Love has come
>   to pay his tribute of fine traits.

Fresh-petaled flowers—
    a new battalion of many hues—
Crowd together
    on every lovely vine:
Bows are in their hands,
    and quivers at their waists
Like the bodies of warriors
    arrayed in battle armor.
Cuckoos are the elephant ranks;
    geese and peacocks, cavalry;
Mountain cliffs are the chariots;
    chakor birds, the infantry.
Banana trees and palms
    become poles and battle flags;
Waterfalls are herald drums,
    and bees that buzz there, kettledrums.
Wise lieutenants proffer
    sandal-breeze advice
And the forest, pleased,
    titters with rustling leaves.
Beauty's cavalcade comes
    galloping in so swiftly
That the horsemen's garments
    flutter like flags.
Surdas says,
    this is the girl's plea:
"Here is Kama cowering
    as at the time of Shiva's anger,
Imploring
    with vast, quick-moving eyes:
Calm him now, Gopal,
    with a gesture of your hand".[4]

In its final verses this poem recalls an archetypal battle between Kama and Shiva, in which the verdant expressiveness of love (kāma) was defeated—rendered bodiless—by the heat amasses in the world's greatest yogi (Shiva) through eons of rigorous self-restraint. But it was a pyrrhic victory, as every practiced listener knows. Bodiless Kama dispersed himself throughout that very world, as Krishna's love-making presence in Braj attests. Any battle between Shiva and Kama is really no battle at all; we are awash in a world of love. Spring is its perpetual symbol, as here, but the rains of summer also have a special romantic flavor, and the full moon of autumn is beyond compare. This is the eternal wilderness that the workaday world of adulthood should never forget.

Just Where Is Vrindavan?

As we have begun to sense, the great transformation of Vrindavan from story to place happened in the course of the sixteenth century, and the key to much of it lay in the arrival of visitors from far away who attempted to discover just where the mythical tulsi forest could be located in physical space. Chaitanya, the Bengali ecstatic, was the most important of them, for he couldn't resist putting his ear to the ground. Where did Krishna's lila-games really happen? he asked. There was something in him that had to know, and his followers reported that he could detect each site with unerring accuracy. They reverberated through his soul since he was, in his followers' perception, a latter-day Krishna himself—Radha and Krishna in a single person. Others had other commitments—the Vallabhites located their Vrindavan where Chaitanya did not—but such disagreements notwithstanding, it is remarkable how many people travelled to Braj as the sixteenth century progressed. Not the least of these were the Mughals, who arrived from central Asia with a different purpose. They soon allied and intermarried with Hindus and came to play crucial roles in this broader plot of religious and cultural reclamation.

Thus it was that sixteenth-century Vrindavan began to emerge. Its red sandstone temples, classic in their simplicity because they lack external sculpture (perhaps a gesture to Muslim sensibilities), date back to this period. These temples were built to honor specific locales. A hillock might be perceived as a place where the Goddess dwells, or there was a pre-existing village or pile of ancient ruins that suggested the right location for another. In addition there were plenty of glades and ponds that might have attracted the divine couple. Krishna and Radha danced *here*, someone felt; he stole the milkmaids' clothes *there*; *this* is where he jumped into the river to tame the black cobra called Kaliya. All this was identified as Krishna's forest playground, for sure, but its proximity to worldly Mathura was no accident. A garden is a garden because it is marked off from the byways of ordinary life. A wilderness is a wilderness because it is not owned, not plotted, not a city. And childhood is childhood, or loveplay play, not because these are primordial facts but because adults recognize their independence from the dutiful, routinized lives into which they have settled. The purpose of the built Vrindavan was to make this contrast real, to give it physical and institutional boundaries, and one of the remarkable facets of its history is that this major focus for Hindu pilgrimage could not have materialized as it did were it not for the implicit and explicit support provided by Muslims—that is, the court of the Mughal emperor Akbar (r. 1556–1605).

These were the movements of history, but they echoed to the rhythms of myth, and Vrindavan's mythic reach has for centuries extended throughout the Indian subcontinent—sometimes even beyond. In the language of UNESCO, this is a World Heritage Site, although local and state-level politics have prevented its being declared so and thus preserved. We can begin to take the measure of Vrindavan's reach by traveling to the extreme southern tip of the subcontinent. There we find ourselves in Tamil-speaking country, and several of Tamil's key monuments evoke the Vrindavan that existed in people's minds long before those sixteenth-century temples began to rise on the shores of the Yamuna. The Tamil epic *Shilappadikaram* (*Tale of an Anklet*), for example, includes an episode in which herds-women perform a circle dance associated with Krishna's youth (vālacarita nāṭakaṅkal). We have butter in hanging pots, plenty of milk ready in cows' udders, and a dance enactment of the roles of Krishna, Balaram, and the southern gopi Nappinnai.[5] Vrindavan does not appear by name there, but the epic has a close association to the city of Madurai, and that name is the Tamil equivalent of Mathura. The echoing is intentional.[6] We find the same pattern taking shape in the *Tiruppavai* of the female Tamil poet Andal (ninth century?), who is also closely associated with Madurai. Even more pointedly her other poem, the *Nachiyar Tirumoli*, concludes with a "song of questions and answers" in which the herdswomen repeatedly ask where Krishna is and receive some form of the same response: "We glimpsed him in Vrindavan".[7]

The idea of Vrindavan is no less present elsewhere. We meet it, for instance, in the name that has been given to an island in Tungabhadra River in southwest India where the bodies of nine celibate leaders of the Madhva Sampraday, Vyasatirtha the most important among them,

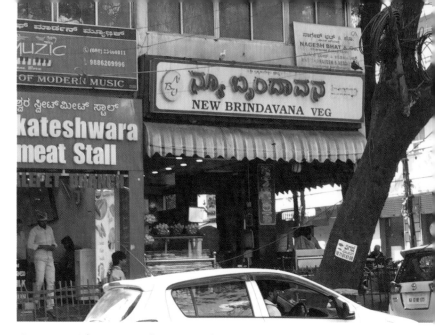

Figure 1.5.   The New Brindavana (Vrindavan) restaurant in Malleshwaram, Bengaluru—vegetarian, of course. January 29, 2019.

are entombed. This is Nava Vrindavan, a term that might seem to mean "the new Vrindavan" but actually refers to the number nine (nava), in that each of these burial shrines is its own Vrindavan. The affirmation being made is that each of these saints has assumed a form of heavenly presence that defies death: they are alive to Krishna.[8] Far across the state, near Mysore and adjoining the Krishnarajasagara dam, we find quite a different sort of site: Brindavan (that is, Vrindavan) Gardens, a 60-acre nature preserve that opened in 1932. It features fountains illuminated at night and other tourist-friendly wonders. And in Whitefield, on the IT outskirts of Karnataka's capital city Bengaluru, there is an entire complex built by and around the charismatic god-man Sathya Sai Baba (d. 2011) for his immense international following. It too bears the name. Or would you like some breakfast or lunch in Bengaluru's venerable Malleshwaram neighborhood? Try the New Brindavana (Fig. 1.5).

Vrindavan is also keenly marked at the other extremity of India. It makes its appearance already in Jayadeva's *Gitagovinda*, composed in Sanskrit at the Sena court of twelfth-century Bengal and soon performed throughout the subcontinent.[9] Vrindavan's ambience is omnipresent in that text, but it comes in the form of a private tryst between Krishna and Radha rather than in the more widely shared erotic mood we often meet in the south. This continues to course through the poetry of Mithila and Bengal, and in Manipur we have a ras lila tradition that is largely independent of what we find in Braj itself.[10] Assam has given us the remarkable textile tradition called vrindāvanī vastra, the "Vrindavan garb" whose most famous exemplar dates to the late seventeenth century and resides in the British Museum. Into it are woven scenes from Krishna's life in guess where—the defeats of Kaliya the snake and Baka the heron, along with the theft of the gopis' clothes.[11] Meanwhile, back in Bengal itself, we have a whole culture invested in discovering self-styled gupta (hidden or secret) Vrindavans, either within the physical and emotional bodies of devotees themselves or somehow replicated in a shared landscape. One such gupta Vrindavan emerged in the course of the seventeenth and eighteenth centuries at Vishnupur in southwest Bengal. Its Malla rulers specifically had "our" Vrindavan in mind as they created their own local versions of temples that the Gaudiyas had built in Braj.[12] But even more important in the long term was the small city of Nabadvip, hometown to Chaitanya himself.[13] When in 1894 the Gaudiya modernizer Kedarnath Datta identified Mayapur, just across the river, as the true site of Chaitanya's birth, it was part of a larger project by means of which he hoped to display the fact that the whole area of Nabadvip ought to be seen as Bengali version of Vrindavan.[14]

Datta's work would inspire a frenzy of building a century later on the part of the Hare Krishna movement—more properly the International Society for Krishna Consciousness, ISKCON. We will hear more about that in Chapter 4. For now, though, let us merely observe that ISKCON was active elsewhere too, and again in the cause of establishing a Vrindavan presence in places that lay far from the Braj original. Already in 1968, just two years after its incorporation in New York, ISKCON started building a New Vrindavan (called just that but with a slightly different spelling) in rural West Virginia, so that urban devotees could taste Vrindavan's pastoral delights. More recently ISKCON has established "New Vrajes" (that is, Braj) not only in and around Mumbai but in Hungary and Spain.[15] Another attempt to replicate the glories of Braj has been built by the followers of Kripaluji Maharaj just outside Austin, Texas. This complex is called

Barsana Dham after the name of Radha's hometown. Then too we have a retreat center in rural Pennsylvania called simply Vraj, this one established by Vallabhites.[16] Suddenly Vrindavan and its surrounding terrain are everywhere and very global indeed, but the roots of the urge to enact Vrindavan far from Braj itself are deeply Indian. They show what a hold it has held over Hindus' imaginations for a millennium or more.[17]

But what about now? What happens when the focus of all that recognition is in danger of becoming unrecognizable?

Certain readers, especially Indian ones, may expect that a book with "Vrindavan in the 21st Century" as its subtitle should aspire to offer an objectively neutral view of the place. To such readers I must apologize. I cannot offer the comprehensive, systematic examination that we might expect from a sociologist—caste, class, gender, religious affiliation, economics—nor the determinedly even-handed approach of a top-flight externally based journalist. My own circumstances are too personal. This is a town where I have been a guest over the course of many decades, and always a guest of the same family—Brahmins with deep roots in Vrindavan's traditional culture. What I see happening around me is conditioned by that past and by a hospitality and intellectual companionship for which I remain ever grateful. In many readers' minds, no doubt, the idea of the twenty-first century stands for a set of ideals—economic, social, and gender parity, and secular governance in the best possible sense. I share those ideals. But my primary purpose here is not to see how well Vrindavan measures up to general standards such as these. Rather, I hope to report on the dramatic changes that are actually happening.

Vrindavan Then and Now

When I arrived in Vrindavan in the fall of 1974, I felt I had stepped back in time—not exactly to some former era, but to a place running on primordial rules. Pilgrims often came by horse cart or by foot (Fig. 1.6). Everyone bathed in the Yamuna; that simply went without saying. Newcomers approached one of Vrindavan's traditional Brahmin guides to get a sense of how they should negotiate the three days they were expected to stay in town. Pilgrimage was seasonal— heavy in the summer monsoon, the autumn month of Karttik, and

Figure 1.6.   Pilgrims arriving in Vrindavan by horse-drawn tonga cart, mid-1970s.

the springtime season of Holi, but much reduced at other times. Everyone expected to see at least one of the ras lila plays if possible, and during the monsoon they were particularly abundant. Then there were the gardens that enshrined the trysts of Krishna and Radha, especially Sevakunj and Nidhiban, where these two and the other gopis once performed the rās dance—and still do, for those who have the eyes to see. It was well known which were the great temples in town, the ones you just had to visit: Banke Bihari, the local favorite and aligned with no trans-regional sectarian group; Rangji, the big tall one named after the great Vaishnava temple that resides at the heart of Tamil Nadu in Shrirangam; and several of the old red sandstone temples that date to the sixteenth or early seventeenth century. Radharamanji's current temple was built later, but it too belongs in this group.

The menu wasn't exactly prix fixe, but there was fair consensus on what it contained. Pilgrims would typically stay at one of the big dharamshalas; that was where you connected with your guide. And if you were not one of those visitors, a pilgrim, chances are you belonged somehow to the pilgrim trade nonetheless—as a temple priest or gosvāmī; as a guide or paṇḍā; or perhaps as a merchant dependent on the business pilgrims provided. This was the Vrindavan I met way back then—too busy and commercial to be a full-time paradise, perhaps, but a town firmly dedicated to making that image accessible to others.

Today every one of the features on that grid has changed, many drastically. The horse carts are nearly gone, and with them the old, quiet cycle rickshaws. Instead there are battery-powered auto rickshaws, and three-wheeler tempos and private cars zoom noisily everywhere. The motorcycles' horns are particularly deafening, and their speed especially life-threatening. Buses still arrive, as they did back in the 1970s, but the chartered ones rarely stay as long as three days anymore. Because of the greatly improved highways, tourist buses from Delhi can include a quick taste of Vrindavan as part of a day trip centered on Jaipur and Agra. This means there's not much need for the local pandas, since the bus companies themselves arrange what the visitors will see. Individual pilgrims no longer do much of the seeking and negotiating. Is "pilgrim" even the right word? These travelers are headed for Jaipur and Agra, too—secular destinations. Of course, there are exceptions, yet but the trend is unmistakable.

Vrindavan is still a destination—a big one—but the patterns of access are new. Hordes of visitors now arrive by car, mostly from Delhi or nearby Haryana or Punjab. The old seasonal rhythms are obsolete, polluted by the culture of the weekend, which simply didn't exist 45 years ago; Saturday was still a workday. Nowadays those private cars are particularly in evidence on Saturdays, Sundays, and one-day holidays.

As for the ras lilas, that distinctive art form so beautifully tailored to the image of Vrindavan as a paradise of childhood, they're alive but they're faltering. The crowds are much diminished, and the plays themselves have adopted a rather different personality. As I've said, the central roles used to be taken by children; today the key performers tend to be older adolescents and young men. To me, it seems jarring—all wrong for a theatrical form I associate with children's earnest, piping voices and an audience of delighted devotees.

Sevakunj and Nidhiban are still jammed—even more so, since India's population has more than doubled since the 1970s—but these days people also like to spend time in a different sort of garden, the kind that comes as part of an attraction park. Such places cluster on the outskirts of town and have a very different flavor from the older retreats. Some of the big dharamshalas are still there, but a host of hotels now crowds around them—commercial establishments rather than religious ones, and some quite upscale. As for the temple trade, Banke Bihari and the others I have mentioned are still big draws—Banke Bihari especially—but the ISKCON temple is just as popular and new temples that we have yet to mention, such as Prem Mandir, draw eager throngs. Prem Mandir opened in 2012, in a part of town that didn't even exist in 1974, except as wilderness.

Changes like these—the motorized traffic, the urban sprawl, the increased pollution—are hardly novelties in the twenty-first century. But for a place that has built its identity as a religious retreat in a mythic wilderness, they are jaw-dropping. Whether they're debilitating or enabling, entirely destructive or leaving some room for hope, are matters we will gauge in the chapters ahead. But one such change has certainly altered Vrindavan in a fundamental way, and this has to do with the river. Almost nobody bathes in it these days, and fewer still dare to drink its water. The heartbeat of pilgrimage in Vrindavan is in danger of disappearing entirely.

Of course, Vrindavan is not the only place to have experienced such rapid transformations. Other arcadias and Ozes have also lost their purchase on anything pristine. Jerusalem is flanked by a heinous wall; Mecca's high-rise hotels surround and obscure the Ka'bah; and the Chinese government has thrown a dam across the gorgeous Yangtze gorge, perennial inspiration for painters. Venice sinks into a sea of cruise liners. And look at the bigger picture. The air we breathe doesn't have enough air in it; the food we think is food is really the food industry; water wears a sheath of plastic; and silence is defenseless against noise. Americans think reality TV is so real that they've elected a president to prove it. All of this we know from everywhere.

Yet Vrindavan deserves our special attention because it is such an eloquent bellwether—self-consciously sited as a wilderness, and a wilderness in plain view of major cities. There were three of these—Mathura, Delhi, and Agra—but the whole point of dignifying Vrindavan as a special built domain was to have its essence accessible to yet separate from these. It was to be in conversation with the ongoing rhythms of civilization and empire, certainly, but not engulfed by them. From the point of view of Hindu rulers such as the Kachvahas to the west or the Bundelas to the east, this hands-off approach was a necessity: the realm of Krishna had passed out of the control of Hindu kings already in the thirteenth century. Yet it was also true from the point of view of the Mughal rulers and their Muslim predecessors. They expected that a spiritual preceptor would exercise his other-than-worldly authority by keeping at a distance from the seat of secular power, a distance that nonetheless should not be too great. Hence armies and merchants might pass through Vrindavan as they knitted together the empires of which they were part, but if Vrindavan were to become an urban area just like any other, a secular space, it would lose the special identity upon which its own particular form of power depended. It would become a parody of itself, a fountain of youth gone dry.

All over the world the thing we call religion has tried to serve as a bulwark against assaults like these. Religion fends them off with a set of realities it trumpets as its own. Critics ridicule it and say it's just another theater of cultural production—especially egregious because it pretends to ride above it all in a bubble of holy independence. Religious people don't accept this judgment. They answer that if religion sometimes has intricate, aging structures, it's nonetheless in the service of a higher, greater truth. But the critics will have none of it. Religion has always been some bloated, super-sized Las Vegas, they say—a theme park just like any other. It's hard to disagree when the Vrindavan Chandrodaya Mandir (VCM) currently under construction—Vrindavan's Moonrise Temple, our subject in Chapter 4—actually boasts a Krishna Theme Park as part of its enormous temple complex. The grounds that are projected to surround it will constitute a kind of virtual Vrindavan, made necessary because the real town—centuries old, the place where Shrivatsa Goswami grew up—has come to seem irredeemable, or in any case quite some distance away.

I'm trying to figure out what to make of all this, as I explore the new Vrindavan and take refuge in what remains of the old. Maybe Vrindavan always offered more of a Marie Antoinette retreat than a genuine sojourn away from real life, real adulthood. Maybe I have been too blind to the fact that members of the oppressed classes have always found it hard to feel welcome in such a Brahmin-dominated place—or Muslims in such a Hindu one. And maybe Vrindavan is simply reinventing itself as it's done before, this time a "city upon a hill" that is a man-made hill and has finally achieved its global glow.

Or is the new Vrindavan the canary in our ever darkening anthropocene cave, its last and saddest song?

I need a decent and useful perspective on this debate, and that's why I have come back. I hope that perspective will emerge in the course of this book, which begins—as it must—with water. The desperate state of the River Yamuna is the crisis that has polarized the town more than any other. What happens if the river is no longer essential to Vrindavan's identity, no longer connected to it as if by an umbilical cord (Chapter 2)? Then we look more closely into the town itself, new and old, and ask whether the two can—or should—be reconciled (Chapter 3). After that comes a visit to the skyscraper temple, the Vrindavan Chandrodaya Mandir—grand symbol of Vrindavan's future, and perhaps a death knell to all that was (Chapter 4). Then we turn to the Vrindavan that has long been associated with women—specifically, widows. For centuries women who survive their husbands in certain parts of India have been cast out of their homes by family members who see them as inauspicious or simply don't want to support them. Old Vrindavan has always offered refuge, or at least a mouthful of food and a place to pray; new Vrindavan has other ideas (Chapter 5). And finally, we meet with my friend and mentor, Shrivatsa Goswami. How has he dealt with these changes? Is he less relevant than his father was to Vrindavan's process of self-discovery? Or is it that, as new storms develop, he's steering with a different rudder (Chapter 6)? For me, and for generations of students after me, the sight of Shrivatsa in Radharamanji's temple is the sight of Vrindavan itself.

But now? Into what sort of reality is Vrindavan now heading? Is it hyper or diminished or just plain virtual? You could say that religion has been about virtual reality all along, but how is that virtuality twisting as the Anthropocene Age descends? In a seventh and final chapter I reach for answers that will place the new Vrindavan on a global stage.

2

The Battle of Keshi Ghat

From my room in the old Vrindavan, I can see the river. By spring it will be a trickle, but now, in the fall, it flows freely with the aftermath of last summer's monsoon. The water is that special dark gray color—shyām—that has been immortalized in several of Krishna's most familiar names: he too is dark, dark as a raincloud (ghanshyām). The alluvial plains on the other side of the river add a lighter shade of gray to this perfectly horizontal scene, and as evening falls and cooking fires are lit, a third striation appears: another band of gray, this one ashen, almost white. The wind gathers the smoke and sweeps it against a distant line of trees; it seems to form a parallel river.

This sort of spectacle has made Vrindavan famous throughout India, and now, by means of books, videos, and websites, throughout the world (Fig. 2.1). As darkness falls, the Yamuna becomes more luminous and mysterious still. Especially in the month of Karttik (October–November), as the moon wanes to the point of disappearance and then slowly waxes again, people gather after sunset and set tiny oil lamps afloat on the river's blackened surface. These pinpoints of light are an elemental offering to the River Yamuna

Figure 2.1.   The Vrindavan waterfront, 1998, showing, from the center toward the right, Keshi Ghat, Pandavala Ghat, the temple of Yugal Kishor (in the background), and Bhramar Ghat. Photo by Abhinav Goswami.

herself. Once launched, they form a long, long phalanx of minuscule lantern-soldiers advancing at a single pace against some unknown downstream foe.

The Yamuna makes two striking adjustments as she meets Vrindavan, flowing in from the north. First she turns eastward—these days on a rather diagonal trajectory but earlier with a dramatic pivot that prompted many temples and ghats to be built along her banks, on the town's northern flanks, from the sixteenth century to the nineteenth. Once the Yamuna has passed all these, she rounds the point at the eastern extremity of Vrindavan, then curves back along the town's southern underbelly and departs toward Mathura, that ancient crossroads city. This means that when she flowed in her older riverbed—the one without the diagonal shortcut—the river embraced Vrindavan fully on three sides before proceeding farther south. One can see why Chaitanya and his followers found this such an entrancing site. Later, after Mathura, the Yamuna passes Agra, where the Taj Mahal rises on her right bank, and there, having paid her respects, she takes another dramatic turn and heads east to join the Ganga (Ganges) at Allahabad. These two sisters, Yamuna and Ganga, mix their waters and flow to the Bay of Bengal together.

To gaze at the Yamuna in this way is to survey a legendarily peaceful scene. But the legend includes an enemy, roiling the mood of this picture-perfect pastorale (Fig. 2.2). He lurks at the Yamuna's second

Figure 2.2.   Krishna killing the horse demon Keshi. Fifth century CE, north India, terracotta. In this sequential narrative the dead Keshi is shown at the bottom. Metropolitan Museum of Art, New York, 1991.300.

bend on a bluff called Keshi Ghat, where for centuries the river has formed an especially deep channel. Keshi means "hairy", a reference to the ample mane of a wild horse that Kamsa had sent to battle Krishna, a lad of perhaps seven or eight. The horse's animal wrath proved powerless against the divine boy. As Keshi charged, Krishna thrust his elbow between the horse's jaws, killing him instantly in a paroxysm of pain.

Nowadays Keshi Ghat is the center of another epic confrontation. Two sides are involved, and I'm calling them the Futurists and the Protectors, though they'd each probably claim the right to the other name. They propose very different solutions for the problems that face Vrindavan today, but they do largely agree about the problems:

- the open sewers in the older part of town and the way they spill untreated waste into the river;
- the repellent smells;
- the free-roaming pigs that form a centuries-old part of the sanitation staff;
- the plastic bags thrown everywhere; they also end up in the river;
- the mass of billboards that line the streets—almost all religious events and real estate;
- the intractable traffic jams in both the older and the newer parts of town;
- the loudspeakers that spew forth religion at all hours of the day and night;
- the corruption at every level;
- and the water.

That's where Keshi Ghat especially comes in. Only a few people dare to bathe in the river these days—ordinarily a pilgrim's first impetus— since so much of it has been polluted upstream by industries, agriculture, and the vast population of Delhi. Vrindavan's own untreated sewage makes matters worse.

And then there is the problem of the monkeys—a universal complaint. In the forty years since I have been coming to Vrindavan, these brown-and-red bandars have grown from pranksters focused on a single intersection to a band of militant predators that go just about everywhere in the old part of town. (They are utterly distinct from the elegant long-tailed gray langūrs that also belong to the species, which are entirely absent from Vrindavan except for one or two imports who have been trained to combat the bandars.) These days you cannot wear your glasses outside because a monkey will hurtle down from a wall or rooftop and rip them off. I once left a car window 3 inches open and lost my glasses instantly: a semi-human hand darted in. Luckily the driver knew the ropes. He got a banana and offered it in exchange. We used to joke that the monkeys were in cahoots with the opticians—a circular trade—but now it is widely believed that local boys train cadres of monkeys to withhold the glasses until the victims supply their ransom. The urchin sees it happen; the monkey waits on top of a nearby wall; the kid offers the monkey something to eat; the monkey drops the glasses; the victim is very happy, and the kid gets a handsome reward. You may smile from afar, but to live in such an environment, where residents and pilgrims are prisoners, gets old fast. It's a handsome metaphor for how out of control everything seems to be these days.[1]

In the eyes of many, there is an immense, countervailing force to all this chaos and degradation, and it's ISKCON—the Hare Krishna movement. Most Americans associate the term with clusters of orange-clad hippies dancing and chanting "Hare Krishna" on street corners, but the movement has changed quite a bit since it was spawned in the United States in 1965. Its founder, Abhay Charan De, soon to be called A.C. Bhaktivedanta Swami "Prabhupad" by his followers, lived in Vrindavan before undertaking his missionary journey to the West. In a remarkably short time—by the early 1970s—the movement made its way back to Vrindavan, which Prabhupad had always seen as home turf, and in 1975 a major ISKCON temple opened on the outskirts of town in a dusty area called Raman Reti, literally, "the sands of romance". Prabhupad was based there until his death in 1977. Many of the objectionable features of the old Vrindavan are not such a problem around the ISKCON temple, with the notable exception of billboards and traffic jams; the monkeys are doing their best to invade.

The Hare Krishna devotees and I happened to arrive in Vrindavan at more or less the same time in the 1970s, but we lived in different worlds. They were all speaking English on the outskirts of town; I was doing my best to speak Hindi near its center. I tried to keep my distance, but to Vrindavan residents we were all foreigners and pretty much indistinguishable, so they cordially greeted me the same way they greeted the Hare Krishnas—"Hare Krishna!" or "Hari Bol!" I would quickly respond with the real Vrindavan greeting, which is the vocative form of the name of Radha—"Radhe Radhe!" I'm not sure anyone noticed, but I tried hard to stay away from whatever was going on at what people called the "English Temple", the Angrez Mandir, on the far edge of town.

Over the years it has become harder and harder to ignore the massive changes that ISKCON has introduced into the life of Vrindavan. By the 1980s the Angrez Mandir was attracting hordes of visitors; it became one of the most popular sights in town. Today ISKCON is no longer a movement comprised mainly of Westerners but one embraced by many Indians as well, and this has drastically altered the way Vrindavan looks and feels.

The lavish, all-marble ISKCON temple that rose up on donated land along the main road on the western edge of town has become the cornerstone of the new Vrindavan (see Fig. 4.5). First a school and a residential community opened nearby, both ISKCON projects. Then, with the liberalization of India's economy in the early 1990s and the transformation of black money into more negotiable means of exchange, a flood of new properties appeared, mostly outside the ISKCON orbit. Temples, hospitals, ashrams, and residential communities now line the road, and when you look to the horizons, construction cranes and half-built apartment complexes are everywhere. This new Vrindavan is in danger of eclipsing the old.[2]

Prior to ISKCON, the most frequently visited temple in town was clearly Banke Bihari, which houses a surprisingly small image of Krishna as "the lithe enjoyer". The term bānke, the "lithe" part of this moniker, literally means crooked or bent—that is, bent at the ankles, waist, and neck, the classic pose we saw in the case of Radharamanji. The ISKCON temple's location proved providential in the cause of achieving this success—or was it carefully planned? In 1980s and 1990s, as many more people came to own private cars, the most popular access to the town began to shift away from the old road connecting Vrindavan to Mathura (and thus to all of India, especially by rail) towards National Highway 2, which connects Delhi with Agra and points beyond. In the 1970s NH-2 was widened into a four-lane highway, the marvel of its time. Now there are six. Vrindavan lies just 5 miles away, and in 1975, the year the ISKCON temple was inaugurated, it was the first structure you met if you came into town by that route. ISKCON devotees persuaded the municipality to erect a huge arch over the road at this point. On it is an inscription in Hindi saying that the municipality welcomes you, but just below, in English, we learn that this is Bhaktivedanta Swami Gate, celebrating the founder of ISKCON. (No mention is made of the fact that he spent most of his life as a manager in one of India's pharmaceutical companies.) Two recently affixed panels memorialize the fact that ISKCON was incorporated in "New York, USA", as if this distant metropolis had of late become Vrindavan's sister city.

A glistening golden image of Prabhupad is a major draw for visitors to his temple; he reigns in a memorial shrine of his own that is only slightly subsidiary to the main temple. There he is flanked by two similarly golden bas-reliefs celebrating his missionary victories. One, which shows him leading the Jagannath chariot festival down Fifth Avenue in New York, where the Empire State Building and a church are crowded into the background, says it took him only ten years to conquer America. His disconcertingly lifelike presence there is also be found in the main temple—this time as a three-dimensional golden image.

Between ISKCON and the old town, where there used to be a quiet, lightly forested gap, we now have an unbroken row of shops, hotels, ashrams, real-estate offices, and restaurants. Looking the other way from ISKCON, west toward National Highway 2, we see the boldest structure in all Vrindavan—Prem Mandir, built entirely of Italian marble in the classic north Indian style and illuminated in an ever-changing array of floodlit colors at night. Prem Mandir (Love Temple) was inaugurated by the religious leader Kripaluji Maharaj in 2012 and is now said to attract more visitors than the Taj Mahal. But that is not all. Between Prem Mandir and ISKCON there is the Chitrakut Ashram with its 52-foot high statues of Hanuman and Ganesh. On the other side of Prem Mandir, farther out on Chatikara Road, such monuments multiply. There's the pale concrete lotus-shaped temple that serves as anchor to the Shanti Sewa Dham guesthouse; there's the crane-like tower above the Jvala Dham Shri Krishna Ashram that flashes little lights at night; there's the ashram itself with its huge statue of goddess Durga just below; and shortly before the road meets National Highway 2 we encounter an even larger image of goddess Vaishno Devi. Durga's hegemony is general in the Himalayas, where each hill and mountain is apt to be crowned by a temple to some form of this great goddess; Vaishno Devi, by contrast, connects to a specific place in the Jammu region. Both goddesses—and they are connected—now bring their Himalayan homes within the orbit of Vrindavan.

Meanwhile a vast array of apartment complexes and gated communities crowds the landscape, often serving as second homes or retirement retreats for India's new cosmopolites. In 2016 a sign went up announcing the first sale of apartments in a new development called Vrindapuram. The name was written in large Hindi letters, but the rest was in English: "Delhi Distance 120 KM, Noida Distance 120 KM, World fame tourist place, World class educational hub, Industrial hub".

With this extraordinary boomtown in mind, the people I'm calling Futurists are hoping to reorient Vrindavan—literally—so that the crush of new development doesn't entirely wipe out the idyllic style of life once cherished or at least imagined here. This brings us back to the battle of Keshi Ghat. The Futurists have launched a plan that would extend Keshi Ghat out into the Yamuna by another two hundred meters, laying a concrete platform that would serve as a place for tourists and pilgrims to enjoy the spectacle that the beautiful old ghats provide. A promenade for pedestrians, cars, buses, scooters, and rickshaws would run along the river beneath the old ghats. There would be benches to take in the view, kiosks where visitors could relax with a cold drink, and some even suggest a Ferris wheel.

And another feature has also been proposed—a ropeway to ferry visitors across the river in airborne gondolas from the other side.[3] This would provide visitors with a memorable vision of the historic ghats and iconic temples—an access to the town that would be as pure and uncluttered as the present approaches are exactly the opposite.[4] Since 2012 Vrindavan has been on the route of a massive expressway intended to whisk travelers from Delhi to Agra and the Taj Mahal. Built with funds provided by the government of Uttar Pradesh (UP) and its construction partner, the Jaypee Group, it was originally to be called the Taj Expressway, but the name was changed to the more inclusive "Yamuna Expressway", since it turned out that many more vehicles were heading out from Delhi with Mathura and especially Vrindavan as their destination than were continuing on to Agra. In part this is a testament to Vrindavan's ever-growing global fame. In part, though, it merely testifies to the exponential growth of metropolitan Delhi and to a hunger for weekend escapes on the part of its residents. Of course, weekenders can be pilgrims too; we should not think of these as two separate groups. But in either case it makes a difference that Vrindavan is an hour closer to Delhi than Agra.

As the Futurists see it, the development of Keshi Ghat as an attractive and indeed almost iconic point of access to the heart of Vrindavan—the old Vrindavan—would benefit everyone. Visitors' cars and buses could be required to park on the opposite side of the Yamuna, thereby turning Vrindavan's vehicle-choked streets into something of a pedestrian zone. (Residents' cars would still be free to navigate there, it seems.) Prestigious families whose temples and ashrams had been established in the older parts of the town centuries ago—many of them Brahmin and pursuing religious vocations— would now be able to welcome visitors by means of a far clearer and more direct route than before. And those who invested in the new Vrindavan would once again be able to move and breathe; the intolerable congestion on their streets, especially on weekends, could now be managed.

All this thanks to a gondola? No, there's more. Paramadvaiti Swami, one of the major proponents of the plan for Keshi Ghat, has argued that other new means of access—light rail, for example—might also be required to manage the flow. Many others support the building of a Ring Road around Vrindavan, within whose confines cars and buses would not be permitted; or maybe just a Ring Road in any case, one that would connect to a new bridge and funnel traffic more efficiently to the new Yamuna Expressway. Yes, these additional pieces might have to be fitted into the puzzle, but the important thing, says Paramadvaiti Swami, is to move ahead and not drift backward—and to work in concert, not in squabbling factions. Only this will make it possible to create a clean Vrindavan that would match the clean India (Swacch Bharat) campaign that Prime Minister Narendra Modi and his Bharatiya Janata Party (BJP) administration trumpeted as one of their major aims for the country after sweeping the national elections in May 2014.

Working with Mahamantra Das, ISKCON's chief information officer for India and a man with excellent political connections that stretch back to his days in school, Paramadvaiti Swami was able to arrange a meeting in early 2016 with the then Chief Minister of Uttar Pradesh, Akhikesh Yadav. Paramadvaiti Swami believes it was this encounter that persuaded Yadav to move forward with his plan for Vrindavan's riverfront development, but he readily acknowledges that others have also been involved in the planning process. Broadly, they fall into two groups: those concerned about development in pure terms—vikās as it is called in Hindi, bringing Vrindavan into the modern world—and those concerned about saving Vrindavan's beautiful, historic waterfront. As we will see, these aims sometimes come into conflict, but Paramadvaiti Swami thought they had for the moment been brought into alignment. He understood that the local officer in charge, the District Magistrate of Mathura, was being instructed by Chief Minister Yadav to prioritize and implement this project. But just how? Huge concrete pipes 6 feet in diameter had already been brought to the side of the Yamuna, ready to be sunk there for the purpose of channeling drainage water and sewerage past the ghats and downstream: What was the plan as a whole?

To hear the District Magistrate on this point, and to make sure he took into consideration the concerns of Vrindavan's religious leaders, Paramadvaiti orchestrated a meeting in Vrindavan on October 24, 2016. The youthful magistrate and his right-hand man first visited Keshi Ghat, then showed up two-and-a-half hours late—Indian Standard Time, as many quip—on the grounds of the Mayapur Vrindavan Trust (MVT), an ISKCON planned community just behind its temple. MVT's lush, quiet grounds seemed the perfect venue for such an encounter—an image, perhaps, for what all of Vrindavan should look like. The president of the ISKCON temple, a plain-spoken American named Panch Gaur Das, was also there. Garlands abounded, ready to be placed around the necks of the visiting dignitaries, and when it came time for the District Magistrate to speak, he offered assurances all around. He would prepare an action plan within a month's time. He would make efforts to ensure that regulations already on the books—general covenants about loudspeakers, for example, or prohibitions against the use of plastic within the town of Vrindavan—would be enforced. On loudspeakers and plastic subsequently he would try, although policy is never the same as enforcement.

And what about Keshi Ghat? That was a big proposal. He would study the matter, considering land ownership, cost, and general feasibility. He was hearing this idea about a ropeway and gondolas for the first time, he noted. But the UP government in Lucknow was already at work on the general concept. Working through its construction contractor, it had produced a slick 3-minute 3-D video that whisks viewers above the treetops of a riverfront park: strollers enjoy the sylvan delights below as the odd car passes by. What a contrast to the ramshackle congestion that infects or, depending on your perspective, enlivens this part of Vrindavan today! Paramadvaiti Swami had hoped to be able to project this video on the big screen in the meeting room, but it arrived too late for the show to be coordinated. Never mind. You can see it all on your mobile phone, and many people subsequently did.[5] In that video Keshi Ghat and the temple of Yugal Kishor, not far away, are recognizable presences (though Keshi Ghat is oddly formed: it looks like a museum), but there is no indication of anything else along the river—only a set of generic, unmarked white buildings just beyond the park. The beautiful old ghats are invisible. Perhaps they were unknown to whatever tech crew designed the show, or maybe they were simply not significant to the designers. However closely you might look at the video, there didn't seem to be a place for them. The waterfront had been subjected to a total makeover, one that generally followed the pattern of others in the region—Rishikesh and Haridvar on the Ganga and Lucknow, UP's capital, on the Gomti. In each case the riverbed was disciplined into a straight, almost canal-like channel, with areas for pedestrians to walk along the banks. The Yamuna's distinctive boats were replaced by aluminum-style American rowboats, the cumulous clouds are unfamiliar, and the video opened with a shot of big boulders lining the river. Boulders? Where are we? Nowhere near Vrindavan. The software is designed by the Regional Plan Association (RPA), based in New York; Ajay Construction Company had outsourced the job—way, way out.

Enter the Protectors

In many ways it was a beautiful makeover. What a contrast to the total mess of reality that greets you around Keshi Ghat today! I couldn't help being a bit transfixed. But once back in my room, a different world took hold. There too I was surrounded by a vista of calm and beauty, but this time one that was real. Shrivatsa Goswami had made it possible for me to stay on the third floor of the ashram and ras lila performance complex called the Shri Chaitanya Prem Sansthan, which his father had built at a compound located just upstream from Keshi Ghat. The celebrated London fashion photographer Robyn Beeche, who had been drawn to Vrindavan's brilliant display of color and life in the 1990s, lived there until her death in 2015, and she had turned the little flat into a place of wonder: a silver-leaf pillar here, a gold-leaf pillar there, heavy wooden doors carved by a local craftsman, and big windows out to the river. Shrivatsa's hospitality had been responsible for all this—first to Robyn and now to me. How could I not have his eyes lodged somewhere behind my own as I walked around Vrindavan and took in different aspects of the scene?

Shrivatsa has long been a major force in the struggle to clean up Vrindavan, and he's not thinking about gondolas, he's thinking about sewage. When I first came to Vrindavan in the 1970s, the town was actually quite clean. Yes, it is true, the drains were open—then as now—and the removal of sewage and rubble was left to prickly-haired, vacuum-snouted pigs and a company of sweepers who worked with brooms and carts morning and night.[6] But the town was much smaller then. By the time the census was taken in 2011 it had doubled to 65,000, and knowledgeable people estimate that it had easily passed the 100,000 mark in 2018. The crowds of visitors have similarly leapfrogged—to about 35 million a year according to government statistics—as Vrindavan has been drawn into Delhi's megalopolitan orbit. That much more raw sewage gets dumped into the river.

Working with other local activists as far back as 1996, Shrivatsa tried to do something about the problem by helping to pioneer a private initiative by means of which sweepers were paid a bit more than the standard citywide rate. More importantly, perhaps, they were given uniforms to wear as they performed their daily work, and they were supplied with gloves to shield their hands from direct contact with refuse and organic waste. Friends of Vrindavan (in Hindi, Vrindavan Bandhu) was the name of this initiative, and it was remarkably successful in a series of pilot projects—for instance, cleaning up the mess around the Banke Bihari temple. But when it came time for the municipality to step in and support the project, public officials refused to take responsibility. The municipality was finally persuaded to build a sewage treatment plant (STP) a bit downriver from the center of town, but the plant never became fully operational. City fathers failed to staff it with more than one employee, and never organized sewage collection in a way that would make use of the plant. Refuse was dumped elsewhere, some of it into the river, and the STP stood there empty and rusting. Things are a bit better today, in that an additional STP has been built even farther downriver. It went into operation in 2015. It receives most of the effluents it treats from two interconnected pumping stations—one near the Yamuna at Kaliya Deh and another at Rukmini Vihar on the new side of town—but that still only accounts for only about half of the town's waste, and by "town" we mean only the old pre-ISKCON core. These are very slow gains, but a master plan has never been announced. When I visited the plant in the summer of 2018, the seven workers employed there had not received their salaries from the state government for 6 months. Did the fault lie with the state authorities in Lucknow or with the contractor for the project in Agra? The man on the job in Vrindavan didn't know. Later, luckily, these back payments arrived.[7] But the STP only goes so far. In summer 2018 a modest pipe was laid down just beneath the surface of the lane that passes in front of the compound where I stay. A year later its contents still go straight into the river, and the gutter that feeds it is still open to public view—and smell[8] (Fig. 2.3).

Reformers like Shrivatsa and his colleagues have been protesting this kind of mismanagement for years. In 2009 the Mathura Vrindavan Development Authority (MVDA), which drew the Mathura and Vrindavan municipal governments into a single body that would plan for their coordinate futures, authorized the construction of a bridge over the Yamuna, welcoming a tourist-development initiative that was being undertaken by the state government in Lucknow. The construction began with the sinking of eleven huge pylons into the river; these were to support the highway that would run overhead.

Figure 2.3.   Wall painting near Chir Ghat protesting Vrindavan's garbage in words attributed to Shiva and the cow, November, 2016.

It was a colossal eyesore by any measure, but supposedly it would be justified and perhaps even beautified when the bridge was completed. But—a bridge to where?

Not to the other side of the river, it turned out, but right down its center. If a bridge is in its fundamental definition something that connects pieces of land on two sides of a body of water, this was no bridge. Its supporters and builders might call it the Halfmoon Bridge (ardhachandrākār pul), but it was really just a semicircular elevated roadway. Its purpose was to skirt Keshi Ghat and connect up with the rest of what was to be a ring road that would circle the classic old Vrindavan. These pylons ran parallel to part of an ancient path known as the Parikrama Marg that had always been a distinctive feature of Vrindavan's sacred geography; on the other side of Keshi Ghat they would join it.

The Parikrama Marg circumambulates Vrindavan, that is, it runs around the circumference of the town in such a way that pilgrims can follow it while keeping the town on the right-hand side. In Hinduism, the right-hand side is auspicious; the left is not. When Hindus visit a temple, they sometimes begin by walking clockwise around the perimeter, so that the sacred space is always on their right; Vrindavan is treated the same way. People have trod this path barefoot for centuries, and almost 2 kilometers of the route run directly alongside the old channel of the Yamuna, just outside a battalion of historic ghats that march along the riverbank arm in arm—or did before the water receded. For centuries these ghats had afforded people access to the river regardless of the water level that pertained in any particular season. Along with the circumambulatory path, the ghats made it possible not just for people to enjoy the river's beauty as they walked along its banks but actually to partake of it—to bathe.[9] All that was in danger of being destroyed or at least permanently defaced by a highway that would run down the middle of the river. It would presumably leave the footpath intact as it bypassed Keshi Ghat in the river, but in doing so it would turn the pilgrims' experience into the sort one might have on the underside of a flyover. And the process of its construction shoved the river toward the opposite bank. Truck after truckload of sand had been dumped beneath the flyover-to-be, altering the river's main course.

There was considerable public outrage, prompted not just by the bridge project but by the larger problem surrounding it—the increasing degradation of the Yamuna. Standing on the ramparts above Keshi Ghat in 2010 and looking out over a steel-gray river, Paramadvaiti Swami made a pithy video pleading for public support. It's still worth seeing today, and not just because an anonymous monkey provided a surprise ending by grabbing Paramadvaiti's glasses on-screen.[10] In summer of 2011 a group of bicyclists pedaled from the headwaters of the Yamuna all the way down to Vrindavan in a campaign called "Save the Yamuna". They lifted the title from the famous but ultimately failed campaign to "Save the Narmada", a river in middle India that was dammed in such a fashion that 200,000 people had to leave their homes. In 2011 and again in 2013 there were also massive marches by foot. The first began at Allahabad, where the Yamuna meets the Ganga, and continued through Vrindavan to Delhi, where a huge rally was staged outside the lower house of Parliament. Again in 2013 a hundred thousand people marched from Vrindavan to Delhi—to no avail.[11]

Shrivatsa did his part, too. Most of the sandy parikrama path had been turned into a paved road—illegally, according to federal covenants protecting the river's floodplain—and new construction was taking place on illegally dumped landfill. One section of the path, leading from Shrivatsa's own property to Keshi Ghat, was still unpaved, and Shrivatsa intended to make sure it stayed that way, so he took a page from the annals of Gandhian activism and simply sat down on the path. There he stayed from afternoon through evening, and for a time the paving did stop, but that proved not to be the end of it.

The year 2015 saw a minor explosion of events in Vrindavan, celebrating the five hundredth anniversary of the year in which Chaitanya is thought to have made his first pilgrimage to Braj. With funding from the government of Uttar Pradesh for a year-long celebration to celebrate "The Splendor of Vrindavan" (vṛndāvan prakāś), every major temple sponsored something to mark the moment—a more local version of what happened in the Christian world in 2017, five hundred years after Luther pinned his ninety-five theses to the door of the church in Wittenberg. The President of India, Pranab Mukherjee, flew down to grace the occasion, and as a matter of protocol UP's chief minister, Akhilesh Yadav, came into Vrindavan to join him. On that occasion he was heard by his assistants to say, "We have to do something for Vrindavan", perhaps with the 2017 elections in mind, since they might—and did—pose a major challenge to his Samajwadi Party. He needed the "Hindu vote".

And there, it seems, it all began again. In an effort to make it look as if it were doing something for the preservation and development of this highly visible, deeply treasured site, the state government launched a major new wave of construction (Fig. 2.4). It earmarked the equivalent of some 5 million dollars for the project—an amount

Figure 2.4.   Pipe ready to be laid along the Yamuna, as backdrop for the captain of the construction team and his associates, November, 2016.

that had far greater buying power as 330 crore Indian rupees. There was a huge flurry of activity—earthmovers, sheet-piling girders, those enormous concrete pipes, two company field offices on the riverbank, and constant drilling. Activists sued to stop the work, and the High Court of Uttar Pradesh ruled in their favor, issuing an order that any construction altering the current layout of the ghats and riverfront could not proceed. The National Green Tribunal (NGT), the national body established in 2010 to protect India's natural resources and address issues of environmental concern, made a similar ruling, saying that the work on Keshi Ghat compromised the Yamuna's alluvial floodplain, where new construction was not permitted. The Tribunal also noted that the work was violating another provision: anything constructed within 200 meters of a monument protected by the Archeological Survey of India had to receive special permission to proceed. This involved the temple of Yugal Kishor, which was indeed under the jurisdiction of the Archeological Survey—the construction around Keshi Ghat clearly invaded its terrain.

Success? Not for long. Despite the restraining order, the project of paving the Parikrama Marg to Keshi Ghat resumed a week later. I happened by the site on my way to the other side of town, and there it all was—trucks bringing in load after load of earth, an earthmover busy spreading it out to form the new road, and another truck hauling bricks for the pavement. I stopped and asked the young man behind the wheel of one of the dump trucks what was going on. Who was he working for? He was very hesitant to answer. A private construction company, he responded at length. And who was the company working for? Again he wouldn't say, but after a while he conceded it was the municipality. I thought an iPhone picture of one of the dump truck drivers would provide an amiable view of the New India, since he was chatting away on his cell phone as he worked. He threw me a hostile gesture and told me to put the camera away.

Down below, bigger equipment was hammering those sheet pilings back into the riverbed and rooting out the ugly pylons that were no longer needed (Fig. 2.5). That part, at least, was a blessing. When the last of those hideous pillars was gone, you could once

Figure 2.5.   Sinking sheet pilings into the Yamuna, November 2016. In the background is one of the pylons set in place for the projected bridge in 2009, finally removed in spring 2017.

again see the full sweep of the river. But the barrier of sheet piling was doing something else—something subtler but potentially more long-lasting. The Yamuna was being trussed and gussied into the shape of the river of the future—a straighter, more streamlined version of her former self.

With the elections of 2017, Vrindavan for the first time came under the control of a single party—the BJP—at the federal, state and local levels. The Protectors hoped that with this new alignment, officials could be held accountable at last. What's more, Prime Minister Modi had been very vocal about the religious aspects of his Swacch Bharat development campaign. But nothing changed—or rather, everything changed for the worse. All levels of government now sided wholeheartedly with the Futurists. On a visit to Vrindavan in June 2017, the former film star Hema Malini, now the Member of Parliament representing Mathura and Vrindavan, reiterated her plan to create a "unique Krishna Theme Park on the pattern of Disneyland" in Mathura, and said she wanted to see the Yamuna Riverfront Project completed in Vrindavan.[12] Meanwhile, the riverfront project had been adopted with some qualifications by the new government in Lucknow, and Hema Malini hoped for even more—that the Vrindavan area would soon become a part of the continually expanding National Capital Region, which currently encompasses close to 20,000 square miles of land radiating outward from Delhi. The new state government of Uttar Pradesh also announced that it had joined in partnership with Pavan Hans, Ltd., of Noida, the sprawling new mixed-use complex east of Delhi named after its development agency, the New Okhla Industrial Development Authority. The plan was to create an "aerial parikrama" that would enable customers to circumambulate all of Braj in 20–30 minutes from a base in Vrindavan. They would be ferried there from a heliport in Noida. What used to take a full day or two, or even the better part of a month for the full Braj circuit, now could be accomplished in scarcely more than an instant—and a new layer of din was added for anyone living below.

The story is ongoing, and the details still vague: no master plan has yet been seen.[13] Advocates like Paramadvaiti Swami explain that the paved road will be so narrow that only battery-powered e-rikshaws will be able to pass through the eye of the Keshi Ghat needle, not cars and other vehicles, thus preserving the traditional mood for those who circumambulate by foot and minimizing air pollution. Reflecting a somewhat different understanding, the ISKCON officer Mahamantra Das, with whom Paramadvaiti collaborated to organize the MVT meeting, speaks of the benefits that will accrue to the aged, who will be able to perform the pious circumambulation in their private cars. But however the details conflict, I kept hearing the remark, sotto voce, that this fully motorized parikrama was mostly intended to benefit government ministers and their cronies—VIPs. They'll be able to whisk around Vrindavan without ever having to put down their cell phones or dispense with air conditioning if the Ring Road gets completely built.

People still circumambulate the sacred town by foot—Brajbasis especially on the occasion of a new moon, others with a more pan-Hindu perspective on the eleventh day of every lunar fortnight, and both sets during the anomalous intercalary month that comes every three years. But the experience has changed completely. By traditional canons, the benefits of circumambulating Vrindavan are at their height if pilgrims make actual contact with the "dust of Braj" (braj kī raj) by means of their own bare feet. Even better if their foreheads and whole bodies make contact with the earth in this way. This can happen if one turns oneself into a stick (daṇḍavat), as the traditional phrase has it, through a series of successive full-body prostrations (see Fig. 3.15). All this used to be possible because there was a comfortable dirt path underfoot—a path made from the holy dust of Braj, so revered that it has its own name: braj kī raj. Now, though, except for a tiny segment around Keshi Ghat, that path has been paved. It's searingly hot underfoot for many months of the year, and since it's paved, it's become a major artery, especially for the newer side of town. Pilgrims on their walk now confront a barrage of chaotic motorized traffic, and injuries to both people and animals are common. This pattern will only increase if the whole extent of the Parikrama Marg is paved. Meanwhile, some young men have adopted a version of the "stick" prostration that seems better suited to the street. You throw down a sheet of durable plastic, sling yourself onto it sideways for a second, then leap up ready for the next landing. It's all one stylish motion—necessity, the mother of invention. Urban living at its best!

But there's the serious matter of infrastructure. An array of parking lots is proposed for the opposite bank of the Yamuna and because the sweep of the river confines development in Vrindavan itself, land values have shot up on the other side of the river. Soon that too will be an aspect of the new Vrindavan, destroying the town's currently unbuilt beauty. Shrivatsa and those with whom he has been working over the years feel this is incredibly short-sighted, even in economic terms. The historic buildings, the historic feel of the place, and that beautiful view out across the Yamuna will be lost forever. Vrindavan will no longer be Vrindavan, they fear, and people shouldn't kid themselves into believing that theme parks will keep the pilgrims and tourists coming once the real thing is gone. Bigger and better theme parks will go up somewhere else. If Vrindavan abandons its historic core, to use the biblical metaphor, it will have sold its birthright for a mess of pottage.

Nonetheless, most people in Vrindavan continue to side with the Futurists. Construction is always messy, they realize, but they're enthusiastic about the immediate economic gains. These provide hope for one of the poorest areas of India—actual employment, right now. And more tourists and pilgrims will come, they are sure, adding to the 35 million annually whom we have already mentioned. How can that be bad?

Such views find an eloquent spokesman in an unusual source— Jai Krishna Baba, a sinewy, middle-aged ascetic who wraps his head in the simple white cloth that workers and villagers wear, and has a well-earned reputation as an environmental activist. With heartfelt indignation he once explained to me about all the insults to which the Yamuna is submitted these days after she descends from the Himalayas to the plains—the dams, the water-leaching, the outright poisoning. These are the issues he raised time and time again when he was a fiery leader of the great protest march from Vrindavan to Delhi. Yet on the subject of Vrindavan itself, he was brisk and unsentimental. He accused Shrivatsa of opposing development chiefly to protect his family's land on the Yamuna, and he had no patience with what he saw as a lot of fawning over old buildings. Come on, he demanded, were all those temples around in Krishna's time? Of course not. It was just the river and ancient Mount Govardhan and the land itself, he said, enumerating Braj's classic tirthas (sacred locales). This plan to make new ghats on the Yamuna and create a buffer between the river and all those old buildings would return the Yamuna to its pristine state. If that was development, he was all for it—and at that point, as if an image would indeed be worth a thousand words, he pulled out his phone to show me the 3-D video image of the new riverfront, with its park-like environment and plenty of water coursing through the Yamuna. Who could be against all that?

Shrivatsa is not, in fact, opposed to development; he just wants it to focus on the fundamentals. When he looks at that 3-D video, what he sees is an image of a generic, much prettified India that has little to do with Vrindavan. Where is the bountiful Yamuna it pictures going to get all this water, since it increasingly has had so little? The Futurists don't seem to have worked this out very diligently, but they talk about the village of Mant, on the other side of the river. Farms around Mant get some water from the canal system that was established in the middle of the nineteenth century to spread the Ganga's water throughout the plain she traverses.[14] Futurists say a little drain would be used to extend the canal system to the Yamuna. But the drain is tiny—barely three feet wide, Shrivatsa observes—and he doesn't believe for a minute that the fast-growing population of Delhi is going to let a significant amount of water bypass them and go to Vrindavan. Back in the 1980s there was a court order to save some 60 cusecs of Yamuna water for Vrindavan. That water has never arrived. Or perhaps a new pipeline is to be laid down as part of a region-wide project intended to use Ganga's water to alleviate problems in the Yamuna basin. Such a plan was adopted in 2005 with significant financial backing from the Japan Bank of International Cooperation—a pipe from Palra to Mathura to Agra. No results have yet been seen.[15]

And what about sewage? What is this pathology about forgetting the sewage?[16] As 2016 turned to 2017, it seemed that nothing in the new development plans dealt with channeling it appropriately. Those huge pipes, it seems, were just intended to contain the river—to channel it beyond any pressure points—rather than to contribute to its cleansing. Or, if these pipes were in fact meant for sewage (no plan emerged to make this clear), Shrivatsa feared they might give way during flood season and leak their contents back out into the Yamuna. He found it hard to take seriously any plan that refused to be straightforward about these crucial, if unglamorous, aspects of development. So he was elated when the National Green Tribunal ruled that the current Keshi Ghat initiative was illegal. To him it seemed as if the death of the river had been once more averted. The scene repeated itself a year and a half later. The proponents of development had put forward the view that theirs was precisely a plan to beautify the waterfront. The NGT rejected that point of view explicitly on July 12, 2018, and on January 21, 2019, it followed up with a ruling that all construction materials that had been sunk into the river must be removed.[17]

Again it was a victory for the Protectors, but again it was hard to tell how long the victory would last, or how closely its dictates would be observed. To the "progressive" faction—the great majority—it seems the Yamuna is caught in the grasp of a stubborn, backward-looking group unwilling to let the resources of modern engineering and urban planning release her from her distress. Or, in any case, just release her—and the rest of the town with her—so that they can all ride the tide of modernity as modulated by the rhythms of elections and real estate investment. More than once there's been a sort of truce, but it is not a principled one; it reflects no agreement.

In July of 2018 a row of sandbags marked the point at which the construction had arrived. The plateau of the new "ghat" stopped there; only one crane was nearby, and it too had stopped working. By January 2019 the ghat had inched forward. The girders behind this vanguard now supported a long walkway that curved with the bend of the river (Fig. 2.6), and up ahead a narrow slab of concrete had been sunk

Figure 2.6.   Newly created "jetty" beside the platform taking shape atop the girders, looking downriver toward Keshi Ghat. January 23, 2019.

offshore from Keshi Ghat, proclaiming that more was yet to come. Along the shore there was lots of activity. Several young men with pickaxes were digging a trench along the jerrybuilt parikrama path so that pipes could be laid for a new sewer line that would be completely independent of the great pipes along the river. It would carry sewage from the town upriver to Kaliya Deh and over to the STP plant, replacing the older system built in the 1960s. As for its more glamorous cousins—those 6-foot-wide pipes directly along the river—I now heard the explanation that their purpose was to transport industrially contaminated waters from the Kosi Nala, a manmade channel that empties into the Yamuna just upstream, so that they would no longer pollute the river that flows beside Vrindavan. The poisoned water would be dumped into the Yamuna some distance beyond Keshi Ghat instead. Thanks!

And please take a look at those pipes. In the substantial but hardly colossal monsoon of August 2018, the Yamuna had already shredded the new pipeline. It lay in ruins at Keshi Ghat and elsewhere—pipes unhitched from their pipe-mates, filled with silt and garbage or sunken way below. It was all just as Shrivatsa had predicted. Such realities confirmed the wisdom of the National Green Tribunal's conclusive January 2019 decision, but no one seemed to be listening. And that's just part of the picture. Nothing in the MVDA's development efforts tried to serve the broader goals of the National Trapezium Zone, which India's Supreme Court created in 1996 to reduce the pollutants that had become so damaging to the walls of the Taj Mahal downstream. Vrindavan falls clearly within the jurisdiction of the National Trapezium Zone, and the NGT took note.

Miracles, Money, Mastery

As we recall, the first ruling from the National Green Tribunal ruling came down on November 1, 2016. This was not just any day. According to the lunar calendar, the one most Vrindavan people use, this was Yama Dvitiya, "Yama's Second", the second day of the waxing half of the month of Karttik. This is an important festival on which the Yamuna, as a deity, is asked to intercede on behalf of human beings with the god of death Yama, who is understood to be her brother. Actually their mythologies diverge, but their names make it sound as if they must be related. Traditionally brothers and sisters join hands and wade out into the Yamuna on this day, with the sisters beseeching the goddess to intercede with Yama on behalf of their brothers in the year that lies ahead. The brothers thank them for their prayers with gifts. Was the NGT ruling, then, to be understood as a divine blessing on this day—a benefaction from the river herself to her poor beleaguered human brothers and sisters?

If so, it wouldn't be the first time a miracle had been wrought on the banks of the Yamuna. The compound where Shrivatsa Goswami and his family live is built on a plot of land that was acquired from local owners way back in 1699 by Maharaja Jaisingh II of the Kachvaha lineage that ruled much of eastern Rajasthan. It was Jaisingh who built the fabled "Pink City" of Jaipur; it bears his name. The princely state of Jaipur was disbanded when India became an independent nation in 1947, and in 1992 the State of Rajasthan, its successor, sold land that the royal family had elsewhere—including Jaisingh's estate in Vrindavan. Shrivatsa's father, Purushottam Goswami, was able to acquire the main part of the Vrindavan plot and return it to the orbit of the Radharaman temple, with which it had always been associated. One parcel did escape—the land where the small temple of Nityagopal stands (this the Rajasthan government allows the municipality of Vrindavan to maintain)—but the rest was reconsolidated, including an important stretch of land along the river.

This is called Bhramar Ghat, the bee's ghat, because such a big black bhramar bee is said in both Sanskrit and Brajbhasha literature to have been perceived by the forlorn gopis as a messenger from Krishna. The bee shared the beloved's dark color and even had flecks of gold that reminded these young women of Krishna's yellow dhoti. In their distraught condition they couldn't help ask: mustn't this be his messenger? And then it happened. On the day Bhramar Ghat, restored to its former glory, was being ritually rededicated, an inch-and-a-half-long winged black beetle bee flew in, utterly without expectation and not once but twice. This living expression of the bhramar bee insisted on becoming part of the ceremony in which Bhramar Ghat was resacralized.[18] That was a quarter century ago, and it seemed to herald a new relationship between ghat and river, but if the new road along the Yamuna continues to be built, Bhramar Ghat will no longer possibly extend to the river. Already the Yamuna laps its shores only at the height of the monsoon because so much water has been extracted upstream, Delhi being the biggest offender, but this would be the death-knell—as for Keshi Ghat nearby. More than once the NGT's rulings have provided hope that the seemingly overwhelming powers of development with a capital D could be forestalled. If so, it would be another miracle, amplifying the first.

And what about the river? For a time, at least, it seemed that another sort of miracle had happened at Keshi Ghat. This wonder was called Chandi Heffner, and as the name suggests, she is American. Her birth name was Charlene—Chandi is its Indian adaptation—and her presence at Keshi Ghat for the better part of two decades served as a remarkable testimony to the power of money and the value of political influence. That and the fact that it was exerted from so far away. There is a palace at Keshi Ghat, and Chandi Heffner made it her home (Fig. 2.7).

Vrindavan is full of palaces. Most of them date to the eighteenth and nineteenth centuries, when kings and queens from all over northern and eastern India—Gwalior, Indore, Munger, Tripura,

Figure 2.7.   Bharatpur Raja's palace at Keshi Ghat, the Lakshmi Rani Kunj Haveli, occupied until 2017 by Chandi Heffner, photographed in July 2018. A group of Gujarati pilgrims has gathered at the right. Note the pipes intact.

Manipur—built residences for themselves in Vrindavan, but the tradition extended into the twentieth century as well. Jaisingh's retreat house was peanuts compared to these, and one of the most impressive among them was built at Keshi Ghat—later, Chandi Heffner's palace. She is a new kind of royalty—not by birth but by money. Chandi owes her wealth and power to a relationship with Doris Duke, the tobacco heiress whose father's name is enshrined in that of Duke University. She secured her chunk of that vast inheritance by means of a messy, well-publicized court battle in the mid-1990s, shortly after the death of Doris Duke. She is a great fan of Donald Trump. One time, she told me just before he won the elections of 2016, she was present at a dinner in Manhattan that he attended. How proud she was to have been the only woman in a bevy of men!

Chandi Heffner met Doris Duke in Hawaii in bhakti and yoga settings. Polo and horseback riding were also part of the scene, and they apparently shared a belly-dancing class. For a number of years they were very close. Doris explained their innate attraction to each other by believing that Chandi was an incarnation of the daughter she had lost in childbirth, but Chandi did not tell me any of this when we talked for several hours in her splendid mansion in October 2016. Certainly there was no mention of the court battle. Rather, I was left to form the impression that she had grown up in a moneyed old Maryland family, later tasting the outdoor joys of Hawaii as a result of her own freedom—and desire—to navigate the world as she pleased. She told me she came to Vrindavan in the early 1970s because she was searching out monuments that had been photographed in the course of the nineteenth century by Dr. John Murray, an employee of the East India Company. But the 1970s were halcyon days for ISKCON, of course, and Chandi was involved. When she returned to Vrindavan in the first decade of the following century as a fabulously wealthy heiress, she began by living next to the ISKCON temple at MVT. Before long, however, she moved out, objecting to ISKCON's cruel treatment of the poor people who approached the compound's gates looking for help. At that point a close friendship she had developed with a well-known public figure, an Indian, made it possible for her to stay elsewhere. Until very recently foreigners haven't been able to acquire property in India—it was against federal law—but Chandi found a way in K.P.S. Gill.

Mr. Gill, who died in May 2017, was a renowned public figure in India. He was the government administrator most directly responsible for pacifying his native Punjab—sometimes with startling ruthlessness—after separatist Sikh Khalistani agitators holed up in the Golden Temple at Amritsar in 1984 and Prime Minister Indira Gandhi attacked to get them out. As everyone knows, one of Mrs. Gandhi's Sikh bodyguards responded by assassinating her shortly thereafter. Ever since Gill performed this valuable service for the Government of India, he was able to command a personal security contingent of the highest quality, and at a certain point he extended that protection to Chandi. Two bullet-proof black SUVs kept company with two camels in the palace stables—Chandi is a great lover of animals—and Chandi had guards wherever she went. When we talked in the fall of 2016, Chandi made the point that Vrindavan had really become her home— she would expect to be in the United States only a few months of the year at best—but she left India shortly after Mr. Gill's death and hasn't been back. There's a court case about who actually owns the palace. Is it Gill's family or Chandi or successors of the man who tended to the venerable Hanuman temple built into one of its walls? The camels remain, but the security guard has departed. Without that, how can Chandi return?

The palace where Chandi lived was built in the mid-nineteenth century by Randhir Singh, the Raja of Bharatpur, a small city that lies some 35 miles southwest of Vrindavan.[19] His wife Lakshmi hailed from the royal family of Patiala. It was she who wanted to live in Vrindavan and she who lavished such loving attention on the palace the raja had built for her. By means of a series of careful restorations Chandi brought the old palace back to life, investing many millions of dollars in the process. She also opened a medical clinic just outside the gates. She was keenly interested in its work, but most days she was not there in person because she was off in one of the nearby villages with a mobile medical and veterinary team that served the needs of all who came forward to avail themselves of it—entirely without charge. Chandi footed the bill and was glad to do so. These village people, after all, were the ones she thought of as the real Brajbasis. It was they whom she hired to work around her palace, not residents of the town itself—a little colony all her own, though she thought of it as being inhabited by the real natives. Chandi stressed her connection to these villagers. Like them, she said, she hates being preached to. It's "the Krishna heart" she values instead. As we talked, she stressed the fact that she can do without all the "fake holy stuff" you encounter all the time in Vrindavan—the saffron clothes, the bowing and scraping—and it didn't take her long to name Shrivatsa Goswami as a prime example of the sort of thing she meant. He seemed to her a self-serving hypocrite like all the rest, and she was sure that when he found out that I had visited her at Keshi Ghat, he would throw me out of my lodgings on the spot. Needless to say, nothing like that ever happened.

As for Mr. Gill, I never was able to meet him, but for a time he worked closely with Shrivatsa and others in trying to repel the Bridge-to-Nowhere project, and he and Chandi labored at great cost to restore the Yamuna to her normal course after those pylons created alternate currents. Later Chandi became firmly aligned with the Futurists, yet not with the understanding that they would actually construct a road that would separate her beloved Keshi Ghat from the river—a third shade of opinion on this issue if we think back to Paramadvaiti Swami and Mahamantra Das. Unlike what they had implied, Chandi said it would just be pedestrian. A foot path would form a level on a series of steps that would extend down to the river's edge; the connection between the historic building and the river would remain unbroken. She was confident that the construction company, working on the model of earlier successes such as the reshaping of the ghats along the Ganga at Haridvar, would do the job right.

Chandi Heffner's presence at Keshi Ghat was for me one of its striking mysteries, but you could hardly call it a miracle after the fashion of Yama Dvitiya or the appearance of the bhramar at Bhramar Ghat. No, too much is creepy here. It wasn't just that Chandi had sat at table with Donald Trump, but that she shares his paranoid perspectives. Like the pre-election Trump, she broadcast the view that Islam has become a curse to the planet. And not just in the abstract. The Pakistani secret ISI police, she told me, have long been active in Vrindavan—and still are. No wonder she needed an armed guard! Her world is an emphatic black and white. This too sets her apart from the Vrindavan I know and treasure: most people who live there are far from seeing the world in such polarized terms, no matter the strength of their disagreements. We have been chronicling an important one and we've come to know some of the characters, but these same people, however strong their views, continue to interact at different levels. They continue to hope for the best. There's always the sense that a miracle might descend, and whether you are a Futurist or a Protector or some combination of the two, you try to usher in the day—unless you're too busy taking bribes and lining your pockets.

Chandi stood apart from this general stream of everyday interactions. In a way she had no choice: she was a particular kind of foreign royalty and she didn't really speak the local language either literally or at a more metaphoric level. Still, she had a certain uncanny power. What is one to make of the fact that as she rooted around her unused palace, mired in three feet of mud, she discovered an entirely forgotten image of Balaram? It (or rather, he) had been secreted away in one of the basement storage rooms. Chandi inferred the existence of some secret stash as she crawled around with a flashlight, noticing a slight misalignment in the walls, and out came this forcefully molded Balaram. She installed him next to Krishna and Radha in the sanctuary upstairs, and many Vrindavan Brahmins, wonderstruck at the fact that he had revealed himself to Chandi on his own festival day, attended his re-installation ceremony.

Chandi had little interest in becoming integrated into Vrindavan's spiritual economy, with its heavily brahmanical rhythms. To the contrary, she prized the fact that she had been able to liberate her house temple from exclusive brahmanical control. If her workers want to add their own pictures and images to the temple array, that's just the way it should be—simple and direct. No "fake holy stuff", as we've heard her say. If ever Vrindavan becomes less brahmanical than it is today—more boldly mercantile if not more genuinely proletarian—it would be strange to think that at least some small part of that egalitarian sea-change had been envisioned by an eccentric, half-adopted, determinedly philanthropic, fully capitalist queen.

Do we live in a world with sufficiently mysterious contours that this might be? Certainly the people of Vrindavan have always believed that the place itself—and especially the deities who live there, like Gopal Bhatt's Radharaman and Chandi's Balaram—have potencies that continue to reveal themselves in unexpected, uncharted ways. What might this ultimately mean for the battle of Keshi Ghat?

Figure 2.8.   Encroachments—including a newly built whitewashed temple—along the paved Parikrama Marg that borders the Yamuna, December 23, 2017.

It's hard to look at everyday realities and think the revolution (whatever revolution that might be) is just about getting ready to arrive. Huge amounts of money earmarked at several stages for the development and beautification of Vrindavan have promptly disappeared into the pockets of politicians and politically connected actors at both state and local levels. Then there's all the money that has passed under the table so that officials would look the other way as protected public lands were being massively encroached (Fig. 2.8). At certain points, particularly as elections approached, this caused a bit of desperation at the state level. The government had to be able to suggest that it exercised some level of control over all the change Vrindavan was experiencing—something visible, beautified, big. But successive administrations were never able to show that they actually had a development plan. Or, just as likely, they were unwilling to do so since aspects of it were patently in defiance of pre-existing law and the court orders that had been issued to defend it. Time and again the courts intervened in response to suits made on the basis of existing water management and environmental regulations. Time and again government officials ignored those interventions, while claiming in court that they had stopped construction in the sensitive riverbed area. Several officers of the local municipality have been fined by the courts on grounds of perjury—and the list continues to grow right up to the present day. But the construction continues, even though the state government says it is not happening. That's always been the pattern: a court order might cause a temporary delay, but work proceeded, even so.

December 23, 2017, provides an example. On the day before, responding to a suit mounted by several of the Protectors, the state High Court in Allahabad had issued an order that all construction within 200 meters of the Yamuna's old riverbank must be stopped, from upriver of the Banke Bihari temple all the way around Keshi Ghat, a distance of more than a half a mile.[20] Aside from the fact that such construction violated environmental regulations governing the riverbed, the court reasoned, the whole area fell within the area adjoining monuments under the protection of the Archaeological Survey of India—the temple of Madan Mohan at one end and the temple of Yugal Kishor at the other. No construction is allowed within 100 meters of those monuments without a specific variance from the government. Shrivatsa and his family, who had worked hard and long to stop the development project, received the news with elation.

So I went out to the river to see what was going on. Indeed, plenty was going on—three cranes were hard at work and two huge flatbed trucks had brought in more pipes to build the sewer line. A great deal was already in place—the pipes at a level just below the Parikrama Marg and beneath them the girders intended to separate the river from the platform where the park and esplanade would be built. The last pipe in the line created an unusual bit of "found art", trapping flowers someone had offered to the river and a little bit of added detritus so that they formed a delicate tableau. I asked bystanders and workers how long it would take for the construction to be complete, receiving answers from one year to five. It was a man who worked for Ajay Construction who offered the most "optimistic" answer. Vijay Kumar estimated it to take four months, and being very aware of what the court had ruled the day before, he assured me that that ruling applied only to the ghats themselves, that is, to the stairs that would connect the lower level, the platform those earthmovers were constructing, with the existing (if jerrybuilt) road at the level of the town itself—the circumambulatory road. And as if to confirm what Chandi Heffner had been led to believe, he specifically denied that this Parikrama Marg would be extended around Keshi Ghat so as to connect with the Parikrama Marg that resumes on the other side. Visitors would have to get out of their cars and walk. If I wanted specifics about that, he said, I'd better check with the field office up at Keshi Ghat itself. Really, does the right hand not know what the left hand is doing?[21]

In all this, Vijay Kumar seemed to want to create the impression that the court ruling had no effect on the work in which his crew was engaged. Similarly—unbelievably, you might think—a whole string of statements from local and state governments had denied in court that any work was proceeding. When the court was presented with photographs that showed in a single frame a clearly dated newspaper (or more than one) and the work of these construction crews, it had to render a decision in favor of the Protectors. With its ruling of December 22, 2017 it effectively determined that those statements from the government side were simply lies. No wonder one of the biggest cranes worked at night—under cover of darkness—and was still doing so after the verdict had been rendered. I happened to pass by this floodlit beehive of activity two days later. It evidently didn't matter what the court had said or what one read in the local Hindi-language papers. The real power lies elsewhere, and it is determined to create facts on the ground that no court or self-righteous bureaucrat will have the gumption to undo.

Actually, from the Protectors' point of view, things are even worse. They may have hoped, as Shrivatsa did, that the BJP's electoral success at the state level would streamline things from Delhi all the way down to the local municipality. The massive local corruption, a product of many years, could be countermanded by strong leadership on the part of Narendra Modi. Yet the opposite seemed to occur. There was streamlining, yes, but it looked like it all aligned with the moneyed interests that favor exactly the development the Futurists want to impose. Following a shift that could happen because all levels of government were now under the control of one party, a new regulation was issued with the effect that Vrindavan's local government would be subsumed by the Mathura municipal corporation. This happened with lightning speed, as if the developers and their government partners had been planning for it all along. It transpired within the first two weeks after the BJP's victory in Lucknow.[22] This change means that any zoning protections enacted by the prior incarnation of the Mathura Vrindavan Development Authority now stand to be renegotiated. Earlier a developer might bend the truth by saying that he was building an ashram with a major garden component so as to qualify for a construction permit in what had been marked out as a green zone, even when said developer was actually planning to construct no such garden at all. Chicanery of this sort would no longer be necessary, and the biggest concern is that the government might abandon the regulation that buildings in certain areas of Vrindavan must not exceed appropriate heights, from four or five stories in the old part of town (even fewer if a venerable temple is nearby) to fifteen or so on the periphery. Instead, the rules governing Mathura would extend to Vrindavan—rules that make it easy to build buildings twice that height.[23] Such structures would chop up and choke the historical "heritage" part of Vrindavan. Before long they would wipe out the centuries-long contrast between Vrindavan, the pastoral wilderness, and Mathura, the densely inhabited city. The old story had it that Krishna and Balaram, fresh from their lives as cowherds, were easily able to overcome Kamsa and his minions in a great battle at the royal palace itself. But that was then. Kamsa, it seems, now carries the day. Vrindavan is in danger of becoming just an extension of Mathura, or so the Protectors understandably fear.

Who needs Vrindavan's beautiful ghats and historic temples, actually? The BJP member of parliament for the whole area, Hema Malini, seems to think a Krishna Theme Park built between Mathura and Vrindavan could nicely replace them. Or at least, that's where her energy is going.

The River After All

One afternoon in the spring of 2017 I went down to the river where an earthmover was busy scooping out a load of sand and struck up a conversation with a man who was standing and watching. Keshi Ghat was just downriver, beautifully in view. "What's happening?" I asked. His answer was straightforward. "There's going to be a ghat", he said. "They're building a ghat. Oh, and a park". He didn't express any worries or objections; he saw a ghat underway, and he saw progress.

Maybe he wasn't thinking about the mythical battle of Keshi Ghat, but I was—I was thinking about the fearsome horse sent to vanquish the child god in this very place. The heavy mane shakes chaos into a gentle, pastoral people. But which side is which? Is that heavy mane the burdensome weight of the Protectors, keepers of Vrindavan's heritage and a damaged status quo? Or has Kamsa sent the Futurists, with their furious energy, eager to upend what has always been?

Standing by the river with my new acquaintance, I try to imagine what it will be like when I find a park here instead. To him, the park is an afterthought, but in truth it's much more than that. That park, a cheerful esplanade between the town and the Yamuna, will become the big new thing you'll see when you approach the river from the town. You'll emerge from one of the little lanes breaking through the ramparts that the beautiful old ghats provide. You'll cross the new road and the new pedestrian pilgrimage path that borders it, then you'll cross the park, and there you'll find steps leading down to the water's edge—the new ghat. Such a pleasant prospect, we are led to believe. All this is what its sponsors call "beautification". It will reestablish a connection to the river—a river that for whatever reason has chosen (or been forced) to move away from the old ghats she used to touch.

And what river is that? A much diminished, deeply polluted Yamuna, but the hope is that this will change. In January of 2019 Nitin Gadkari, the Union Minister for River Development and Ganga Rejuvenation (among other portfolios), announced a grant of more than 500 crores—some 7 million dollars— to provide clean Yamuna drinking water for Mathura and environs by the year 2020. Vrindavan's STP would be expanded, others built, and an elaborate system of new sewage channels would be created all over Braj. So far, so good. But no mention was made of the industrially polluted Kosi Nala, and there was also no mention of the massive pipes that were not long ago intended to control it. Are they still? Their broken carcasses festoon Keshi Ghat[24] (Fig. 2.11). One wonders, too, whether

Gadkari's massive Band-Aid actually cures the disease. As long as Vrindavan's untreated sewage is allowed to flow past the old ghats and toward the river, disaster is just waiting to happen. Shouldn't it be pumped back in the other direction before it sinks that low?[25]

These things, to follow the metaphor, are deep. Whereas the old ghats were built on pylons that allowed the river to ebb and flow in response to the monsoon rains, the new system, with those 70-foot vertical girders, has disrupted the aquifers that provide the town with its underground water supply. In the year that followed the sinking of those girders in fall 2016, the water level beneath Vrindavan suddenly sank fifty or sixty feet.[26] And what do we get in return? This disciplining project is intended to make Vrindavan's Yamuna look like the Seine in Paris or the Gomti in Lucknow or the Sabarmati in Ahmedabad. The last is Narendra Modi's signature masterpiece. But look behind the scenes. The rejuvenation of the Sabarmati was achieved thanks to a massive damming project on the Narmada about which we have already spoken. Starting in 1999, it upended the lives of hundreds of thousands of people. Ironically, the struggle to prevent this from happening—the "Save the Narmada" campaign—is sometimes invoked not just by groups committed to stopping development along the Yamuna, but by those who see such efforts as key to the river's salvation. There's plenty of ambiguity to go around—or is the writing already on the wall? Very few people want to read it.

The massive project of reshaping the Yamuna (if it proceeds, as seems likely) will further parch the town that once stood on its banks, making Vrindavan a museum of itself. There will be no chance for the Yamuna to return to her former course along the old ghats. It will be like Ayodhya, where they actually had to create the ghats they thought belonged in every pilgrimage town. Thanks to a development and beautification project begun decades ago and recently expanded, Ayodhya now has its ghats, but they lead to the River Sarayu at some distance from the town itself. So it will be in Vrindavan—ghats separated from the river rather than leading to the water. But in this case the ghats were already there! Encroachment and "beautification" have separated them from the river—and, of course, the river itself has inched away.

The MVDA, working with funds provided by the central government's Ministry of Housing and Urban Affairs under its much-heralded HRIDAY program (Heritage City Development and Augmentation Yojana), is trying to deal with this anomaly, but again the term Band-Aid comes to mind. Taking a page from the efforts of the Protectors, the MVDA is excavating some of the old ghats to display their handsome architecture. The Protectors had wanted to reveal this beauty so as to show what was being lost from encroachment and construction along the parikrama path, separating the old ghats from the river. The Futurists, however, have turned this goal on its head by accepting the status quo. The MVDA is making these classic ghats into decorations—ornaments of the past—embellishing them with murals and hollowing out ponds in front (Fig. 2.9). These

Figure 2.9.   Improvements along the Parikrama Marg in the portion built on landfill next to the Yamuna. The steps of the old ghats lead downward, but not to the river. Traditional Braj block prints are the model for the mural seen at the rear. March 4, 2019.

will flank a level-paved Parikrama Marg, the real object of the game, and pedestrians will be confined to sidewalks as cars hold right of way. That in turn will lead to the Riverfront—I capitalize the word advisedly—a plateau with parks and a Ferris wheel, which will remind you of Paris, London, and Ahmedabad, the Futurists say. Or the grand sweep and public amusements of Chowpatty Beach in Mumbai. A Vrindavan of somewhere else.[27] But long before that could happen, we would have the newly enhanced Parikrama Marg ready for Election Day in May 2019.[28]

Elections apart, something is wrong here. The Yamuna, like the other great rivers of India, has always stood for the forces of ongoing life, a never-ending flow that sweeps humanity through time (Fig. 2.10). Pilgrims have perennially longed to touch it, and be touched in return. As they bathe, they physically enter the medium that Krishna himself so enjoyed—and, as the story goes, worked so hard to protect. That is the deepest meaning of coming to Vrindavan, but what can one do when the water is laced with poison and there are so many thirsty people standing on the bank? Few people any longer bathe in the Yamuna, and the image of a woman washing her

Figure 2.10. Pilgrims on the banks of the as yet untouched Yamuna just below Keshi Ghat. Photographed in 1975.

mouth at Keshi Ghat—a common sight when my camera captured it in the late 1970s—would be hard to replicate today.[29] People do still come, of course, sometimes from very far away. The elegant nineteenth-century ghat provides a handsome place to mount an arati, an evening offering of lamps to the river. Someone films it and the loudspeakers do the rest.[30] But it must be disappointing to offer one's flowers—and prayers—in sight of a sewer pipe, and once offered, the flowers just sit there. There's no current to take them away. As for those huge pipes that were supposed to keep the water flowing and clean, they're broken in many spots. The Yamuna trashed them in the 2018 monsoon (Fig. 2.11).

"There's going to be a ghat", they say—a new ghat, that is. But will it actually lead to the river or is it all an elaborate camouflage?

Figure 2.11.   The area around Keshi Ghat, as of January 25, 2019, showing pipes destroyed in the 2018 monsoon.

Can civilization from here on out have a direct and symbiotic relation to nature, or does it get ever more virtual and self-absorbed as it follows its own priorities? This is the question embedded in the battle of Keshi Ghat, whether we read this story in its ancient, scriptural form or live it out in real time today. The fury of Kamsa's horse, it seems, is ours.

3

Mall of Vrindavan

Approaching Town

Way back in 1981, when I worked with Shrivatsa Goswami in writing *At Play with Krishna*, my main purpose was to introduce the ras lilas of Vrindavan to readers who might never have heard of the place where I had been seeing them performed. And the purpose of that, in turn, was to get beyond some disembodied "book knowledge" of Hinduism to a sense of what it feels like to be Hindu in real life. Of course, this wouldn't be everyone's Hinduism—the term embraces such a wondrous diversity that no single place could represent the whole—but Krishna is such a major divinity that Vrindavan matters in a special way. Here I found a chance to avoid remix and homogenization and let Krishna speak for himself in direct and local terms, as he does from every ras lila stage, whether in Vrindavan, elsewhere in Braj, or farther afield. That "stage", in fact, is scarcely a stage. If the ras lila is performed in the way tradition says it ought to be, it will emerge from a much more natural setting—a circular spot in the village commons, or perhaps at a place where two roads meet, and the actors will scarcely be actors but kids raised in the village itself, or perhaps part of a troupe that's visiting from nearby (Fig. 3.1). *At Play with Krishna* was intended to move beyond some predigested standard image of Krishna and make it possible to hear the way he speaks to the people

Figure 3.1. Rās līlā performed in the open. Photograph by Jagdish Lal Goswami, courtesy of the archive of the Shri Chaitanya Prem Sansthan, glass negative, prior to 1945.

who ought to know best—the no-nonsense Brajbasis among whom he came to live, at least for the duration of his childhood. It's theater, yes, but a form of theater that is simultaneously local and universal. By means of it Krishna's childhood becomes a symbol of the childhood of us all.

But how do visitors move into that charmed world, the world left behind by the adulthoods and modernities of every age? How do they find the Vrindavan that keeps it alive? In the years leading up to 1981 most visitors took a bus or train to Mathura, seven or eight miles from Vrindavan. From there, they took another bus, or a horse-cart or tempo, or even came by foot, the most time-honored way. And where would they land? In some dharamshala, typically—a pilgrim guest house where they could rent a room for next to nothing. Vrindavan had many of these. The biggest and best known was the one that had been built as an act of piety around the turn of the twentieth century by a merchant from Mirzapur, a town located in eastern Uttar Pradesh near Banaras. Behind its ornate exterior it could house up to three or four thousand pilgrims a night, and it was hard to miss, since it greeted travelers near the edge of town on the Mathura Road. In our book, Shrivatsa and I chose it as the point of entrance for a hypothetical set of visitors because at that time so many travelers did put up there.

Not anymore. In February of 2015 the Mirzapuri Dharamshala was dismantled, and now more modern, and of course considerably pricier, accommodations are under construction. The financial benefits will largely make their way into the pockets of one of the gosvāmī Brahmin families who already own some of the most valuable real estate in town. It's not a laudable thing to destroy a structure built for the welfare of pilgrims, so the actual task of demolition was passed on to a construction company owned by Muslims. A Shiva temple had formed part of the Mirzapuri compound. That was spared the wrecking ball, but the guardian spirits of the place objected nonetheless. Local people reported that snakes became very active and bit more than a few victims on and around the site, and eight of the ten people involved in the project died of various causes in the months that followed. But the damage was done: the Mirzapuri Dharamshala is gone.[1]

What replaces it is not just the structure being built on that site itself but an entirely new physical and conceptual geography of the town. Mathura Road is no longer the royal road to Vrindavan. It has been replaced by the Chatikara Road, which enters the town from National Highway (NH-2) and thus, primarily, from Delhi—the road that passes the ISKCON temple. There a very different sort of scene opens before the visitor's eyes.

First of all, it opens by car. Buses still find it most convenient to come in by the Mathura Road or even by the new expressway and deposit their travelers on the older side of town, but on the Chatikara Road the automobile is king. To deal with the flood of cars, the Mathura Vrindavan Development Authority has built a huge parking structure as part of its Rukmini Vihar apartment complex; there are also jerry-built parking lots everywhere along the road. In addition to professionally painted signs advertising car parking in both English and Hindi, there are a number of hand-lettered ones content with Hindi only: this is not a high-end trade. Guest houses—dharamshalas, but they rarely use that traditional word—still exist, but it is usually presumed that guests will come by car, which alters the economics significantly. Looking around the penitentiary-like interior of Ma Jvala Dham, which also calls itself Shri Krishna Ashram, you might well think you were at a dharamshala. But no, as the manager told me, "It's a business"—Rs 1000 per night including food, and bookings come in online.[2] As for buses, the backbone of the pilgrimage trade only twenty years before, several parked along the Chatikara Road have brought school children, or they may have brought day visitors of other kinds. It's a day trip: they'll be back in Delhi or Agra by midnight.

Other visitors arrive jammed eight or ten at a time into three-wheeler tempos and smaller, more sedate battery-operated rickshaws. Hailing one of the latter, I might well find myself sharing the journey with a couple from Delhi or Mumbai or Surat who had contracted with one another to come to Vrindavan for two or three days every month as a religious obligation, usually on a weekend. They are apt to be disciples of one of the gurus whose establishments line the road—ISKCON devotees or followers of Swami Kripalu, especially—and to stay at guest accommodations associated with those institutions. And of course many come by private cars from Delhi or Agra, near enough to be able to make it down for a single day or, if they have a place to stay, the weekend.

Until recently, an experience of Vrindavan would have been inconceivable without a trip to the banks of the Yamuna to bathe. Today that impetus is all but gone—a shocking development, considering the importance of rivers to India's sacred geography.[3] In part, as we've seen, the river is just too polluted and everyone knows it.[4] In part, the whole process of stripping down, drying off, or changing saris no longer appeals to most pilgrims. The excitement of a shared visual experience (darshan) of a temple deity, the joy of singing simple chants and songs along with vast numbers of other people—these experiences of bhakti immersion largely supplant a dip in the Yamuna. A similar thing has happened with the land. While some people do still perform the circumambulation of Vrindavan barefoot, the fact that the Parikrama Marg has been almost entirely paved changes the experience fundamentally.[5] Now the words Parikrama Marg appear on official green signboards alongside, say, ISKCON Temple, Keshi Ghat, or Raman Reti, with arrows directing the driver to each. The old circumambulatory path, a three-hour walk, has become a major artery of motorized traffic (Fig. 3.2).

Figure 3.2.   Signage and traffic along the Parikrama Road as it intersects with the Chatikara Road, looking west, March 2017.

But the memory of what was—even in the very recent past—is not lost. A couplet exalting the powers of braj kī raj is still frequently recited as an explanation for why so many people come to Vrindavan and why it is regarded by locals as such a privilege to have been born in the Braj country:

chitrakūṭ kā rām rāj, vrindāvan kī dhūl
yah raj jab mastak lage, pāp hoeṅ sab dūr.[6]

Chitrakut has the rule of Ram. Vrindavan has a cloud of dust.
Rub that powder on your forehead once and every last sin is lost.

The eleventh day of one particular lunar fortnight—the one following Holi—is still celebrated as an especially auspicious time to circumambulate Vrindavan, for that is the day when sins melt away, but it's much harder to engage with the physical substance of Braj than it used to be. To feel the pleasures of that soft and granular dust on your feet as you honor the sacred space by this ever so basic means, you have to go to a place like Mount Govardhan, where a special effort has been made to preserve the earthen path alongside the paved road that now accompanies it. Many people do make that trip. Govardhan and the places near it, especially the old pond-side settlement called Radhakund, preserve a sense of what the old Vrindavan was like in a way that cannot happen along the Chatikara Road. The Gaudiya scholar Jan Brzezinski—who is known in Vrindavan and to readers of *Vrindavan Today*, the online journal he has established, as "Jagat", short for Jagadananda—reports that quite a number of ISKCON devotees and those who belong to closely related groups have given up living in Vrindavan itself because it has become too congested, too loud, too compromised by the outside world.[7] The irony is painful. ISKCON and its Krishna Balaram Temple actually spearheaded the creation of the new Vrindavan from which these devotees are fleeing. But this, of course, is the theme song of suburbanization around the world. Here it is played in a sacred key.

For others it is all quite different. They live in or visit the new Vrindavan not to escape the crush of contemporary life but to supplement and refine its ethos. The old understanding was that to undertake a true pilgrimage to Vrindavan you had to abandon the stable things of life—family, job, and home—and become a virtual renunciant for a limited period of time. Now, though, the real estate agents and planners of utopian religious communities who are creating the new Vrindavan project a very different sort of vision. "Live like a king in the Lord's own kingdom", as one ad puts it. In this view creature comforts, far from being a hindrance to religious practice and insight, actually serve to keep the spiritual senses alive.[8] It's not quite the Gospel of Pure Prosperity that has become a major leitmotif in contemporary American religion, but it's not as far removed as you might think.

Let's survey this new Vrindavan—I propose we do it in three related ways. First we'll take a stroll down the road that has become the physical spine of the new Vrindavan, the Chatikara Road. We will see how the structures that line it—all recently built, many still under construction—do or don't reflect the old Vrindavan. Then we'll motor around the real-estate developments that surround the Chatikara Road, getting a more complete sense of this new ecosystem. Finally we'll do the same thing at a spiritual level: Who are the new gurus who flourish here? How have they developed and split off from an earlier, single ISKCON axis? Our guiding metaphor will be the mall.

The Chatikara Road and the New Vrindavan

I've never been to the Mall of America, in Bloomington, Minnesota, but everything I've read about it is coming to mind as I make my way along the Chatikara Road through the new Vrindavan. With more than 520 shops, a year-round roster of events including parades, concerts and sound-and-light shows, a seven-acre amusement park and an aquarium featuring a "swim with sharks" enclosure (they're behind glass), the Mall of America represents American commerce at its most feverish. Here on the Chatikara Road, the array of attractions is on a considerably smaller scale, but the style of entrepreneurship is remarkably similar and so is the taste for head-spinning public display. It's the Mall of Vrindavan.

Sure enough, the first major structure I meet, turning down the Chatikara Road en route from Delhi, is a temple complex so gigantic it's visible well before I make the turn (Fig. 3.3). Even more striking, at least to those familiar with Vrindavan's temples, is the fact that

Figure 3.3.   Maa Vaishno Devi Dham, showing the Goddess herself, her lion mount, and Hanuman in attendance, December 2016.

Krishna is all but missing from this one. I'm gazing at the Vaishno Devi temple, or more formally Maa Vaishno Devi Dham, which honors a goddess traditionally associated with the western Himalayas, where she manifests herself in a mountain cave. Here in Vrindavan, Vaishno Devi is a hundred feet tall, mounted on a fierce lion, and smiling as she displays an array of weapons—sword, mace, trident, conch, discus, and bow. She also holds a lotus, which is traditional for a goddess. Greeting you as she does from her prominent place on the road, Vaishno Devi seems to play the role of a giant gatekeeper (dvārapāl) to a Vaishnava "temple", Vrindavan itself. In some classic Vaishnava temples the river goddesses Yamuna and Ganga perform this gatekeeping function: they stand on either side of the door as worshipers enter. Vaishno Devi has no opposite number yet, but one is planned—a shrine to Shiva will soon appear on the other side of the road. Unlike most of the wealthy donors who build temples in Vrindavan, the man behind this enormous display, an entrepreneur from Delhi named J.C. Chaudhury, is not primarily a Krishna devotee. His religious orientation tends more toward Shakta and Shaiva sensibilities. But his temple suggests that the great Vaishno Devi has made her own pilgrimage to Vrindavan, and that her presence glorifies the town in new and dazzling ways.

One of the most important rituals at the Vaishno Devi shrine concerns security measures, which are wildly different from anything in the old Vrindavan. You must check everything at the door—not just your shoes and socks, as is the case in all temples, but anything else you may be carrying, including your mobile phone. To check your phone, you stand in line at an office where young men, seated like bank tellers behind glass partitions, ask your name and phone number, then give you a printed receipt stamped with the time. There will be no photography, you are warned, either in the temple or anywhere in its precincts. I'm getting the sense of a major bureaucratic apparatus, rigidly observed, as if one were coming into the presence of a very high government official. Before arriving at the feet of the Goddess, we must leave behind these symbols of our ordinary existence, passing through a metal detector that secures the realm beyond this one, the realm outside daily life. And yet, once I am inside that sacred realm, I see that not much in the way of peace or devotion was being cultivated. Suddenly I am in the middle of a group of schoolchildren from Agra whose teachers were whipping them up into team-style shouts of "jay mātā dī" ("Victory to the Goddess!"). It quickly becomes a game—whose team can shout the loudest? It's true, the historic temples of Vrindavan are full of enthusiasm and noise. When Banke Bihari appears from behind a curtain to offer darshan, the crowd responds in full voice. But here at Vaishno Devi—among the kids, at least—the language of piety sounds like something you could hear at a soccer game. It really is a bit different.

About half the monumental structures along the Chatikara Road evince a clear Vrindavan connection, the way the town's historic temples do. We will visit some of these before long. But just as many are more like Vaishno Devi—hybrid. They belong at least as much to the general orbit of modern Hindu religiosity, particularly as one might meet it in Punjab-infused Delhi, as they do to Vrindavan's special heritage.[9] Vaishno Devi exemplifies this clearly. On the one hand there's a background story that ties her to the Vaishnava side of the Hindu pantheon where Krishna is also to be located, but that's not the primary mood. If you venture into the cave-like temple that lies buried within the mountain on which her lion stands, you won't find much reference to Krishna. Out of the ten scenes depicted on its inner walls, fashioned so as to suggest a cave, only three are devoted to him. The rest show Ram, Hanuman, Shirdi Sai Baba, and Guru Nanak. Conceptually and architecturally speaking, this means that Vrindavan's Vaishno Devi temple is closer to a Hindu temple called Divya Dham in the Woodside neighborhood of Queens, New York City, than it is to the old and historic Vrindavan. In Queens too, Vaishno Devi's Jammu cave has been recreated—this time in a former warehouse—and again the temple's main altar features an array of divinities that is intentionally wide-reaching. If you were blindfolded before coming in, you wouldn't know which temple belonged to which country, except for the language mostly spoken by those around you.

Another example of such a hybrid Punjabi temple is provided by the Jvala Dham Shri Krishna Ashram some way down the Chatikara Road. We stopped there briefly in the previous chapter. "Shrī Krishnā", as it is spelled in Hindi, ties it to Vrindavan, of course,[10] but "Jvālā Dhām" identifies it with a famous cave in the Himalayas where three eternal flames signify three aspects of the Goddess. Jvala Mukhi is "the Mother with the Glowing Face", that is, volcanic. She is a sister mountain goddess to Vaishno Devi, and visitors can sometimes be heard to confuse the two, or rather not to see much difference between them. This is so despite the fact that a model of the Jvala Mukhi cave, clearly labeled and flanked by other clearly labeled goddesses including Vaishno Devi, has been constructed to one side of the ashram's front door. So that is one side of the ashram's personality—the Himalayan, Shakta point of reference—but on the other side of the main entrance we have its counterpoint, something that connects it clearly to Braj. The mountain motif persists, but this time it's Braj's own Mount Govardhan rather than anything imported from the Himalayas. Krishna lifts the ancient mountain with his customary ease.

As in other representations of this iconic moment, whether sculptural or painted, a number of Brajbasi cowherds (this time made of fiberglass) try to help him do his job: they lift their cowherds' sticks toward the mountain overhead. As elsewhere, Krishna has no trouble doing the job himself. He lifts the mountain on an upraised arm—indeed, an upraised pinkie. In more traditional versions of this scene a hint of verisimilitude is provided by the fact that you can see animals nestled among the crags along the mountain's surface. These animals are completely undisturbed by the dramatic action below: they have no idea the mountain has been severed from the land on which it used to stand. Ma Jvala Dham takes all this a bit farther by adding a couple of giraffes beneath the mountain, their torsos adorned in Christmas-tree lights (Fig. 3.4). But that doesn't mean there's no attention to what's going on up above. What looks from underneath

Figure 3.4.   Diorama of Krishna lifting Mount Govardhan, joined by cowherds and giraffes. Ma Jvala Dham Ashram, Chatikara Road, March 2017.

like a mountain turns out to be also a helipad. Kids can go up a flight of stairs and see what's landed (Fig. 3.5).

A very different expression of Punjabi sensibility that can be tasted in either of these two goddess-focused institutions can be found farther down the Chatikara Road, well beyond the ISKCON temple. Here too there has been lots of new construction over the course of the last ten or twenty years. This time the Punjabi land-mark is a Sikh gurdwara called Nanak Tila, so named because Guru Nanak himself, the founder of the religion, is said to have come to that spot in the year 1512 and sat on a mound of earth (ṭīlā) there to preach his message. It opened its doors in September 2015. Because there is a mention of the name Vrindavan in the Sikhs' scriptural anthology, the Guru Granth Sahib, and because some Sikhs have concluded that it must have been uttered here, it was natural that

Figure 3.5.   The rest of the mountain. Ma Jvala Dham Ashram, March 4, 2019.

Baba Hanbans Singh, a recently deceased Sikh sant based in Delhi, should have wanted to include Vrindavan among the gurdwaras he was determined to establish at every site Guru Nanak ever visited, if one had not already been built.

Whether the Vrindavan mentioned in the Guru Granth had any association with the Vrindavan that is the subject of this book may fairly be doubted. In the poem in question, Nanak associates Vrindavan with an age that is now past, the yug or epoch preceding our own and not the one in which Nanak himself lived. This we know because he associates each of these epochs with one of the Vedas, and the one mentioned here, the Yajur Veda, is given as the third among them, not the fourth:

> In the Yajur Veda he made off with Chandravali
>   as Kanh Krishna the Yadav.
> He brought a gopi the wish-granting Parijata tree
>   and enjoyed himself in Vrindavan.[11]

Nanak is generous about the value of meditating on such things, though he ultimately heads for higher ground. He says that some truth or another can be learned from each of the classical four yugs and bows before bhaktas who seek to ascertain what that message might be in each case. They are his actual focus, not the object of their bhakti. But whether Nanak was inspired to speak this way by actually traveling to Vrindavan is dubious—there is no mention of such a stop anywhere in the early accounts of his journeys. And if he did go, it seems he didn't like what he saw. There is another passage in his writings, traditionally sung to the same raga (āsā), in which he disparages performance traditions that sound very much like the ras lilas and their ram lila cousins. The performers of these plays, he says, go out into the market and drum up business for themselves before donning uselessly expensive costumes to dance and sing and play the roles of gopis, Krishna, Sita, and Ram. All this is just to make a buck—or rather, a rupee. Nanak himself prefers a simpler brew.[12]

Without quoting that passage from the Guru Granth or citing any of its particulars, the men in charge of the Vrindavan gurdwara, a granthi and a caretaker, do seem to share a similar perspective. The contrast they draw between their tradition and the Hindus' focuses on monotheism (in the Sikh case) or its absence (in the Hindu) and matters of personal cleanliness. They are eager to point out the spick-and-span bathroom they have placed just behind the gurdwara, right there within the sacred compound. "If this were a Hindu temple, you'd have to go somewhere outside to answer nature's call", they say. "What kind of awareness of the body is that? What if someone is old?"[13] But despite these differences of perspective, Baba Harbans Singh and his cohort have been eager to see the Sikh community open a shop in the Mall of Vrindavan. As with every franchise in a mall, their purpose is not to contribute to the glory of the overall establishment, but to have a chance to market their own goods. If religion is on offer, they should be there.

Metaphors have their limits, and I do not mean to be disrespectful. But I think there is something appropriate about the commercial analogy, not so much in regard to sales as in regard to shared conventions of display and anticipated patterns of traffic on the part of "customers".[14] This is hardly novel—many consumption-oriented, commodified forms of religiosity have existed in the past. Yet clearly there has been a shift. Over the past thirty or forty years the new Vrindavan has created a self-referential world that separates it appreciably from the old, as a mall is separated from the pre-existing settlements nearby. All the structures we have so far visited feel like stores that belong in that mall, and once again the Vaishno Devi temple leads the way. The prasad it offers—normally an edible expression of the visual contact a worshiper achieves through darshan—comes here in the form of a small silver coin. On the front side is an image of the goddess; on the back you see the inscription MAA VAISHNO DEVI ASHRAM VRINDAVAN (UP), with the date 2014 and the temple's logo embossed in the middle. Both commerce and branding are built into this expression of divine grace; it's prasad and simultaneously a souvenir. Too hybrid for some? Yes, one staunch devotee of Shrivatsa Goswami who lives not far away on the new side of Vrindavan told me with considerable rue that she'd been to the Vaishno Devi temple once and would never go back. Hybridity of this sort is not for everyone—too new, too materialistic, too cut off from Krishna and his world.

Do we leave such things behind if we visit the more specifically Krishna-oriented structures that line the Chatikara Road? Not entirely. Suppose we stop in at the Priyākānt temple, the immediate neighbor of the Vaishno Devi shrine: an outdoor gift shop is immediately to our right as we make our way in. It's filled with CDs that have been recorded by the well-known singer Nandininandan Thakur, a local Brajbasi who has gone on a much more global career in the bhajan business. The temple itself seems less self-promoting. There, in the sanctum, we find standard images of Radha and Krishna—bigger and brighter than what we would see in most of the temples in the old Vrindavan, yet belonging clearly to the type—but consider the context. The temple is surrounded on three sides by a handsome guesthouse, and the guesthouse is flanked on one side by a performance hall where Nandininandan Thakur performs when he is in town. Most of all, when you look up you see that the temple itself takes the form of a giant white lotus bud 125 feet high (Fig. 3.6). At night it's

Figure 3.6.   Priyakant Temple and its ashram, Chatikara Road, December 2016.

illuminated in various colors. We've hardly left the orbit of its Vaishno Devi neighbor.

Another example of a specifically Krishna-themed temple that forms part of the new Vrindavan is the celebrated Prem Mandir built by Kripaluji Maharaj. Remember? A rival to the Taj Mahal! The images it houses are definitely those of Radha and Krishna, breathing Vrindavan's local air, but once again, after the general fashion of the Mall of Vrindavan, the Prem Mandir also broadcasts something more generic. This time it is a vision of the iconic north Indian nāgara temple—graceful, and with its soaring spire—that appeals to a much more widely shared image of what a Hindu temple ought to look like than what we typically find in the old Vrindavan with its more Mughal sensibilities. The clearest model for this sort of building comes from Khajuraho, that great temple complex built a millennium ago in what today is Madhya Pradesh. But Prem Mandir does Khajuraho one better. It's constructed entirely of Carrara Italian marble—whiter than the driven snow—and once again that pure white hue by day enables the temple to adopt the color of whatever spotlight is trained on it at night. These follow a regular succession of seven—blue, green, yellow, gray, salmon, purple, lavender, plus plenty of contrasting highlights focused on individual parts of the temple. These floodlights display a structure that is at once clearly classical and at the same time open to the multicolor tastes of the modern world. By day it's Vrindavan's answer to the Taj Mahal; by night, to Times Square (Fig. 3.7). Indeed the comparison to the Taj Mahal is not incidental. Those associated with the Prem Mandir are very proud to claim that of late it has attracted more visitors per year than the Taj itself. If Vaishno Devi is Penney's to the great religious mall laid out along the Chatikara Road, then Prem Mandir is the much classier Nordstrom.

Well, not too classy: the temple and its grounds have a thoroughly popular feel (Fig. 3.8). Visitors range from very young to very old, with the center of gravity falling somewhere near what it would be for the Indian population as a whole—25 or so. Largely speaking, it's a boisterous group ("Have fun!" one teenage boy shouted to his friend), moving quickly so as to take in all the sights, though just outside the restrooms I did hear a woman who was confined to a wheelchair celebrate the fact that the canteen was the next thing up ahead—chance for a rest. The language of visitors to the Prem Mandir is almost

Figure 3.7. Prem Mandir by night, December 2016.

entirely Hindi, and the sights themselves have a demotic feel. Once you've passed through one of the eight metal detectors (half Ladies, half Gents) and been frisked, you find yourself walking up a wide path situated to one side of a large grassy area. Straight ahead, on a vast plinth, lies the temple itself. Practiced Indian tourists feel right at home. They're making their way into a layout they've seen many times before, at sites under the care of the Archaeological Survey of India—extensive grassy grounds surrounding a central monument. Again, one thinks of the Taj. This time, though, the monument is alive, as is signaled by the play of lights across its surface at night and at any hour by the constant movement of crowds.

There's even life where life is not alive. On the right side of the entry area we see another grassy field and across it, a fiberglass evocation of pastoral Braj—cows, cowherd girls, Radha and Krishna on a swing, and a few attentive bunnies that never managed to make their way into the classical accounts. "Daddy, look! Cows!" exclaimed one little boy to his father in Hindi. What is the universal miracle of recognizing something animate in the man-made? Just beyond, a large painting of Kripaluji Maharaj (1922–2013) beams down, together

Figure 3.8. Taking photos of the Prem Mandir, with lawns and murals visible in the background, December 2015.

with a painting of Prem Mandir. Opposite these, on the other side of this outdoor "foyer", Krishna strikes a classic pose, playing his flute while dancing on the many heads of the black serpent Kaliya, or Shesh Nag, as many visitors call him, conflating this snake with the one that supports the recumbent Vishnu at the beginning of cosmic time. Krishna, however, standing atop him, is clearly living in Braj. He rules over a watery basin intended to evoke the Yamuna, and at a certain point the seven-headed cobra starts spitting blood (that is, red water) from each of his seven mouths. His eyes also glow in that ubiquitous theme-park red.

Later, on the way to the place where you can leave your shoes so as to enter the temple itself, you find yourself in a domain that focuses your attention on increasingly specific matters. The first of four dioramas, on your right, presents a scene in the life of Krishna that connects to whatever the current festival might be. A village woman near me calls her friend's attention to Krishna's foster father Nanda, whom she has recognized—again, the "Look!" instinct. Again people pause to take selfies. The next diorama, though, is more formal, more demanding. It features an image of Kripaluji flanked by four other eminences, two on each side. A label identifies each of these as a jagatguru—a world-class teacher, and much is made in books sold on site of the fact that at the tender age of thirty-four, Kripalu was recognized as deserving of this title. It was conferred on him in 1957 by an assembly of Brahmin intellectuals gathered in Banaras, the Kashi Vidvat Parishad. A bright glow emerges from behind his own image, the largest of the set. The others are the acharyas or preceptors classically represented as standing at the heads of four sectarian communities: the four sampradays, though viewers are not asked to deal with this technical designation. These men are, from left to right, Shankara, Nimbarka, Madhva (properly Madhva but misspelled Mādhva), and Ramanuja; the signs are only in Hindi. Shankara doesn't actually belong within this set, since he is popularly considered to be Shaiva rather than Vaishnava, but his widely recognized presence adds weight to the message that Kripalu belongs to a very august company. No one within it outshines him.[15]

Not many selfies immortalize this rather austere scene, but once we move to the next scene the smart phones are out again. This time it's a diorama featuring a model of Prem Mandir itself. It serves as background for a representation of the circle dance that gives the ras lila its name—the rās—or at least we see Krishna playing his flute and lifting his foot as if he were dancing. Radha is in immediate attendance and her eight principal gopi friends play supporting roles. Finally, there is a diorama in which the publications of the Kripalu organization rotate around an image of Radha and Krishna, as if they too were expressions of the eternal ras lila dance. Progressively, then, we have moved from general to specific, and in the direction of what is actually produced and available here: the temple and its publications. If one stops to think about it, a significant feature of Prem Mandir as a whole is the attention it focuses on itself. It is not just that the site appears in miniature in the third diorama and in one of the wall paintings we see on the way in, but that our vision is trained on the temple even before we make our way through the gates. Three massive signs advertising Prem Mandir and the Kripalu enterprises stretch across the other side of the road like sheets that a film crew might use to concentrate the light when a shoot is about to begin. It's all just that—a scene, a scene featuring a temple as the lead actor.

Other arms of the Kripalu organization are considered worthy of our attention, and since not all of them are immediately visible at the temple itself, big signs explain what they are. Just next door is a state-of-the-art hospital where those suffering from many kinds of illness are treated at no cost; the doctors are devotees who volunteer their services. But we may not notice that if we've come to see the temple, so a sign tells us what we may be missing. Other signs advertise the two Kripalu ashrams in town, and that there are more to be found elsewhere in Uttar Pradesh and abroad. There are signs featuring education, too. "Educating Girls: 50,000 underprivileged girls educated", one boasts.

But nothing outshines the temple itself, which is said to have been Kripalu's wish ever since he first visited Vrindavan with schoolmates as a young man. He wanted a temple that would be taller than the Rangji temple, and at 125 feet (including the flag at the top of the spire) he got it.[16] Lest you think this is one man's effort to aggrandize himself, one of the books for sale at the bookstore on site makes it clear that it was only in response to the repeated and impassioned pleas of his devotees that he allowed a statue of himself to be placed within the temple's walls. Nor was it Kripalu who drew attention to the strong resemblance between himself and Chaitanya ("God doesn't proclaim himself", a bookstore volunteer declared), yet devotees find the connection self-evident and undeniable. Kripalu to them is Chaitanya for our present age. Even in the most famous tale of this type, Kripalu does not speak for himself; God speaks for him. The story goes that along about the turn of the millennium (the dates are not always precise) Kripalu went to Banke Bihari, Vrindavan's most important temple, and shooed out everyone else so that he and the deity could have a private moment together. He slipped behind the curtain that separates Banke Bihari from his throngs of loving devotees. It was then that Bihariji was able to speak to Kripalu in confidence, telling him that it had just gotten to be too crowded where he was living—too much aggravation. "Build me a new temple!" he commanded.[17] Construction began in 2001.

Prem Mandir, then, is supposed to be the new Bihariji temple. A great many people who visit it also include Banke Bihari on the roster of temples they see while in Vrindavan, but if that doesn't happen, well, they've made it to the new Bihari temple in any case—or so the builders of Prem Mandir hope they will feel. They're eager to focus our energies on this temple and it alone. As is said in the English-language book for sale at the bookstore:

> Just circumambulate this, the sanctum of all sanctorums. No more spiritual practice is required; no more wandering in Braj or Ayodhya, for now all is unified. You will be rewarded with pilgrimages to all holy places, and perfection in all spiritual practices as LOVE is the soul of all. Chanting with LOVE comprises the complete way towards your ultimate goal—TOWARDS DIVINE LOVE.[18]

Not far away, an easy walk eastward, one passes into the thriving neighborhood that has grown up around the "Angrez Mandir", ISKCON's Krishna Balaram Temple. This area includes a number of ISKCON offshoots, of which we will speak soon, but visitors may also notice another interesting presence: the art gallery of Kanhai Chitrakar, not far from the ISKCON temple. Among his many achievements as a "heritage artist" embedding gold leaf and gold powder in his paintings, Kanhai Chitrakar (1934–2013) was commissioned by Akhilesh Yadav, the chief minister of Uttar Pradesh from 2012 to 2017, to do portraits of Yadav and all his predecessors for the Vidhan Sabha building in Lucknow. Their unveiling in 2016 became an occasion for Yadav to rechristen Chatikara Road in the name of Kanhai Chitrakar, thereby displacing its earlier designation as Bhaktivedanta Marg. Devotees of Kripaluji have taken the occasion to smash and remove the roadside marker that used to announce Bhaktivedanta Marg just across from their own temple, as a gaggle of boys reluctantly explained when I noticed it lying on the ground. Temple rivalries do exist, and they have even played a role in inspiring the creation of the grandest temple in the new Vrindavan, the Krishna Chandrodaya Mandir now under construction, as we will see in Chapter 4.

Vrindavan was always been more hybrid than you might think—and more cosmopolitan (Fig. 3.9). Still, there is something about this new Vrindavan that sets it apart from the old. Part of it is the self-referentiality we've observed—the implicit imitations linking the franchises that compete for our attention, yet at the same time benefit from one another's presence. Part of it is the sheer competition

Figure 3.9.   Old-style performer with his one-stringed instrument across from the ISKCON temple, Chatikara Road, March 2017.

for size—what Philip Lutgendorf identified as the "My Hanuman Is Bigger than Yours" syndrome he noticed along the Mehrauli Road between Delhi and Gurgaon a quarter century ago, a sacred symbol of a rapidly expanding metropolis.[19] And part of it has to do not with a vertical dimension but a horizontal one—the suburbs that create a distinctive hinterland for the Chatikara Mall.

Behind the Mall

The Chatikara Road is the spine of the new Vrindavan, and a whole body takes shape around that spine. From ISKCON almost all the way out to NH-2, and with appendages that stretch out along it, clumps of look-alike apartments dot the landscape. Farmers' green fields end abruptly at fences that border these colonies, as they are called. They have names like Shri Krishna Heights, Hare Krishna Orchid (not Orchard, as you might think), Vrindapuram, and NRI Greens. NRI means Non-Resident Indian, someone who has emigrated to greener pastures abroad, but NRI Greens suggests, by its name, that there is greenery here at home too—a second home, perhaps, or a retirement retreat.

NRI Greens opened its doors in 2009 and has long been fully occupied; only resales are possible. Laundry hangs from balconies and the swimming pool looks as if it's been well used. By no means are all residents NRIs, but I am told that there are quite a number. It looks like a Miami Beach condominium minus the ocean view. A particular attraction here is that residents can easily walk to the ISKCON temple for morning and evening darshan. Many do observe that sacred ritual, but I noticed an "English wine" shop not far away, which led to a discussion about who might be going to such a store. The man in charge at NRI Greens explained that his community's ethos would hardly suggest that sort of thing, but he emphasized that the management had no interest in controlling what people do in the privacy of their own homes. In public, though, liquor is verboten. Up the road at Hare Krishna Orchid there is another wine and beer establishment, whose owner said local people might buy something for a party or a wedding, the implication being both that this was something for outsiders and restricted to special occasions (Fig. 3.10). Hare Krishna Orchid does indeed advertise itself as an excellent venue for weddings and the like: they have special rooms for that purpose in addition to their flats and the little houses called villas. And why would someone want to arrange for a wedding in Vrindavan, perhaps even serving a little wine? So that the marriage would last, a guard told me, clasping together two fingers on one hand by means of two that the other provided.[20]

Complexes like these are what people think of as the heart of the new Vrindavan, and some of them have explicit ties with religious

Figure 3.10.   Sales staff, Hare Krishna Orchid, December 2016.

organizations, as does the Mayapur Vrindavan Trust, which is right
next to the ISKCON temple and part of the same organization. Sales
agents for others under construction often emphasize that people
who buy flats there will doubtless be making regular visits to temples
in the neighborhood and they may be especially associated with
one or another of these. The brochure for Shri Krishna Heights, for
instance, extends the darshan concept to the darshan that can be had
of a temple from its own premises. Some of its rooms will offer a view
of the VCM skyscraper now under construction along the Chatikara
Road. A picture in Shri Krishna Heights' brochure shows nothing but
trees between it and the new temple, and the text reads "Super luxuri-
ous flats in facing of Shri Vrindavan Chandroday temple [sic]". Sure
enough, we see a not-too-graying couple gazing out a window with
a game of chess ready to be played on the bed, and the caption says
"Maximum Flat Windows Chandrodaya Mandir Facing".

My introduction to Shri Krishna Heights came at a tea stall across from the ISKCON temple. The very affable salesman was so persistent in his efforts to sell me a flat (there are now ways for foreigners to buy what had earlier been reserved for Indian citizens and NRIs) that I asked if he was being paid by commission. No, he proudly explained, he was salaried, and his sales boss—confident, garrulous, no-pressure Amit Rajpoot, hailing from Mathura—was right there to load me on his scooter and take me out to the place itself. This fifteen-story complex, consisting of two quite massive buildings, is still under construction—the first building is scheduled to open in 2020—but more than half of the apartments have sold on the strength of the company's reputation at similar sites, two of them in Vrindavan itself. The sales office of Shri Krishna Heights has a little shrine of its own. It is not connected to the temple that will form a part of the VCM but dedicated to Bihariji, Vrindavan's old stand-by, and the Bihariji temple also anchors a corner of the map of places relevant to the new development. A least for marketing purposes, the new Vrindavan is not yet separate from the old.

Shri Krishna Heights boasts some handsome amenities—a bus that will take residents wherever they want to go (temple visits are especially in mind), two stories of underground parking, and a jogging track. The management specifies that the new complex practices "water harvesting", has its own sewage treatment plant, and will offer "Radha Krishna chanting in common area"—piped in through the ceiling, of course, not a troupe of live musicians. Sales happen mainly on weekends, when whole families, three generations' worth, come down in their cars from Delhi. The kids like the picnic, the elder generation likes the temples, and the middle generation likes having the whole family intact. For those who can afford it, a flat in a place like Shri Krishna Heights is a beautiful solution to stresses that often arise in the life of a middle-class semi-nuclear family: the younger part stays in Delhi, the older part in Vrindavan, and they are within easy contact of each other by car. About half of the apartments sold have gone to Delhi people; the rest to buyers from elsewhere around India. I was interested to know whether apartments facing the Vrindavan Chandrodaya Mandir would cost more on account of the dramatic view. No, I was told, it's more about whether someone likes to have the apartment flooded with sun in the morning or the evening—and besides, estimates of when the VCM tower would actually be completed were not very confident. Eight years perhaps? Ten?[21]

Then there's the investment angle. On advertising signs and in its printed materials Shri Krishna Heights assures you of "monthly assured return" on your investment, and over at Hare Krishna Orchid, Rajdeep Singh, one of the sales agents on duty, says values increased more than 100% in the four years since the complex opened. In a rollicking conversation he spoke of the basics, switching from Hindi to English: "availability of the things—you can have anything here ... food of your choice, clothes of your choice, rent you want, culture", and especially a "choice in accommodations—hotel, ashram, dharamshalas, three or two star hotels. Before, there didn't used to be all these choices".[22] He looked over his shoulder in the direction of the old Vrindavan with a slight gesture of pity. I thought of what I'd heard about the restaurant at ISKCON's Mayapur Vrindavan Trust: it's renowned for its pizza. For many readers all this may seem less than miraculous, but please remember as a point of reference the pilgrims who arrived at the Mirzapuri Dharamshala around 1980. They belonged to a different world—and still do. Even today hordes of pilgrims fit that description, minus the horse carts, but you won't find them anywhere close to Hare Krishna Orchid.

One group of new Vrindavan residents does in some way bridge this gap between the old Vrindavan and the new, and perhaps it's the one you might expect: ISKCON devotees. You'll see them buying Ayurvedic products in the stores of Loi Bazaar at the heart of old Vrindavan (admittedly more expensive stores than ordinary visitors can afford), but you may just as well find them dancing and singing in front of Prem Mandir. What are they doing there? They haven't come for darshan—they don't go inside. They're drumming up business for themselves. On many an evening when night falls, they pulse to Hare Krishna rhythms that first were heard in New York, singing the mantra and selling books. Oh pardon—giving them out: you make whatever donation you might like. These people are young (30 at the most, I would guess), mixed by gender (though largely male), and almost all of them Russian. At most times of year there are about a hundred and fifty Russians in town, all of them ISKCON-ites, but the number swells impressively in the month of Karttik. ISKCON devotees know there is special merit associated with that season and like to spend it in Vrindavan if they can.

As among the guards and salesmen who sit around the gates of Hare Krishna Orchid, there is a palpable sense of affability just outside Prem Mandir, and one meets it elsewhere, too. Just in front of the shops across from the ISKCON temple one Russian in his twenties—clean shaven head, a little pig-tail in back, Brahmin-style, and wearing the signature dhoti of a celibate brahmachari—seems only to have to hold out his little pouch with a smile and people eagerly stuff in ten-rupee notes. In a temple mood, who wouldn't want to support such cheerful religious abandon? In front of Prem Mandir reactions are a bit more studied. Little circles of onlookers take photos with their mobile phones and pose in front of the devotees—or among them. One of the younger men among these spectators submits to a brother-to-brother hug from the ISKCON guy with the face-mike and accordion. He joins the dance for a moment, too. The spectacle of light-skinned Hare Krishna dancers is certainly not new to Indians— they've been a regular enough fixture in Bollywood movies—but here are some real live specimens. Why not join the fun?[23]

A general feeling of self-confidence and a desire to be part of the future seem to bind the "colony" sales agents into a single group with young Russians such as these, and a number of the young men living in the Russian House (formally, Vrindavan Dham) near the ISKCON temple do indeed participate in the same expanding global economy that makes places like Hare Krishna Orchid flourish. These Russians may come to India as refugees from rapacious, godless capitalist values, but they keep their hand in the game. Quite a few conduct online businesses from their quarters at Vrindavan Dham. They sell garments and perfume on eBay, broker gems and crystals on Instagram, and even manage online counseling services. And they do the standard ISKCON things. Devotees of all ages are constantly showing up at Apex Computers, located at the nearest intersection, to print out color posters advertising some upcoming ISKCON event—or simply to invest in an external hard-drive. One boy stood out from this steady stream because he was able to converse with the owner in perfectly idiomatic Hindi, crossing a line that few local ISKCON devotees can. It turned out that he was born in Vrindavan itself—one parent was Russian—and was being educated in ISKCON's gurukulam school,

Figure 3.11.   Jiva Das (right) with his friend and co-worker Ananda Chaitanya Das at Vrindavan Dham, December 2016.

which, according to a special announcement on the cover of its annual magazine for 2014–15, is "ranked No. 13 school in India". You have to read a bit further to ascertain that this is not an official rating and that it only applies to residential boys' schools, but still, it's something to boast about.

Such an enthusiastic embrace of upwardly mobile marketing, however, is just what another Russian devotee was eager to leave behind. His birth name was Evgeni, and that birth took place at Murmansk, on the other side of the Arctic Circle. Here he is known as Jiva Das, meaning, as he explained, servant of the soul (Fig. 3.11). Jiva too lives at Vrindavan Dham, and I was introduced to him by the young woman who manages the office so that he could converse with me in English. On the new side of Vrindavan English is often the language of ordinary communication, far more so than in the older part of town, though Hindi is still the norm. This layering of languages is an important aspect of the divide between the new Vrindavan and the old.

Jiva is tall, generously built, and a little on the shy side. Though he smiles and laughs easily, he is quick to dip his head and cover it over. His eyes are light green, to the point of being almost yellow, all of which seems more naturally attuned to Murmansk than to Vrindavan, but Vrindavan is where he loves to be. Things move FASTER here, he says. There's kirtan all the time, people talk about their lives more openly (as for instance in the course of making the lunch meal, one of his duties at Vrindavan Dham), and sure enough, the food goes bad far more quickly than it does in Russia. Jiva is no stranger to the wider world. Somehow he managed, after finishing school, to spend five years working at a series of jobs in Sheepshead Bay on the outer side of Brooklyn—everything from being a lifeguard to cutting hair. Hence his fine, modestly colloquial English. He met ISKCON just after that in Baltimore, where he spent two years with a friend, and that was what soon brought him here.

In a way, what Jiva had to say was by the book—the Prabhupad book—and he was eager to press into my hands a handsome Hindi translation of *The Bhagavad Gītā As It Is*, which was written in English and first published in the United States. There, perhaps, I would find what he had found: that the purpose of life is to remember, and to remember that one truly belongs to Krishna. To cultivate that sense is the purpose of jap, the constant repetition of the Lord's names. It is also the purpose of sambandh, he said—the intense ties that come from being with like-minded people—and of eating together and eating prasadam.[24] And it all leads to purification, a term that came up frequently in what Jiva had to say about his life in Vrindavan. It was hard to imagine that he had much to purify, but that is the human condition, he assured me, and here he had the chance to burn off bad karma from this life and former lives so as not to come back as a dog the next time around. To pipe into Krishna's knowledge of trikal, the three times (past, present, future)—that was the security achieved by Krishna consciousness. And the power of Vrindavan as a dham, a place of extraordinary energy and focus, made that possible at high speed. Here, as he said, everything is faster. This rigorously theologized understanding of what lies at the bottom of the ecstatic displays one sees at the Krishna Balaram Temple several hundred yards away is something one might never guess from the phenomenon itself. It is book knowledge, not body language, that Jiva wants to impart to me, a condensation of correct teaching that is understood to go right back to Krishna himself. By means of this "disciplic succession" one finds a unified frame of reference that explains what life is all about.

Each person has a story to tell, Jiva emphasized, but each also needs to have access to far more wisdom than any individual's experience can provide.

If the liberalization of India's economy at the end of the twentieth century and the acceleration of globalization in the twenty-first are chiefly responsible for the creation of our new Vrindavan in one sense—as we can so plainly see in the real estate revolution—this kernel of evangelical truth is responsible for it in another. The new Vrindavan could not have developed in the way it has without the particular vision of globalization that the Hare Krishna movement has fostered. Hence it is appropriate that in a physical sense too, the Krishna Balaram Temple now stands as the gateway to the new Vrindavan. But the picture is more complex. The most recent residential project of ISKCON's Russian community is located quite some distance away on the Yamuna's floodplain; it is by far the most prominent structure to have been built on the illegal landfill that now supports and amplifies the parikrama road. This element of illegality means that its future is not entirely secure. Rulings from the National Green Tribunal could demand that it be dismantled, and then we would have to see whether local under-the-table arrangements could render such judgments moot, as they have so often done in the past.

Another symbol of uncertainty can be found in the yet-to-be-built spur road intended to link the new Vrindavan directly to a new exit that is being built on the Yamuna Expressway at Bajna not far north of the one that leads to Vrindavan. Just as the ISKCON temple bypassed so much of Vrindavan's traditional culture, so will this new road bypass ISKCON. At present ISKCON's Krishna Balaram Temple benefits from traffic coming not only from NH-2 but from the Yamuna Expressway: the link provided by the Parikrama Marg's flyover-expedited link brings cars quickly here. The new road, though, will be some distance away. Once built, it will improve access from Delhi to the new, more suburban-style complex that is growing up along the outer reaches of the Chatikara Road—the Chandrodaya Mandir, for example—but it will skirt ISKCON, which lies much farther in. The new road will connect directly to a new development called Mayavan, which is now being heralded as the best of the best of the new Vrindavan. One weekend I found an ad for Mayavan on the floorboards of a battery-powered e-rickshaw, discarded by a previous passenger:

> Mayavan Plots are a larger part of the large world class residential development comprising exceptional lifestyle, leisure and hospitality facilities. Meticulously planned layout inside the safe and secure gated community with proper access roads, ample greens and utility distribution points will make living a joy. Plot owners will enjoy access to extensive services and facilities at Mayavan along with assistance in quality villa design.

What is being marketed here is well beyond the apartment blocks that are the bread and butter of developments such as Shri Krishna Heights and Hare Krishna Orchid, though they are nearby. It's all private plots and villas. The ad gives us a picture of two older women greeting each other at a park bench—one's cane is clearly in view. It's the generational utopia Amit Rajpoot invoked, but this time there is no particular bhakti point of reference. "Discover World Class Living by the Yamuna", it says, as if advertising a totally new Vrindavan.

The Yamuna! These plots do indeed lie closer to the river than most of what counts as New Vrindavan, but Vrindavan as we know it has disappeared from the scene. In Mayavan's brochure, as in some of the promotional materials emerging from the Vrindavan Chandrodaya Mandir, one sees the massive temple rising mistily in the distance behind a strangely uninhabited photograph of Keshi Ghat, but all the real-world mess that lies between these two sites has been conveniently elided. It's a classic picture of how the great historic ghats looked before things went ecologically and developmentally haywire. Mayavan Plots is projected as a world apart from all that—entirely separate from the problems and complications that have attended earlier iterations of the built Vrindavan.

The New Gurus and the Spiritual New Vrindavan

The physical layout of the new Vrindavan—accomplished, under construction, projected—raises an important question at a less physical level. Have there also been streamlined end-runs around the scandals and mutually conflicting orthodoxies that created spiritual traffic jams in earlier times? In particular, what about the internal dissentions that have disrupted life at ISKCON? Are we beyond all that now? Here the terrain is complex, and as we bring it into view we must remember that for 99% of the people who course through Vrindavan, it really doesn't matter. They love the throbbing energy of the ISKCON temple, which is still very real, as they love the mood of its affiliate temples in Delhi, Mumbai, and elsewhere. ISKCON has a lot to offer, and sells itself well.

But there have been problems too, and over the years several important leaders have left the main ISKCON fold while remaining active in Vrindavan itself. One of these dissenters is Paramadvaiti Swami, about whom we have spoken already, a loyal yet independent force on the Vrindavan scene. While his position on the Keshi Ghat controversy allies him with the Futurists, he also has good conservationist credentials. With immaculate attention to detail he has restored to their former glory the buildings and grounds of the palace erected by the king of Tripura and his Manipuri queen, calling it Vrinda Kunj, and has used that compound as a place to gather his global following—principally Spanish and German speakers in their 20s and 30s—for a month each year of uplifting talks, hearty vegetarian food, kirtan, and education about the sacred sites of Braj.

Vrinda Kunj is situated in the old Vrindavan, not far from a number of other royal residences (with their inbuilt temples) that were established in the course of the nineteenth century. But these days the spirit of Vrinda Kunj is anything but old. Assembled under the rising full moon of Karttik at the end of their stay, Paramadvaiti Swami's devotees tell one another what has moved them in the course of their month-long sojourn with new friends from around the world. It could be the final fireside meeting at a Christian summer camp, except that here campers testify to their deepening Vaishnava faith and their growing love for Vrindavan. During their month together they play games, they sing, they even have their own version of lila: I've seen fifteen or twenty at once jumping and clapping in a circular formation as they shouted various divine names. It was all in a religious mode, but they were clearly having fun. Other times they simply talk about their lives. The mood is free.

Paramadvaiti Swami has long been involved in an effort to expand the borders of the Vaishnavism he learned from Prabhupad, which became increasingly doctrinaire after its first, more purely charismatic phase. First he tried to develop a World Vaishnava Association that would go well beyond ISKCON's carefully policed conceptual borders. Later he joined an interfaith movement called United Nations of the Spirit, which intends to bring people around the world back in touch with the earth's intrinsic sacredness. Ample, smiley, quick to embrace, and constantly reaching out to others in Spanish, English, and his native German, he embodies the spiritual generosity in which he believes. Images of Prabhupad do decorate the Vrinda Kunj ashram in several places and Paramadvaiti has even given Prabhupad a little chapel of his own, but these are gestures of gratitude to a man who made a difference in world history and in personal guru-to-pupil teaching, not expressions of ongoing fealty to the organization he established.

You do not have to be a European like Paramadvaiti to claim this kind of independence. Two of the most important dissenters from mainline institutional ISKCON are Indian, and their Indianness contributes substantially to the authority they project. One of them, Satyanarayan Das, lives in Vrindavan—not just occasionally like Paramadvaiti Swami who has devotees to call on around the world, but more or less year-round. When he travels it is sometimes in the company of his brother, who has a business in Ayurvedic products. One of the brothers sells products that contribute to the physical side of personal health; the other, through his lectures, makes things come together on the spiritual front. The business is called Jiva Ayurveda, which has as its base a medical center in Faridabad, halfway between Delhi and Vrindavan, where a staff of several hundred doctors answers calls that come in from around the country. Ayurvedic products are often sold in consequence of these free consultations. As we now know, the Sanskrit word jīva designates an individual living person, so the name makes perfect sense in an Ayurvedic context, but Satyanarayan Das has also turned to it in establishing his own spiritual clinic in the Sheetal Chhaya neighborhood not far from ISKCON's "mother church".

This is the Jiva Institute. True to its name, it is devoted to developing the wholeness of any living being. It houses a program of academic and spiritual instruction as well as dormitory rooms, a gaushala or pen for cows, plenty of simple vegetarian food, and kirtan. But the term "jīva" also has another meaning in this context. It refers to the person many people regard as the most important theologian ever to have emerged in the Gaudiya Sampraday—Jiva Gosvami (1511–1596), who belonged to the second generation of intellectuals Chaitanya dispatched to Vrindavan and who succeeded in drawing together the theological and institutional initiatives of the generation that preceded his, not only in Vrindavan but in far-away Bengal and Orissa. In a moment we will return to Satyanarayan Das and the Jiva Institute, but first we must mention the other great ISKCON dissenter of Indian origin.

His name is Madhu Pandit Das and he lives a thousand miles away from Vrindavan, in Bangalore. It was he who led the most important breakaway faction from the greater international ISKCON fold—not to establish something new, he believed, but to return to the actual wishes of the founder. In Madhu Pandit Das's view, Prabhupad never intended that the twelve Westerners he appointed to positions on his Governing Board Commission would assume the role of spiritual successor, initiating new devotees into the faith. Rather, they were supposed to be ritviks, priests who officiated on Prabhupad's behalf.[25] To belong to the exciting new Krishna community that Prabhupad established was at its deepest level not about accepting a particular succession of gurus but responding to one's own inner conversion. Matters of succession, including the initiation of newcomers into the ISKCON fold, were to be more broadly vested, Madhu Pandit Das believed, not only in a person such as Prabhupad himself but in local leaders who might establish new ISKCON presences anywhere around the world. Madhu Pandit Das's call to a new way of understanding the movement was thus global in its reach, but very importantly the person who broadcast this global wisdom was Indian. As with Satyanarayan Das, this boosted both his personal charisma and the authority that came with his sense of religious and cultural belonging. In both their cases ISKCON was being reclaimed for India.

As we shall see in the next chapter, the Bangalore ISKCON temple led by Madhu Pandit Das was to have an enormous impact on the reshaping of Vrindavan. He and his close associate Chanchalapati Das have been the most important visionaries for the Vrindavan Chandrodaya Mandir. Yet Satyanarayan Das is also a significant presence in the new Vrindavan. If you visit his Jiva Institute any weekday morning, you will find an amiable group of thirty or forty souls gathered in the basement, a large, cool space with a library spread out along the walls. They come from around the world—Poland, Russia, Germany, the Americas—and several of them, often somewhat older or visiting with their families, hail from India itself. Whole families are included, and the crowd is racially diverse. Satyanarayan Das—Babaji or Baba, as he is familiarly called—will be holding forth in his engaging, affectionate way. He has placid, observant eyes and a wispy beard that suggests something of a Confucian inner presence. He teaches a range of subjects. The day often starts with an introductory course in Sanskrit. He is a master of the subject, and served for many years as the Sanskritist attached to ISKCON's boarding school down the road. Or perhaps the Sanskrit class has been supplanted by an introduction to Hinduism for a class visiting from Rutgers or by the Bhagavad Gita for a yoga group just arrived from New York. Later in the morning one might have a class on the Yoga Sutras of Patanjali or the philosophy of logic, nyāya. Whatever the subject, Babaji's own modeling of how it can have an impact on an individual life makes it a general introduction to the life of faith. He sits up front on the dais, comfortably ensconced on a cushion behind a short little desk that rests on the floor. Sometimes he stands up and writes on the whiteboard. Someone videotapes. Students mostly listen from an array of desks that face the front in a traditional, ordered classroom fashion; others sit at the side. When Babaji has finished, they ask lots of questions—more or less knowledgable, it doesn't matter. He answers each one patiently and with a glint in his eye. There is tenderness in the room. For many, Baba is not just academic guide but guru. Yet you never lose the sense that you are in class, and some aspect of Jiva Gosvami's textual corpus—Baba has produced many volumes in a bilingual Sanskrit and English format—is apt to serve as an example for this or that grammatical or theological point.

For Babaji, Vrindavan is good. It provides an environment in which students can explore the many things that lie beyond the safe green walls of the Jiva Institute, and it contains the burial place of Jiva Gosvami himself. But Vrindavan has also become loud and busy. Baba thinks of moving the institute an hour away to a more rural part of Braj—off in a world by itself, a true retreat, as ashrams were meant to be. If he does, he will have no trouble selling his land at the highest prices Vrindavan can command. They equal the best in Delhi.

Listening to Babaji's gentle voice and observing his devotion to the values of concentrated study, you might never guess what brought him here—a full-dress confrontation with the most important people in ISKCON. Baba first encountered ISKCON through a friend in Miami, where he was working in 1981 as an engineer after completing his engineering degree in India. In Detroit, two years later, he was initiated. At that point he launched a second academic life with a degree in Sanskrit at Agra University, and continued it by teaching Sanskrit and a few major texts for ISKCON, first in Tirupati and then in Vrindavan. The subject of his study in Agra was the theological writings (sandarbhas) of Jiva Gosvami, and there the trouble began.

Prabhupad, who like Baba and many Gaudiya Vashnavas saw Jiva Gosvami as the ultimate arbiter of religious truth, had on several occasions said that Jiva regarded human souls (again the word is jīva) as having once been pure and complete entities in the presence of Krishna before being trapped in the delusory realities (māyā) of this world. This, clearly, was a Vaishnava doctrine of the fall, different from but comparable to what is taught by the Christian church. Indeed, Prabhupad made these remarks while addressing Westerners, doubtless in an effort to aid his pupils' passage into Vaishnava teaching and sometimes directly in response to their questions. The problem was, as Baba learned through his close study of Jiva's own writings, that such a doctrine was not Jiva's own. Indeed, as Baba pointed out, Prabhupad had represented Jiva quite differently on other occasions, saying correctly that jīvas in the supernal and eternal Golok Vrindavan, being entirely focused on the Lord, do not depart from that state. There is no occasion for them to do so—the classic problem of the origin of evil in a world that God controls. Their simultaneous existence as much more qualified (compromised, you might say) "atomic" souls, the sorts that inhabit human bodies, has to be explained in other ways, perhaps in consequence of proximity to maya, the universal force of collective self-delusion, or perhaps as part of the intrinsic drama entailed by Krishna's taste for and existence in the mode of play, lila. As with the Christian doctrine of the fall, efforts to explain human beings' simultaneous consciousness of the divine and rejection of it—sometimes willfully, sometimes inescapably—are mysterious and difficult. But what was clear to Babaji was that Jiva conceived Golok Vrindavan to be in principle separate from any qualifying, diluting agency.

Others did not agree, and were troubled by any suggestion that Prabhupad may not have been infallible in his every utterance. They reaffirmed what they understood to be his doctrine of the fall. This meant that when Babaji, in the course of his ISKCON-authorized translation and explication of Jiva's teachings, found it necessary to record Jiva's own position otherwise, there was an uproar. Various possibilities for dealing with the problem presented themselves. He might record his disagreement with Prabhupad's representation of Jiva in a footnote when it came up, still publishing through ISKCON's Bhaktivedanta Book Trust, or being blocked from that, he might publish through the Swedish branch, where the leadership was more sympathetic. Or he could simply remain silent. The first option was unacceptable to the ISKCON higher-ups; the last was impossible for Baba; so he chose the intermediary Swedish path. Hearing that the work was going forward in this way, however, a group of powerful ISKCON people, led by direct initiates of Prabhupad, caucused in the United States and sent to all the important people what Baba calls a "heavy letter" saying that he was in effect "a dangerous person".[26] In consequence, everything stopped in Sweden. Drutakarma Das, the leader of Baba's opposition, prepared to publish a book called *Once We Were with Kṛṣṇa*—the title states its position succinctly. Baba felt he had to reply, and did so in a book called *In Vaikuṇṭha Not Even the Leaves Fall;* there too the title captures in a nutshell the author's view of Jiva's position. And all that led to Baba's being called before ISKCON's General Body Commission when it met in Mayapur, in Bengal, in 1995. They felt they had to put out the fire.

It must have been a dramatic event. I cannot help comparing it to Luther's famous appearance before the diet of the Holy Roman Empire at the Council of Worms in 1521, where he had to answer to charges of heresy and uttered his famous words "Here I stand. I can do no other". Satyanarayan Das, hardly a flamboyant figure, found himself standing at the right hand of the General Body Commission president, who was seated at the head of a long table at which were gathered the entire upper ISKCON leadership. They asked questions, he answered—and in the end they effectively excommunicated him.

They told him not to teach or publish and required him to stop studying with the Vrindavan scholar with whom he had been working. Baba
was shocked and for a long time depressed, but he regrouped, feeling
ultimately that Krishna had plans for him outside of ISKCON—divine
grace was behind the whole thing. With financial support from his
own family, he established the Jiva Institute so that he could continue
his work, and slowly but surely it flourished.

In a letter to the ISKCON leadership, Drutakarma Das had characterized Baba as "just doing his own thing—just one more Sanskrit
scholar who has gone off the deep end". "Word-juggling Sanskrit
experts" were apt to do just this.[27] Baba saw things otherwise. "People
don't like the truth", he said, unless it is "mixed with falsity. Then it
will be very successful". It's like offering condensed milk to people
who are unprepared for its strength; they will reject it. Or diamonds.
A good fake is better than the original: it's just as shiny and it costs
less. "If you have the truth, people would like to kill you", he said.[28]
And so it was that Satyanarayan Das was set loose from ISKCON's
worldwide moorings and confined to Vrindavan, but increasing numbers of people from around the world have found their way to his door.

There is a third interesting figure who straddles the border between
the Indian and the global, though this time not a direct contestant in
ISKCON debates. This is a good friend of Babaji's who seems different
from him in every way—Shri Swami Vishwananda. The title is meant
to connote a particular sort of joy (ānanda) that can be experienced in
a global, worldwide (vishwa = viśva) manner; alternatively the name
can mean "joy in everything" or even, to be a bit mischievous, "Joy to
the World". Born in Mauritius and with an early career that had both
Hindu and Christian dimensions—in some settings, until recently, he
could still be addressed as Bishop Michael—Vishwananda ultimately
decided, after travels in many parts of Africa and Europe, to oper-
ate from a base in northern Europe.[29] This was the part of the world
he perceived as being most in need of his message of unconditional
love, and Germany especially: fortress of chill rationalism, apostle of
efficiency, and the nation most completely alienated from its religious
moorings.[30]

It was in Germany that Vishwananda established the principal
headquarters of his organization, Bhakti Marga, in a sprawling, close-
to-the-ground building of sleek contemporary design that is located in

Figure 3.12.   "Just Love" vehicle, Springen, Germany, July 2018.

the beautiful Taunus hills outside Springen, not far from Wiesbaden. Before Vishwananda bought it, this building had served as a retreat center for a labor organization in the region, before being abandoned. Now, much refurbished, it is home to more dramatic retreats. Once a year, in June, devotees from around the world gather there for a three-day lovefest called (what else?) "Just Love", which has created for itself a special niche on Europe's summer circuit of kirtan-chanting, yoga-practicing events (Fig. 3.12). In the summer of 2018 the numbers were even greater than usual—well into the thousands—because the swami was celebrating his fortieth birthday with the inauguration of an entirely new temple that would henceforth be the focus of its worship life. In its labor-union days this room had been an indoor swimming pool. Now it swims with souls.

Vishwananda has centers elsewhere, too. In South Africa he is constructing the biggest Hindu ashram in the southern hemisphere, as he is pleased to announce, and at the end of 2016 he inaugurated a center in Vrindavan. This new center is just down the street from the Jiva Institute, and the building that was expanded and reshaped to house it used to belong to one of Satyanarayan Das's earliest and closest disciples. It was Babaji himself who suggested Vishwananda establish his beachhead in Vrindavan by acquiring it. Already it's being expanded with a new structure next door, so as to accommodate the many pilgrims Bhakti Marga will bring to town, especially when the swami himself is there.

To look at the two of them, you would never guess that Satyanarayan Das and Swami Vishwananda might be close friends. Satyanarayan Das is understated, scholarly, and modest; he seems intentionally spare in all his ways. Swami Vishwananda, by contrast, positively glistens with charisma; an immense white-picket-fence smile bursts across his handsome dark face. Satyanarayan Das is always clad in simple monochrome white, emblematic of his sadhu's calling, while Vishwananda is a cloud of yellow, orange, maroon, and occasionally blue. Earrings, garlands, embroidery, and saffron globbed across his brow make him seem a living, life-size murti, an image of ideal beauty adorned for worship.

Satyanarayan Das recalls that he first became aware of Swami Vishwananda on a Jiva trip to Europe with his brother in the summer of 2007. One of Vishwananda's close disciples—Anuprabha, an airline hostess with Lufthansa who lived nearby—came to hear Baba speak and invited him to a kirtan session at her house the next day. As it turned out, this was to celebrate Vishwananda's twenty-ninth birthday; her altar was suitably adorned. So this was Vishwananda, but not yet in person. The following year there was a mirror-image meeting in Vrindavan. Anuprabha was visiting and happened to meet Kamala, a close disciple of Babaji's, who was shopping just opposite the ISKCON temple, something she rarely does. This time it was Anuprabha who was invited home, but Vishwananda himself was still absent. The two men must meet, of course—both disciples felt that keenly—and the meeting was arranged for Babaji's next summer trip to Germany. On that occasion, Baba recalls, Vishwananda lined up all the disciples living there in a double row to give him a welcome. They chanted mantras and threw flowers in his direction as he passed between the two lines. Talk about a contrast to Mayapur! Satyanarayan

Das and Swami Vishwananda became instant friends, and they began to exchange regular semiannual visits, with Baba staying in Springen for a couple days in the summer and Vishwananda visiting the Jiva Institute at some point in the colder months. Some of Babaji's devotees, seeing the friendship blossom, were worried: "He'll take over the Jiva Institute". Baba had a quick response. "Let him, then. He is my friend!"[31]

And a most unusual friendship it has become. Several times Babaji has traveled with Vishwananda in Europe for occasions that Vishwananda calls darshan sessions. A large group of his disciples gathers—there can be a thousand—and wait to have an individual face-to-face moment with him in which, says Babaji, "he does some mystical thing". Meanwhile Babaji lectures, which makes the long wait profitable in a different way. It is a remarkable partnership. I find it hard to resist an image of Krishna with his older brother Balaram, the one very dark (the word Krishna means literally "black"), the other white, and both striding forth to conquer demons or just herd cows. I admit that the analogy is flawed—Balaram was less intellectual than his brother and quite the drinker—but still, I can't resist the thought. They make an unusual, deeply bonded pair, and the fun they have shared is real.

One night in the course of the inaugural ceremonies for Swami Vishwananda's new center in Vrindavan you could see this brotherly bond being physically enacted. There under a vast orange-and-white tent filled with musicians and devotees—mostly Vishwananda's but some of Baba's too—Satyanarayan Das was drawn into a dance with Vishwananda. Their hands and arms locked, they swirled with centrifugal energy, and a host of bhajan-singing, drum-beating, clapping devotees cheered them on. Will young people belonging to Swami Vishwananda's community now start coming to the Jiva Institute to study Sanskrit and Gaudiya theology? And will Baba's disciples drink in the aura of Vishwananda? Perhaps—and if so, in either case, they will only have to travel a few steps down the road.[32]

The link to Satyanarayan Das played a definite role in precipitating Vishwananda's decision to open shop in Vrindavan, but the bigger picture relates to the mall—not the specific physical mall on the Chatikara Road, but the broader spiritual mall it represents. If Shiva and Shakti and Big Hanuman could be accommodated in the "Mall of Vrindavan", why not also Vishwananda's special bhakti elixir? Here is the man who according to his community has spent his life "effortlessly connecting principles of eastern spirituality with elements of western spiritual tradition. Swami Vishwananda reveals the underlying oneness of the Divine and inspires a unique experience of spirituality regardless of culture, religion, gender, or age".[33] This does not mean that actual Christian images will ever be installed in Vishwananda's Vrindavan temple as they have been at Springen, where parallel Hindu and Christian chapels used to flank a single airy hall. With the opening of the new temple room in a different part of the complex—very definitely Hindu and centered on a large image of Narasimha, Vishnu's Lion-Man avatar—the erstwhile Hindu temple has been transformed into a "Hindu Saint Museum". It still stands in a balanced relationship to the Christian chapel just across the hall. Both rooms are crammed with icons, images, and relics, but these are drawn from different traditions. The fact that the erstwhile Hindu temple has been "museumized", however, reveals something else—that the ashram has become increasingly, self-confidently Hindu even in the few years since it was founded. The new temple is far larger and far more dramatic as an open space expecting large crowds. There used to be daily services in both Hindu and Christian settings, but now the Christian service has been reduced to a weekly affair.[34]

Understandably, this trend within the Bhakti Marga movement is openly to be seen in Vrindavan, where there is no explicitly Christian worship setting—in part, a gesture to Vrindavan's specifically Hindu sensibilities.[35] Yet the interreligious, even universalist orientation of Swami Vishwananda's message has not been lost. To me, at least, it finds expression in the rather special nature of the deity who was installed there in December 2016—a seemingly world-encompassing figure with distinctly personal sense of appeal. This is Giridhari, Krishna as the lifter (dhārī) of Mount (giri) Govardhan, but now this Giridhari has been reinterpreted as "the uplifter of hearts". Quite unusually, he is shown with the Yamuna as his consort.[36] The name Giridhari is often closely associated with that of the iconic female Rajasthani poet Mirabai, whose legend circulated already in the sixteenth century and whose claim on hearts ever since has been immense. Though we have written access to only a single Mirabai poem from the sixteenth century, people have no trouble connecting to her through the many poems that have come to bear her name since.[37] Many of them bind her own name to that of urbane (nāgar) Giridhari in a single, composite oral signature: "Mira's Lord is the clever Mountain-Lifter". Since the mountain lifted by Krishna is located right here in the Braj country, it is no surprise that he is frequently venerated by means of stones that people take home.[38] In the new Vishwananda temple, however, we have something additional—a strapping 6-foot Giridhari whose pose recalls Mountain-Lifter images that can be traced back as far as the fourth century CE in the Braj area itself. Elsewhere, on occasion, they could indeed become monumental in size. I am not claiming that Swami Vishwananda was specifically drawing on this early history in commissioning his new Mountain-Lifter, but he must have known what an innovation it was to reinsert this image into a religious culture that had long since preferred worshiping Krishna as an amorous, flute-playing cowherd. There is something quietly revolutionary here—something that connects discreetly and perhaps unknowingly to the monumental tendencies on display along the nearby Chatikara Road. At Swami Vishwananda's new temple-ashram we are also swimming in the moods of the new Vrindavan, but in ways that appeal to a substantially new international crowd. The very fact that this temple need not be on the Chatikara Road to be noticed by the right people already indicates as much. The Internet does the advertising, if advertising is required, and Bhakti Marga's international following already knows.

On Sunday, December 4, 2016, the new Giridhari image in Sheetal Chhaya was inaugurated in a rite of abhishek whereby, in the style of the temples of South India, a succession of liquid substances is showered over the head of the deity. In the case of the most viscous among these substances, sandalwood paste, the "liquid" is smeared across his body. Then a shower of water clears away that offering, and the deity is bathed in another substance. Repeat, repeat, repeat (Fig. 3.13). And not just for this image but also for the statue of the River Yamuna, who stands as his left side in the spousal position that the Vallabh Sampraday sometimes celebrates, and for smaller images across and below—one of Ramanuja, to whom Swami Vishwananda claims ties via his initiation into the Shri Vaishnava Sampraday, and once again an image of the Lion-Man avatar of Vishnu-Krishna.

Figure 3.13.   Swamini Vishwamohini placing sandal-paste marks (a form of prasād, since it had earlier been offered to Giridhari Krishna himself) on the forehead of a female devotee, December 4, 2016.

This Narasimha—moved to the center in Springen but a second-order divinity in Vrindavan—is a vivid, sheer-strength presence that is felt with special force among some members of Vishwananda's community. Swami Vishwananda once manifested a hot metal image of this Narasimha out of his own flesh. The recipient was a young man, Brazilian by birth and forceful by temperament, who was to join Vishwananda's circle of innermost companions and become the movement's principal theorist. Once initiated, he became Swami Vishwarevatikaantananda, or more simply Revatikaant; all of Vishwananda's sub-swamis wrap their names in his (Fig. 4.13).

At a certain point in the Vrindavan ceremony these larger statues were joined by a much smaller image who completes the array—and in a way outclasses any of them. This is Vishwananda's personal murti, the very deity who is said to have been worshipped by Mirabai herself, the one she brought to her own wedding and from whom she vowed never to be separated. Though he is called Giridhari or Giridhar, the mountain-lifter, in most Mirabai songs, he somehow has come to be thought of in visual terms not with his arm heroically uplifted (Fig. 7.4) but rather playing the flute (Fig. 6.8). In the popular imagination, then, this flute-playing Krishna must have been the deity Mirabai brought with her when she made her own pilgrimage to Vrindavan in the course of the sixteenth century. She hoped to engage one of its great Gauḍīya theologians in conversation. In the *Bhaktirasabodhinī* commentary on the *Bhaktamāl* of Nabhadas, Priyadas tells this story as a meeting with Jiva Gosvami. Mirabai asks why he will not abandon his ascetic pretensions, his vow to have no interaction with women, and talk with her. As far as she can see there is only one true man in Vrindavan anyway—Krishna; the rest of us are sakhis, his female servants. Hearing this, Jiva relents.[39] How appropriate, then, that Vishwananda's abhishek ceremony transpired not a hundred yards from the Jiva Institute. Conches blared, music sounded, and only the luckiest of devotees could be accommodated inside the temple itself. The rest had to listen through loudspeakers installed for the benefit of those who stood in the lane outside.

They too got to participate, however, when the ceremony drew to its conclusion. (By then Vishwananda's Mirabai murti had retired to his private quarters.) Swami Vishwananda invited all present to join him in showering the sacred liquids on the deities a final time. Such general participation would be unheard of in the old Vrindavan, where only specially initiated Braj Brahmins belonging to this or that gosvami lineage are afforded such a privilege. But in this context the meaning of initiation had changed. It had been liberated from that history of specific successions and relocated in a living global guru whose authority is clearly charismatic—an apostle of the present. It was a bit of a balancing act. On this formal initiatory occasion—not just for the murtis but for Vishwananda himself as he made his debut in Vrindavan society—it also seemed important to Vishwananda that he display the approbation of other gurus in the local Gaudiya fold. This he achieved through the participation of Sadhu Maharaj, whom we have mentioned, along with Abhishek Goswami from the Radharaman temple lineage and a well-beloved sadhu from Barsana called Vinod Bihari Baba. These men, whose respective credentials are royalty, lineage, and affect, in that order, provided for Vishwananda what the local community of Vrindavan scholars had provided for Satyanarayan Das several years before when they recognized him as a bona fide preceptor, an acharya. Or at least they did so in the eyes of his own followers.

With all of Vishvananda's devotees participating in the act of sprinkling liquid substances on the deities, this abhishek was a remarkable occasion—the priesthood of all believers, if we may once again reach for a Lutheran comparison, enacted right here in Vrindavan. But there were conditions. Vishwananda made sure to tell all who wished to come forward that they would need to wash themselves before entering the sanctum sanctorum. Following traditional Hindu practice, too, menstruating women would have to stay away. Thus the line formed, and it took well over an hour before each person had made her or his way forward into the presence of the deities.

This matter of physical connection is central to Swami Vishwananda's message and to his style. The moment when Revatikaant received his Narasimha idol in Springen at 2:00 in the morning is a telling example. Frustrated that his critical approach to life would forever separate him from the simple ability to feel, he laid out his grief to Vishwananda. They were alone together at the end of a very long day. "Do you want a spiritual experience?" his guru asked him warily. Yes. He asked again later: "Are you sure?" Revatikaant did not know what it would mean, but yes, he was sure. At that point the older man—older, but only by a dozen years—invited the younger to touch his chest, directly over his heart. Only an undershirt stood between them. Revatikaant could feel an inner heat that went beyond anything he'd ever imagined, and the throb of his guru's heartbeat was fast and machinelike, like a fusillade of bullets. Soon Vishwananda reached beneath his left sleeve and produced the Narasimha image. Revatikaant took it in his hand. It was searing to the touch.[40]

Not every encounter with Vishwananda's fleshly presence is that dramatic, of course. As I found myself sitting at table with him and a few others on the uppermost story of his newly opened Vrindavan ashram, Swami Vishwananda offered me a scaly brown bulb he called snake-fruit and invited me to eat. I had never before seen this exotic thing—it turned out to be from Bali—and was a little hesitant about what to do with it. Reluctant to accept what seemed like a playful personal challenge, I asked if someone would like to share the snake-fruit with me. Two of his lieutenant swamis stepped forward and helped me peel back the skin. The inside had soft, moist, cream-colored surfaces—delicious, too, as I was to discover—and one of the swamis, in the course of peeling, joked about the fact that the fruit shaped itself into two little balls. I thought they looked a bit like bulging eyes, but he was thinking of something else. And what about Vishwananda? How did he know I've always been afraid of snakes?

Is this too the new Vrindavan? In a way, perhaps, it is. Vrindavan has always been a symbol of love—a physical symbol of love—and the thrills, terrors, and deep rewards of love clearly swirl around this newly emergent guru. One of his acolytes, a curly-haired German named Akshaj with a technical background, who served as one of the entrance guards for the space where the inauguration happened, stressed this theme as he looked back on his own seven-year history with Bhakti Marga. Akshaj's first contact with Vishwananda had been at a distance. A friend had told him about Vishwananda, and he somehow chanced to see his picture. When it happened—at that very moment—he heard these words ringing in his ear: "Hier is dein Meister. Hier is dein Meister. Hier is dein Meister". "Here is your master"—three times over—and it's been that way ever since. It's not easy to have a guru, Akshaj explains. At first it seems so, especially with someone like this, since Vishwananda is obviously so loving and accepting. But once you get into it, as he said, "it's the hardest thing I ever did in my life". This guru is finely attuned to any sign of ego and pride, and supremely able to knock it away, either by himself or through others at the ashram. "It's like walking through the fire". It burns. His purpose is to destroy "mind", which gets in the way of everything—and specifically in the way of love. Here Akshaj's imagery was very strong. Vishwananda takes a hammer to that mind, he said—a huge cudgel. Any hint of self-satisfaction is enough to incite the blow. His purpose is to shake you to the core.[41]

Was that Krishna's purpose, I wondered, in deserting the gopis? There, as here, it happened in the context of a sense of material certainty: the gopis were unwilling to accept any substitute for

Krishna's physical presence. After he departed for Mathura and farther west, Vrindavan devolved into what the gopis felt to be a desert. Seeing that, Krishna sent his messenger Udho to persuade them to accept an ever-present spirituality denuded of any specific sense of place or body, but this seemed useless to them. Similarly for Akshaj—it was the body. What Vishwananda said in his commentary on the Bhagavad Gita about the body's being an electromagnetic field—apropos of the chapter on field (kṣetra)—made sense to the engineer in Akshaj, but the main thing was that you could tell Vishwananda had been physically present at the epic battle the Gita described. "He was there!" For Akshaj, here is the Krishna of our present moment.

Personally, I would be happy to call this an alternate sense of materiality, yet I am sure that Akshaj would reject the "alternate" part. For him, there actually is no other. This is bodily truth, and only that can open the way to conceptual truth. No wonder Akshaj first heard about Swami Vishwananda while visiting the ashram of the miracle-worker saint Satya Sai Baba in Puttaparathi, just outside Bangalore. Vishwanand had been there before him, as a teenager.[42] But the bigger picture is Krishna—Krishna powerfully, locally, physically represented. It makes sense that, unbeknownst to Akshaj at the time, Vishwananda had been to that very place before him. What Akshaj was hearing in his inner ear was not just hearsay.

This material access to Krishna, and specifically to the Krishna of Braj, is proclaimed as nowhere else by the murti Vishwananda personally worships—Mirabai's murti, the Krishna of her own personal bhakti. The story of how this image came into his possession takes us to the Himalayas. Swami Vishwananda and some of his close disciples, having visited Vaishno Devi in Kashmir and the Dalai Lama in Dharamsala, happened to notice an obscure sign as they traveled along a mountain road in the Kangra region. It claimed to point to an old Krishna temple connected with Mirabai. Vishwananda, of course, wanted to see it. The road narrowed and narrowed for five miles or so and finally ended in a tiny village. At first they saw no temple at all, but the villagers had them lift their eyes in the direction of a ruined castle on the hill—seemingly at the end of the world, Vishwananda said. He then summoned the old temple priest, who showed them its main image, explaining that it was the very one into which Mirabai had disappeared at the end of her life in Dvaraka. He also showed them the contents of the bag she always kept with her, explaining that the king who once lived in this ruined palace had acquired it as a gift when he went to Rajasthan and visited the royal family into which Mirabai had married—distant relatives of his own. The Rajasthani king (Vishwananda was no more specific than that) offered his visitor whatever he wanted—the requisite royal hospitality—but the visiting king demurred. Pressed, though, he asked for something whimsical: Mirabai's Krishna, the one she used to carry everywhere. He knew this was an impossible demand. The king's wife had taken this image into her personal possession, worshiping it daily, and certainly could not be parted from it. To ask for it was a way to accept the offer of royal largess without actually requiring that the donor to follow through. Thus the Kangra king was happily ready to go his way, knowing the image would stay in Rajasthan where it had always been.

That night, though, the queen unexpectedly died. "Did the deity arrange it?", Vishwananda asked with a chuckle. "It's possible, you know". And that meant the tiny flute-playing Krishna went to Kangra with the visiting king after all. Then, with many smiles and laughs, Vishwananda revealed how he himself unwittingly walked into the story. He too found it impossible not to ask for one of Mirabai's Gopals—either the big one from Dvaraka or the small flute-playing one she kept with her at all times. The pujari said that both options would be impossible. The big Giridhari was rooted in the temple, and as for the smaller one, only the president of the temple trust could grant such a wish, and she was away. Suddenly, though, she materialized among them saying "Give him whatever he asks". Thus Vishwananda went off with the smaller, flute-playing Giridhari, and he has served him unstintingly ever since. Wherever Vishwananda goes, so does he, just as it had always been for Mirabai. In a way, Vishwananda became both the Kangra king and the Rajasthani princess-saint as the old story acted itself out in present time, though he claimed neither role explicitly as he told the tale.[43] In both regards Mirabai's Krishna has claimed Vishwananda as his own—not doctrinally or in the spirit, but body to body.

The little book *Giridhari: The Uplifter of Hearts*, created to accompany the inauguration of the Vrindavan temple, focuses on this murti of Giridhari rather than the larger public one that was the main focus of the abhishek offerings. Just as at the ruined Kangra temple, the larger Giridhari stands as background to the image who is actually present with Vishwananda all the time. To inculcate the intimacy surrounding this latter Giridhari was the editors' purpose in assembling the *Uplifter of Hearts* book. All the words it contains are Vishwananda's own, and they exude an unvarnished practicality. Consider the following three-step guruvākya (guru's words) meditation formula, which is printed on the page opposite a photograph of "Meerabai's Giridhari Gopal":

1. Gaze at the Divine form of Giridhari on the opposite page and silently and continuously repeat to yourself 'Giridhari.' (One minute)
2. Continue chanting His name, but now close your eyes and visualize His form on your third eye, chanting 'Giridhari' with each inhalation and exhalation. On your own timing, move this visualization down to your heart. (Two minutes)
3. Open your eyes and read one Guruvakya from the Giridhari Guruvakyas section slowly to yourself three times and let its wisdom speak to you. Simply reflect on the meaning that comes to you, and enjoy these most intimate moments with the Divine, sitting in His presence. There's only Him and you in the chamber of your heart, so feel embraced by His love and send the Love He gives you back to him. (2 minutes).[44]

Thus Giridhari passes from Vishwananda's possession into that of everyone who undertakes this practice. This, no doubt, is a mediated practice—mediated by the book—but Swami Vishwananda himself requires no such mediation. He carries the murti with him wherever he goes. He is always, you could say, in Braj. He was in Vrindavan a long time before he arrived (Fig. 3.14).

Vrindavan and the New Generation

It may be regarded as a failing that a foreigner appraising what is new about the new Vrindavan should spend so much time talking about other foreigners. I concede the point. And one could also be critical of the fact that so much of the information given in this chapter has been mediated by the English language. Yet I am convinced, to my own dismay, that the natural medium for much that

Figure 3.14.   Swami Vishwananda with Mirabai and the flute-playing Giridhari image they share, painted by a devotee. Bhakti Marga Ashram, Springen, Germany, June 28, 2018.

has happened in the new Vrindavan is both foreign and English, and that the town's rapidly expanding access to an international world is responsible for a great deal of what makes the new Vrindavan new. Even if the language of one of its major institutions, the Vaishno Devi temple, is entirely Hindi, the resources that made its construction possible are dependent on English. The Aadesh Institute founded by J.C. Chaudhury aspires to funnel students entirely in the direction of schools whose medium is English only. Similarly, though the language almost always spoken at Prem Mandir is Hindi, the funding that made its construction possible came also from abroad, and the doctors in its hospital all speak English. The Russian accent of present-day ISKCON in Vrindavan provides an interesting twist, but when such people interact with locals they do so largely in English. The texts on which they rely to guide their own spiritual lives and which they try to sell to others are publications that emerged first in English. Prabhupad's books are translated into Russian not from any language originally Indic, but English.

Thus the "English Temple" I tried so hard to tune out in the 1970s has won the game—or rather, the playing field on which it played has won the game. ISKCON's Angrez Mandir has become the obvious pivotal point that separates the new Vrindavan from the old, and this is true both geographically and cultural speaking. In physical terms the old Vrindavan stands on one side, the new Vrindavan on the other. In cultural terms it mediates between Vrindavan's Gaudiya past, which Prabhupad tried so hard to graft onto the West, and the new gurus who have found it necessary to go beyond ISKCON. We have seen that none of the old Vrindavan lineages was present at the inauguration of Swami Vishwananda's temple; neither was anyone from ISKCON.

Yet if we imagine the new Vrindavan as being entirely separate from the old or think that everything now happens in English—linguistically, culturally, and religiously—we have definitely gone too far. Just visit Vrindavan on New Year's Eve and you'll find you're floating in a sea of Hindi-speaking humanity. The roads are jammed and the police have thrown up barriers here and there (definitely around the ISKCON temple) to create zones reserved for pedestrians. In 2016, New Year's Eve and New Year's Day happened to fall on a Saturday and Sunday, so New Year's traffic was compounded by the jams that every weekend produces. It was total gridlock in several places, the worst probably being the place near Prem Mandir on the Chatikara Road where a parking lot receives cars forbidden to proceed farther. Cars were the cause of the jam, and the fact that they were useless made it all the more fun for the young. It wasn't just that tires had been exchanged for shoes. Whole troupes of boys in their teens and twenties left their shoes behind, as if participating in some vow that would bring them back in touch with the dust of Braj. But that wasn't it at all. They simply found they could get in and out of temples better if they were barefoot. They would have to leave their shoes at the door in any case, and you can imagine what a pile they would have to sift through to find their own upon exiting—or how long they would have to wait if the shoe-keeping service was organized and regulated instead.

Which temples were they going to? Prem Mandir and ISKCON, of course, but if there was a single ground zero for this pedestrian surge, it was the temple of Banke Bihari in the center of town. This is the old Vrindavan for sure, but actually the place is older than that. Banke Bihari stands on the site that was once the village of Dosaich, which is mentioned in the Mughal records as one of three hamlets that preceded what we now call Vrindavan. Somehow the memory of that primordiality has survived to the present day, not just for old-timers but for the young. About a dozen years ago, when Delhi people went over completely to the "British" calendar and started celebrating New Year's Day wholeheartedly, making it a new beachhead in their own sense of time, many turned to Bihariji to do so. They flocked to Vrindavan for January 1. New beginnings should start with his blessing.

Another venerable feature of Vrindavan's religious rhythms comes to life on New Year's Day: circumambulating the town along the parikrama path (Fig. 3.15). That path has now become the paved Parikrama Marg, as we know—its ancient form is gone—but still it gets a lot of foot traffic, and not just on the part of traditional pilgrims

Figure 3.15   Preparing to perform a daṇḍavat praṇām, a stick-like prostration, on the Parikrama Marg, New Year's Day, 2017.

who have come in for the day from surrounding towns or are staying
overnight in one of the old dharamshalas. All sorts of people join the
fray. There are little bands of ISKCON devotees, Russian and otherwise, usually young but sometimes led by an old sadhu who knows
the terrain. I also spotted a woman of perhaps thirty who has dressed
herself in a red and white sari and was performing her circumambulation by spreading out like a stick on the ground in the classical
way, edging forward body-length by body-length. Occasionally, when
she was upright between prostrations, she would stop to speak with
someone on her cellphone. Nearby I encountered three young men
in their mid-twenties from Kurukshetra in Haryana. They too had
come down to be a part of the action. One runs a bike repair shop,
another has opened a confectionary (he used the English word), and
the third mans a dance academy (again he imported the English
expression). "Bharat Natyam?" I asked. He looked at me with pity.
"No, all western"—the English word again.

In an environment like this we are on the border between two
languages and two calendars, and between a metropolitan world
and a local one—seemingly the new Vrindavan and the old—but
the whole point is that these divisions are so little honored at this
moment. Take the merchant from one of Delhi's largest vegetable
markets who is here because he has made it a feature of his religious
discipline to come to Vrindavan each weekend that precedes the
night of the full moon. Thus he makes his own accommodation to
the way the secular "British" business calendar has intersected with
the older, more distinctly religious lunar one. This weekend qualifies
on both fronts, and it's New Year's to boot. Or consider the energetic
set of circumambulators, middle-aged and younger, who stop in front
of a shop along the Parikrama Marg to sing bhajans as they make
their way around the town. They are devotees of Pundrik Goswami of
the Radharaman lineage, captain of an international following. His
English is excellent and he performs week-long expositions of the
Bhagavata Purana (Bhagavat Saptahs) around the world, sometimes
in that language. Even when he speaks in Hindi, which is more usual,
he inserts plenty of English accents. "He's coming, he's coming!" two
or three young men tell me with plenty of excitement, and they say
it, for sure, in Hindi. But in doing so they welcome an international,
cosmopolitan celebrity.

So despite all the things that separate the old Vrindavan and the new, Vrindavan is still a single fluid entity—or so it seems at the height of this particular festival season. It's as young as India is young, and just as old, as well. It's liminal in its way, but it's also surprisingly normal—normal as measured by what counts as normal in India today. It's what Durkheim was trying to get at when he spoke of the fundamental nature of religion being collective effervescence—something insubstantial with a substantiality all its own.[45] At times like New Year's the new and the old unite, and the brew seems always fresh when they do.

But how does it feel to the old-timers? you might ask—people who have seen the old Vrindavan become so radically new. Do they feel regret (Fig. 3.16)? I cannot speak for all, but let me report the perspective of a woman of about 60 who shared a tempo with me as she traveled out of Vrindavan on the first leg of her trip back to Delhi that very same New Year's Day. She was bundled up in woolens against the cold. She had been in Vrindavan for three days, having darshan

Figure 3.16   Vendor of pictures of Vrindavan and vestments for images of Krishna, Chatikara Road, New Year's Day, 2017.

of Banke Bihari twice a day, as she had done for one weekend of every lunar month over the course of many years. When I asked if it wasn't an arduous trip to make time and time again, she smiled and said she came because Bihari called her—what could be the difficulty in that? She had a wondrous sense of being sought out by the Lord. "Come see me!" she quoted him as saying. "I live here!" "Āo, maiṅ yahīṅ baithā hūṅ!" I asked her what she thought of all the new construction on the Chatikara Road, knowing she'd seen a lot more of it over the years than I had. I expected she might long a bit for the good old days, but her response was anything but wistful. "What do we know?" she said. "It's just vāh vāh", a celebratory affirmation meaning something like "oh boy", or to go for the cognate, "oh wow!" It's all Banke Bihari's doing, she wanted to affirm.

And a little crooked to the end, I thought. That's what the word "bāṅke" means.

4

The Skyscraper Temple

Reaching to the Sky

In January 2017 I found myself in the Chennai airport, plunged into that special pre-departure daze that every traveler knows. Blankly I looked around at the walls, the halls, the little stalls, until my ever-observant wife pointed to a big sign and said to me, "Isn't that...?" Indeed it was—a sign that alerted travelers to a new tourist destination in Vrindavan: "a skyscraper temple for Lord Sri Krishna, height 210 meters, 700 ft. or 70 stories". At this height, the new temple will be the tallest building in India and the tallest religious structure in the world. A ceremony to placate the gods of the earth was performed in November of 2014 and there's now a huge hole in the ground where the foundations for the new temple are to be laid. By mid-2018, some 400 of a total of 511 pillars had been sunk in the ground, each of them three times as big as those that support the Delhi Metro.[1] Nothing of the building itself has yet begun to emerge. The signs urging travelers to "visit" are inviting them to visit a website.

The skyscraper temple in question is the Vrindavan Chandrodaya Mandir (VCM), and as we know, it is a project of the Hare Krishna movement—specifically, ISKCON's prosperous Bangalore temple. There was a day back in the 1960s and 70s when the Hare Krishna Movement's airport presence was rather different. Trying to catch a flight in London, Los Angeles, or Dallas, you might be accosted by a band of youthful, chanting, saffron-clad ISKCON devotees eager to sell you a copy of Prabhupad's *The Bhagavad Gītā As It Is*. Today in the Chennai airport it's all different. No saffron, no chanting; instead you see up-to-date advertising in the language of progress and prestige. Chandrodaya means "moonrise", and is especially associated in Vrindavan circles with the gentle, luminous skin tone of Chaitanya and his appearance on the world stage some 500 years ago.[2] Although this temple is touted as "The Rising Moon of Vrindavan", however, that rising moon was first sighted in India's premier IT city—Bangalore. It was there in 2004 that the ISKCON temple president, Madhu Pandit Das, announced plans to construct in Vrindavan a structure even more extraordinary than the one already built in Bangalore. This one, he said, would be sited in the spiritual center of India as a whole—and it would be visible worldwide.[3]

To launch the VCM, he and his working partner Chanchalapati Das, the Bangalore temple's vice president and president of the VCM, culled from their leadership ranks a team of young men who would dedicate their lives to building the world's tallest religious structure. Working together, they developed a plan, signed on an architect, and set about raising funds. The idea was that funding would come from three main sources: individuals, Indian corporations, and a variety of real estate projects that would make it possible for the faithful to stay or live in the immediate vicinity of the temple. The total budget was never publicly announced (Wikipedia said 300 crores of rupees, the equivalent of some 43 million dollars), but whatever funds were in hand by the middle of 2019, they were not enough to enable the ISKCON team to start building—at least, not the skyscraper itself.

Still, a lot is happening on the 5.5-acre campus that immediately surrounds the temple. (When you add in the cluster of associated real estate developments, some owned by ISKCON itself and some by its real estate partner, The Infinity Group, the number rises to almost a hundred.) Visitors along the Chatikara Road are welcome to come in and have a look. Right up front there's a parking lot for cars and buses, and a heliport farther back suggests that VIPs sometimes drop in by air. Once you've shut the car doors you find you're in a park—a grassy expanse that invites a stroll, and there's plenty of room for children to play. A sunken amphitheater partially ringed by water stands ready for outdoor performances, and sparkling-clean public restrooms adorn the scene. A little farther back, near the heliport, a huge rectangular shell has been built for lectures and outdoor darshans, and stretching into the distance there is more. A fence and gatehouse guard a hardhat zone and suggest that construction work for the actual temple should soon begin. At this writing it's a vast hole, but a row of prototype "villas" has begun to be constructed around it so as to flank the new temple at close range. Otherwise, however, they look very much like what you might see in Washington DC, San Diego, or Naperville; one of these has been painted and decorated to serve as a model home. On the other side of the great pit an enormous apartment complex is coming up; it too has its "villas". It's just a mirage of replicating gray cubes at the moment, but billboards beyond the parking lot show you what's ahead "at the feet of Vrindavan Chandrodaya Mandir". "Live blessed!" in this Krishna Bhūmi complex, they urge. And why wouldn't you? At the end of 2016 there were pictures of the elder care facility, the Ayurvedic spa, the airy apartments, the food court, the "family lounge", and the gym. Also a young woman dressed in a skirt and top who stands outside in the sun. She throws back her head and spreads her arms wide, while the ad bids you to "Soak in acres of Greenery".

Finally, last but not least, there's a temple. It's temporary, to be sure, housed in a fiberglass geodesic dome, yet the deities are permanent. They'll be transferred to the skyscraper once the temple to house them there is sufficiently complete to welcome them. There they will reign over a vast space two-and-a-half times that of the Bangalore temple. To approach these deities in their present location you leave your shoes at a well-maintained facility beneath the portico out front and climb the stairs to a welcoming, arched toran gateway. From there, as you look inside down a long hallway, you see that darshan times have been posted, telling you whether you're permitted to mount the semicircular stairs that lead up into the sanctuary. As at all Vrindavan's temples, the deities nap at midday. If the deities are awake, however, you mount those stairs and emerge into their dome-shaped presence, finding much-bedecked images of Radha and Krishna surrounded by a host of other Gaudiya luminaries. In some ways it's a lusher version of every other temple in the New Vrindavan, but the dome gives it a special charge, as if you were in a planetarium waiting for the planets to emerge along the ceiling. Indeed, as the arati ceremony proceeds, the room is filled with a myriad of little flames, and it seems they're standing in for the stars. All so beautifully orchestrated! And once you've taken in this darshan, an attendant and a sign lead you down the one-way stair going out. Making your way down the curving stairway you might think you were descending to the street after the opera.

But there's no need to leave just yet. In the vestibule area just outside the temple proper, you'll find several young men sitting behind a fifteen-foot-long table ready to answer any questions you may have about the VCM project. (They're also sales agents, in case you're interested in buying one of the new apartments.) Video displays are mounted on the wall behind them, and there's a glassed-in model of the planned temple just across the way. It's raised on a platform decorated with crimson ruffles after the fashion of a stage where dignitaries might sit. On the way out toward the entrance you'll find a gift shop selling books, memento images, and all kinds of incense starting with "Celestial Sandal". Opposite there's a counter where you can buy prasad to take home—sanctified food. If you keep exploring the area you'll come upon a projection room where you can see one of the seven-minute videos showing Madhu Pandit Das and his associates as they describe their vision for the skyscraper. Perhaps one of the reception staff has invited you to do so. The whole vestibule—with its board room, seminar hall, and "Annakoot" restaurant—has a brisk, corporate feel to it. You're not just bidden to visit a temple here; you're invited to be part of a shinier, better world. Krishna is the name of that future, and Vrindavan—*this* Vrindavan, heliport and all—is going to be its sign and its exemplar. Just as Bangalore's IT parks surround the central city, maintaining it as a point of reference while decentering and outclassing it at the same time, so this bright, clean, new Vrindavan sublimates the old.

Before you step outside, take a look at a massive coffee-table book called *Reaching to the Sky*. There's a copy lying somewhere on the long reception desk. Here you'll find temple elevations, a diagram of the complex's various parts, and an artist's rendering of the museums and theme parks the temple encompasses, together with its pristine and lovely grounds. But perhaps the most revealing section is a two-page spread that puts the entire project in perspective. It's a full-color march through time headed "Some World's Iconic Buildings", starting with a picture of the pyramid of Cheops at Giza and continuing with the Roman Colosseum, Angkor Wat, the Qutab Minar, the Minakshi temple in Madurai, the Blue Mosque in Istanbul, St. Peter's Basilica in the Vatican, the Taj Mahal, the Potala Palace in Lhasa, the United States Capitol building, the Akshardham temple in Delhi, and finally, yes, the Vrindavan Chandrodaya Mandir. The concept of "iconic buildings" is of prime importance to the VCM leadership, who created the book. As Sarvanand Gaurang Das, head of the communications office in Delhi, once said to me, "Iconic structures attract people".[4]

An icon or image (mūrti, vigraha) is obviously one of the central realities of Hindu religion, but here we have something different. At the Chandrodaya Mandir we are concerned less with the icon than with the iconic. Sarvanand was implicitly articulating the distinction between temple and spectacle—darshan and pradarshan—upon which Kavita Singh focused when speaking of the monumental new architecture that has been sweeping India in the course of the last two or three decades. She is thinking especially of the Akshardham temple that rose on the floodplains just across the Yamuna from Delhi in 2005, and she finds it easy to establish that display has been prioritized over worship in that place, since the central structure, though it looks like a temple, is not actually understood that way on the part of its Swaminarayan builders. There is indeed an actual temple on site, but it is distinct from this monumental temple-for-show.[5] Kajri Jain, surveying a much broader range of macro-statues and buildings in north India and elsewhere, has taken a somewhat different approach, firmly straddling both sides of the fence that separates darshan and pradarshan. She points out a number of ways in which these two functions, which correspond roughly to Walter Benjamin's "cult value" and "exhibition value", go together naturally as part of the large and complex pattern of circuitry that sustains such flashy, oversized sculptures and buildings.[6] At the Chandrodaya Mandir, similarly, icon and this more spectacular sense of "the iconic" also act in concert. It would be unthinkable for the plot where the new monolith is being built in Vrindavan not to be sanctified first by means of a temple, even if temporary. For ISKCON, the deities must lead, but they lead in the cause of display.

Size is not all that is involved here. "Iconic structures attract people", as we have heard, and this project is intended to create a global field of attraction. It has an unabashedly Disney aspect—attractions in the country-fair sense.[7] Hence there is no implicit sacred–secular boundary that gives a second order of significance to "theme park attractions". The ground floor of the projected Mandir is planned as an area that will be full of them—the Krishna Lila Theme Park—and with a special emphasis on the kids. There will be an Aghasur water slide, offering an experience of the child Krishna's victory over a python-sized snake; a little car that routes you beneath "Bakasura, assault of the lethal bird" (the reference is to the heron who attacked him, here depicted as being quite enormous); and a cave-like pathway that gives you a sense of "Trnavarta, the vicious whirlwind" (Fig. 4.1).

Figure 4.1.   Tṛṇāvarta, the whirlwind demon, as he is to be encountered in the Krishna Theme Park on the grounds of the Vrindavan Chandrodaya Mandir, from *Reaching to the Sky*. Courtesy of the Vrindavan Chandrodaya Mandir.

All these demonic beings were dispatched by Kamsa to do away with the child who was destined to dethrone and kill him once he had matured into adolescence. In the theme park, in each case, there will be plenty of sound effects, and there is sure to be a regular typhoon blowing around Trnavarta. Other segments of the theme park will be found on the grounds outside. In one of these Kamsa himself will stand menacingly on the battlements of the fort of Mathura—a distinctly Anglo-Saxon-looking affair that houses the dungeon where the evil king imprisoned Krishna's parents in anticipation of his much-feared birth. You'll enter this frightening realm on a bridge that crosses a moat. Inside you'll be able to see the "Birth of Krishna: Dark Ride", which features the sacred moment by showing how the newborn child was bathed by his mother. It's a classic abhishek scene, akin to what Vishwananda performed and following general temple practice throughout Braj on Krishnajanmashtami, his birthday—except that here we can see the babe himself, lying in his little tub. A friend of mine, seeing this depicted in *Reaching to the Sky*, said it reminded him strongly of Christian depictions of Bethlehem. If so, the bathing tub stands in for the crèche and a well-positioned calf replaces the "ox and ass before him" of Christian iconography.[8]

It is true that the mythology of Krishna's birth shares many features with other narratives of divine and royal birth that circulated in the ancient world—not just Jesus but Moses, Sargon, and more—but the creators of these "attractions" at the VCM believe they are depicting something specific and truly historical. Any analogies that may connect this scene with the religious tales and experiences of others are secondary. Yet this sense of standing apart from the rest of the scenery of global religion hardly prevents them from sending out Christmas greetings on Christmas Day, and they are proud of the ecumenicity that is represented among those involved in the designing of the temple itself. A Sikh, Jagminder Jit Singh, serves as chief architect under Rimpesh Sharma, and Aarif Mohammad, a Muslim, is also a part of the team.[9]

Against the background of this interreligious global canvas "attraction" is a major theme, and it has a certain theological depth. In far more than a theme-park sense, the Vrindavan Chandrodaya Mandir is expected to serve as akarshan (ākarṣaṇ: attraction), a word closely related to Krishna's own name. The VCM is intended to reflect the fact that in a host of ways Krishna was the greatest force of attraction ever known to man—or woman. In the view of its communications staff, Krishna exerts that force today as well, and specifically through this project, this building. "The purpose of technological development is to connect the world to bhakti", says Sarvanand Gaurang Das. "Krishna wants this". He means to continue to attract, now more than ever. The new Mandir "is going to be ever fresh—because it's about Krishna, because it's about spiritual life. It's going to be eternal".[10]

Some of this work of attraction happens on the ground, through the humanitarian, people-pleasing power of VCM's Akshay Patra Project, which occupies a building all its own just behind the temporary temple and its showroom facilities. In fact, since the actual temple is still only in the initial stages of construction, locals tend to refer to the whole site as Akshay Patra. This is a public-facing aspect of its activities that has been up and running for some time. The phrase akshay patra (akṣay pātra) means "inexhaustible vessel", and refers to the miraculous feeding bowl that the sun-god Surya gave to Arjuna's elder brother Yudhishthira so that all the Pandava forces would be fed continuously on every day of the epic battle recorded in the Mahabharata, the one the Bhagavad Gita portends. At today's Akshay Patra, this "inexhaustible vessel" is indeed being continually refilled. According to the annual report for 2017, some 168,000 children enrolled in 1870 schools all over Braj were sent free lunches. A factory that stands just behind the temporary temple produces these lunches daily, and a fleet of vans dispatches them to hungry kids (Fig. 4.2).

It is a remarkable sight, this factory, and people from all over come to see it. School children themselves top the list, but you might also encounter, as I once did, a delegation from the Kalyankari Mahila Samiti (Women's Welfare Organization) of Agra, a group of twenty or so women aged 50 to 70 who have been doing good works in that nearby city for many years. They arrived by bus, and after they had visited the temporary temple they proceeded to the Akshay Patra building and donned blue plastic hats and slippers, as required, so that they would not be in danger of compromising the sanitary standards of the facility. Their tour was led by an affable and pedagogically practiced young man hailing from Jaipur, and it started in the chapatti-making

EACH SMILE
EMPOWERS US TO
KEEP STRIVING
TOWARDS OUR GOAL
OF REACHING
5 MILLION
CHILDREN BY 2020

Figure 4.2.   One of the Akshay Patra trucks that deliver lunches to school children, photographed just inside the main entrance to the VCM complex, July 2018.

part of the operation. He explained in detail what happened when the "Broken Rice Segregator" weighing two tons—all this clearly displayed in labels affixed to the machine itself (they're expecting visitors)—went into operation before dawn each morning. And so on down the line, all the way from the "dry kitchen", where the tour began, into the "wet kitchen" where the day's vegetables and pulses are processed and cooked. Some women became a little tired after a few stages of the tour and retreated to the restaurant where lunch would be served, explaining to their friends that "This is going to take a long time—I'm going", but on the whole they stuck it out, and the guide was very effective in holding their attention. This too, then, is "attraction", not just the good works involved but an eagerness to display how they are performed, attracting the interest of others. It is hoped that the acts themselves will serve to draw people into Krishna's orbit—especially children, who have their lives before them.

The Akshay Patra program is one of the signature projects of ISKCON Bangalore, not only here but in sixteen temple locations around the country (the number continues to grow), each functioning independently but under the inspiration and loose supervision of the Bangalore headquarters. If you count the Akshay Patra programs of all these temples, more than three billion lunches have now been served—mostly with money provided by a program initiated by the central government, but with about a third of the cost being borne by ISKCON adherents themselves: private–public partnerships in the official lingo. It is the largest food-distribution program in the world. There's no denying that this is impressive, and from a nutritional point of view it's better by a long shot than the other food organization that counts its output in the billions—McDonald's—or at least used to before the numbers became so overwhelming they lost their meaning.[11] The President of India, Pranab Mukherjee, attended a celebration of the two-billionth lunch in Bangalore in 2016, and when the three-billionth was served in 2019, the ceremonial feeding was relocated to Vrindavan. The Prime Minister himself, Narendra Modi, helicoptered down from Delhi to do the honors.

Modi was joined at the ceremony by Yogi Adityanath, who 'coptered in from Lucknow. A crowd of eleven thousand greeted them—donors, politicians, religious dignitaries, locals, and hundreds of school children who'd been eating Akshay Patra meals. A vast temporary structure resembling an open-air airplane hangar had been quickly assembled for the occasion, and when Modi's helicopter appeared on huge screens around the hall, the crowd burst into eager applause. Modi spoke in steely, commanding tones about his government's Swacch Bharat Abhiyan ("Clean India Mission") and its efforts to better the lot of mothers and children, expositing the Bhagavad Gita as he went. He applauded the "oceanic tradition" of the Mathura area in its service of that symbol of motherhood, the cow. At the end, with a flourish, he expressed the hope that Akshay Patra's works of service would indeed remain akshay—inexhaustible.[12] Several days before this event took place, the VCM's president, Chanchapalati Das, said categorically that the temple stood neutral with respect to political parties.[13] But it was hard to be there on that brisk February day and not sense an echo between the VCM–Akshay Patra alignment and the Hindu-friendly stance of the BJP. ISKCON

Bangalore is indeed the parent of Akshay Patra: billboards all around the site proclaim the connection. What Vrindavan adds to this parent-child relationship is a lineage that stretches back millennia. Several months before the national elections would take place, this was no inconsiderable gift.[14]

Things are hardly static in the VCM promotional world. This too is an aspect of its attraction. On New Year's Day 2017 in Vrindavan at the same locale I had the good luck to meet two young men who are crucial to the VCM effort, both of them vice presidents in the Communications wing. Yudhishthira Krishna Das, whose vice-presidential title associates him with several aspects of the VCM including Akshay Patra and the Krishna Lila Theme Park, is a generously built man of about forty who travels the world in service of the VCM project. Bharatarshabha Das, the actual vice president for communications, has a somewhat more studious air: you can easily sense his IT background. Both men have Bangalore histories.

Yudhishthira explained that they were about to launch a new phase of marketing, a sort of VCM 2.0. There would be a brand-new promotional video in which the language of iconicity would be amplified or even supplanted by that of heritage, most bluntly by bestowing a second name on the Vrindavan Chandrodaya Mandir—the "Vrindavan Heritage Tower".[15] This, Yudhishthira said, is a more attractive concept to donors from countries outside India than the "iconic" pitch had been, in that it signals an attention to preserving the past.[16] The hope is that it will deflect attention from the fact that it is actually a temple being built here, though it's hard to avoid that fact. Foreigners—non-resident Indians, that is—are apt to react sourly to the idea of building a new temple. One Los Angeles businessman, after he'd heard Yudhishthira's sales pitch, said the idea of building yet another temple was "just plain ridiculous", but he felt much better about the Akshay Patra aspect of things. Yudhishthira's job was to bring him on board by persuading him that the new "heritage" angle built on that base, adding a cultural component that had become an urgent form of social service in an India changing so rapidly that people are apt to forget their roots. A connection to the resources of the land should not disappear either—hence the work of Akshay Patra—but great effort was also needed to strengthen a sense of how the past had given the country its special heritage.

Heritage is an international buzzword, thanks in part to UNESCO and a host of NGOs around the world. No wonder there's an apartment building in Mathura called Heritage Greens or that a forward-looking school has just opened its doors in Vrindavan under the name Heritage Public School (as in Britain, "public" means what Americans would call "private"). But the Vrindavan Chandrodaya Mandir sees itself as bearing a particularly urgent heritage responsibility. Yudhishthira acknowledges that there's a history behind each of the world's heritage towers, by which he means the Eiffel Tower and all the rest, but Vrindavan's claim to heritage is unique. The town itself, he says, being a dham—indeed the central dham in all of India—constitutes a deeply rooted and intrinsically sacred locale that has a crucial role to play in creating a sense of balance and coherent structure not just for India but for the entire world. As we have seen, the term dham is used all over Vrindavan, but here we are faced with a special irony—or so it seems in the eyes of the VCM's detractors. The structure is so massive, so obviously self-aggrandizing and separate from the rest of Vrindavan's dham, such people say, that it threatens to drown out the thing itself. They positively choke on the idea that such a mammoth, newfangled structure could possibly contribute to the preservation of Vrindavan's heritage. Nalini Thakur of the School of Planning and Architecture in Delhi, someone who has thought a good bit about what ought to be meant by "heritage", was livid on the subject. "There is no New Vrindavan", she declared. "Vrindavan has nothing to do with what's going on over there".[17] From the inside, however, it all looks different. For the VCM team "heritage" means something integrally contained in the structure they are building—heritage in a sensory language that twenty-first-century people can understand, heritage that connects to *them*.

Vedic Cosmology on the Chatikara Road

As the Vrindavan Chandrodaya Mandir was initially conceived, the building was supposed to house a cluster of heritage elements at and around its base—a Krishna Heritage Museum, a park-style evocation of Braj's classic "twelve forests", and a representation of the Yamuna herself in the form of a "Yamuna Creek". (The name of this manmade stream eerily mimics the diminution of the Yamuna herself, but turns it from something sad and dispiriting into something charming and manageable: a creek.) There would also be a "Krishna Lila Park" at the base of the structure indoors. Then up above, we would have heritage on a completely different scale and in a somewhat different mode. The VCM would offer an immersive experience of "Vedic cosmology"—heritage in the broadest, oldest sense—by means of a bank of high-speed elevators whisking visitors to the top of the Mandir (Fig. 4.3). There you would have an incomparable experience of Vrindavan as dham. In the original design only the lower stories were to have been habitable, housing temples, museums, offices, and flats. After that you would soar into a different world—or worlds. Upon entering one of the VCM's translucent capsule elevators, you would find yourself in a hollow space resembling a vastly elongated Hyatt atrium, and as if that were not awesome enough, your Vedic experience would be orchestrated in a 5-D medium. State-of-the-art cinemas make possible a four-dimensional experience by providing their patrons seats that move in response to the drama being projected all around, but here you would also be engaging with a fifth—smells, clouds, rain, and so forth. As Sarvanand explained these things, I found him reaching for other examples, but in the end, he exclaimed, it was "just everything!"[18] The mention of the moving seat made me a little apprehensive, considering that this time the "seat" would apparently be the elevator itself, but he assured me the architects didn't have a vibrating capsule in mind.

Figure 4.3.   Vedic cosmology in the atrium trunk, from *Reaching to the Sky*. Courtesy of the Vrindavan Chandrodaya Mandir.

As for the conceptual element of the design, that too would follow the motif of dham.[19] As explained in *Reaching to the Sky*, you would ascend through a progression of four of these dhams. Ayodhya, the peaceable kingdom where Ram established his reign, would be first. Its domain hovers near the bottom of the tower. In the three dhams that rise above it, each more exalted than the last, one would find a vertical expression of the concentric trajectory the designers perceive to have structured Krishna's life on earth. The second dham along this concentric but now vertical gradient is Dvaraka, the city on the shores of the Arabian Sea where Krishna established an ideal kingdom that more or less corresponds to Ram's Ayodhya. Then farther in—or in the VCM's transposition, farther up—you would encounter the dham of Mathura. It too is an earthly domain—a kingdom with all the accoutrements of government—but it is given a specially exalted quality by being situated inside Braj. It was here in Mathura that Krishna toppled the evil Kamsa from his ill-gotten throne by assuming human birth; like Ram, he fought the battle of dharma. This third dham, then, is both political and familial, but because of its location at the center of the Braj country, it was not just public and adult but also private and infantile. It was in Mathura, after all, that Krishna was born. Next and last, you would come into the tender realm of intimate, amorous, and friendly relationships that Vrindavan itself comprises—the fourth dham. In the VCM it would be called Golok Vrindavan.[20] On a concentric, horizontal model, Vrindavan dham lies at the center of the universe, but now that horizontal "pinnacle" takes shape vertically as well—as a pinnacle literally speaking. Golok Vrindavan would be situated at the top of the Vrindavan Chandrodaya Mandir.

Golok (goloka in Sanskrit) is the name given by the Bhagavata Purana to the most supernal of any realm in which Krishna expresses himself, but that name, meaning "cow world" or "domain of cattle", indicates at the same time that it is intimately tied to the pastoral realm where Krishna chose to live in simple harmony with simple people. Golok, then, is a supernal location with the most intimate human and animal face—transcendent and immanent at the same time. To enter this densest, tenderest core of reality is a peak experience, and the Vrindavan Chandrodaya Mandir projects it literally as such.

This four-dham scheme makes an additional contribution, too. It leverages the India-wide concept of the char dham (chār dhām: four splendid dwellings, four points of fundamental orientation) in such a way that it pertains specifically to Vrindavan. A Vrindavan-centered view of the four dhams gets beyond the element of intersectarian miscegenation that characterizes the dhams that mark the subcontinent's four directional points: both Vaishnava and Shaiva institutions are to be found at Badrinath (north), Puri (east), Rameshvaram (south), and Dvaraka (west). The VCM design, with its new four-dham cosmology, sweeps away this more traditional view of the holy directional points that anchor the Indian subcontinent. Contrary to what visitors experience at the dhams of Vaishno Devi or Jvala Mukhi, people who get whisked upward at the VCM find themselves in a purely, strictly Vaishnava cosmos.[21]

Another common way of conceiving the four dhams in north India is to think of the term as referring to four sacred sites in the Himalayas—the source of the Ganges, the source of the Yamuna, and the temples at Badrinath and Kedarnath. Here too, however, Vaishnava purity is absent. Kedarnath refers specifically to Shiva, and the Ganges is ambiguous as to her associations, being claimed mythologically as belonging to Shiva and Vishnu both. The VCM once again escapes these problems. Vaishnava through and through, it implicitly testifies to that great and best-known affirmation of the Bhagavata Purana, that "kṛṣṇastu bhagavān svayam": Krishna is God himself.

Thus the concept of four dhams does a great deal of conceptual work at the VCM, but another quartet is also involved. This second four-part hierarchy is articulated in the language of loks (the Sanskrit loka, denoting "world"). According to the original vision of the temple announced in Reaching to the Sky, those who ascend to Golok Vrindavan in the clear-glass capsule elevator would rise above the world in which we are now situated by passing not only through two intermediary dhams but two intermediary loks before arriving at the fourth and last level, the destination of each journey. One of these intermediary loks is Svarga Lok, a term that is familiarly construed as a "heavenly realm", but which has been explained by Chanchalapati Das, one of its principal designers, as being, rather, the "transitory place for righteous souls".[22] Then there would be Vaikuntha Lok, a traditional designation for the heavenly abode of Vishnu, but because it is hierarchically conceived and is associated more with Vishnu than Krishna, it remains subordinate to Golok Vrindavan itself. That is where, at the pinnacle, one finally arrives. Hence we have a second system for understanding the stack of realms for which Golok Vrindavan serves as the summit—equally Vaishnava, but differently imagined.

People who come to the Vrindavan Chandrodaya Mandir were intended somehow to experience both of these ascending four-part sequences—the dhams and the loks—but I had trouble understanding exactly how. My interlocutors in north India resisted becoming too specific about how it all would work, either practically or theologically. Yet their fealty to what they called the "Vedic system" was clear. It was demanded by the Bhagavata Purana, they said. That master text, revered not just in Vrindavan but by Vaishnavas worldwide, does indeed proclaim itself the fifth Veda, placing itself above the other four in so doing. It is fifth in a temporal sense: it was composed after the original four Vedas were. It is fifth in a textual sense: it goes beyond the ordinary four Vedas after the manner of the epics, which like the Bhagavata assume a narrative format that is quite different from anything we find in the four Vedas. And it is fifth in a philosophical sense, compressing the messages of the prior four into a single system—or so its devotees like to claim. In similar fashion, if we return to the layout of the Chandrodaya Mandir, the lok directly associated with Krishna—Golok Vrindavan—stands above each of the other, historically earlier conceptions of heaven. Lok supersedes loks just as Veda supersedes Vedas, and while the designers of the Chandrodaya Mandir did not explicitly announce these historical progressions, they seemed bent on enshrining them in glass. They were trying to create a visible fact that would stick in people's minds. By analogy, I suppose, the Vrindavan Chandrodaya Mandir itself becomes the new Bhagavata Purana, its equivalent.[23]

Or, if you were to follow the Bhagavata Purana itself, you might think of the building of the Vrindavan Chandrodaya Mandir as a modern-day analogue to what Krishna did when he displayed his fully divine nature to the cowherds who had begun to sense it.[24] But the whole point of that episode was to repel any sense that heaven lay anywhere but here on earth and indeed in their very midst. All this reflects suspiciously on the erection of a massive structure that outclasses the down-to-earth Vrindavan Krishna seemed to love. On another occasion Krishna revealed himself to Akrur, the messenger of Kamsa, and as understood today, that happened at the edge of town.[25] But this peripheral position on the road to Mathura seems quite different from the one the Chandrodaya Mandir occupies on the other side of town. Akrur's vision of the cosmos was occasioned by depth, not height. It happened by surprise as he bathed in the Yamuna, not while climbing determinedly in the opposite direction.

That brings us to a final dimension of the VCM experience. If you gaze out from the observation deck at the top of the spire, what do you see? If the day is very clear, the Taj Mahal. It lies seventy kilometers to the south in Agra. This does not mean that the Taj has been transmuted into a Hindu temple, as happened in the mind of P.N. Oak and his protégés, who have claimed quite fantastically that the Taj Mahal is not really the Taj Mahal at all but the Tejo Mahalaya—the Great Abode of Tapas (ascetically concentrated energy), a Hindu temple to Shiva. Yet here too the Taj is fundamentally reoriented and re-cognized. From the pinnacle of the Vrindavan Chandrodaya Mandir you will look *down* on the Taj. A Hindu monument will literally top a Muslim one.

Yogi Adityanath, the man appointed chief minister of Uttar Pradesh by Narendra Modi after the BJP victory in the spring 2017 state elections, has expressed the view that the Taj Mahal is not sufficiently Indian. Such negative views about the value of the Taj Mahal as a superlative distillation of north India's distinctive Hindu–Muslim culture may be lamentable, but their spirit is hardly new. There have been many efforts in north–central India to erect a structure that would out-Taj the Taj. In Agra itself we have the Soamibagh temple of the Radhasoami Satsang, which has been under construction since 1904. Somewhat farther north there is the huge temple of Jai Gurudev, which arose along the Agra–Delhi highway near Mathura in 2000 and also seems to take the Taj as its template.[26] At the gateway of Vrindavan itself, if you enter by the Mathura Road, stands the temple of Pagal Baba, completed in 1981. It too is supposed to be a new and better version of the Taj, with certain architectural echoes. And finally, of course, there is Prem Mandir. Its design is quite distinct from that of the Taj, but it boasts a comparison nonetheless. It is more flawlessly white in its marble, say its promoters, and it is already being touted as drawing more visitors.[27] Yet for all these earlier efforts, nothing tops the Taj so literally and conclusively as the Vrindavan Chandrodaya Mandir. Unlike all of the other "Tajes", it abandons any effort to replicate the Taj in any of its design or material features; rather, it sets its own terms. It is tall enough to reshape the landscape of the region as a whole, and the Taj will come literally under its spell. Some promoters have said they look forward to the day when the VCM will become Number One on the bucket list of every tourist who comes to India, replacing the Taj as the seventh new wonder of the world.[28] I hasten to add, however, that the VCM's president denies any such Muslim-besting intent. With a knowing smile he's also skeptical about how many days will be clear enough to see the Taj from his new Mandir.[29]

The New True ISKCON

At many points—in print and on the Web and in conversation—I heard that the idea for a skyscraper temple originated in the mind of ISKCON's founder, the man familiarly known as Prabhupad. The references that support this assertion are carefully documented. One points to October 29, 1972, when, in the course of a class he held in front of the burial place (samādhi) of Rupa Gosvami in Vrindavan, Prabhupad addressed himself to the Americans in the group and said, "Just like we [humanity, evidently] have got a tendency to construct a skyscraper building. As in your country, you do. So you should not be attached to the skyscraper building, but you can utilize the tendency by constructing a big temple like skyscraper for Krishna. In this way, you have to purify your material activities". The other moment that seemed to call for the building of a structure like the Vrindavan Chandrodaya Mandir occurred in Mumbai on February 25, 1974—again in the last years of Prabhupad's life. He was heard to say, "This is a Krishna conscious vision: 'Oh, there are so many skyscrapers. Why not construct a nice skyscraper temple of Krishna?' This is Krishna consciousness".[30]

So there are these two, but I have also heard this moment remembered as having happened in New York, when Prabhupad was actually surrounded by skyscrapers. No one has mentioned the interesting fact that there was indeed a whole movement to build "skyscraper churches" in that city in the course of the 1920s and

1930s—probably Prabhupad didn't know.[31] The Western influence on ISKCON Bangalore is visible elsewhere too. Chanchalapati's gloss on Svarga Lok as "the transitory place for righteous souls" calls to mind the medieval Christian idea of Purgatory as much as it does any traditional Indian usage of the term.[32]

We are squarely in the present here, a present that features an encounter with the West. Otherwise how to explain the presence of a lovely blonde woman in one of the advertisements for Krishna Bhūmi, the real-estate arm of the VCM—a billboard that once formed part of a set displayed on the property of the VCM itself (Fig. 4.4)? Her husband (presumably he is her husband) gazes out the window of their apartment to the Chandrodaya Mandir while he talks on his cell phone. Yet in the minds of the men whose lives are devoted to promoting that Mandir, this structure is simultaneously intended to project the past—to exert, as if in a magnetic way, a field of "attraction" that will draw people to what Yudhishthira Krishna Das

Figure 4.4.   Couple with view of the Vrindavan Chandrodaya Mandir. Billboard on the VCM grounds advertising real estate in the Śrī Krishna Bhūmi apartments, December 2016.

called "the historical personality of Krishna".[33] This, he emphasized, was by contrast to anything imaginary. It's not the sort of thing you might encounter in any garden-variety amusement park in the USA or even at Universal Studios or Disneyland. He ought to know. Members of his team and he himself did indeed visit and study these carefully in preparing the way for the Chandrodaya Mandir. When kids see Krishna's heroic feats as a child—his "pastimes", to use the word Prabhupad always did—they are intended to see the real thing, "how it was in history", not something invented in Hollywood or in any other-wood closer to home.[34]

To me, this confidence that what was recorded in the scriptures—preeminently the Bhagavata Purana—has to have the stature of historical fact is a remarkable thing. It contrasts broadly to the more playful, subjective valences of lila (Prabhupad's "pastimes"), which is such an important and theologically versatile term in the Bhagavata itself. It resonates to much more recent times. One thinks, for example, of the Krishna that Bankim Chandra Chattopadhyay, that great nineteenth-century Bengali intellectual, was at pains to fashion as he sought to develop a Hindu nationalist narrative theology that would counter the myth of British and Christian supremacy.[35] These ISKCON-ites have not abandoned the Krishna of Vrindavan in the way that Bankim sought to do—in the VCM temple he appears alongside Radha in the glowing, white-faced form that has become so familiar these days—but the rest of the Chandrodaya Mandir is heroic to a fault. It's a soaring expression of masculinity, and in videos depicting its construction we can actually see it rise suddenly, a thing of steel and muscle, from its base.

In this seemingly intentional move away from the saccharine, lovelorn side of the old Vrindavan we see something of a Hegelian Aufhebung: a transformation or sublation of an earlier form of consciousness that is apt to render it inaccessible ever after. It's a shift that runs parallel to the way Prabhupad recast the Bhagavad Gita in his own image by asserting in his title that his own definitely modern version of the ancient text simply presented the Bhagavad Gita "as it is". At the Chandrodaya Mandir, similarly, structures that follow earlier Hindu norms of temple-building are grouped at the bottom and then overshadowed by an immense, soaring superstructure that assumes and incorporates them into something else.

All this is reinforced in the domain of media too, and it's in this environment that the idea of building the Vrindavan Chandrodaya Mandir first arose. In the opening decade of the twenty-first century Chanchalapati Das and others at ISKCON Bangalore worked with BIG Animation, an arm of the Mumbai-based Reliance communications group, to produce an animated series called "Little Krishna". The animation writer Jeffrey Scott, winner of an Emmy award, was centrally involved, and "Little Krishna" was launched on Indian television by Nickelodeon in 2009. It was an instant, runaway success. This had a deep impact on Chanchalapati Das and his Bangalore cohort. They could see that there was a vast distance between the primitive sorts of animation they and all of India had seen in the "Ramayan" and "Shri Krishna" series of Ramanand Sagar, broadcast on Indian public television in late 1980s, and what was possible now. The question naturally arose: What if you animated Vrindavan itself in a similar way? They came to feel that Krishna himself was secretly at the helm of this particular sort of technological advance. Sarvanand found the sense of verisimilitude he experienced when King Kong hovered overhead at Universal Studios "amazing", but he could only think how much more powerful it would be to experience the joy of being protected by Krishna from Indra's torrential rains as one huddled beneath a hand-held Mount Govardhan. That was what the Vrindavan Chandrodaya Mandir would achieve. It was almost as if these new cinematic representations of experience (*experience* was a term of art) were being unleashed in the service of the divine Artist himself. And perhaps they were. They made possible a new form of divinely inflected history—a new sense of being simultaneous with scripture, even more powerful than the immediacy one feels every time one opens the Bhagavad Gita.[36]

Technology makes everything easier, more convincing, as many members of the VCM team keep saying. They cherish a sense that technology is on their side. These men—they are in fact all men, many quite young—boast technological backgrounds that effectively render them the new Brahmins of the world in which we live. They are not just Brahmins of the pujari (priestly) type, techies with respect to a much older brand of ritual expertise, but pracharaks (preachers) and aspiring intellectuals (acharyas) for our present-day world.[37]

Several of them came to ISKCON straight out of the IT institutions for which Bangalore is famous, or from one of the city's secondary schools. Some were trained at technical institutions located elsewhere, perhaps one of the campuses of the prestigious Indian Institute of Technology, but then they too became part of the Bangalore story in a literal fashion. Every young man who becomes a sadhu has to go to Bangalore itself to train, so its special aura of technological superiority becomes a part of each initiate's personal past. The cardinal theme of "technology left behind"—or rather, "technology integrated"—in the life of such an individual is not exclusively the property of ISKCON Bengal; we see it also among the young sadhus of the Swaminarayan Sampraday, for instance. But it is deeply coded into the VCM's myth of origins and into the lives of those who serve the new Mandir.

Among the VCM's professional sadhus there is an overwhelming sense of the kindness and potential of the future, and as if to herald it, the present too seems saturated with miracles. I have heard that word again and again. Yet for all this forward focusing, the past has not been left behind. To the contrary, its glories need to be reclaimed. To our friend Sarvanand it seemed the historical Vrindavan had been "overrun with Buddhist philosophy" at a certain point in time—the period that gave us the beautiful stupas of Sanchi and the fine Buddhist relics of Mathura itself, in fact. For him such things were not worthy of praise but distractions from Braj's essentially Vaishnava identity, and the game was lost until Chaitanya came along, reviving Krishna consciousness in the region. But even that did not prevent Vrindavan from once again descending into "a shambles". Look how dirty it is even around the Radharaman temple, he charged, and as for Bihariji, "just give those gosvamis enough money and they'll do anything!"[38] The VCM's purpose was to bring all this back inside the Vedic system, and to cultivate people who could make that happen. The communications staff would first pursue the wealthy and influential, working their way down from there—a strategy for which a basis is claimed in the Bhagavad Gita:

> Whatever it is the best person does, others follow suit.
> The standard such a person sets is sure
>   to serve as other people's guide.[39]

Following this method the VCM created a roster of "founder patrons"; in the VCM's temporary headquarters their names are displayed on a plaque next to a big model of the temple being built. These are men and women who would be committed to a life free of meat, alcohol, and extramarital sex—pillars of the wider community being forged by the VCM campaign. Often I heard that special quarters would be built for them in the lower stories of the Mandir, not for them to own—one cannot own a temple—but where they would be exclusive guests, mixing with others of their stature and vision.

A new Vrindavan, indeed! This would be truly a cashless economy—the noblest form of the "demonetization" (noṭbandī) that Prime Minister Modi released throughout the country in the fall of 2106. The VCM is intended to be a place untainted by the blackness that always seems to go with money and commerce. I didn't have the chutzpah to ask where these exemplary people actually got their money in the first place, but one thing is plain. By and large they come not from Bangalore or Kolkata, as the VCM's most important visionaries and entrepreneurs do, but from places like Delhi and Agra. The temple's vision may be global, but locals are the ones apt to travel to the Mandir on a regular basis. Like New Yorkers heading for the Hamptons, they can easily make the trip.

This is something down to earth, and there's another down-to-earth reality that hovers over the VCM project—sibling rivalry. It's hard to miss the fact that the concept of the VCM has a lot to do with its proximity to the Krishna Balaram Temple just down the road (Fig. 4.5). These two joust with one another. Regionally speaking, it's the south and west of the Bangalore group versus the north and east of the "original" ISKCON represented in the Angrez Mandir. Nationally speaking, it's indigenously Indian versus foreign. These days the Krishna Balaram Temple is not as "English" as it used to be. Busloads of Indian schoolchildren come from considerable distances to see it; Indian women sit in the corner threading garlands while darshan happens up front; all the temple stores are staffed by Indians, and they comprise a good part of the ritual staff, as well. But the temple president is still an American: Panch Gaur Das from Buffalo, who was born in Macedonia, and the Slavic connection is interesting since plenty of Russians hover about, as we have seen.[40] For many of the Indians present—they must be at least 95% of the whole—this

Figure 4.5.   Taking selfies at ISKCON's busy Angrez (Krishna Balaram) Mandir, November 2016.

international flavor is part of the place's charm, but historically speaking, as in the case of Satyanarayan Das, things were not always so amicable. Foreigners sat in seats of power; locals had to pay tribute.

Far more visible than the controversy surrounding Babaji was the conflict that arose between the Governing Body Commission and Madhu Pandit Das, the president of ISKCON's extremely successful Bangalore temple, as we saw in the last chapter. Bangalore, with its indigenous Indian leadership, split off from ISKCON international at the turn of the current century. Their right to do so was ratified by the Indian courts in 2002, and they obtained legal ownership of the Bangalore ISKCON temple in 2014, though their adversaries continue to pursue the case at the level of the Supreme Court. One also sees the results in Vrindavan. Confident now of their southern base, President Madhu Pandit Das and Vice President Chanchalapati

Das are projecting their internationally visible yet distinctly national temple—and the "indigenous" form of organization it represents—into the annals of ISKCON history at large. They and their group proclaim that they are being servants of Prabhupad in the way he intended: "Srila Prabhupada's ISKCON, Bangalore", as their publications say.[41] Their ritvik philosophy of organization lays out the scheme—each new group inspired to join ISKCON forms a temple with its own leadership—but just as the Bangalore temple's glittering success provides an image of what can happen when such a group forms, so the skyscraper temple will broadcast that success to the world.

There is one more twist to the story. When Madhu Pandit Das and his associates declared their independence from international ISKCON as it had developed after the death of the founder, they were also declaring their independence from Bengal. It was Mayapur, just across the Ganges from Nabadvip where Chaitanya had spent his early years, that had been adopted as the international center of the Hare Krishna movement. Mayapur was where the Governing Body Commission met annually, with Jayapataka Swami at its head. When Madhu Pandit Das said goodbye to the international ISKCON conglomerate, the parting happened there. He was also separating himself from its specifically Bengali roots. The very name of Vrindavan's skyscraper temple makes this obvious. A Mayapur Chandrodaya Mandir has been in existence at ISKCON Mayapur since 1974, and a newer, grander version has been under construction there since 2009. The Mayapur ISKCON establishment also has a Pushpa Samadhi Mandir, whose purpose is to memorialize the life of Prabhupad, replicating the memorial shrine (again, samādhi mandir) that forms a part of the Angrez Mandir complex in Vrindavan and showing how tightly connected are the Vrindavan and Mayapur "seats" of international ISKCON. Without explicitly replicating all of that, the new Vrindavan Chandrodaya Temple clearly intends to "sublate" and supersede it.[42]

In some ways the temples under construction in Vrindavan and Mayapur are quite different. The Mayapur temple is being built to look like the Capitol building in Washington, DC. Prabhupad once expressed a longing to have a capitol-style ISKCON temple, too. Its dome does indeed suggest a certain resemblance, although this dome will be colored a vibrant blue—Fabergé, says one of its students,

Figure 4.6.   Artist's rendering of the completed Mayapur Chandrodaya Mandir, with its "Fabergé" effect, https://tovp.org, accessed March 2017.

Urmila Mohan, thinking of the famous Russian imperial Easter eggs, and indeed a team of Russian technicians is installing some Russian-made kalasha finials (Fig. 4.6).[43] The Vrindavan Chandrodaya Mandir leaves behind Prabhupad's desire for a Krishna dome, following his skyscraper fantasy instead, but in other ways the imitative aspects of a sibling rivalry come out more clearly. As the name of the Temple of the Vedic Planetarium implies, there's plenty of talk about Vedic cosmology at Mayapur, so it's no wonder something like a planetarium also shows up in the VCM design. At Mayapur a shimmering gold representation of the cosmic Mount Meru is to be suspended beneath the dome along with other primal elements in an elaborate "universal chandelier". All this is as one would have it on the basis of what is recounted in the Bhagavata Purana, a main subject of its exposition on the second day of a Bhagavat Saptah.[44] At the VCM, by contrast, the planetarium effect will be more virtual, but in the minds of the temple's designers equally effective. It will be achieved by projection devices installed in an auditorium.

Another feature also makes these two structures candidates for comparison—one that we've recently been reviewing. As at Vrindavan, Mayapur's mandir will incorporate four loks, though these are not the same four as are projected for Vrindavan.[45] Instead we have, in ascending order, Devi Lok (our present, this-worldly position), Mahesh Lok, Hari Lok, and at the end, of course, Golok. The first three recapitulate the three great categories of Bengali religiosity from Shaktism to Shaivism to Vaishnavism, and there is Krishna to top it all. Vrindavan traces a different progression and couples the lok vocabulary with dham, but it is hard to miss the analogy with what's going on in Mayapur. All this takes a regional, theological competition and expresses it in structural terms.

In one way this rivalry is new and ISKCON-specific, but in another way it echoes a tension that is centuries old. There has long been a characteristic difference of perspective separating Gaudiya Vaishnavism as we find it in Bengal and Puri—east—from the sort of Gaudiya Vaishnavism that developed in Braj—west. This is part of the historical DNA of the Gaudiya movement, extending back to the sixteenth century. For all the world it seems as if this remarkably long-lived sibling rivalry is casting about for new ways to express itself, this time with the armies of international finance arrayed on both sides. The Bangalore IT firm Infosys, global in its reach, is a notable contributor to Madhu Pandit Das's enterprises, and the wealth of the Ford Motor Company of Detroit undergirds much of what's happening in Mayapur. The chairman of Mayapur Chandrodaya Temple of the Vedic Planetarium is known as Ambarisa Das, but no attempt is made to hide the fact that he began life as Alfred B. Ford, grandson of Henry. He has been a major donor to ISKCON Mayapur for many years and is providing many millions for this specific structure. It is as if these corporate icons of technological innovation—the more recent, Indian; the earlier, American—were jostling with one another to be the Pandavas or Kauravas of the new spiritual global economy as they understand it. Not that the family connection is entirely suppressed. On June 30, 2017, I received a VCM WhatsApp post that forwarded an earlier one clearly originating elsewhere. In the corner was the medallion of an organization called "The Youth" and the photo showed a man clad in an ample white shawl performing arati, I believe at Mayapur (Fig. 4.7). A red circle had been drawn around

The man doing Puja of lord Krishna is no ordinary man..

He is the owner of world's richest Car company Ford's in USA. His name is Alfred Ford

Please Share this maximum so that all atheists can see it.
by TheYouth team

Figure 4.7.   WhatsApp forward of Alfred Ford from "The Youth" team, received as part of my daily VCM feed, June 30, 2017.

his head and the following explanation appeared, written as it was the original: "The man doing Puja of lord Krishna is no ordinary man. He is the owner of world's richest Car company Ford's in USA. His name is Alfred Ford". And in red: "Please share this maximum so that all atheists can see it". I suspect the author was Russian.

This act of forwarding seems a conciliatory gesture from west to east, from Vrindavan to Mayapur, yet the rivalry persists. We see traces of it within Vrindavan itself. To project their image of being more ISKCON than ISKCON, the architects of the VCM have affixed Prabhupad's image everywhere, as if to outdo the Angrez Mandir down the street. Prabhupad smiles down from huge billboards as you enter the VCM complex, and the signs affirm that this skyscraper project was specifically his idea. The same statement is being made outside the compound, too. Wherever you go on the outer reaches of the Chatikara Road, you see evidence of the Bangalorewalas' desire to reshape Prabhupad's legacy in the direction of the Chandrodaya

Mandir. It seems A.C. Bhaktivedanta Swami Marg, as cited on that sign in the Chennai airport, should be *their* A.C. Bhaktivedanta Swami Marg. Advertisements for the VCM and its associated real estate venture Krishna Bhūmi, sponsored by The Infinity Group, have entirely captured the median strip that bisects the Chatikara Road. Large well-lit billboards appear from time to time, and a set of smaller ones whisks by at quick intervals, one every fifteen feet, as you drive down the road. They've been posted on Mathura Road too, Vrindavan's other point of entry—the Yamuna Expressway—feeds in there. These signs are lit from the inside and therefore easily visible whether you come into town by day or night. You are made to feel the force of an India that is neither too local nor too Bengali nor too westernized. It's the real India—the real new India. However you approach the Chandrodaya Mandir, Bangalore and Gurgaon converge.

Precedent and Present—the South

All this looks and sounds like a complete makeover of the Vrindavan that has existed in this place since the sixteenth century, and for sure we are witnessing a major rupture. But if we think of this arrival of the south in Vrindavan as something alien and unprecedented, we have to think again. Put yourself in the position of the farmers who lived in Dosaich and two surrounding hamlets in 1594 when the Kachvaha king, Mansingh of Amer, came calling. He was trying to acquire even more land to surround the temple of Govindadev that he had just completed in 1590 with help from the Mughal emperor Akbar (Fig. 4.8). That temple was the tallest, most massive temple in all of India—some 400 feet long and 300 feet tall.[46] Talk about a radical alteration of the landscape! Talk about a scrapping of old ways! It was one in a series of real estate developments that utterly altered the pastoral character that had drawn Krishna to this place, a legendry that could be read in the names of several nearby towns—Govardhan, of course, and Arith (Hindi "arīth", Sanskrit "ariṣṭha"), named after the bull-demon Kamsa had sent against Krishna. Arith is where this conflict was supposed to have occurred. Imagine how it felt to have that ancient heritage transformed by the newfangled temples that shot up in Vrindavan in the sixteenth and early seventeenth centuries,

Figure 4.8.   Temple of Govindadev as depicted in the dining quarters (bhojanśālā) of Raja Jaisingh II in his palace at Amer, near what was soon to be Jaipur, ca. 1710. Note that the temple's tower, above the altar room (garbhagṛha), is shown intact.

Govindadev being the grandest of the lot. Anyone whose family had been living there for a period of time must have wondered how the real Vrindavan could survive this onslaught.

King Mansingh was from Amer in Rajasthan, but some of the most important religious entrepreneurs he patronized in Vrindavan, and with whom he worked, were southerners. Rupa and Sanatana Gosvami came from Gaur (Gauḍ), where they served at the court of Hussain Shah. That city was by now within the Mughal domain, but Rupa and Sanatana's forebears had migrated there from Karnataka and they themselves had been involved in sustaining a community of Karnataka expatriates in Gaur. Or what about Gopal Bhatt, the man behind the founding of the Radharaman temple in "old" Vrindavan? He too was a southerner—recruited by Chaitanya at Shrirangam, we are told. When in his *Haribhaktivilāsa* he framed the laws of ritual practice that would be widely followed in the then-new Vrindavan, he was largely transporting southern norms northward. A third influential southerner was Narayan Bhatt, otherwise known as Ghamandi, who settled at Arith, joining a group of ascetics from eastern Indian who had camped there and renamed the place after the pattern of their own devotional sensibilities: Radhakund. It was there, in 1552, that he completed his *Vrajabhaktivilāsa*, the great treatise that created a new sacred geography for Braj—describing it, all the while, as an old geography rediscovered and clarified for modern times. A late seventeenth-century biography written by one of Narayan Bhatt's descendants reports that Narayan's father hailed from Madurai in the far south, but there may have been an intermediary stop. According to this same account and to the *Vrajotsavachandrikā*, a work reportedly written by Narayan himself, Narayan Bhatt was born in 1531 on the banks of the Godavari. That would imply a more gradual northward migration. But the point remains that he too came from the south from which so many sixteenth-century gosvamis hailed, and indeed, then as now the idea of Vrindavan was important in the south. As we have noted earlier, Madurai is the Tamil form of Mathura, after which it was named.[47]

Narayan Bhatt's *Vrajabhaktivilāsa* is a remarkable treatise, cataloguing every conceivable forest, grove, or ford in the Braj countryside, connecting each with a deity or character in the life of Krishna, and instructing potential visitors about the mantra to be uttered at each place and the time that would be optimal for intoning it. This encyclopedic work reads, in the words of Alan Entwistle, "not so much as a description of actual circumstances, but as a prospectus for a full reclamation of Braj, making use of any existing objects, however trivial, and inventing the rest".[48] It provides a prospectus for a full reclamation of Braj—and doesn't that sound like what we have in the design of the Chandrodaya Mandir? Evidently it was partly Narayan Bhatt's distance from local ways and conventions that made it possible for him to see such a different Braj from what the locals saw, and thereby to provide much of the basis for the ongoing reformulation of Braj and Vrindavan that was enacted as

landscape surrounding it looks much more like Gurgaon than like anything around Banke Bihari or Keshi Ghat. This is the same sprawl that has made it bureaucratically necessary for Delhi to expand itself into the National Capital Region. No wonder Hema Malini thinks Vrindavan should sign on.[55]

The mood of the times is everywhere, and we know a lot about it already—the real estate, the relentless commercial construction along National Highway 2, the faint smell of liquor on someone's breath. But perhaps the most telling expression of the way this new NCR identity might engulf the culture of Braj is that a recent chief minister of Uttar Pradesh, Mayawati (r. 2007–12), had the idea of transposing the great pilgrimage places of the Braj onto NH-2 itself. They would become roadside rest-stop oases along the Delhi–Agra highway—one would be themed Barsana, another Nandagaon, and there would certainly be a place for Mount Govardhan. These rest stops, with their miniature amusement parts, would be fun for the family and heritage at the same time—a type of heritage that meant you didn't have to leave the main road to access it.[56] Precedents for this sort of spatial transposition go deep into Hindu religious history; Mathura and Banaras have their miniature versions of the south Indian pilgrimage center called Gokarn, for example.[57] But the significant change in this case is that the transfer is not from one sacred locale to another, but from sacred place to the side of a newly expanded thoroughfare. This is the culture of bypass.

Let's try another angle on this emerging megalopolis and the way it's wired to Vrindavan. Let's visit the office of the VCM's chief architect, Rimpesh Sharma, in Gurgaon. It's a glistening affair situated in one of the city's spanking new glass-sheathed office buildings, and that, in turn, belongs to a newly built corporate compound called Spaze IT Park. It's one of Gurgaon's trendiest business destinations, and the "z" spelling prepares you for just that. At first it may seem distinctive, but before long you see that it's also conventional—a convention, precisely, of the Now. This "z" is used all over Gurgaon and elsewhere to add a little zest to tired old spellings—tired old English spellings, that is.[58] "We're distinctive, we're hip", it proclaims, but it turns out we're also generic. Etched into the glass doors you open to enter the building is the following ukase: "SPAZE. Invoke the Future".

Figure 4.10.   Rimpesh Sharma at his Gurgaon offices, January 2, 2017.

Rimpesh Sharma is one of two founding directors of the architectural firm InGenious Studio Pvt. Ltd., and the whole feel of the place
is young and well designed (Fig. 4.10). A conference room opens on
your left as you make your way through the pass-coded door. There
are two banks of cubicles just ahead, where somewhat older hands
(approaching 40?) offer guidance to their juniors, and off to the
side there's a handsome office for the two directors. If you look out
the window to the park-like landscape below, you see a few 20- and
30-somethings chatting with one another on a break or walking
between buildings. For all the world, it looks just like an architect's
drawing, with those few dreamlike figures serving as casual decora-
tion for a sleek structure still in the mind's eye. Is this Houston or
San Diego? Is it reality? The gates of this corporate park do their best
to keep the ordinary world of north India at bay. Three-wheelers stand
ready to ferry you down the highway to what is presently the last stop on
the Delhi Metro—they wait dutifully at the corner outside, and outside
is where you have to go if you want to sample India's delicious, freshly
cooked street food. An enterprising young man offered me a flyer for

a thali app that makes it possible to have "homely food at your door step"—or, presumably, delivered through those carefully guarded gates to your office. I'm not sure the sense of home will survive.

Gurgaon has been thrown up overnight—this part of town in the last decade.[59] But lest it sound as if InGenious Studio is showing off by choosing to inhabit such a fancy exurban location, let me point out how sensibly its offices are positioned. Far from being perched on some "executive" upper floor, they hug the ground just one floor up, which means you're not at the mercy of the elevators that serve the building as a whole. It's easy to use the stairs. A similar down-to-earth-ness characterizes Rimpesh Sharma himself. Trim and of medium height, he is consummately dapper in his dark tailored suit. A beautifully patterned handkerchief peeks out of his jacket pocket, its three carefully ironed triangular peaks marching smartly along their shared black battlement. Yet for all this obvious elegance (I hasten to add that on other days he dresses more informally), he is a practical man. His mobile phone would constantly beg for attention if it weren't on silent mode, but he is cordial, composed, plain-spoken. His manner puts you immediately at ease. Rimpesh grew up in a village in Punjab and did his architectural training at one of Punjab's nearby government colleges. But his father was a military man who knew someone in Dubai, so when it came time for Rimpesh to launch his architectural career, he did so in the shadow of the Burj Khalifa. A decade later he was back in India, still only 33. Now he has made his way into his early forties, and the brochures, blueprints, and promotional books festooning his conference table give plenty of assurance that much, much more is still to come.

The way Rimpesh talks about this rise makes it sound far more whimsical than you might expect. It was only a word at the right time from an old friend that made him aware that architecture even existed as a field—this just before he had to decide what sort of academic program to pursue—and his very name Rimpesh seemed to have no model or plot behind it. Was it somehow connected with the Tibetan Rimpoche? I asked. No, his parents just put the sounds and syllables together because they liked them, without their having any particular meaning. That would have to come later—if there actually was any meaning to come. And things kept on happening to him in this experimental way. A friend in Jaipur, Archana Surana, started a school of design in two rooms in her house when Rimpesh was just a young man, so he jumped in to teach interior design and vastu, the ancient Indian practice of auspicious positioning that corresponds in part to Chinese feng shui. He had to teach himself what it was about, since he had no access to the Sanskrit in which the classical texts were written. Then the two of them lost touch, but years later this same friend was looking for an architect. Her school was now 600 students strong and they needed a new building, so she asked a friend to suggest a firm. InGenious came to mind—and sure enough, to her surprise, there was Rimpesh at the helm of the ship.

A similar pattern characterizes Rimpesh's relationship with the Chandrodaya temple. It was only in 2013, actually, that he visited Vrindavan for the first time, accompanied by his wife and son. They drove down from Gurgaon first thing in the morning, arriving sometime around 6:30 or 6:45 a.m. Turning in from NH-2, they stopped to ask someone who would be the first to open for breakfast. The answer was the restaurant at Akshay Patra, and there one of the VCM staff gave Rimpesh advice about what temples his family ought to visit in Vrindavan before they pressed on to Mathura and Agra. The two talked and Rimpesh left his card. A year later he got a call as he was packing his bags to get on a plane: Could a group of VCM people come to see him? Yes, if they'd come to his house in Gurgaon's Sector 46. He had to catch his plane. And so it all happened. They'd done their research on him, of course—he later found out that they'd gone to others first with their ideas—but in the end it was the everyday magic of that early-morning encounter in Vrindavan that set the right wheels turning. Rimpesh got the job.

As we have seen, serendipity is also built into the sense of life that a number of the VCM staff possess, but there it's called "miracle" instead. How but for a sense of the miraculous could one be open to Krishna's surprising initiatives? Not quite so, Rimpesh. He is simply, amusedly nonchalant about what life throws in his path. Similarly brainstorming is a big part of what he thinks it takes to make plans work—it's "mindset" that matters most, not a given template or blueprint, and particularly with a building like a temple, the plans themselves need to have an element of flexibility built in. "Certain things flow with time", he says, "and temples are one of them. They're donation-based. You can't force anybody. ...

People join you after seeing it", and you really don't even know how many people you're planning for. Yes, he's living for the moment when he can see "the stone ... cast in front of us", but at the same time it all has to be dynamic: there are sure to be new "plug-ins" not far down the road. The art of architectural management is to develop a structure that makes it possible to plug them in when the time comes.[60]

An architect's job is to create an overall design that will respond flexibly to specialists' solutions to individual aspects of the conundrum the building in question may present, and the bigger the project, the more this flexibility is key. "We may not even know what all the parts are when we begin", he says. In regard to the VCM, take the matter of fire regulations. There actually is no code for a structure taller than thirty meters, Rimpesh explains, so in this case you have to forget your normal contacts with people at the building authority and start knocking on the fire department's door—at the state level. When Rimpesh did this, it turned out to be determinative. Floors and landings were nowhere in the minds of the VCM visionaries—it was all to be a grand theater of animation—but flesh-and-blood people would be there to take it all in. Where would they take refuge if something went wrong? Suddenly the building had to be transformed into something that had a semblance of stories all the way up, or at least platforms people could use in case of emergency. As for the top two floors, dedicated to Golok Vrindavan and the observation level for viewing Braj and the Taj, they had to be designed simultaneously so that they could serve as a sanctuary in case there was a disaster somewhere below. Was the meaning of Golok Vrindavan thereby altered? In his view, not a bit.

Where is religion in all this? Can we find it anywhere? Surprisingly, it surfaces in Rimpesh's sense of what is meant by "Vedic". Vedic, for him, has little to do with texts: "Whatever is logical, I would say, is Vedic. It is not something cast in stone. It's like a calculator". He demonstrates with the one he has in his hand. "You can see there are nine keys and you can also see solving all kinds of problems with just this set of keys". Veda is dynamic in the sense that no one knows the whole picture, so you have to make your own way experimentally. "The whole picture is stable", he says—it's just that we only know part. Somehow the whole is designed to allow for that fact. Here the image that came to mind—and again he shaped it with his hands—was a conical structure with a central pillar that is stable but with a horizontal dimension that rotates. Similarly, what's Vedic is ancient but constantly changing.

Rimpesh was amused to notice that he hadn't prepared his calculator analogy in advance, it just came to him on the spur of the moment. But it nicely suits his solid-yet-dynamic vision for the Chandrodaya temple itself, something that has to have an enormous foundation and a very resilient shell yet also serve the purpose of projecting "maybe 5-D laser shows". The calculator comparison also aligns with Rimpesh's conviction that he is not working with any actual model here. There may be things to be learned from buildings constructed earlier, but what would be the point in just building another one? He firmly rejected the idea that the riverway anticipated at the base of the Chandrodaya Mandir had anything to do with the one they constructed underground at Akshardham. "We have not benchmarked ourselves".

Is this sense of "Vedic" really religion? There's a fair amount of pop-Veda thinking in Hindu India these days—Vedic mathematics and the like—but one doubts that it would satisfy the ideologues and theologues with whom Rimpesh is working at the VCM. As their "Vedic cosmology" shows, they have a stricter sense of things. Yet their predilections and Rimpesh's make for a happy synergy. In its way Rimpesh's perspective is the more wide-ranging—certainly less confined by sectarian canons of interpretation. From his point of view it's no conceptual problem that the designs for the new Shiva temple being constructed just down the road, Shankar Dham Vrindavan, also lie on his desk along with many others all over north India. The four kingdoms that give Disney World its character look completely distinct—otherwise they would not exert the attraction they do—but a massive set of passageways and a single massive kitchen connect them underground.

Not all of InGenious's clients are in the National Capital Region itself, of course—they can be as far away as Saudi Arabia—and not all of the specialists involved in designing the Chandrodaya Mandir live any closer. The man in charge of structural issues works out of Mumbai and the lighting consultant is in Australia. Yet this is no anomaly. A national and international modus operandi such as this is precisely what Gurgaon stands for in India today—far more so than its neighbor, Delhi. In that sense too Gurgaon is what the Vrindavan Chandrodaya Mandir is about—even more than anything in Vrindavan itself. The structure being built here, says Rimpesh, has to be worthy of "pride from the whole of the country". It's really not that Vrindavan stands for the end that the Vrindavan Chandrodaya Mandir seeks to achieve, while Gurgaon serves as the means. Rather, means and end turn out to be surprisingly the same. The public relations staff of the VCM seem to have perceived this in their own way. They made Rimpesh into the host and star of a promotional video they produced in the early months of 2017. It showed up on my Facebook page on June 27 of that year. Nor was that his only appearance.

The connection between the VCM and all that Gurgaon stands for has been solidified in another way, as well. On April 29, 2018 the Vrindavan Chandrodaya Mandir launched its first "satellite center" in Gurgaon itself with ground-breaking exercises anticipating the construction there of a temple dedicated to Krishna as Radharaman, the deity who revealed himself to Gopal Bhatt in the sixteenth century.[61] This new tie between Vrindavan and Gurgaon is meaningful in many ways, with the momentous power and innovation flowing both directions. We've recently had our eye on the Gurgaon-to-Vrindavan flow, but the construction of this new center asserts the other—the hope that cosmopolitan, globally wired Gurgaon will come to stand in Vrindavan's shadow. In one way this new "satellite center" obviously stands in the shadow of American Express and many other multinational firms; they are its immediate neighbors. But it is also intended as a seed and a corrective, a gleaming Vaishnava "mission church". There are already six or seven wine shops (liquor stores) in the vicinity, said one VCM interlocutor.[62] This temple will remind the world of Gurgaon what must never be left out, and as in Bangalore it is to be more than just a reminder—a magnet, a lodestone, a compass.

Repeated Retrofittings

For those most deeply involved in the VCM project, one of its deepest fascinations is that the bulk of it lies always ahead of them. It is never done until it's done, and there is the expectation that it will continue to evolve even then. For members of the core design team who come from within ISKCON itself, this has a theological meaning: Krishna runs out in front, a leader urging them on. For the architects, however, there is a more immediately structural dimension. Once one has fixed the outlines for a project that covers 200 million square feet—the outer shell of marble and glass and the immense pillars that support the weight of everything within—it is the interior parts that remain to be adjusted, assigned, imagined in detail. There precisely one feels Rimpesh's excitement as a space theologian: How to give *meaning* to these parts? How to envision them in a way that they will excite the imagination of donors and patrons and thus take on a life of their own? The design elements of this project are vastly different from other temple projects that he is also shepherding—the height!—but he often stresses that floor plans often look remarkably generic. It's what goes inside that makes the difference.

Despite his early disclaimer about being personally religious in a general sense only, and despite a subsequent remark that "This project is not for us religious", I have come to feel that whenever Rimpesh's energies are focused on planning the Chandrodaya Mandir, it comes to serve in some special way as an architect's personal regime of discipline, what in religious terms would be called sādhanā. By virtue of its special demands, the VCM imposes a discipline that makes it natural for Rimpesh to work his way into Krishna, and while it lasts, at least, this is a process he eagerly embraces. When he is talking about this project he happily adopts the greeting "Hare Krishna". His job is to make this structure and the landscaped complex that surrounds it echo the reality of Krishna, and in his elegant nonsectarian way he eagerly leans into the role.

The "real world" also has its say, however. Indian corporations with annual net profits in excess of 50 million rupees (approximately $725,000 at 2019 rates) have since 2013 been required to donate 2% of their earnings to the cause of corporate social responsibility, and donations made under that rubric cannot be specifically religious. A corporation cannot receive public credit for helping to build a temple. To attract such donations, the Vrindavan Chandrodaya Mandir must be something more than a mandir—in fact, something *other* than a mandir. No wonder that it is now to be known—in certain public contexts, at least—as the Vrindavan Heritage Tower.

A Google search using this phrase yields ample results, but I did not find the word "Hindu" anywhere in publicity issued by the VCM (or if you prefer, VHT) itself. The "cultural" term Vedic—as in "Vedic values"—replaces it, and there is a tendency to shy away from the adjective "religious" in favor of "spiritual". The Vrindavan Heritage Tower is to be not just a temple but a seat of learning in which students can absorb "our" spiritual values and the meanings of the texts that best represent them, the Bhagavad Gita and the Bhagavata Purana. "Uplift" is also involved, we hear. There is a no more Gandhian term. Here it is applied to the work of Akshay Patra and a general devotion to cleaning up Vrindavan. The last word of one of the videos produced for broadcast in 2017 is indeed, with appropriate *gravitas* as it is declaimed, "heritage". And a notable effort is made to situate the project outside the realm of Hinduism itself—at least for certain viewers. A special feature shows Yudhishthira in the company of, I quote, "Suhail Mohd Al Zarooni, Guinness World Record Holder, Chairman Al Zarooni Foundation & the Emirati Entrepreneur at Al Zarooni Palace". There are several formal shots in which we see the two men standing opposite one another facing the camera and holding a plastic-wrapped example of the "neo-Vedic" art for which ISKCON is famous along with one of the large-format publications about the Mandir—or rather, Heritage Tower. Elsewhere Mr. Al Zarooni receives a copy of *The Bhagavad Gītā As It Is*.

Rimpesh Sharma is dissatisfied with the VHT moniker. He doesn't like the "tower" designation—too rough, too heartless—and he is trying to find the right substitute. "Lord Krishna's Peacock?" he once mused.[63] Indeed, the motif of the peacock feather is built into the general design Rimpesh has adopted for the plot of land on which the building rests, and one of his desires is to foreground "horizontal" aspects of the project along with the vertical statement it makes. The plans for the walls and height of the VCM are fixed, he observes, but the life of the place will be generated from within. That life opens onto what Rimpesh thinks of as the building's horizontal dimensions. These reflect, anticipate, and shape the experience of people who will be involved with the site; they are organic. But how to experience this organic reality before it exists? The second part of the 2.0 name that had now been assigned to the project—"and Krishna Lila Theme Park"—makes an attempt to capture this dimension, but it only begins to suggest what that experience will be. In March 2017 Rimpesh was still waiting for the right concept to manifest itself. He keeps working toward it from within.

To begin with, it is a space of many parts. The "Vedic cosmology" aspect fits into a much larger scheme than its own cosmic claims and earlier conceptual prominence suggest. Using a distinctively Indian metaphor, Rimpesh says we're talking here of an "extended family" of processes he is content to call tourism—recreational, educational, spiritual, and even cultural heritage tourism—and the whole matter of the tower comes at the end of that. That's even the way it is literally. Visitors will first explore this "extended family" realm and only later ascend the tower. And as of March 2017 there would be a "widow feeding facility", a range of themed "food festival venues", and a great deal else—a world of its own, but truly a world.

To me, one of the most striking aspects of the new Vrindavan Heritage Tower is its "Anchorage Hall of Values", a scheme by means of which the pillars bearing the vast weight of the tower's vertical structure will be integrated into the horizontality of the base complex—this time a horizontality that is not touristic but ethical. This is a step up (figuratively speaking) from the fourth-place status that the lowest of the dhams, ethical Ayodhya, was granted in the original vision. In this major conceptual retrofitting, the four main weight-bearing pillars surrounding the central core will be the pillars of truth, compassion, austerity, and purity (satya, dayā, tapasyā, śaucha), these being "the four pillars of civilized life", principles ISKCON theorists have specifically extracted from the Bhagavad Gita. Indeed, the structure will include an Institute on the Bhagavad Gita along with an Institute for Ethics and Values. But the striking thing is that Rimpesh and his team have found a way to encode these values into the structure of the building itself—on the floor just below the actual temple. The four great pillars are objects for charitable contributions too: you can have your name (or that of your family or company) inscribed on each to immortalize your support for the enterprise as a whole or perhaps to record your appreciation for the particular importance of one of these four dimensions. First come, first served—you may not be able to get your choice unless you act quickly! It is already projected that the names of Henry David Thoreau and Ralph Waldo Emerson will be featured on plaques in the central hall that surrounds these pillars, recognizing their reverence for the Gita. To theirs you can add your own.[64]

This VCM 2.0 (or rather, VHT 2.0) approach obviously reshapes the concept of Vedic cosmology. Earlier we saw the world—indeed the cosmos—being aligned in relation to the special emphases of the Bhagavata Purana, which in turn had featured the special wonders of the Braj countryside and its roles in the life of Krishna. Now, though, we have the far more sober claims of the Bhagavad Gita, the text that is the Bhagavata Purana's older sister. From an ISKCON point of view it shifts the center of attention toward the scripture that initially "sold" the Hare Krishna movement to the world and away from the more inward-facing purana that occupied Prabhupad's energies after he had fashioned *The Bhagavad Gītā As It Is*. In VCM 2.0 the force of attraction as such is no longer expected to exercise the almost magical draw that earlier had been hoped. The root metaphor for the communications and advertising process has shifted from attraction to construction. Perhaps it would be fairer to say that there has been a recalibrating of the balance between the two, but it does seem that the "weight" of the structure itself is much more prominently featured, as if it had turned out to be more essential to the shape of things than had been anticipated by VCM 1.0. There is no denying, as Rimpesh concedes, that "the structure is very dominating". Acknowledging this, the "Krishna Lila Theme Park" obbligato is not gone, but it has been put in its place—a new place—and in that act of conceptual transition the Vrindavan Chandrodaya Mandir has moved a giant step away from the rest of Vrindavan. In its design it was always more muscular, more masculine—dare one say more phallic?—than any other structure in town, but now it's trying to get its financial feet on the ground.

There are other examples of the same changed, more pragmatic mood. As Sarvanand emphasized, there will be a hotel school—or as he put it, a "Hospitality Institute" where young local people in need of a livelihood can be given the skills that will enable them to be employable far from Vrindavan. For Sarvanand, the manners and professional interpersonal behavior they are to be taught will contrast broadly to the crude and imperious habits of the pandas who so offended him when he first visited Vrindavan from south India in 2002. Nobody in this Hospitality Institute is going to use the "filthy language" these local guides employed in the presence of the elderly women of Sarvanand's family who travelled with him.[65] To the contrary, the new trainees will become immaculately trained ambassadors for ISKCON and Krishna no matter what positions they end up assuming after they graduate. And there are statistics to be cited. Several of the slides that Rimpesh and his team have designed emphasize the fact that a new manufacturing facility creates on average 45 jobs, while a new tourism facility creates 78. I have seen similar figures in the context of the World Bank's Pro-poor Growth initiative. As for the immediate relationship between the VCM monolith and its many real estate satellites, whether they be formally related to the VCM or not, the Chandrodaya Tower will serve as the USB for all of them, says Rimpesh.[66] In fact, he adds, it already is.

In the first wave of promotional material touting the great new VCM complex—in *Reaching to the Sky*, say—there was a clear relationship between the narrative imagery that gave substance to the Chandrodaya Mandir and the motifs that feature prominently in the "old" Vrindavan. For the sake of the kids there might be an emphasis on certain lilas that play no role in the old Vrindavan, but at least there was a connection. The episode in which Krishna vanquishes the snake demon Aghasur, for example, supersedes but has a tie to the more famous episode in which Krishna dances on the head of the black snake Kaliya, this being immortalized at a place called Kaliya Deh ("the black snake's hole") along Parikrama Marg. Now, though, in VCM 2.0, if we think about the complex as a whole, the copy has become so far removed from the original that the relationship is a relation in name only. More and more, the Chandrodaya Tower epitomizes Delhi and the nation, not Vrindavan, and this partly in response to the exigencies of public funding. A conversation with Sarvanand Das in late March 2017 marked a great shift from earlier ones in this regard. I was surprised to find how little reference he made to Krishna and his miraculous powers in the course of that encounter. Instead I heard about the secular practicalities that would make this still obviously religious project succeed. Rimpesh Sharma's stance at the time was somewhat different. His job is less circumscribed by the exigencies of salesmanship, so he can be more expansive, less concerned to watch his words. But with him too I sensed a shift—the shift toward what he called the horizontal. Rimpesh seemed far more attentive to this world and its intricately interlocking domains than he had been in a conversation three months before.

After another year had passed, there was yet another shift of mood—this with both horizontal and vertical facets. In a conversation of July 2018 Sarvanand Das reported enthusiastically about several ways in which the VCM project had diversified—spread out, as if horizontally. Not only had it broken ground in Gurgaon for the new Radharaman "mission" temple (the term is mine, not his), but it had opened a very popular English-language "Culture Camp" based in Gurgaon and Faridabad. Both of these lie on the peripheries of "classic" Delhi; more such camps are projected throughout the city. Parents feel the need for their children to be educated in aspects of India's religious heritage that often do not form part of the curriculum of the English-medium private schools these kids attend. This is to my mind a horizontal development not only in the sense that it is based in the expanding metropole rather than Vrindavan itself, but also because it expands the original VCM mission into areas that are of utterly common concern to upper-middle-class Indian parents and their diasporic counterparts. Here the VCM organization does not create the orbit it inhabits, as in the earlier "attraction" model, but absorbs it. When a "Braj Heritage Fest" came on the scene, as it first did in August 2018, it was based in Vrindavan but it was part of this more general "horizontal" field. It featured competitions for young people in music, theater, and dance, and there were chances for them to display their knowledge of the Gita and stories from the puranas. Such competitions had been a huge success at ISKCON Bangalore, and sure enough, as the VCM planners expected, some 10,000 youths from schools in the Mathura-Vrindavan region were involved. It's the competition feature that locates this new project so firmly in a "horizontal" field: this is a hallmark of extra-curricular private Indian education, and again there are potent resonances abroad. It's no accident that American Hindu kids have recently played a dominant role in national spelling bees.[67]

As for the vertical dimension of things, there too the VCM witnessed an important adjustment to its earlier plans. It had been brewing beneath the surface for some time in response to the fact that the targeting of Indian corporations through the 2% Corporate Social Responsibility requirement had so far failed to bring in the vast increments of cash that had been hoped for when the "heritage" rebranding campaign was launched. Even worse, perhaps, was the fact that Prime Minister Modi's demonetization campaign cut off many of the large cash donations that had been expected to flow in from India's "informal" economy. In a dramatic bow to these uncomfortable fiscal realities, the whole plan to project Vedic cosmology on the inner walls of a largely empty VCM tower was quietly abandoned. For a time it seemed that the space would be filled instead with what you'd find on many floors of all the other needle towers had have recently sprouted up around the world—apartments (Fig. 4.11). Earlier the VCM tower had been envisioned as a giant object of darshan. This shift reversed the gaze, at least partially. Now you would have darshan of all of Vrindavan from inside your apartment, and a good chunk of Braj, as well.

Some of the apartments commanding this view would be owned outright, Sarvanand said; others would be time-share arrangements.[68] And the higher you went, the greater your status—financial status, that is. Higher floors would cost more, putting you in the company of persons just as elite as you are yourself. In the going management lingo, this means you have been identified as a High Network Individual, valuable not just for the resources you personally command but also for the connections you have to others of your status. As Sarvanand Das put it, "if you want that kind of funding ... they will expect good treatment". But still, this focus on "premium pilgrimage" would not be mere secular marketing. "You're staying in a tirtha", Sarvanand wished to stress. In doing so he used the classic Sanskrit word that denotes places of pilgrimage, heavy with religious significance. Earlier on, private ownership, whether individual or shared, had seemed an obstacle. There was an insistence that the property owned by the Vrindavan Chandrodaya Mandir would be different in principle from what you had at Krishna Bhūmi (always written with the ū), even though the two enterprises are neighbors and financial partners. By contrast to the real estate development just opposite, there was to be no ownership as such on these temple premises. As with all Vrindavan temples, the actual owners would be the deities installed there—the ownership would be vested in God. But now the lines would be blurred, replicating the blurring that was required to amass the temple's land in the first place.

Figure 4.11.   North–south section of the Vrindavan Chandrodaya Mandir from an intermediary version of *Reaching to the Sky*, showing apartments ("Goloka Suites") on the upper floors of the tower, just before the blue ("Viewing Gallery") floors begin. Courtesy of the Vrindavan Chandrodaya Mandir.

Was this to cave in to secularity, to abrogate the earlier ideals of ritual and moral purity? The question also arises in relation to the theme-park aspect of things. These "lila parks" were now to be marketed as for-profit operations sold as franchises to external buyers, who would develop them and eventually relinquish them to the management of the temple itself, perhaps after a fifteen-year period. In the meantime, admission would be charged, helping the financial cause. Of course, content restraints would be imposed. The VCM team would insist on approving what was shown in the theme-park attractions, and would continue to enforce standards of purity in relation to the temple's residential life. You would have to pass a moral test to buy in: no drinking, no meat, no loud parties. Thus we were still a big step removed from the wedding venues that have sprung up all over the New Vrindavan.

I sensed a certain level of repressed anxiety as Sarvanand outlined marketing strategies such as these—an earlier innocence had been lost—but an additional level of theological innovation flowed in. As regards real estate private ownership, for example, Sarvanand was pleased to refer to a passage in Rupa Gosvami's sixteenth-century *Bhaktirasāmṛtasindhu*, one that he had found no reason to quote before. Gaudiya theologians, he pointed out, had combed this gargantuan work and laid emphasis on the fact that Rupa was putting forth five main principles for the living of a holy life. One of these—the fourth—was mathurā vāsam, literally "living in Mathura", which for Rupa must have meant not just the Mathura tirtha but also Vrindavan, he urged.[69] This was where Rupa himself had settled when he came from Bengal to live in the holy land, and this is exactly what the VCM wanted to make possible for High Network Individuals by offering them a Vrindavan that matched their standard of living—and more. It's a story of horizontal ingathering, all right—secular in its aims and tone—but with a dramatically vertical, sacred component.

Half a year later things changed again. These real estate compromises weren't bringing in the revenues they were supposed to, and the VCM leadership again shifted course—this time at the highest levels. They headed for something simpler, sleeker, and, they thought, truer to the original vision. There would still be state-of-the-art flats where donors could stay, of course, but they would be located just beneath the level of the temple, not obstructing its upward rise. So said Rimpesh when I talked with him in Gurgaon in mid-January 2019. But by the time I got to Bangalore at the end of the same month and spoke with Chanchalapati Das at the top of the management pyramid, I learned that these apartments would be housed in entirely separate buildings, leaving the temple-tower to itself.[70] The Sanskrit word "mandira" can mean both a house and house of God, but these two would now be kept distinct, as in modern usage (Hindi: mandir). The tower would be left empty except for four high-speed elevators and the few concrete slabs required at intervals for structural and safety reasons. The elevators would whisk visitors to viewing galleries twenty or thirty people at a time. Three would be located at about 450 feet and two more just below the finial on top. That finial would now replicate a more traditional model than what originally appeared in *Reaching to the Sky,* and though the rest of the structure still exemplifies the "unified statement" to which Rimpesh Sharma has always aspired, it has a less thoroughly modernist look. Rimpesh had worked with trapezoids as his overall vertical unit. They marched skyward like a giant banana, peeling apart from the more complex temple structure at their base. Now, though, the Bangalore leadership preferred octagons instead, since they would more comfortably echo the traditional nāgara temple architecture.

This may seem fussier, more ornate than the foursquare plan originally envisioned, but as he talked about it Chanchalapati stressed that the overall effect would be toward simplification, since there would now be but a single temple. The four ancillary ones—to Prabhupad; Chaitanya and the gosvamis; Krishna, Balaram, and their male friends; and Krishna, Radha, and the gopis—had now been entirely scrapped. This was a gesture not to conceptual purity but to the exigencies of finance, though it did have a structural meaning: the earlier architectural break between tower and temple had been rethought. Now the whole thing was to look like a temple. For a while the Bangalore leadership debated whether to convert Rimpesh's sky-blue spire into something beige that might harmonize better with Vrindavan's signature sandstone temples, but in the end blue and white won out (Fig. 4.12).[71] This was a victory for the modern and international by contrast to the "mixed vegetable" hodgepodge Rimpesh saw at Mayapur.[72] It would be an unmistakably global building, standing apart from any local company.

These changes did not happen in a vacuum. Chanchalapati Das was entirely open about that fact. The main driving force was the bottom line. There would be no apartments with various degrees of height and luxury—too costly—and no expensive Vedic projections

Figure 4.12. Chanchalapati Das, President of the Vrindavan Chandrodaya
Mandir and Vice Chairman of the Akshay Patra Foundation, displays
a poster showing the redesign of the Vrindavan Chandrodaya Mandir.
Bangalore, January 30, 2019.

on the inner walls. Donations were not coming in as had been hoped. Chanchapati revealed that the initial budget for the Chandrodaya Mandir had been 1200 crores—some 200 million dollars—but it was now being reduced to a sixth of that, and even then they would need a bank loan to get things going. That was no easy sales pitch: "The risks of a high-value project are high". But once they got that loan, construction would begin, and once people saw it was happening, they would climb aboard. Even in the "dampened financial environment" that followed from the Modi government's revised tax regulations, people with "religious inclinations" would come forward and join the cause, just as they had done in Bangalore itself. They just had to see that it was really happening.

Chanchalapati announced this with no bravado—only the steady tensile strength of his elegant speech. But as he thought about how the sparer design would project a clearer message, he warmed to the rhetorical task of the moment. "Message" moved front and center, and he proclaimed that the very existence of this new structure would be a message—Krishna's message to times like ours. The Hare Krishna mantra and the novel chanting style Chaitanya fashioned to proclaim it—spare, elegant, public, bold—were assuming this age-appropriate new form. All the great sources—the Gita, Rupa Gosvami, and Chaitanya himself—spoke of the cardinal importance of remembering Krishna, thinking of him all the time.[73] This temple was to be that very remembrance, and to cause it to arise in others—the "moonrise" temple indeed. Love in the form of a skyscraper: how could the world not respond?

Legibility was very much on Chanchalapati's mind as he developed these thoughts. "Just look at how everything has changed!" When people go to shop, especially the young ones, where do they go? To malls, with all those "glittering features". And it's just the same for hospitals, schools, and airports. There's "high quality infrastructure" all throughout "the glitter of modern India". We have to make our message like that, he explained—interesting, modern, and clean, not some dirty rumpled relic of the past. Otherwise people won't get the message and see who Krishna is. I asked if he thought it was Bangalore's particular mission as India's vanguard of technological change to bring Vrindavan into the present like this. No, he demurred, it's only that "the Lord has blessed us, inspiring us to do something". You could see he felt the Lord meant business. With the bank loan coming soon and the Prime Minister gracing the Vrindavan premises, the construction work would surely soon commence. By Karttik of 2020 the temple could be finished. They would issue contracts so that it could be constructed in parts more or less anywhere in the world—"computer-controlled precision fabrications". The results would be assembled in Vrindavan and the tower would shoot up in a mere six months, a visual marvel if ever there was one.

The deities would already be on site, housed in the northern wing of the temple, for that would be built first, once the loan came in. These deities would serve as anchors for the "Experience Center" where they'd be housed—the *experience* word once again! Visitors could also have a "walk-through" of the entire structure thanks to models and visual projections, and some theme-park features would also be involved.[74] I asked what had happened to the idea of Vedic cosmology, and Chanchalapati assured me that aspect would be retained—just transposed to screens lining the elevators. Visitors would still get a taste of the Veda (at least as ISKCON conceives it), but it would be ever so much less expensive. Good from a psychological point of view, too. As Rimpesh once remarked, two or three minutes in an elevator with twenty or thirty people can seem like a very long time.

The peak experience will be saved for the top, of course. You will emerge from your elevator into an open gallery that offers a vision of all of Braj (braj darshan), the Braj you see in the present day. Through telescopes you'll be able to zoom in on Krishna's birthplace in Mathura or focus on Radha's home in Barsana or follow the meandering course of the Yamuna. By this means you'll be able to circumambulate Braj in a single moment, a lofty parikrama But that's not quite the summit experience. Go one floor higher and you'll enter a completely different realm—different but complementary. You'll take your seat in one of many specially rigged chairs and enter the 5-D "virtual reality experience" that's always been a part of the plan. With your special CGI (computer graphics imagery) goggles, you'll be able to see not just the Barsana of the present but the place that Radha and Krishna saw themselves—or Krishna's town of Nandagaon, if you prefer. Or Gokul or Mathura or Vrindavan itself. Whatever it would be, you could *choose* it—that proud independent variable of modern life—but Chanchalapati hoped you'd especially want to compare what is with what was. Portals on the computer screen would allow you to see either or both, or toggle freely between them. Surely the "lush green forests" of the original Braj would seem more vivid and real than what you'd see if you got in a car and went today. Chanchalapati was careful not to demean what present-day pilgrims do, but his energy leapt toward the future, the ideal—or rather, the Barsana or Vrindavan that once was. What for me seemed clouded in myth was for him instead the vivid stuff of factual history. He imagined how it would all seem from the perspective of a radically refashioned panopticon, ever so much more humane than Foucault's. He was taking himself on a "flying experience" as he laid it all out, and he looked forward to the day when others could join him.[75]

As he talked, one feature seemed to beg for attention, and I couldn't fail to bring it up. Theologically its name is aiśvarya—lordliness or mastery—and the Chandrodaya Mandir seemed fairly to embody it. Wasn't this exactly what Krishna sought to escape when he wrapped himself in Vrindavan? Hadn't he abandoned divinity, hierarchy, and height to swim in a sea of on-the-ground, this-world intimacy?[76] Chanchalapati acknowledged the problem, but he was quick and nimble in dispatching it. He turned to the theology of Kedarnath Datta, great-guru to Prabhupad and familiarly known under his initiated name Bhakti Vinod Thakur. This man, as we saw in Chapter 1, was a very great builder himself. It was he who created Mayapur across the Ganga from Chaitanya's Nabadvip, heralding a brand new era. That's exactly what was happening here—another requisite mission to present time. It was just "an enhancement of Prabhupad's wishes, not an effort to dwarf anything else". Not everyone is sufficiently refined to appreciate the love-drenched essence of Krishna in relation to Radha, he said. Many have to focus on things big and royal instead—Krishna as Vishnu and Radha as his consort queen Lakshmi. Our times may seem advanced, but these habits of mind persist. They have to be properly directed to Krishna. In the world in which we live, awe has its place.

As Chanchalapati Das laid all this out at the end of January 2019, he made it seem the best was about to come. Two weeks earlier Rimpesh had sounded a similar note. But when I talked to Sarvanand

Das on the same day as Rimpesh, it seemed a very different story. Ever the soul of optimism, Sarvanand admitted to feeling glum. It had really hit him that people just weren't coming through with their donations. They hadn't made the real estate purchases everyone had hoped. So he found himself asking "What does Krishna want?" "We do our best", he said with a brave sigh, "and then we have to await his sanction". As Sarvanand talked on, he spoke about the 100+ story skyscrapers going up in Taipei or Qatar, conceding they'd always be taller than Krishna's skyscraper. And the specter was inching closer to home. Supertech Capetown, an apartment complex going up in Noida, was trumpeting a tower that would rise to 300 meters. The VCM's will be only 210. Encouraged by the central office in Bangalore, Sarvanand had always secretly hoped for more—108 stories, perhaps. But he stepped back from these worries with a philosophical turn once he had given them voice. He was ready for whatever might come. In all this, he hastened to affirm, "We have a ringside view of Krishna lila".[77]

Perhaps the concept of lila is generous enough to encompass it all—a playful sense of bemusement about the workings of reality. Reality is never all that real. But isn't something fundamental getting lost here? It's not just the overwhelming height that gives me pause— I can see how that fits with everything that's happening on the ground in places like Gurgaon or Noida. I accept Chanchalapati's judgment that the world is changing, "whether you like it or not". But when it comes to heritage and leisure and the way they ought to be connected, I find myself really getting stuck. Heritage is being Disneyfied at the VCM, there's no question about that. It's a stroll around a manmade creek or a device you strap on your head in a souped-up high-rise theatre. I resist.

It's all very different for Chanchalapati. He lives in an exquisite cloud of Krishna consciousness, and his business keeps that foremost in his mind. (I mean no disrespect in putting it so.) But what about the rest of us? With its sylvan layout and vertical pyrotechnics the Chandrodaya Mandir hopes to establish a new kind of lila as experience, taking its cues from our increasingly virtual world. But how can it be heritage at the same time? It seems the new Mandir can only sustain its message if it's separate from the Vrindavan that has been. That precious Vrindavan reeks of the real world.

The Timings of Time

One day, coming back to Vrindavan after a few weeks out of town, I found myself taking notes on different senses of time. Being in Vrindavan again called forth this activity. I had re-entered a world of the familiar, and it was set amid buildings that, like me, had aged. The old Vrindavan met the old Jack—at least in the memory of the Jack who lives right now. First I noticed my old friend Pulin, who takes his seat every evening in the photo studio just next to the temple of Radharamanji. It's the same studio where his father sat every evening for decades as worshipers came and went. Different as they are in temperament and voice, I could clearly see Jagdish in Pulin—two times, two generations, superimposed. As to the time marked and celebrated in the temple not far away, that's another kind of time—the archetypal progression of Krishna's day, ever the same in its eight daily moments, varying only by season. It played its great continuo as background for the humbler, more delicate events that transpired in the Praveen Photo Studio.

Not far away there's the time inhabited by Suresh Chand, the man who does my laundry. Sometimes in the last business hours of the day he will stretch out on top of his display case like a Cheshire cat and read the paper—an early-evening tryst with printed truth. This has a special benefit. Thanks to him today's paper will become the paper that appears between the front and the back of my shirts tomorrow— an excellent venue for catching up on yesterday's news. This is laundry time, a tempo all its own.

Then there's family time. As I talked with the young man who stopped by to fix some electrical things in the kitchen, I asked about his family. This lit a little spark in the intelligent eyes of Bhakta Haridas. I learned that he had a baby girl who would soon be five months old. How could he so easily remember? Because he is her father, of course, but also because she happened to be born on Radhashtami, that is, Radha's birthday, so the lunar calculations are easy. And by the way, was it just happenstance that she was born on that day? No, as he sees it, there's a hand turning the wheel of time. It belongs to Thakurji, to Krishna, Radha's mate.

There was one more family moment that day, this one enacted by Radhika, the beautiful daughter of Samrat Schmiem Kumar and his

Figure 4.13. Radhika, queen of foreheads, November 28, 2016—two months before she discovered the wrinkles in mine. The forehead she focuses on here belongs to Swami Revatikaant of the Bhakti Marga community.

wife Elida Jacobsen (Fig. 4.13). Samrat and Elida are a mix of Indian and European, and he is the author of a major study called *Vrindavan's Encounter with Modernity: Changing Environment and Life-worlds in an Indian Temple Town.* Whenever I was in Vrindavan, I would go over to talk with Samrat and Elida. Radhika and her younger brother Mohan would be scooting around on all sides unless Radhika, then 4, was engrossed in a video. When I walked in the door on January 29, 2017, however, I'd been away for a full month and Radhika looked up with interest. In the intervening weeks she had suddenly discovered the fascinating reality of wrinkles on the faces of adults. It was a gold mine, she seemed to feel, and I offered her plenty of new mine-shafts to explore. As we sat together she opened the subject by saying I had something on my face, so I tried to wipe it off, but had no luck. Then it became clear what was smeared there—my age. Gently and with a sense of wonder she started tracing the creases around my mouth and eyes, not knowing what to call them. What did they mean? I told her each of them hid a story that even I did not know. "A story about going into the forest?" she asked. What manner of intergenerational time were we keeping together as she imagined such a journey?

I suppose there will eventually be a place for each of these times to be enacted somewhere within the orbit of the Vrindavan Chandrodaya Mandir, but you would never know it from the thrill of presentness that animates the lives of its most devoted devotees. An imminent future, a past disciplined by doctrine, and a vivid appreciation for the value of virtuality—all these things course through the life and work of people deeply connected with the VCM. In talking with them, particularly early in each conversation, my normal sense of time always speeded up as I drank in their sense of everyday global purpose. Perhaps it is a necessary orientation in what amounts to a business—salespeople have to be enthusiastic—but they say, to the contrary, that it's the constant sense of release that comes from doing Krishna's work. No wonder it's the responsibility of one of them to send out WhatsApp messages that will bring the rest of us up to speed—"Today's Special Darshan of Sri Sri Radha Vrindavan Chandra", special day after day after day. It may be a simple suprabhatam greeting that arrives with a ding at sunrise (or if you happen to be on the other side of the world, at night) or it may be yet another installment of "Vrindavan Memories", the projected past of this utterly new VCM endeavor. But whatever it is, the underlying message is clear. Keep your mind on the goal. Keep time with the purposeful future that's unfolding in the now. Be leveraged into a new reality—Krishna's VCM reality. Where virtual and real are all the same.[78]

It's a heady feeling, this wind at the back of the new Vrindavan. There's plenty of magic being worked at the Chandrodaya Mandir— by promoters and architects alike, and even in a climate where the "real" demands of funding have reasserted their claims. It's magic, the VCM. But I confess that I miss magic of a different kind. It's found in the wrinkles that line my face, and as little Radhika stops to trace them with her finger, it glows intensely from hers. This is what I would call heritage, and after I've been swimming for a while in the Mandir's swirling stream, there's nothing I want more than to have it back.

5

A Different Refuge for Women

Overwhelmingly in this book we have been following the activities, the thoughts, and indeed the disputes of men. Yet in the imaginations of many people Vrindavan is a place where women are very much in the limelight—women who have come here not by choice but out of necessity. Vrindavan is known for its widows—women shunned for their inauspiciousness by those who accept the values of a deeply patriarchal society, women shunted off into Krishna's world. The contrast between this hateful reality and the ideals of love that stand at the heart of the myth of Vrindavan is stark. It will be our job in this chapter to see how valid the contrast is, and whether it is shifting and changing as years pass. We will ultimately meet a range of women, but begin with the women everyone knows: the widows.

The press—especially the English-language press—has long been devoted to measuring the distance between the ideal Vrindavan, the pastoral locale of Krishna's youth, and the one we see in the real world. At some level it's always an exposé. On March 29, 1998 *The New York Times* ran such an article on the front page: "Once Widowed in India, Twice Scorned". The BBC contributed "The Indian Town with 6000 Widows" on May 2, 2013. Al Jazeera reported on efforts to ameliorate

widows' lives there in June 12, 2014. *National Geographic* produced a
beautifully illustrated "For Widows, Life After Loss" in its February,
2017 issue. *The Hindu,* top-of-the-line among Indian newspapers, ran
"Forgotten Widows of Vrindavan" on August 28, 2017. And one day
short of a year later *The New York Times* returned to the subject with an
articled entitled "A Sanctuary for India's Abused and Exiled Widows".

This is only a small sampling. Even amid change, the persistence
of this old, harsh Vrindavan is much bemoaned, not just in India
but around the world—a curiosity and far more. There are novels,
photo-essays, films, and here is a poem by the diplomat Pavan Varma:

> And then they said:
> She must wear white
> Cut her hair
> Break her bangles
> Remove the Kajal
> Wash the sindoor
> Let her renounce meat, give up spice,
> Adopt white! White, the color white!
> Bleach the mehndi; or anything else
> Recalling
> Even remotely
> The dreams of a bride.
> She is dumped in an ashram in Vrindavan and laments:
> I cannot find Krishna
> In this temple town
> Of overflowing sewage,
> Where pandas breed
> In concrete cess pools,
> And devotees walk on filth
> Without anyone noticing
> I cannot find Krishna
> In this holy city.
> Although I chant His name.
> From seven to ten
> In the morning.
> Every evening.
> She ends up as a common whore:
> We live in the shadow
> or whore houses,
> Prey for priests

Landlords, rickshaw drivers
Policemen, shopkeepers
In fact, any male in sight.[1]

This kind of coverage upends the myth of eternal youth that envisions a world where Krishna is always surrounded by a crowd of eager gopis (Fig. 5.1), yet it is indeed this myth and its institutional expressions that have brought so many lonely, needy women to Vrindavan (Fig. 5.2). In Bengal, particularly, which had much to do with the fact that Vrindavan was built in the first place, the Gaudiya Math lets women who have been exiled by their families upon the deaths of their husbands know that there is a place where they can go to pull

Figure 5.1. The rās līlā as depicted in a Sukhsāgar ("Ocean of Happiness") painting seemingly attributed to both Gang and Surdas. Virginia Museum of Fine Arts, "Krishna and His Friends Celebrate Holi in the Forests of Vrindavan", object no. 96.33, detail.

Figure 5.2.   Widow of Vrindavan, photographed in the 1970s.

their lives back together—and it often provides the means to get them there. Other players also chime in. Of these the most visible is Bhajan Ashram, founded by Janki Dasji Patodia in 1914 in response to the ravages of a severe famine. This is how I described it decades ago in *At Play with Krishna*: it seemed an integral part of the old Vrindavan.

> The members of the International Society for Krishna Consciousness ... are not the group most responsible for filling the air with the constant ring of the *mahāmantra*. That honor ... would have to go to the twelve hundred widows who chant the great mantra eight hours a day at ... Bhajan Ashram. Every day they come in from all corners of the town, wherever they have been able to find a tiny room for two rupees a month, to sit in long rows and sing the names of Krishna; every so often a lead singer varies the tune, but the point of the whole exercise is repetition. There are other assemblies in Vrindavan where

the *mahāmantra* is sung with joy and verve, but not here. An air of
boredom and confinement pervades the hall. Eyes look up as strang-
ers come in; there is little sense of community evident. The reason
is that the motivation is largely economic. For eight hours of song,
each woman is entitled to 250 grams of rice—sometimes there are also
lentils—and forty pice, enough money to buy a single vegetable or a
few chilis. There are officers who make sure that everyone sings the
allotted time. Bhajan Ashram is sustained by contributions from the
wealthy Marwari community that owns businesses all over India, and
they see it not as a prison but as an organ of charity. They, after all,
are responsible for the fact that Vrindavan is filled with such auspicious sounds, not for the fact that—particularly in Bengal—a woman
becomes an outcaste in her own home where her husband dies. Her
presence is ominous in the absence of the man whose service provided
her a place in society, and in an extremely poor society she is an economic drain as well.

Perhaps a quarter of the population of Vrindavan is composed of
widows, almost all of them Bengalis or Nepalis, and the great majority near destitution. They have come to spend their last days—almost
whole lives in the case of some of the younger widows, of whom
there are quite a number among the Nepalis—sheltered at the feet
of Krishna and Radha. It is not easy to praise their condition—the
colorless, borderless white saris and absence of jewelry and shaven
heads that spell widowhood—but here at least, far from Bengal, they
are relieved of the burden of their own inauspiciousness. They join
the ranks of all the *gopīs*. Some, the more wealthy, are provided for by
some pension, and come by choice. Others come because here they
can beg. Still others are not really widows at all; perhaps they have
taken their children and fled a husband who beats his wife. Whatever
the reason, they come for refuge, and Vrindavan offers it because
its holiness absorbs the inauspicious and because its central myth,
the *rās*, expresses the vision of an alternative to society rather than a
validation of the ways of the world. The *gopīs* who come to Krishna
leave house and home, pulled into the forest against their will by
the call of his flute. These women, often at least equally unwillingly,
swell their number—superannuated *gopīs*, many of them, and bent
with age. And many do find solace in giving up their lives to Queen
Radha's will.[2]

Does this sound too respectful, too airbrushed, too accepting of a
terrible reality? If so, I plead not guilty on two grounds. First, I wanted

to honor the good intentions of Bhajan Ashram's donors and many people's belief in the healing power of the Hare Krishna mantra. No one of us lives a life that will not come to an end, or a life untouched by suffering and sorrow. In a world like that, song provides a refuge, access to a different way of living. Such an alternative way of living is called lila in Vrindavan—play.

Second, I had hoped not to blame Vrindavan for the ills of a particularly vicious form of patriarchal society, as so often seems to happen when the media fix their lights on the town. Religion exists to deflect attention from society's evils, they seem to suggest. I think it's far too easy to be content with that. Consider Sharada Ma, the wife of the nineteenth-century Bengali ecstatic Sri Ramakrishna, who is considered by many people to have been a saint. Ramakrishna urged Sharada to take refuge in Vrindavan after his death, and she did so willingly to all reports. Sectarian accounts of her life emphasize the fact that she loved being there in 1886–87, not just because it provided a place where she could disengage from the memory of her husband's death and simultaneously feel his presence but because she began to fall into trances just as he had done, and to awake from them in the same manner as he had, asking simply for food. She had a freedom she hadn't had in Kolkata. To many this may seem a too male-dominated narrative, but we also have accounts of her wandering happily alone along the Yamuna, and asking Radharamanji to release her from her tendency to criticize others. When she learned that they had revoked her pension at the Dakshineshvar Kali Temple in Kolkata, her devotion to Vrindavan seemed to help her take it in stride. It's surely not a feisty feminist narrative, but on the other hand she was hardly rejected and alone. She began to initiate others, assuming this mantle from her departed husband, hence it was in a sense the beginning of her professional life. And it seems she felt Vrindavan to be a balm.[3]

Other women's stories are more active and, because more recent, easier to disentangle from the embrace of sacred memory. In the mid-twentieth century Anandamayi Ma, the formidable female spiritual leader who for years observed a vow of silence and communicated with her disciples only by means of her eyes, chose to build an ashram in Vrindavan. This was a woman who had the likes of Indira Gandhi as a pupil; once, under cover of darkness, she secretly came to meet her there. Anandamayi Ma's choice to retreat to Vrindavan was not constrained, but the fact that she came from Kolkata reveals a familiar path.

There are many other less well known instances. One that I happen to know about concerns the wife of Triloki Nath Madan, one of India's most celebrated sociologists and someone deeply interested in religion. From their home in the Delhi area, where Madan was based at the Institute for Economic Growth, his beloved Uma traveled often to Vrindavan. "Loki" Madan was a transplanted Kashmiri, but Uma came from a family with Mathura roots. Her mother was most comfortable speaking the language of Braj, and Uma loved to recall bits of poetry that connected to Krishna or had a Braj ring:

> The Merciful One reveals himself
>   through everyone living in this world.
> Says Rahim: Someone you meet, just happen to meet,
>   might really be Narayan.

For Uma Chaturvedi Madan there was something about Vrindavan— something reassuring—that she didn't want to do without. Whenever she was there she would make it a point to be present in the temple of Radharamanji: Shrivatsa Goswami and his family had become good friends. When she died, at her instructions, her ashes went to Vrindavan. A tulsi tree was planted in her memory in the courtyard of the Gokulanand Mandir, where she joins a centuries-old group of revered Vrindavan bhaktas.[4]

I wish to honor women such as these who have found in Vrindavan a true refuge, but there's no denying that for many other women the picture is anything but rosy. The media are right. Where women are concerned, Vrindavan lives under a dark shadow. Some of its most distinguished citizens, historically speaking, hailed from Bengal and eastern India—from Chaitanya to Jiva Gosvami to Sharada Ma to Prabhupad—and what do we find there? A system of marriage and inheritance peculiarly destructive to girls and women. From the point of view of inheritance, this was the dayabhag system, which was embraced by British colonial authorities as the basis for family law in Bengal. It had the seeming advantage of apportioning certain rights of inheritance to a widow upon the death of her husband, but that sometimes made her the object of envy and resentment on the part of her sons and their families. Meanwhile, the upper levels of Bengali society came to embrace an ideal according to which a man of thirty, marrying for the first time, was expected to find an ideal bride in a girl who had just passed puberty. Hence one had powerful widows and young ones—a troubling population best kept out of sight. Add to this the fact that Vrindavan, with its scads of gopis, occupied a vivid place in the Bengali imagination, and you have an assortment of sticks and carrots that explains why over the course of many years Bengal and its neighboring regions have sent so many widows to Vrindavan.[5]

It used to be that these accounted for almost all of Bhajan Ashram's widows, as reported above—all dressed in white and many with shaven heads. Now it's rather different (Fig. 5.3). One sees other colors than white and the place has a much more spirited feel than it used to. A youngish woman was leading the women in song when

Figure 5.3.   Bhajan Ashram as it appeared on July 12, 2018.

I visited one day in the summer of 2018, and she danced a bit as she did so. I had the sense that many of the women knew each other as friends—quite different from what I thought I saw forty years ago—and they're at least a little better paid than they used to be. Still, their lives are severely circumscribed, and by them Vrindavan is known.

Mohini Giri and Ma Dham

Not many years ago Oprah Winfrey came to Vrindavan, as an expression of her general concern for women around the world, and as she planned the trip she got in touch with Dr. V. Mohini Giri, a practical and magisterial woman who celebrated her eightieth birthday in January 2018. Mohini Giri is not too sure how Oprah got her name—perhaps because she has frequently lectured in the United States on women's issues.[6] In any case, Oprah simply called her on the phone one day, and by January 2012 she was in Vrindavan. Her principal destination was Mohini Giri's ashram for rejected women, called Ma Dham—"Mother's (or Mothers') Home", "Home for Mothers". It was a warm and cordial meeting, beginning with a garlanding ceremony and ending in a shot that showed the two women making their way hand in hand down the walkway—Mohini Giri in red, her white hair pulled straight back; Oprah in beige and yellow with a luxuriant mass of black curls. The camera caught Mohini Giri's benediction: "God bless you. Keep empowering women like you are doing. You have been a great inspiration to the world and you will be an inspiration to womanhood". Later, as Oprah framed the scene for airing on TV, she returned the compliment. Somehow the spirit of Mother Teresa had come upon Dr. Giri, she mused.[7]

Not surprisingly, perhaps, there were a few intercultural wrinkles along the way. Mohini Giri spoke with pride about the fact that the women in her ashram do all their work for themselves—they cook for themselves, they clean for themselves, they have and wash their own plates. These were all signs of empowerment in Mohini Giri's eyes, but for Oprah that mention of plates was a red flag. She couldn't get over the fact that what's left of these women's lives, as she put it, "comes into that cabinet and boils down to a single tin plate". Mohini Giri, for her part, remembered a moment when Oprah had seen one of Ma Dham's women peeling boiled potatoes with her fingers and suggested that a potato-peeler would do a better job. Oprah offered to send one from the States when she got back. Mohini Giri wryly assured her they were also available in India, but she was very happy to accept Oprah's offer of a 25,000-dollar donation for a new program of vocational training.[8]

Ma Dham's present ashram is located way out on the Chatikara Road, on a modest piece of land that happens to be just behind the Chandrodaya Mandir's massive property. There's a sign on the road that you have to know to watch for; it points you to a rocky little lane. The surrounding fields still have the open feel that used to be common around here. You can even see the peacocks that used to live in the old town of Vrindavan before they fled its monkey regimes.

Ma Dham is an unusual institution. In one way it belongs to Vrindavan in a very traditional sense—a home for women who haven't any other resource, who have come to Vrindavan for refuge. As such, it takes its place alongside a number of better-known institutions that fan out from the older part of town. Bhajan Ashram is foremost among them, but there are many others. Shrivatsa Goswami's wife Sandhya, for example, serves as the secretary for a small home for widows and other needy women that her family has established on the ground floor of the house where they all grew up. This family charity takes its place among many similar homes, many of the ashram type.

Other institutions follow the Bhajan Ashram model more closely. Near ISKCON, for example, there is a well-kept dharamshala that offers accommodation to visitors at the rate of 900 or 950 rupees a night, depending on whether you stay in the older part of the complex or the new. This is the Balaji Ashram, which faces the Chatikara Road. It was established by Mangeram Agrawal, the founder and CEO of Action Shoes, in the name of his parents. He himself lives in Delhi, but his family came from Hissar in Haryana. Every day from 2:30 to 5:00 p.m. poor women living in the neighborhood gather in the court-yard to sing the Hare Krishna mantra—very much after the Bhajan Ashram fashion. At the end of their singing they receive 100 grams of lentils, 200 grams of rice, and ten rupees to take away. When I stopped in on December 29, 2017, I learned that 430 women had signed in at 2:30 to take part—the warden was able to retrieve the figure instantly with a click of his mobile phone. You have to have signed in punctually to participate, he explained. This makes it possible to calculate the numbers exactly, and he did so in an absolutely straightforward way, without either pride or embarrassment. It's not a business, of course, it's a work of charity and sentiment, but it's run in a businesslike way. To critics this has always seemed offensive, as if these business types were clocking in spiritual profits from the widows.

Ma Dham's profile is quite different, and very much a part of the new Vrindavan—separated from the old not only by physical distance but by a distinctively different conceptual orientation. At Ma Dham you see none of the signs of a widow's inauspiciousness. No heads are shaved, no dietary restrictions are enforced, and nobody wears a white sari. Instead there are blues and yellows and plenty of pink. Though living at some distance from the rhythms of Vrindavan's daily life, these women are not cordoned off from the life of others. Mohini Giri has designed the home in such way that younger generations are always present. A school serving girls from nearby villages is on-site, and their sounds bubble into the air every school day. In addition the older generation has educational opportunities all its own. Ma Dham's residents can take classes that teach office and computer skills or prepare them, say, to become beauticians. A more iconoclastic specter than a widow-beautician is hard to imagine.

A new crafts department has also opened at Ma Dham, and one of its features is that it enables women to sew garments that will be worn by girls in the Sannidhi School. Thus they see the fruits of their own labor. Sewing can take other directions, too. Some of the women integrate themselves into Vrindavan's special economy by making tiny bright-colored garments—clothing and crowns—for images of Krishna. Pilgrims have long wanted to buy such Vrindavan-branded goods to decorate their own personal Krishnas once home, and the trade brings in a pretty good income (Fig. 5.4).

At the same time, Ma Dham defies some of the special—if implicit—restrictions that its location in Vrindavan might suggest, for it is an interreligious space, welcoming women of all religious backgrounds. In practice the overwhelming majority of the women who live there come from Hindu backgrounds—these are the women who would be naturally attracted to Vrindavan in the first place—but Mohini Giri is pleased to report, if sotto voce, that among the eighty-five widows and women living there now, there are indeed a few Muslims. The space in which they live invites this broader view

Figure 5.4.   V. Mohini Giri displaying Ma Dham women's handiwork—clothes for Krishna images sold to Vrindavan visitors. Delhi, February 1, 2019.

of religion. Ma Dham has two chapels—one centering on an image of the ambiguously Muslim-Hindu saint Sai Baba of Shirdi and the other explicitly intersectarian, with Muslim, Buddhist, Sikh, Hindu, and Christian writings, each in its appropriate language and script (English and roman for Christianity), lining the octagonal walls. In the view of Mohini Giri, anything more restricted is "not what Hinduism is. It is vasudhaiva kutumbh", she says—pertaining to the whole family of Earth.[9]

Of course, Ma Dham isn't heaven, and Mohini Giri is quite aware of that fact. When I visited the ashram in late 2017, one woman with whom I spoke—in her sixties perhaps, or late fifties—complained that there were lots of squabbles among the residents, and she still lacked what she simply called her "papers" (kāgaz).[10] These pieces of paper—or perhaps just one—would make her a person again. Tears continued to wash across this Brahmin woman's eyes as she explained how, five months earlier, she had been ejected by her children from her family home in Kanpur. The young man who performs Bhagavat Katha each evening and lives not far away explained that her husband had died and thirty hectares of land were at stake. Switching from Hindi to English, he said—a bit cloyingly, I thought—that such stories broke his heart and had motivated him to adopt a life of service. Perhaps it was the fact that he was not altogether comfortable in English that made it sound a little stilted; he could not very well advertise his devotion to cause in the presence of and language spoken by the very women who had occasioned it. But service indeed is what Ma Dham is all about: Mohini Giri rarely strayed from this message when we talked. In the end, she said, "Service is God", and those were the words with which we concluded.[11]

As for the matter at hand, however, there is more to be said. When I mentioned the delayed and missing papers to the ashram's administrator, Manjeet Singh, he took quite a different tone. He explained a bit impatiently that it took time to straighten out women's identity papers and that they had to get it right, since this would have repercussions for her claim to government services. One had to go through channels, but eventually it would all be resolved, as he knew from years of working in this field. In the meantime, though, this particular woman, one of the most recent arrivals, was unusually depressed. She had indeed been deprived of her identity: she was worried about her papers and her pension. Others were considerably more cheerful, sometimes giving thanks to the grace of Queen Radha that had brought them here, but this woman had not arrived because she wished to do so. Perhaps she was one of those who had been referred by the police; such a referral could also come from the district court or from a hospital. She was railing inside against the injustice of it all; she was openly in mourning for herself.

Mohini Giri herself has been a young widow, though in very different circumstances. She is the daughter-in-law of V.V. Giri, who served as President of India from 1969 to 1974 when Indira Gandhi was Prime Minister. After the death of her husband, Mohini acted as her father-in-law's professional companion, but the experience of being widowed, even at such elite levels, opened her eyes to the plight of widows throughout India. Indeed, her own mother had been widowed in middle age.

Mohini Giri was one of seven children. Her father was the vice-chancellor (president, in American terms) of the University of Lucknow, so it was a privileged way to begin a life, but her father died when she was just ten. Her mother took the family to Rishikesh, where her spiritual teacher, a medical doctor, was the head of the famous Shivanand Ashram. It was there, at the age of twelve, that Mohini Giri learned what service was: she helped him as he cared for lepers and performed eye operations. Years later, as she circulated in high administrative circles in Delhi, she was confronted by the tragedy of the Bangladesh–Pakistan war of 1971. Working in military hospitals, she came to know many widows and ultimately founded an organization designed to help them, the War Widows Association. In the 1990s she served as chairperson of the National Commission for Women, a rank equivalent to that of a minister in the central government, and in that capacity toured the country widely. By then (1995) she herself was a widow.

The first time she traveled to Vrindavan happened to fall on the day before Holi two or three years later, and there she came across a scene that would stay with her for the rest of her life. A widow had just died and her corpse lay on the road, hounded by dogs and threatened by vultures. No one did anything; the men nearby explained that they could not, since it was a religious holiday. Mohini Giri was outraged, so she appealed to members of her own sex, a number of shaven-headed, white-clad widows who had also gathered to take in the scene. "Could this happen to you tomorrow?" Mohini challenged. At this, unlike the men, the women responded. They found a pallet on which the body could be laid and took turns bearing it away to the river, where the body could be submerged.[12] Mohini Giri was inspired by their response and simultaneously appalled by their condition. Clearly they were capable of more action than their rigidly circumscribed role was intended to suggest. Shouldn't they be doing more with their lives?

This was the start of Ma Dham, a project on which Mohini Giri embarked with Swaraj Lata Goel, a local resident. First there was a private house with five widows, but before long Mohini Giri had appealed to the owner of a large, dilapidated, unused haveli and was able to accommodate three hundred. Then, when the owner wanted it back (much improved) she began a determined searched for a new location. This involved transmuting a plot of agricultural land that lay on the outskirts of town into municipal property so that it could become the site of a charitable organization. Mohini was no stranger to getting things done in governmental circles, and she's also all along been good at asking for help from individuals and public agencies. The new building opened in 2006.

Much goes on there, as we already know, but I want to report on one of the most startling events I have ever witnessed in Vrindavan, old or new. The occasion was a Christmas party held on December 24, 2017. Mohini Giri, who gets around with the help of a walker, had driven down from Delhi to preside over a program featuring a contribution by "German musicians", as the advance publicity billed them. This turned out to be a string quartet composed of extraordinary young professionals gathered by the renowned violinist Midori for the specific purpose of making a ten-day tour of India. And there they were in Vrindavan, playing the overture to "The Marriage of Figaro". My jaw dropped. What was I hearing? Gathered in Germany but with backgrounds that ranged from Latvia to France and in Midori's case Japan, these young musicians were stunning. Where does one have a chance to hear such performers at such close range, and what in the world were they doing in Vrindavan (Fig. 5.5)?

It wasn't easy for much of the crowd to enjoy this unfamiliar music, but Mohini Giri's younger colleague and "right hand woman" Meera Khanna did her best to close the cultural gap. As each of the musicians introduced one of the pieces to be performed, she provided a spirited translation into Hindi, sometimes supplementing the literal meaning with a bit of context that would enable the audience to appreciate the spirit of the music. The most rousing moment came when Khanna, translating the words of introduction that had just been spoken by the quartet's violist, Benjamin Beck, explained that the melody of the

Figure 5.5.   Residents of Ma Dham listening to the Christmas concert
presented by Midori's quartet, December 24, 2017.

Haydn string quartet they were about to perform was so beloved that
it had been adopted as Germany's national anthem. Hearing Khanna
report this, the ladies burst into spontaneous applause, and at the end
of the concert everyone stood to sing India's own national anthem.

It was a wonderfully chaotic encore to an exquisite concert. The
more the women sang, the harder it was to determine in what key
they did so. Afterward several of the guests rushed up to pose for selfies with the musicians, sometimes pulling one of the residents by the
hand (Fig. 5.6). Then, as the excitement died away and tea was served,
the musicians packed their instruments and set out for the return
to Delhi. Mohini Giri, Meera Khanna, and their Delhi-based coterie
also made their departure. Mohini's daughter, who lives in the Detroit

Figure 5.6.   Selfies and bowstrings after the concert.

area, rode shotgun in the SUV. She and her husband were visiting
India to help celebrate her mother's eightieth birthday.

It hardly needs to be said that Ma Dham is quite a different expression of "the new Vrindavan" from anything else we have seen so far.
The way it is grafted onto the rest of Vrindavan is unique. This is true
not only of the old Vrindavan, where Ma Dham was incubated for a
decade, but also for the new. The women of Ma Dham receive their
midday meals thanks to a van that comes over from Akshay Patra just
next door, and to that extent they are connected with their neighbors.
But otherwise, these women's lives play out at a huge distance from
the showy displays we encounter along the Chatikara Road. It seems
appropriate that you have to turn off the main road if you're following
the sign to Ma Dham. In just this way Ma Dham stands for something
off the beaten path—something independent and progressive that is

Figure 5.7.   Mahadevi Ma, one of the residents of Ma Dham, December 24, 2017.

still in the early stages of exercising much influence over the rest of the life of Vrindavan, new or old. Mohini Giri hopes that it will serve as an example of what needs to be done elsewhere to improve the lives of Indian women, and within the Guild for Service orbit it has already spawned some copies—in areas of need such as Kashmir, Uttarakhand, parts of Delhi, and the region where a tsunami hit Tamil Nadu in 2004. But whether Ma Dham's example will be copied elsewhere in Vrindavan remains to be seen (Fig. 5.7).

Sadhvi Ritambhara and Vatsalya Gram

Ma Dham's closest equivalent among the institutions that constitute the new Vrindavan sits at the other end of town, but all you have to do to see the contrast is drive up to the front gate. There it is in full view on the Mathura–Vrindavan Road, not stuck away along some country lane, sporting a grand heraldic entrance wide enough to accommodate two lanes of traffic and a generous median in between.

The gates that regulate access are decorated with stone-built triangular shapes on the lintel above, suggesting a bit of classical temple architecture. Once inside, you find a sprawling 52-acre campus where you can roam among a dozen or so substantial buildings, all carefully labeled. These include, among others, a lower school for girls and boys (named after an American donor, Krishna Brahamratan), a secondary school that continues the educational process for girls (Samvid Gurukulam, where tuition-paying students from all over north India mix with a number of locals who come free), a separate hostel for upper-age boarders, a residential complex for children and their mothers, and a sizeable guesthouse billed as a "spiritual resort". Guests pay a thousand rupees per night to rent a room, and many come from quite a distance.

This impressive complex is Vatsalya Gram. The term is somewhat difficult to translate, since vātsalya refers broadly to the relationship between parents and children, so it is "Parent–Child Village", you might say. But the founder, Sadhvi Ritambhara, is thinking along the female side of this gradient. The literature of her organization translates the name as "A Village of Maternal Love". Vatsalya Gram does have an impressive English-language website, but up until 2018 its distinctively Indian format and Hindi-language preference seemed designed to engage quite a different readership from that anticipated by the Guild For Service website that directs you to Ma Dham (www.guild.org.in). Even with the dramatic update, however, www.vatsalyagram.org has none of the sharply crafted photographs of women in distress that appear on the Guild For Service counterpart. Rather, it's a feel-good website. Instead of Mohini Giri intervening in the lives of unfortunate women with a big hug, we find ourselves in the presence of a stately saffron- or crimson-clad woman with a bright red tilak and long black hair. Her broad and sparkling smile is often on display—either that or a studied, serious gaze. She is the heart and head of the organization—"The Divinity" as one English-language brochure says, divinity in the form of a mother.[13]

Mohini Giri is a figure to be reckoned with in Delhi's NGO circles, but Sadhvi Ritambhara is even more renowned. She goes by Didi Ma—"Elder-Sister Mother"—both on the website and in person. It's a family term, intimate yet respectful. Vatsalya Gram and the other institutions with which it is connected are meant to represent a larger-than-life family, an Indian joint family in the broadest sense. Indianness is very much on display, and Vedic Hinduness before all else. Whereas Mohini Giri hails from the inner circles of the Congress Party, with its avowedly secular orientation, Sadhvi Ritambhara has spent her life in the service of the BJP. She is one of its best-known female members. In the days of the assault on the Babri Mosque in the early 1990s no one gave more fiery speeches to galvanize the young Hindu-right activists than the equally young Sadhvi Ritambhara, unless it was her sister-in-the-faith Uma Bharti, now the Minister for Drinking Water and Sanitation in the national BJP government and the party's vice president. Unlike Uma Bharti, Sadhvi Ritambhara has withdrawn from the conduct of politics as such and settled into life as a religious leader. Like Mohini Giri, rather, she retains a quasi-political identity—but on exactly the opposite side of the political spectrum.

It may seem remarkable that two women as different as Mohini Giri and Sadhvi Ritambhara should have established women's institutions in Vrindavan, and they do, in fact, relate to Vrindavan in strikingly different ways. Ma Dham focuses on elderly women who have no other option, making this traditional mission serve new ends. Vatsalya Gram focuses far more on female children than on their elders, making room for boys as well at the primary school on campus. Both institutions believe that the generations ought not to be separated, but Vatsalya Gram goes further: it not only emphasizes children but it reconfigures the family itself. The organization's very name calls attention to the specific set of emotions that attend the care of children, since "vātsalya" is literally the way a cow looks after her calves (vatsa).

The new kind of family that forms the symbolic core of Vatsalya Gram is either called simply "family" (parivār) or a specifically "maternal family" (vātsalya parivār) (Fig. 5.8). In each such family there are three adults and seven children, all unrelated—a "mother", a "maternal aunt" (the Hindi term is mausī), an older woman who serves as "maternal grandmother" (Hindi: nānī), and as to the children, five girls and two boys. Together they make a unit of ten, and they are allocated a flat in the building called Gokulam—Gokul with a fancy Sanskrit ending. The adults all come from nearby. The mothers may be as young as in their twenties—perhaps widows who had been married to a much older man; aunts and grandmothers may be

Figure 5.8. Didi Ma shown caring for a girl child. Poster inside the Vatsalya Gram complex, December 26, 2017.

much older. What's crucial is not age but education. These women must have the capacity to raise children properly, so that can't possibly include one of those women you might see begging by the side of the road in Vrindavan, as one representative told me emphatically. And dismissively, I thought—the backside of Vatsalya Gram.

As for the children, they are young, up to fifth-grade age, and they all go to the elementary school on campus. After the fifth grade the girls advance to the secondary school and move into its hostel, coming under the care of its gurus—according (so the publicity says) to the Vedic plan. In the literature of ancient India this separation of children from their natal families was prescribed only with boys in mind. Here, though, girls are included in the rubric, and the teaching institution on site is in fact specifically for them. Boys have to leave the campus to go elsewhere for their schooling—to one of the highly rated boarding schools located outside Vrindavan.[14] In any case, the emphasis here is clearly on the girls, who are being trained to be the mainstay of Hindu society. Vatsalya Dham is very proud that a few of the girls who come from these families are now old enough to have been married—arranged marriages, that is, and the person who arranges them is Didi Ma herself.

This invented family is Sadhvi Ritambhara's response not only to what's called the "widow problem" in Vrindavan, but to a larger crisis affecting females across north India. The birth of a girl in this part of the country is rarely welcomed with the same enthusiasm as the birth of a boy. This has to do with the crushing financial reality of the dowry system, the need for a boy to continue to serve as the generational link in a joint family (girls will depart to live with their in-laws), and even the traditional ritual need for a son to perform his parents' obsequies. Families who can afford ultrasound procedures have often used that tool to tell the sex of the child in the womb, and girls are far more likely to be aborted than boys. The use of such procedures has been banned by federal law, but they persist. Vatsalya Gram takes both these problems and tries to solve them together by creating mini joint families that will embrace both the elderly and the young.[15]

Both Ma Dham and Vatsalya Gram actively reject the more venerable institution of the charitable Vaishnava widows' home. Both see themselves as belonging more to the future than to the past. And yet those futures are quite different. For Mohini Giri it involves a rejection of the evils of patriarchy and the similarly oppressive claims of majoritarian religions. She believes that Krishna himself led this charge, saving Rukmini, whom he wed after leaving Braj, from a life with a man she did not desire and "according equal respect to all" as he interacted with Vrindavan's women. He "empowered women's gender justice", she says.[16] For Didi Ma the frame is quite different: there is nothing to be overcome, only something to be restored. It's a Vedic whole imagined as having originally included everyone.[17] There simply were no minorities in this vision of the Vedic past; no one was excluded. Through Didi Ma's compelling religious persona Vatsalya Gram finds the resources to make this kind of appeal to a golden past, and her own life path suggests the importance of one of the buildings located on campus. It is called Sadguru Sannidhi and is officially described as "a pious place for saints to stay while they visit Vatsalya Gram", but it seems in fact to serve as a center where some twenty-five women who have renounced the householder life to learn to be preachers and teachers for a Hindu India.[18] They follow the example of Didi Ma herself.

Vrindavan's Vatsalya Gram is the standard-bearer for a cluster of charitable institutions established by Param Shakti Peeth, headquartered in Delhi. That name invokes the invincible power (param śakti) of the Great Goddess and the fact that there are particular places (pīṭh) that exhibit the Goddess's power—places where, according to texts like the Devi Mahatmya, her power is distributed around the Indian subcontinent. This is one of the things that makes Mother India (Bhārat Mātā in Hindi) live. In the eyes of her followers and seemingly in her own, Didi Ma herself plays a major role in reconstituting that lost national Motherhood. The lineage she celebrates and in fact integrates into Vatsalya Gram itself is not a specifically Vaishnava one. Rather, if anything, it is Shaiva. Her own personal guru is an ascetic named Paramanand Giri, who belongs to a Shaiva order, and the concrete tableau that greets you in the big roundabout as you drive into the grounds of Vatsalya Gram is called Mangal Manas.[19] There we see Shiva and Parvati (also called Shakti) enthroned on their faux-Himalayan heights. At the base of this pretend mountain lies a pool intended to represent Lake Mansarovar, the lake that is fed by the snows from Mount Kailas. It is Shiva's eternal home, so a huge trident and linga, his emblems, stand on its concrete shores. Unfortunately, as in so many Indian models of this kind, the lake doesn't always hold water. Water is a precious thing.

This Shaiva space is bordered by a small Shakta shrine. It is dedicated to a female deity called Shri Sarvamangala, whose name is also registered in that of the Mangal Manas. Vatsalya Gram's publicity brochures report that from gazing upon her many devotees have had remarkable experiences, testimony to her miraculous powers. In one way this is a new goddess, in that it was only quite recently that she announced herself to Sadhvi Ritambhara in a dream. But after the fashion of other "new" goddesss who have appeared in recent years— Santoshi Ma is perhaps the best known—she is really very old, a summation of the feminine power that has always lain at the heart of India's perennial religion, Sanatana Dharma. I have used the normal term in translating the Sanskrit phrase "sanātana dharma" (Hindi: sanātan dharm), but it is significant that the literature describing Shri Sarvamangala takes a slightly different tack. Like the recent developments at the Vrindavan Chandrodaya Mandir, there has been a shift from the language of religion (one of the meanings of dharma) to that of culture (saṅskṛti). Sanatana Dharma is transformed into "India's perennial cultural heritage" (bhārat kī sanātan sāṅskṛtik virāsat). Whether this is for conceptual or fund-raising reasons I cannot say, but one has to concede that the distance between the two is not great. The Shiva-Shakti monument that greets visitors to Vatsalya Gram will soon be superseded by something greater still—a Shri Pitham, for which funds are now being sought. It will be a huge domed structure giving recognition to the much-vaunted scientific glories of Indian civilization, accompanied by a vast museum with the same purpose— all of this under a feminine, Shakta banner.

But where is the Vaishnavism in all this? That's where Yashoda comes in, and through her, the vast Krishna tradition. Sadhvi Ritambhara is a spellbinding orator, and she sometimes exposits the Goddess-oriented Devi Mahatmya we have just mentioned—all over Hindi-speaking India and abroad. She frequently chooses the Ramayan as her subject, too, which fits with involvements that stretch way back to the years in which she helped spearhead efforts to pull down the Babri Mosque and build a massive temple to Ram on the spot. But in Vrindavan she naturally exposits the Bhagavata Purana instead. Typically she sits on a little dais at the front of the great assembly hall of Vatsalya Gram's secondary school, as she did in the final week of 2017 when she sponsored a Bhagavat Katha that would culminate on the first day of the new year, her birthday. As she spoke and sang, Didi Ma was resplendent in red and attended by a silent young man who passed her a gourd of water whenever she needed it. The scene was evidently intended to project a specifically Vedic aura— something like what one might see on the cover of a book where the

Upanishads are to be found. In that case, however, the teaching guru is inevitably male. Here Sadhvi Ritambhara takes his place.

The auditorium holds about 650 people, and many have come from as far away as Mumbai to hear her talk. The donor of the day is also from Mumbai. Sadhvi Ritambhara is miked, of course; musicians sit at the side of the stage; and there's a big screen on one wall of the auditorium where a simultaneous video version is broadcast, making it possible for people sitting at a distance to follow her words and facial expressions in detail. She performs this seven-day Bhagavat Saptah in the traditional manner, observing the divisions that are marked in the standard Gita Press edition, but she takes every occasion to turn the subject to the glorification of what motherhood does for the world. Yashoda is very often her model—significantly, the love of a foster mother rather than her biological analogue, in tune with the new sort of family Sadhvi Ritambhara wishes to project. "Yashoda's feeling is the root inspiration for Vatsalya Gram", as she proclaims in a little booklet for sale onsite.[20] When Didi Ma evokes such motherhood in her preaching, tears often come to her eyes. She is very much at home on stage; she draws the entire crowd into her presence. Many know the songs she sings. They join in gladly, and the voices of the women donors who have been given a place in the front of the hall (the audience is separated by sex) sound out over all the rest. Their confidence is notable—a public women's confidence.

At the end there are two rousing kirtans—one addressed to Krishna and one to the Bhagavata Purana itself. Assistants distribute a page on which the words of both songs are written. Pictures of a smiling Didi Ma and Ma Sarvamangala appear in the upper corners as heralds. Between them at the center we see Radha, Krishna, and a cow on one side of the page. On the reverse side in the same central position and with the same framing is an image of a garlanded Bhagavata. The songs ring out as a concluding arati is performed:

> Offer the lamp to the Mountain-Lifter,
>   offer the lamp to the Forest-Dweller,
> Offer the lamp to India the Mother,
>   offer the lamp to the Bhagavata.

As the sound crescendos, Didi Ma herself seems to become the focus of the arati, though in formal terms it is being addressed to the

Bhagavata Purana that lies on a low table before her. There is incense, there is hubbub, and then from a group of men at the side we hear the sound of Vedic chanting.

This is the signal that the crowd may rise to go—back to the guesthouse and the midday meal, which is served from a big tent that has been raised at the back of the guesthouse. Inside the hotel lobby there's a model of the entire grounds for inspection under glass, showing how everything will look when the complex is complete. It's remarkably close to that goal: only the central Shri Sarvamangala Pitham remains to be constructed. As the guests file in and out of the dining area for lunch, Channel 2020 broadcasts endless "breaking news" in Hindi. At the reception desk people ask when darshan will open at the Bihariji temple or how long it will take to get to Agra, where the Taj Mahal is located. Some, though, seem content to stay where they are. They wander into the anteroom of the Krishna-Mirabai temple around which the guest rooms are built. It's surrounded by a moat in a glass enclosure that smells of many flowers. A recently initiated devotee from Bihar prostrates himself on the carpeted floor in front of a little altar where two copies of the Gita Press Bhagavata Purana are also be seen. Afterwards he sits on one of the sofas and reads the paper.

There are other buildings on site, like the Martyrs' Museum (śahīd saṅgrahālay) focused on those who gave their lives in the cause of Indian independence. The moment of martyrdom, however, is extended and expanded beyond the founding of the nation in 1947. From Didi Ma's point of view, the work of nation-building is ongoing, hence the museum has been named after Bhanupratap Shukla, a writer and ideologue who played a major role in galvanizing Hindus around the country to join the cause of destroying the Babri Mosque in 1992. Again we see the effort to shape a history that follows the contours of Sadhvi Ritambhara's own life and bears out the message of the most important and ideologically committed group in the party to which she belongs. On the cover of a Divali issue of Vatsalya Gram's monthly magazine *Vātsalya Nirjhar* ("Cascade of Motherhood") we see three young women of the Indian army in combat dress carrying automatic rifles. "India resides in the souls of its soldiers", the title proclaims.[21]

Not everything faces toward the public, however. Over in the reception building that sits just inside the compound gate, one of the

Figure 5.9.   Room in Vatsalya Gram with a window that can be opened from the outside, so that a mother wishing to give up a small child can place it in the crib.

attendants shows me a place I hadn't yet seen, a spare little room that is not often featured in brochures or in monthly issues of *Vātsalya Nirjhar*. This room has a poignant appeal. In it sits a rectangular crib that Didi Ma has personally designed, and this cradle sits beneath a window (Fig. 5.9). Initially I supposed the crib was there to catch the light that the window would let in, but I was wrong. The window, it turns out, is a portal. In the middle it has a section that can be opened by swinging apart the two panes, and someone standing on other side, in a sheltered passageway that leads to the street, could do just that. If someone wanted to give up a newborn baby, this would be the place—probably in the darkness of night. When a baby is placed in the crib this way, a signal sounds in a nearby room and a qualified person knows to come and see what has happened. If the baby needs medical attention, that can immediately be had. Most such babies are girls—they are the ones least wanted out there in the world—and before long the infant in question will join one of the vatsalya families of ten.[22] The gender imbalance explains why Vatsalya Gram's families have five girls and only two boys. My guide explains that the child might have been born out of wedlock, but he doesn't explain why so many are girls. There's no need to: this is common knowledge. In any case, some twenty-five families have now been formed to take in these infants, and it's stressed that a child who comes in will never be given up for adoption. Vatsalya Gram is not a pass-through; that child has now come home.

Beyond the World of Widows

It is striking how infrequently Radha and the gopis figure in Vatsalya Gram's imagined landscape, but perhaps that is no surprise. Efforts to expunge that side of the worship of Krishna from his public image have a strong and well-known history dating back to the second half of the nineteenth century. At that point, especially after there was so much commotion about the alleged Vallabhite practice of offering brides on their first wedding night to the community's male leaders so that they would return to their new husbands as prasad, nationalist intellectuals such as Bankim Chandra Chattopadhyay sought to recover a Krishna who was masculine in a very different way.[23] This, of course, was the muscular, politically engaged Krishna of the Bhagavad Gita, as opposed to his flute-playing, lovemaking Bhagavata Purana alter-ego. One has only to travel a little distance toward Mathura along the road that passes Vatsalya Gram to come to the huge temple that the Birla family built in the mid-twentieth century to memorialize the Gita's Krishna and the world-famous "song" he preached to Arjuna. Vatsalya Gram chooses a different means of reconstructing Vrindavan's youthful ras-lila Krishna, but it too is a reconstruction. It seems fitting that these two variations on a reformist theme stand relatively close together on the Mathura Road—and relatively far from the center of Vrindavan.

Several of the women with whom I have spoken in Vrindavan think Vatsalya Gram is actually quite peripheral to the mission of the town as they understand it. More than once I have heard such women separate themselves from Sadhvi Ritambhara and her institution by noting that she represents the RSS (Rashtriya Svayamsevak Sangh) or the VHP (Vishwa Hindu Parishad), institutions relating closely to the organizational and ideological core of the BJP. The three of them join in the so-called sangh parivar, a family of three that stands at the core of India's right-wing Hindu nationalist politics. Unlike many in Vrindavan, the women I have mentioned wanted to stand at a distance from all that, preserving Vrindavan as a zone above the political fray. A glance at some of Vatsalya Gram's publications shows why they might well be concerned about such an infringement. In June of 2017, for example, *Vātsalya Nirjhar* devoted itself to memorializing the "twenty-five years of motherhood pilgrimage" (vātsalya yātrā ke 25 varṣ) that had brought Sadhvi Ritambhara from her leadership role in the campaign to level the Babri Mosque and on to her role at the core of Vatsalya Gram and its sister institutions. The cause of the rule of Ram had been increasingly clarified as concerning equally the motherhood of the nation, the magazine explained, so Sadhvi Ritambhara's transition from one campaign to the other made perfect sense. Some women are worried about the implications of all that. They propound a "softer" vision of what constitutes the essence of Vrindavan—and a more distinctively Vaishnava one, at that.

One such gentle critic is Usha Didi, who has long played a leadership role at Prem Mandir. She is a cheerful, ample woman in her early seventies, who came to live in Vrindavan when her grandparents settled there in the late 1950s. Obviously, she has seen a lot, and continues to see it close-up at Prem Mandir. She has done a great deal in Kripalu Maharaj's organization. For a number of years, while she taught English in one of Mathura's women's colleges, she also served as a principal liaison between Swami Kripalu and the public. Later he enlisted her in some of the crucial bookkeeping functions of the institution, trusting her fair-minded competence. It was important to keep a complete and accurate record of all donations, however small. Sometimes this meant counting change, she said.[24] That actuarial sensibility was one side of things, but the other was Kripalu's immense sense of personal generosity, and one of the ways it was expressed was in a twice-annual gathering in which he would dispense basic bodily requirements to the widows of Vrindavan—blankets, items of clothing, and staples of food. These bhandara occasions continue as a well-known feature of Prem Mandir's work.

However generous its motive, Usha Didi has some doubts about the feasibility of this traditional institution—doubts that Kripalu's close disciples expressed to him while he was still alive, to no effect. The worry was that their master was often being duped. The women who showed up for these massive giveaways were not always really widows, it turned out, and not always really destitute, either. Usha Didi said she kept hearing reports that some of the women who received such donations would later turn around and sell what they had been given; it was a racket. Nonetheless the practice continues, and Usha Didi has tried to set up a new system to make it serve its intended purpose. She distributes tickets to the bhandara in advance—to women who are in real need. Thus she comes, for example, to the Munger Mandir in the days just preceding the give-away to offer tickets to the poor women who gather in the presence of Sadhu Maharaj. A few Bengali widows still elect to sing for their supper in the Bhajan Ashram fashion, taking six-hour shifts that keep the mantra in the air and receiving regular allotments of nourishing food for having done so. It is just such women Usha hopes to reach. But this new system for managing entrance to Kripalu's grand bhandara has also now become known. When Usha came to the Munger Mandir in 2017 to distribute forty tickets, she was mobbed before she could scarcely begin. Outsiders pushed many insiders aside.

Despite such scenes—or because of them—the lot of Vrindavan's impoverished women has gradually improved in recent years. Since the early 2000s the state government has established a set of homes specifically intended for their use in a section of town called Chaitanya Vihar, also near the Mathura Road. For those awarded them, this is a major resource. A more dramatic and far-reaching development, however, occurred in 2012, when a major set of donations to destitute women was made by Bindeshwar Pathak, founder of the company that builds the low-cost Sulabh toilet systems that can be seen all over north India. Each Vrindavan woman who qualified—that is, was registered with the government as indigent—was eligible to receive 2000 rupees a month as charity. Pathak's motives were surely laudable, and many women have benefited from the generosity of the Sulabh Hope Foundation, but I have also heard its grants derided as a system that gives too much to too few, or criticized on the grounds that they offer only a temporary fix rather than the kind of vocational training whose effects would lead to genuine independence. It's also true, people say, that this has led to a situation in which the very family members who turned these women out of their homes in the first place—men and women of the younger generation—are now swarming around them to take away their newfound gains.

I happen to know one of the residents of Chaitanya Vihar, and I've been able to see first-hand how it's made her life more manageable. In 2016–17, when I lived principally in Vrindavan, Subhadra Dasi did some cleaning for me and made me a daily meal, coming to my rooms at 5:00 p.m. after working a day in the kitchen at the Radha Damodar temple, where she cut vegetables with a group of other women. She arrived in Vrindavan as a woman in her forties; her husband had gone off with another woman. From her small income she sent money back to help her son, and she worried about how she could assemble a dowry for her younger daughter, who was yet to be married. Once while I was there, she had to leave work for a month to cook and keep house for her son when his wife became bedridden after a spine operation. Subhadra was such a valuable presence in Vrindavan that the Radha Damodar temple kept her job open until she returned and I certainly did the same. Housework aside, I'd grown pleasantly accustomed to the cheerful, commanding "Radhe Shyam" greeting that sounded from the door when she arrived.

Undoubtedly it's misleading to put forward Subhadra Dasi as representative of most women who have fled to Vrindavan. Yet the increments in housing and income from which she benefits are not insubstantial, even if they represent slow, sporadic change rather than rapid, fully predictable progress. The fact that India's Supreme Court has recently taken a specific interest in Vrindavan's widows is also a good sign—and this under the general umbrella provided by the state's commitment to improving the lives of groups of people who are systematically disadvantaged.[25]

One can see such changes in other ways too, not centrally managed but just as real. In the mid-1970s, when my wife and I arrived to live in Vrindavan, it was almost unthinkable for a woman to ride a bicycle in town. Laura did so anyway, sometimes traveling with me by bike down the road that connects Vrindavan to Mathura. As we passed the technical college called Prem Mahavidyalay, the young men who studied there came out and taunted us with shouts, grabbing at her bike as she rode by. One day she was so exasperated that she spat at a group of them, prompting a contingent of their friends and family to visit me the next day and deliver a massive protest at the insult. Laura was utterly unrepentant. Who had been wronged here, after all? Forty years later bikes are still not an easy thing for a girl to manage in Vrindavan—they're dangerous in traffic and the threat from male passersby remains—but women are seen on motorcycles with surprising regularity. It's arguably the most efficient way to get around town, and the power component is quite visible. And audible.

A different example of womanhood in contemporary Vrindavan comes in the quietly charismatic personality of Swamini Vishwamohini who, though she was born into an Indian family who had lived a century in South Africa, settled into Vrindavan on the instructions of Swami Vishwananda in 2014 (Fig. 5.10). Her charge was to work with local builders and contractors and do everything else necessary

Figure 5.10.   Swamini Vishwamohini at the inauguration of the ashram temple of Swami Vishwananda, daubing sandal-paste prasād on the foreheads of female devotees, December 4, 2016.

to get his Vrindavan ashram-temple built in time for its inauguration two years later. She succeeded admirably, as you must have judged in the preceding chapter, and that success has already produced a sequel. A substantial addition to the ashram is being built under her direction; land has been acquired next door. In addition Swamini Vishwamohini heads a household of ten or so young female members of Bhakti Marga who have made Vrindavan their home.

We shouldn't form the impression that she's in this game to display her managerial capabilities, evident as they are, or even to discover a new setting for her strong maternal instincts (she has two grown children of her own). Rather, as she repeatedly emphasized in telling her story, it is the inner management that matters—sincerity of design and emotion, absence of pride, and the nonjudgmental practice of love—and that management actually comes from being tenderly, sometimes unpredictably "managed" by a guru who knows everything about you before you do. "He made me see beauty in places I had never seen it", she said. Swamini Vishwamohini complains that the sense of humble purpose she has learned from her relationship to her guru is often absent from the worldview of Vrindavan's permanent residents, especially the men. They broadcast the message that simply to be born in Vrindavan is the most important thing—pride of birthright—but pride, she thinks, is the deadliest of enemies. To hear her tell it, her guru spent years undermining hers. At a number of points on the hot, damp morning when we talked, I found myself thinking about the gopis and the painful lesson taught by Krishna's absence—either absent from Braj after he had dealt with King Kamsa and moved on to Gujarat, or absent from one of his Braj sweethearts because he was busy in the arms of another. This is the lesson of longing, and a humbling lesson it is. The question is which of the sexes needs most to learn it.[26]

As I left the lovely drawing room where Vishwamohini and I talked that hot and damp July morning, quite another vision of Vrindavan womanhood came to the eye: a row of women carrying bricks on their heads—bricks that would form part of the walls of the ashram's new wing. All across north India women form part of construction crews. They do some of the most physically demanding and poorly remunerated work. A memorable Hindi poem by Suryakanth Tripathi "Nirala" makes this basic fact of labor stand out. Describing a woman who is part of a road-construction gang, he says starkly in the opening line "She splits rocks"—except the gendered verb in Hindi means he doesn't even need to say the "she".[27] She's just there, and she works hard.

Such women, however, are not the only women contributing to Vrindavan's labor force. There's the dentist from Pune, for example, who moved to Vrindavan to be close to her parents and for her own spiritual reasons, and found that her Pune dental degree translated into greater prestige in the Mathura area than it did back home. And then there are the women doctors who work at the well-equipped hospital adjoining Prem Mandir. Comprising half the medical staff, they are a young and energetic group; they offer their services at no charge either to the Kripalu organization or to the public. Here is quite a different model of service from that represented by Swamini Vishwamohini—a regimen of physical examinations, syringes, and operations rather than kirtan, lessons on the Gita, and Om-chanting at different places around town. Yet once again that special female element in Vrindavan mythology is relevant—the example the gopis provide. Others may deplore it as demeaning and patriarchal, but here it projects an enduring appeal.

Then too, there is the realm of art and music. In the ras lila, Vrindavan's signature performance tradition, all the roles continue to be performed by men and—crucially—boys.[28] Here is a culture that hasn't wanted women performing in public, but nowadays things are slowly changing. As we know, Sandhya Goswami, wife of Shrivatsa, joins him onstage whenever he performs Bhagavat Katha. She is the singer in a now much celebrated duo. Most Bhagavat Kathas are still performed by men, but this is a significant innovation. Sandhya also did away with the family tradition that Goswami women had to cover their heads when they ventured out in public, even if they continue to do so in Radharamanji's temple. Her daughter-in-law Aastha Goswami continues to break the traditional mold. A superbly trained and elegant vocal musician, she is the first woman in the extended family of Radharaman priests to be allowed to sing for the deity inside the temple. She describes it as an experience like no other, but that very experience has been transvalued by her role as a performer.[29] Perhaps it goes without saying that when she performs elsewhere, her head is uncovered. If modesty is called for, she expresses it in the subtleties of the voice, not her dress. For such a woman to enter the performance stream at the temple of Radharamanji is a major thing.

And there's more on the public front. When I first came to Vrindavan there was not a single woman among the kathavachaks who sing and comment on the Bhagavata Purana in a weeklong series of performances. Now, though, we begin to see a few, and they're not all stars who rose in a different sky, as Sadhvi Ritambhara did. It is true that many women kathavachaks who mount performances in Vrindavan—women with names like Sadhvi Shri Ashanand Shastri—do in fact come from elsewhere, so they are perhaps not the best measure of how public womanhood has changed in Vrindavan itself, though forty years ago they were simply nonexistent. More significant may be the fact that at least one performer I have seen comes from a local family. She is Devi Shri Shail Kishori, still in her teenage years, and she began her weeklong performance with many verbal genuflections to the distinguished males who had preceded her in the Bhagavata-performing family to which she belongs. Then she offered her own katha before family who had proudly gathered to hear it and an audience disproportionately weighted toward women and girls. Gender taboos, thus, are beginning to break, but the harder line to cross seems to be caste. I have yet to hear of a Bhagavat Katha performed in Vrindavan by anyone other than a Brahmin.[30] Even there, however, questions are being asked—questions persistent enough to make one wonder what changes the future might hold.

Shrivatsa and Sandhya Goswami have two sons, both initiated into the special canons of knowledge and practice that make it possible for them to serve Radharamanji at close range in his temple—touching his feet (charanspars), as the local expression puts it. So far so good from the point of view of cross-generation transmission. But as it happens, the Goswamis' two sons and their wives have given birth only to daughters—between the two families, there are three. From the point of view of traditions practiced for five hundred years in the Radharaman temple, this would mean the family's share in the cycle of ritual service (sevā) there will terminate after the sons' own generation. Only the three girls—grown to women—will remain, and no woman has ever been seen on the platform inside the temple where Radharaman resides. I wonder if this might change in the course of these three girls' lives, and I have heard Shrivatsa wonder the same.

Figure 5.11.   Vishnupriya Goswami on her seventeenth birthday, February 10, 2019, with her younger sister Jayati.

One thing, though, is already clear. If the new Vrindavan becomes new in this intimate, central way, it will bring into the ritual circle one remarkable woman: Vishnupriya Goswami (Fig. 5.11).

Priya, as she is called, is the oldest of the three girls. She was born only in 2002, but already she has big ideas. At one point she thought a bit about becoming an expositor of the Bhagavata like her grandfather and great-grandfather (and, by the way, one of her grandmother's sisters), valuing the impact she might have on her own generation. She was extrapolating from experiences she's already had as an accomplished Odissi dancer, where she often explains the meaning of dance gestures and poses to various groups of her peers. "I make them ask me questions", she says. It's the interactive experience that turns her on, and this has been at the heart of her own education. She knows there's learning to be had in books, and her appetite for books is famous at school. But she'd rather be finding things out for herself. You'd think she'd read John Dewey! Self-questioning, she believes, is the basis and heart of true learning. As an eighth-grader she deleted everything she had stored on her cell phone, determined to make herself over, to start again.

Not too long afterward what she describes as her early "atheism"—
a sense of being not quite invested in religion—began to turn to
something else. It wasn't that she turned to the religion of what everyone else had always done, but that she insisted on asking where and
why her feelings ran deep. "When I dance, I cry", she said. "Why?"
And especially when she dances for Radharamanji in his temple—so
there's the connection with "organized religion". Priya once spoke of
this depth of feeling as "the fear of God", echoing a phrase she'd heard
in the English-language Dominican school where she was educated
up to the age of fifteen. But this "fear" was also something she'd
heard at home as a kid—in Hindi—perhaps in a gentle reprimand:
"Don't do thus and so. Radharamanji might be angry". Fear, though,
is exactly not the issue. The point is to seek a deeper truth—the truth
of one's own deep feelings. By thinking about religion in this way, she
channels the whole Gaudiya tradition.

Priya is very conscious of the unusual position in which she stands.
She's poised at the center of one of Vrindavan's oldest institutions, yet
by gender she is also poised athwart it. Being a girl, she cannot hope
to serve Radharamanji right up close—to touch his feet, as the traditional phrase has it. Or can she? Might she become the first woman
to mount that high platform and join the select circle of officiants
permitted to go there? It wouldn't be at Priya's own insistence, she
stresses. She doesn't feel deprived. After all, she has dance, her own
true means of closeness to the Divine.[31] But what if? Looking into the
mist of the future, I can't stop asking.

The story goes that Mirabai, the saint who first cared for Swami
Vishwananda's Giridhar Gopal, had to fight her way into Vrindavan.
Everywhere else her songs to Krishna were renowned, but according to the *Bhaktirasabodhinī* written in 1712 in Vrindavan itself, Jiva
Goswami refused to speak with her when she came to town. He'd
taken a vow never to have concourse with women. To this, Mira
had the right response. "Oh, I thought there was only one man in
Vrindavan", she said, and clearly she didn't have Jiva in mind. When
it comes to Krishna, all of us are the women who surround him.
Jiva had no choice but to relent. Shrivatsa Goswami has commented
that if this story were true, it would mean Jiva had profoundly mis-
understood Chaitanya, his own central preceptor, since, after all,
the Gaudiya tradition interprets Chaitanya as being so completely

accomplished and attractive as a male that he was able simultaneously to exude an utterly female presence without diluting it. To his followers, Chaitanya was simultaneously Krishna and Radha—the very bond that holds them together in an inconceivable difference and non-difference (achintyabhedābheda). How could male asceticism belong in such a world?

And yet, somehow, it did—in Jiva and even in the person of Chaitanya himself, who left his mother and wife behind to live with his followers in Puri. In Vrindavan patriarchal perks survive in various ways, and in the leadership of the Vrindavan Chandrodaya Mandir we see an exquisitely updated version of the Gaudiya ascetic tradition. The uppermost leaders and planners are not ascetics, as often happens a level down, but they are certainly male. The temple itself may swirl around gender-balanced images of Radha and Krishna, but these men's engineering and IT degrees trumpet a contemporary version of male hegemony. Not everyone who works at the VCM is an ascetic by any means, yet the people who answer questions at the reception desk, whether celibate or married, are invariably male. The wives of the president and vice president of Bangalore ISKCON were closely involved in planning the Vrindavan Chandrodaya Mandir and designing its publicity, but their spouses still take the lead in the public sphere. What a remarkable thing it would be if the much more traditional Radharaman temple, to which ISKCON leaders have so long turned for historical and ritual guidance, were to cross the feminine finish line before ISKCON. The old Vrindavan would thereby edge out the new. So far there's no suggestion this will occur, but stranger things have happened in Vrindavan.

Back to Basics

What is Vrindavan, after all? It was always meant to be a city of dreams, a town that could capture the searching truths of longing, beauty, and night. Vrindavan invites the erotic rather than submerging it in tales of a virgin birth as Bethlehem does. It thrives on dreams of union with the other, union with the beloved. There divinity waits.

Whose dream is this? The case has been made that this is distinctly a man's dream.[32] It's a fantasy of male irresponsibility, such critics say—an archetype of appetite, a wish for total control. In such a world it's not just the demons who fall under Krishna's powerful sway but the women—they just can't seem to stay away. In Vrindavan's central myth, the ras lila (Fig. 5.1), Krishna is the only man left standing, and he is surrounded by an infinite number of women. They all have direct access to his body and person: he multiplies himself such that each of them feels she has his sole attention. As the circle fragments and dissipates, these women find themselves beset by the tensions and trials that come from focusing on a single, transcendent male. Where has he been the night before? Why does he have nail-mark scratches on his chest? Why do they have to work so hard to escape the proprietary gaze of husbands and in-laws and friends as they try to regain his full presence?

It is easy to think that such quandaries arise because they too are the fantasies of men—narcissists one and all, just as women have always thought them to be. But women also join the game. In any performance of the ras lila they make up at least half the audience. They are there because they want to be. Perhaps this follows from a second aspect of the guiding myth. The presence of but a single male in the central maṇḍala means that all the other actors are women. This yields a space where women can be women with each other—sakhis and sahelis bound by ties of female friendship, and sometimes mothers too. Krishna's Golok heaven becomes in that way their heaven too—not just because he is there but because they have each other.

From a man's point of view this is an alternate world, a mysterious different reality. From a woman's, though, it's the female staff of life. In a patriarchically shaped world this world of women has its tensions, ranks, and envies, but take away the men—allowing a single one to take their place—and you seem to have a different reality altogether: a paradise of women. Each of them holds Krishna's hand in classic representations of the ras lila: he multiplies himself around the circle so that this can be so. But they also have each other. Each woman in the charmed circle surrounding Krishna or Radha-Krishna discovers that after one of her hands has reached out for Krishna and been grasped, another remains. That one holds the hand of another woman.[33] And when Krishna is lost to these women—a metaphor for the deus absconditus that we all know—it's the women who take things in their own hands and make him present by imitating what it was like when he was among them. This is how the ras lila began, we are told—that circle within the circle that is Vrindavan. There they were released from their husbands' patriarchal claims when the very one who made it possible for them to escape disappeared. They brought him back by being him themselves.[34]

It's a story that offers breathing room from patriarchy, but can it be enacted in the real world?

6

Being Shrivatsa

Chapter after chapter, as I've told this tale, I have never stood far from Shrivatsa Goswami. He is the one who, with his father, first made it possible for me to live in Vrindavan in the way I have. He's my landlord, but because it's an ashram I pay no rent. He's my advisor, enlightener, inspirer, correcter. I've watched him fight the battle of Keshi Ghat and heard him pilloried for doing so. I've followed him on ban yātrās with his devotees; I've sat in their midst. I've watched his granddaughters climb onto his lap at the family table. Shrivatsa is far indeed from the new Vrindavan as many people conceive it, but he is by no means a single-minded traditionalist. In many ways he defines what I've come to think of as a genuinely new Vrindavan, one that's anchored in the past but open to the contours of the future.

The Life of a Son

I met Shrivatsa in Vrindavan in 1972, but it was three years later, in the ancient city of Banaras, that I really got to know him (Fig. 6.1). Then 23, he was a postgraduate student in philosophy, working

Figure 6.1.   Shrivatsa Goswami greets the old Vrindavan in the 1970s.

under one of India's most celebrated scholars, T.R.V. Murti, who had recently retired from the faculty of Banaras Hindu University (BHU) but was still going strong. Shrivatsa had completed his M.A., and he and his wife Sandhya, married four years before, had rented a small suite of rooms in the Assi section of town, not far from the main road that leads out to BHU. Their first son Abhinav, whom everyone calls Raju, was still a baby. Sandhya also hails from Vrindavan. A graduate in Sanskrit, Hindi, and philosophy, she is the first of eight daughters (there was finally a son) born to the town's best beloved mayor, Magan Sharma, who held office from 1952 to 1971. He is still remembered for having made the town a paradise of efficiency and cleanliness.

Shrivatsa too had a father everyone looked up to—Purushottam Goswami, a remarkable man. Purushottam had the good fortune to be born into the extended family of Radharaman gosvamis, continuously present in Vrindavan since the temple was founded in 1542;

but his own father had died when Purushottam was only nine, leaving him to have to fend more than usually for himself—and as the oldest child, with many family responsibilities. He chose to undertake them, though, by striking out on his own immediately after finishing his local high-school education, first studying with the famous pundits of Banaras, then performing the Bhagavata in places far and wide. The lore that has grown up around him explains how he once charmed Mansingh, the famous Robin Hood dacoit who lived with his band in the ravines around the Chambal River, and ultimately performed such a remarkable week-long exposition of the Bhagavata in Chennai that he was awarded the title Jagadguru, "teacher to the world". This honorific took on a more institutional aspect after Purushottam represented the Chaitanya Sampraday at a significant gathering of religious leaders at Kurukshetra. Others of similar rank bore the title Jagadguru—it was natural that he should as well. With Purushottam, though, the institutional was never competition for the charismatic. Both as a young man and for years to come he was handsome, outgoing, adventurous, and deeply musical. And as to titles, the one he treasured most was Rajaji. Friends and followers called him this in memory of his father, who had been so called.

When I first met Purushottam on a visit to Vrindavan, I was stunned by his unique combination of vivacity and authority—the force of his physical presence (Fig. 6.2). What must it be like to be the son of such a man, I wondered, with the weight of presumed succession resting on your shoulders? Ruminating about his childhood one February afternoon in Mumbai, however, Shrivatsa dwelt on none of this.[1] Rather, he depicted his father as a helpful and imaginative presence, little inclined to dictate or micromanage. Born in Mathura, like Krishna—it was his mother's city—Shrivatsa started his education at the age of five in a government school near the Rangji Temple in Vrindavan. They tested him as he appeared for admission and determined that the first two grades would be a waste, so he entered the third grade directly—an ill-wished independence, perhaps, but a form of independence nonetheless. When Shrivatsa was 8, his parents made the decision that he should leave the government school and undertake the Sanskrit curriculum provided at a traditional pathshala that operated out of the compound of the Radhavallabh temple not far away. This meant that Shrivatsa spent a year cramming into his

Figure 6.2.   Purushottam Goswami, 1975.

head (for so it seemed to him) the classic *Laghu Siddhānta Kaumudī* that stands at the basis of a Sanskrit education pursued just about anywhere in India. He remembers being rebuffed by his teachers if ever he asked why anything was the way it was: he should merely learn it, they believed, that's all. Questions just got in the way at this stage. Those he could ask much later, when he knew enough to do so intelligently. This is the way Sanskrit has been taught for millennia—and with impressive results for the integrity and resiliency of the tradition. But Shrivatsa rebelled. He left the school—only to find that he would have to come back to Sanskrit much later in life, at twenty, when he needed it for his graduate studies and his brain cells weren't multiplying at the rate they were when he was 8.

His father was disappointed, but understanding and flexible. He arranged for Shrivatsa to go off on his own to Banaras, the city where the most formative stages of his own education had transpired as a young man of 19 or 20. Purushottam had experienced the Banarsi educational tradition in its most traditional form—he attached himself to a single venerable teacher, pleading to be allowed to study. This he did out of conviction, but it is also true that he was almost penniless and had no other choice. A more elaborate institutional structure would not have been possible on account of the fees.

Things were different when Shrivatsa headed for Banaras. There was his age, of course—he was only 9—but it's also true that by contrast to Purushottam's childhood poverty, Shrivatsa was a member of a family that had come to have sufficient financial resources to be able to send him to a boarding school; many of Purushottam's initiated disciples were persons of means. The boarding school in question was not just any boarding school. Purushottam Goswami chose a very progressive institution for his son's education—especially progressive for Banaras. Located in the Rajghat area of town and therefore often called simply the Rajghat School, its formal name was The Foundation for New Education. It had been established by the well-known Theosophical free-thinker J. Krishnamurti, who pioneered a truly experimental approach to education. Yet Rajghat also submitted to a structure of regular examinations that would prepare its pupils to enter other educational institutions upon graduation. Shrivatsa fondly recalls the moment when Krishnamurti himself paid the school a visit, traveling from his home in Chennai. He spoke in the manner that had made him world-famous. The best education, he said, was none at all—children know best what they need to learn. On hearing this, one of the teachers asked the obvious question: Why then were the students regularly required to prepare for various sets of rigorous exams? Krishnamurti stopped for a moment, closed the book that lay open on the table before him, and calmly replied, "Next question?"

But there was indeed a great measure of freedom at Rajghat—parents and teachers had both deliberately chosen such an environment for their charges—and Shrivatsa found that befriending the diverse body of students who had gathered from all over India was an education in itself. They were largely Hindu, he concedes, but Hindu in the very liberal sort of way typical in the Theosophical Society.

This would not be the only time Shrivatsa benefited from the fact that Purushottam was able to put aside his own memories of how hard he had had to struggle to obtain the traditional education that was essential to his own success, encouraging his son to explore the world on his own. Still, as it turned out, a dip in the family's finances meant Shrivatsa had to return to Vrindavan after only a single year at Rajghat, and that was where he stayed for the remainder of his early education. When it came time to go to college at the age of fifteen, Shrivatsa's high scores on the statewide government exams meant that he had the opportunity to join the elite A.N. Jha Hostel at the University of Allahabad, which was by all odds the most highly ranked university in UP at the time. His parents were very pleased that he had the chance. It meant among other things that for the first time in his life Shrivatsa would be immersed in a fully English-speaking environment and using the language that was the key to success in the higher registers of so much that happens in Indian life. English was the language of the ruling class in British times and it remained no less so when they departed. The young men assembled in the Jha Hostel felt this legacy keenly. They were the cream of the Allahabad University crop, plainly destined for careers in law, science, and the higher echelons of government service. That was what they talked about all the time.

Shrivatsa hated it, just as he had hated being recruited for the Sanskrit elite much earlier, and once again he rebelled, this time in very short order. After two weeks he was gone—not far down the road (and down the Ganga) to Banaras, his old academic home. He wanted to go to BHU. Both parents felt a measure of regret when they heard this, but Purushottam dropped everything and went to meet Shrivatsa there. Together they appealed to the all-powerful BHU registrar for late admission to the entering class of the Arts Faculty. As Shrivatsa remembers the incident, the connections his father had forged with the Kashmiri pundit community to whom the registrar belonged and the fact that Purushottam had not long before responded to the vice chancellor's request for two weeks of personal instruction on the ras lila had a lot to do with the fact that answer was positive, but I suspect Shrivatsa must have made quite an impression himself. In any case, he exchanged the Jha Hostel in Allahabad for the Birla Hostel at BHU. Some family friends lamented this perceived lowering of horizons, and indeed Shrivatsa's polished, fluent, and inventive English is not quite the absolutely idiomatic sort he would have had as second nature if he had moved through the Allahabad curriculum (instead he salts the language with idioms of his own), but the change was deeply salutary.

Shrivatsa loved BHU. The university's expansive grounds gave him a sense of freedom. "Sports", he said, "were a form of religion", unknowingly echoing my own father's appraisal of golf on a Sunday morning. In time he became captain of the Arts Faculty's tennis team, and he took up competitive swimming, which was made possible by the Olympic-size pool recently constructed just behind the Vishvanath temple for which the university is famous. "That pool became my mandir", he said.[2] He had never learned to swim back home in the Yamuna. And beyond the athletic fields, too, there was also a sense of expansiveness at BHU. Though a nationally chartered university, BHU was far more regional than Allahabad, drawing many of its students from the Bhojpuri-speaking areas of eastern UP and conducting its normal business in Hindi. This Hindi-language environment made it possible for the student body to embody a degree of class diversity that would never have been possible at that time in elite, English-speaking Allahabad. The same was to some extent true in terms of religious backgrounds, although you might not guess it from the "Hindu" in BHU's name. In the Philosophy Department, for instance, there were Buddhist monks from Sri Lanka, whom Shrivatsa befriended at the Birla Hostel where they both lived.

Diversity came in other ways, too—extra-curricular ones. The university's Hobby Center offered the chance to study photography and Shrivatsa acquired his first camera, the start of a long career in photo-documentation. This he had to pay for by himself, but the university picked up all the other charges. Its renowned music faculty opened further avenues. Shrivatsa studied the sitar for a year, waiting out the painful period in which the necessary callus developed on his third finger. But when asked by his teacher at the end of a year's study whether he was willing to forego some of his other activities—sports in particular—to become really good at music, he answered in the negative. He raced downtown to sell his sitar and buy the Dunlop tennis racquet he'd had his eye on.

All of this served as background for a life he describes as being somehow "holistic". This was rather unusual, since the ideals and practices of a liberal arts education that are taken for granted in North America are ordinarily absent from India's much more closely focused undergraduate curriculum. Shrivatsa regrets this, and he particularly regrets the absence of lively sports programs at most Indian institutions of higher education. Sports are good training for life. A sportsman's attitude means that "If you lose, you don't lose"—you just keep playing all the same. Being in the game is what matters. That kind of resiliency proved crucial for later struggles Shrivatsa was to face, and as to the matter of just what profession he emerged with at the end of his studies, he says it was not altogether clear. Once, in the course of renewing his passport, he was required to state his occupation and none of the options provided by the form seemed to fit. He thought it over for quite some time and finally decided to write something in at the bottom of the page. "Gentleman of leisure", he ventured, recalling some of the English novels he had read.

Shrivatsa recognizes what a privilege it was to have the particular kind of head-start on life that his parents made possible. He's often a sort of "free dealer", as he once said, and his unconventional education prepared him well for that. Even when he was playing "third-fiddle to my father", a fair amount of improvisation was often involved, and his father encouraged it.

At one point in the course of his "fiddling", his mother also played a critical role (Fig. 6.3). It had to do with the musical side of his father's persona. When Shrivatsa began to study music at BHU he headed for an instrument, not voice. To learn an instrument in the Indian system requires that one must first provide a vocal rendering of the raga or phrase about to be attempted on the instrument, but this use of the voice is only an informal tool along the way. And a good thing it was, Shrivatsa thought. Already in childhood he had concluded that his singing voice wasn't worth listening to, and it developed a gravelly quality as he matured. Imagine his relief, then, when his younger

Figure 6.3.   Shrivatsa's mother, Brajkumari Goswami, 1975.

brother Venugopal, fifth of the five children, displayed an aptitude for voice. Here was one aspect of his father's many virtues that Shrivatsa would not be required to replicate.[3]

Purushottam was famous for his singing voice. He often brought it to his roles in the Radharaman temple, performing not just in the ritually circumscribed manner required for the service of the deity up-close, but also, frequently, as the leader of the musical group that assembles at the back of the temple to fill the space with sound and serenade the deity. In Vrindavan's Vaishnava traditions it is believed that all the arts must be engaged in the Lord's service, and music is probably foremost among them. Similarly, Purushottam would sing in the context of the public sankirtan processions he sometimes led through the streets of Banaras—his famous sankirtan yatras commemorating Chaitanya's arrival in that city. They culminated on the open area just outside the Gyan Vapi Mosque. And on top of all that, he was well known for having, as Shrivatsa put it, "musicalized" performances in which the Bhagavata Purana is brought before the public ear, first and foremost in the traditional seven-day Bhagavat Saptah (Bhagavata week) or Bhagavat Katha (Bhagavata recitation) format. It was Purushottam who first surrounded himself with a musical ensemble as he offered his expositions of the text. Thus when Venugopal left home to study with the famous Pandit Jasraj in preparation for a career in which he himself would become a well-known exponent of Bhagavat Katha, Shrivatsa heaved a sigh of relief. The burden of music was lifted.

But not so fast: his mother had other ideas. She said she wanted to hear seven days of Bhagavata exposition from her first son as well—one time, at least, before she died. Surely he would not deny her that.[4] After resisting time and again, Shrivatsa submitted to the yoke. Daily for five or six hours at a stretch in the late 1980s he made it a practice to read the Bhagavata aloud, so as to get a deep feel for the movement of the text. He did this over a period of two years or more. He also studied the Sandarbhas of Jiva Goswami, doctrinal treatises that took much of their inspiration from the Bhagavata Purana, which had been the focus of his postgraduate study with Professor Murti. Finally, if reluctantly, he was ready to give it a try—after all, in seven days it would be over once and for all. Shrivatsa's only condition was that his Bhagavat Katha debut (and swansong) not take place in Vrindavan. All right, then, Dvaraka, his mother declared, and since this site on the shores of the Arabian Sea is just about as far from Vrindavan as you can get, Shrivatsa agreed. The distance brought a certain relief, but just for good measure he made sure to shift the strictly musical responsibilities to his wife Sandhya, thereby producing a mixed-gender version of Bhagavat Katha that remains a great innovation to this day. Even so, when the moment arrived in December 1993, Shrivatsa found he had prepared far too little. How possibly could the brief notes he had assembled for each of the seven days carry him through—such a puny result after his many months of study? It proved to be no problem. The Bhagavata itself took over, as Shrivatsa recalls, and it's a good thing that it did. In addition to his mother and father, who assumed the formal role of sponsors (śrotā) for the event, two or three hundred people made their way to the great Dvarkadhish temple to launch him on his maiden performance journey.

Recall: it was supposed to be his last, but there turned out to be a further complication. The year before, in 1992, his father had acquired Bhramar Ghat and the bee itself—or something very much like a bee—miraculously materialized to play its part in the inauguration. When that happened, Purushottam Goswami took a vow not to leave Vrindavan ever again. All well and good—most noble and fitting—but how would he fulfill another vow he had made, namely, to perform a Bhagavat Katha at the temple of Govindadev in Jaipur once every year in the month of Karttik? The family pressed Shrivatsa to perform this role one more time, and he grudgingly accepted, provided Venugopal would take over after that. But by the time he made his way into that second week of performance, Shrivatsa had been bitten by the Bhagavata bug. Since then, he and Sandhya have performed regularly before audiences big and small. Shrivatsa actually prefers the latter. You can cultivate a genuine sense of dialogue with your audience, he says, responding to their moods and signals as they respond to yours. But it is not always possible. On one occasion he found himself addressing a crowd of ten thousand, much to his distress. He took refuge in the presence of a nearby pillar, gazing at it the whole time and using its blank, calm surface as a way to focus his own racing thoughts. Though he's tried to escape such numbers ever since—the very numbers others seem to crave—this was hardly the last time he had to deal with crowds. Who was in the starring role for a seven-day recitation and performance of the Bhagavata Purana when BHU decided this would be just the way to kick off its centennial celebrations? The student who had turned in his sitar for a tennis racquet.

It must be obvious by now that for Shrivatsa tradition is both a burden and a joy, but we should not imagine that this bifocal relationship to the weight of the past and the promise of the future is new with him. It is deeply encoded in the history of the Radharaman gosvamis. It may indeed make sense to speak of the new Vrindavan as happening on the other side of town at Raman Reti, but the path to a new Vrindavan has also been blazed at the Radharaman temple and Jaisingh Ghera—and blazed for a very long time. The Radharaman gosvamis were the first among Vrindavan gosvamis to install electric lights in their temple. They were also the first to allow cameras to be used while worship was going on and darshan was being received, and the first to make it clear that people of the invidiously called "lower castes" were welcome there.

In the 1930s, furthermore, they weighed in on an issue that had directly to do with the issue of continuity and change. Bhakti Siddhant Sarasvati, the man chosen to succeed Bhakti Vinod Thakur as leader of the Gaudiya Math, a reformist order of Vaishnava ascetics founded in Bengal in 1920, a newcomer to Vrindavan's spiritual economy, had come to the conclusion that the very lineage he had been charged to continue—supposedly going straight back to Krishna himself—was flawed. He discovered that there had centuries before been a break in that very succession. This pulled the rug out from the Gaudiya Math's claim to be not something novel in Vaishnava history but its ancient historical kernel, now come to life after centuries of dormancy. Understandably Bhakti Siddhant Sarasvati's kinsmen were not pleased. At a certain point this dispute arrived on the doorstep of the Radharaman gosvamis, and once again their response showed them to be innovators in certain matters and traditionalists in others. They implicitly stood behind this learned renegade by inviting him to appear in the space just outside the entrance to the Radharaman temple compound, but they did not presume to make a judgment about the succession issue. Rather, they made it clear that they prized Bhakti Siddhant Sarasvati's energetic contributions to modern Vaishnavism through his work at the Gaudiya Math and Mission. This was a "split-level" response to the challenges of modernity.

When Bhakti Siddhant's successor Bhakti Prasad Puri, né Anant Vasudeva, met this same issue in the 1940s, the Radharaman gosvamis once again came to his aid. This time the issue was even more dramatic. Not only did Bhakti Prasad Puri agree with his guru that they represented a broken guru-to-guru lineage, but he concluded that

Chaitanya had not wished his followers to assemble in ascetic communities at all. In conformity with this, he abrogated his position and became a married man, taking the name Puridas. His right-hand man, a Gaudiya Math ascetic named Sundaranand Vidyavinod, wrote a theological treatise justifying this decision by including a chapter on the conditions under which it is justified for a person to disown his own guru, the person responsible for his initiated status as an ascetic.[5] This time the wrath of the Gaudiya Math was even more heated—Puridas's life was threatened—and he decided he had to retreat to the forests of Orissa to conceal his identity. Later, though, when things had cooled somewhat and he returned to Vrindavan, one of the Radharaman gosvamis, Purushottam Goswami, found a secluded place in a garden owned by his own family where Puridas could live.

This distinctive Radharaman role in mediating between past and present took a new form in the 1970s. At that point ISKCON made its presence felt on the Vrindavan scene, and its members made no secret of the fact that they were skeptical of the birth-given authority of gosvamis such as those who served in the Radharaman temple.[6] For this reason and by virtue of their novelty and the money they commanded, they were regularly reviled by many Vrindavanites, who found them strange if not comic. Once again, however, the Radharaman priests took a mediating position. Without either authorizing or challenging ISKCON's claims to legitimate succession—Prabhupad stood in the Gaudiya Math lineage—they willingly offered their services when these new kids on the block (and many were kids) came to them seeking models of appropriate ritual behavior. The effect was that the Radharaman gosvamis pumped their centuries-old, self-consciously conservative practices of serving the Lord out toward the frontier of the new Vrindavan—not as actors themselves, but as supporters in this particular, circumscribed way. However skeptical they may have been at the outset, they did not resist being involved. As a result, even today, when ISKCON is very much up and running on its own terms, one very often sees ISKCON devotees in the Radharaman temple.

These ties between the old and the new are thus many and various, but under the leadership of Purushottam and Shrivatsa Goswami they do not extend to buying up land on the other side of town. In that respect the Jaisingh Ghera subset of the Radharaman gosvamis has been distinctly more conservative than several of its enterprising cousins.[7] Whether this is a principled decision I cannot say, but we certainly know that Shrivatsa has had his hands full trying to keep the old Vrindavan alive on its own, old turf, protecting it against the assaults of the present age. Here again is an area where he might be seen as acting on the basis of his father's generosity, no matter what his development-oriented opponents may think. Against the repeated advice of a devotee who was a commissioner in the income tax department, Purushottam insisted in 1972 that the land and buildings comprising Jaisingh Ghera should become a public charitable trust—the Shri Chaitanya Prem Sansthan—rather than remaining the personal property of himself and his family. Family members would constitute only a quarter of the board of trustees. "Whatever I have received", said Purushottam, "I have received only as a trustee of my devotees. ... Now is my time to give it back".[8]

So then, consider Jaisingh Ghera as an amalgam of old and new. The entryway leading out into the narrow street beyond the Ghera, with its massive wooden doors shaped into a pointed arch, is obviously old, but the largest structure within the compound is much more recent. This concrete building, cantilevered over the large pink-sandstone room where Jaisingh held his royal audiences in the early eighteenth century, contains a performance space, a kitchen, and an office on the ground floor, and accommodates numerous guest rooms and yet more offices in the two stories above. One or two lovely little pavilions adorn the roof. The whole thing bears the name Shri Chaitanya Prem Sansthan, which one might understand to mean either an institution of love dedicated to Chaitanya or a foundation bodying forth his love.

The Sansthan dates back to 1972, and it has played host to a series of events that are strikingly new. There have been a series of academic seminars attracting scholars from around the world—a first for Vrindavan—and other scholars come to make use of its library, one of the finest in all of Braj. In addition, the Sansthan's documentation center keeps a record of performances and gatherings of all kinds that have transpired under its auspices and in the Radharaman temple since 1967. All these have constituted innovations in the service of tradition, and each of them has borne Shrivatsa's imprint. The documentation program began with his own camera and tape recorder, and he has been behind a series of collaborative projects in which the Sansthan has been engaged. There was the Vraja-Nathadvara Prakalpa, launched in 1988, which attempted to reach out to scholars of the Vallabh Sampraday headquartered at Nathdvara in western Rajasthan so as to bring the cultural and religious institutions of that community, which looks to Braj for its origins, into conversation with others that have remained in Braj. There was also the ambitious Braj Mahotsav (great festival in honor of Braj, 2009) organized in cooperation with the Indira Gandhi National Centre for the Arts in Delhi and responsible for a week-long mela and pop-up museum on its grounds right next to the great green mall that connects the President's House to India Gate in the heart of New Delhi.

The list of such enterprises is very long, and one can see linkages between new and old in each. These linkages are not always smooth. On one occasion in early 1994, I remember, there was a tense moment of friction when Purushottam Goswami learned that the New York-based musicologist Peter Manuel was planning to present a paper to the international seminar his son convened on "The Continuing Creation of Braj". Manuel wanted to highlight the fact that traditional songs called rasiyas, typically dedicated to exploring the love between Krishna and Radha or the gopis, were increasingly being mobilized by India's flourishing cassette industry to serve the needs of truck drivers. Their religious content had been overwritten so that truck drivers sitting in their drivers' cabs were singing along to some secular, often pretty raunchy lyrics. Part of the flavor was added by the fact that these songs had begun as Radha–Krishna bhajans.[9] Hearing that this was in the offing, Purushottam Goswami objected. He felt there was no room for such a presentation within the precincts of the Sansthan. Shrivatsa, however, intervened, and Peter Manuel's academic freedom was maintained—with Purushottam Goswami still in attendance.

It is no wonder that Purushottam Goswami could suffer this change in the end. After all, he himself had been responsible for many of the most significant innovations that occurred in Vrindavan's twentieth-century history. He gave renewed attention to Braj's five-hundred-year-old ras lila tradition, expanding its theatrical vocabulary so as to encompass not only the life story of Krishna as child and adolescent, but that of Chaitanya as well. He also played a major role on the team that created these new librettos. The dramas in which they figured were called, after the light-skinned Chaitanya, gaur lilas, and they were first and most characteristically performed on the Sansthan's stage—a morning venture that would anticipate and amplify the afternoon's ras lilas. Even the stage on which these lilas were performed was an innovation. Up until the time it was introduced, traditional ras lilas were always performed in the round. This change was a major gesture to modern forms of theatricality—the traditions of Mumbai's Parsi theater, with Bollywood in the wings. And there was another signal departure too, this one in the direction of the Radharaman temple's traditions of ritual practice, as if to bridge the two realms. Purushottam undertook the enterprise of developing the ras lilas so that they could refer more directly to the canonical eight phases (aṣṭayām) of Krishna's eternal day, thereby producing a separate genre of performance called ashtayam lila for which he himself was the one and only scriptwriter.[10]

Each of these experiments was an innovation for sure, and often with a very public face, and one can see how their example would have encouraged Shrivatsa to develop the capacities of the Sansthan even further, but at the same time one can see a characteristic difference. While his father worked toward the goal of expanding the Vaishnava message and its characteristic art forms toward the widest possible circle of audiences and occasions, with a fair amount of increased internal differentiation along the way, Shrivatsa's innovations have often been aimed at drawing in people who would be quite new to these traditions and sometimes unconcerned about them. Many of these people were not Vaishnavas, or Vaishnavas in quite different ways from the Gaudiyas.

While his father traveled the length and breadth of India many times, branching out to Europe only on the two occasions when a UNESCO program asked for the ras lilas to be performed there, Shrivatsa has made the great wide world his home. His facility in English makes this possible. Often Shrivatsa has traveled the globe to advance interreligious understanding, whether the invitation came from Reverend Sun Myung Moon in Seoul, Pope Benedict in Assisi, the Archbishop of Canterbury, or the United Nations in New York. In 2000 he delivered the centenary lecture on interreligious understanding organized by the Hibbert Trust in honor of the Sanskritist and comparativist J. Estlin Carpenter at Oxford.

If this sounds like a trajectory of endless expansion and liberalization, we should also remember that Shrivatsa has sometimes seen these radically new venues as places to re-encounter things that are very old. In the course of the year he spent as a visiting scholar at Harvard in 1977–8, he was asked if he would present a series of lectures. Here, farther from home than he had ever been in every respect, he chose to speak on what for him was the most traditional subject possible: the ritual manual called *Haribhaktivilāsa* that had been prepared by the founder of the Radharaman temple, Gopal Bhatt, in the middle of the sixteenth century. To expound it at Harvard was certainly something new, but it was supremely traditional. It directed people's attention to his oldest intellectual ancestor in Braj, Gopal Bhatt, and it certainly did the same for Shrivatsa himself.[11] Eight years after delivering these lectures, Shrivatsa took on their subject in an all-or-nothing way. He undertook the training and habits of abnegation (most of them food-related) that would make it possible for him to fulfill that most traditional of gosvami roles, serving Radharaman in the sanctum that bears his name. In doing this he was enacting the mandates of the *Haribhaktivilāsa,* allowing himself to be initiated into the most conservative realm in which the Radharaman gosvamis are active, the theater of ritual practice that surrounds the deity himself.

History and the Self-Renewing Vrindavan

If much of this story of Shrivatsa and his father makes it seem that the "old Vrindavan" is actually not as old as you might think, then we have amplified one of the main messages that Shrivatsa Goswami himself often preaches. But the new, he concedes, is really new. Back in the 1980s there was a master plan for Vrindavan that recognized there would be development, but it was to have been outside the circle formed by the circumambulatory Parikrama Marg—that was sacrosanct. The area inside it was supposed to have been protected by a green zone that surrounded it. "We had that!" he says. "That's what Raman Reti was". But then there was all this corruption. On the pretext that they were building ashrams and gaushalas, to get by the zoning restrictions built into the master plan, people threw up "all these matchbox structures", Shrivatsa says. "It's strikingly ugly, so the whole beauty of the heritage zone gets diluted". And it matters to the old Vrindavan too. "The new Vrindavan and the old Vrindavan—they are seamless. They flow into each other"—and that in a situation where the physical aspect of things really matters. This is, after all, the land that Radha and Krishna chose to touch with their own feet, their own bodies. For this reason if for no other, the Vrindavan of this world matters to the Vrindavan of the other—the eternal Vrindavan.[12]

What a mess this has made, as it turns out. But then, says Shrivatsa with a smile, if we're having trouble digesting the dislocations of the new Vrindavan, we must remember that "The main culprit is Bihariji or Krishna himself". It was he, after all, who left that other world behind to come here:

> If Krishna had not chosen to be in Vrindavan, Vrindavan would have been at peace! The growth even of a heritage site like Vrindavan cannot be constrained, cannot be limited. It's a natural phenomenon. ... Because of Krishna the whole world is descending on Vrindavan. So they need their infrastructure, they need their places to stay, they need places to worship. And more and more sects are coming, more and more charismatic leaders are coming—they need their power bases. All of this is an ongoing process, a natural process. But if people had a little grounding in the spirit of Vrindavan, what I call the vrindāvan bhāv, then the expansion of Vrindavan would have been in consonance with the Vrindavan tradition of ritual and requirements and greenery and what not. If that had naturally flowed in, it would not have been so obscene.

And it's not just the fault of outsiders. It's the Vrindavan people themselves. "They're not even aware of what they are doing. Whether it's a service to Vrindavan or a disservice to Vrindavan—this question does not even arise for them". Hence the constant focus of Shrivatsa's consciousness-raising activities is not just the general public but also close to home. He will talk to anyone who will listen.

One way Shrivatsa tries to raise consciousness is to help people see that they belong to a long and glorious history, a history they have a duty to protect. It does indeed begin with Krishna—"Krishna coming and making a new Vrindavan", as Shrivatsa says—but there are many steps between then and now. The great initiative, in Shrivatsa's understanding, was that of Chaitanya—who, being both Krishna and Radha in some delicate way in his own body, wished to reclaim the land Krishna had claimed so long ago. But "Chaitanya, coming and making a new Vrindavan", wasn't alone. His disciplines were also involved, and they were "joined by this whole galaxy of other saints", among whom Haridas and Hit Harivamsh came to mind, as well as Hariramvyas and "the Nimbarki sadhus coming on the scene, and the nondenominational sadhus ... like Anandaghan who was so brutally murdered by the invading armies—they all built their new Vrindavan". Then there was the era in the eighteenth and nineteenth centuries when so many kings came on the scene, especially from Rajasthan, everywhere building their special places to live in their kunjes, such as the one built by the Holkars of Indore just across the lane from Jaisingh Ghera. "Maharaja Holkar and Maharaja Jaisingh were friends, so they built their places just next to one another".

As Shrivatsa developed this roster, I was struck by how detailed it was—his attention to such specific singer-saints and specific locales. For him Vrindavan is strewn with memory, its very fabric is memory, and so much of that memory is built. If you too knew what he knows, how could you not care about the present moment? He was still going: "Then came the nobles of Bengal in the nineteenth century, especially Raja Nandakumar Basu, and they rebuilt all the structures that had been demolished in the Aurangzeb period. They rebuilt Govindadev and Madan Mohan and Gopinath and Radhavallabh and all". Then came the Marwaris—Rajasthani merchants who had fanned out from their Shekhavati homeland in the course of the nineteenth century and settled in the far corners of India, especially Kolkata. He continued: "By now it was after Independence. Everybody is rebuilding, rebuilding, rebuilding Vrindavan. And in that new moment, who joins? ISKCON. The moment Prabhupad built that temple people started accusing Prabhupad: 'Why in the world have you built that temple so far away? Who will visit it? It was such a distant place.' (His voice rose in emphasis, as if to join this chorus of dissent.) But that was the seed of another new Vrindavan. These are all seeds of new and different Vrindavans. People were coming through all the ages. So that was the process—Vrindavan rejuvenates and recreates itself continuously".

And then, a final comment: "What I see behind all this is that not just Chaitanya but all these saints were building Vrindavan as a kind of human sanctuary. A different kind of place—a place with a different bhāv (sensibility), a place of ras sādhanā (disciplined attention to the emotions), a place where different kinds of aesthetic explosions could take place. These were intended to provide an alternative for a huge segment of humanity that was excluded from political power and had no access to economic well-being, including the suffering part of humanity that is 50% of the whole, called womanhood. These temples and ashrams and all became a sanctuary for all those women".

At the end of this long rumination Shrivatsa concluded by looking back over the whole and saying, "Probably the new Vrindavan that is coming up now also does this job in some way too". But he confessed he couldn't quite see how. "It is all Krishna's lila—a very complex lila".[13]

As I thought about the sequence of thoughts in which Shrivatsa expressed all this, it seemed to me that two apple-carts had been overturned. First, what we have all along been calling "the new Vrindavan" was resituated so that it took its place among many new Vrindavans, going right back to the moment of initial agency that rests with Krishna himself. That was a straightforward part of Shrivatsa's message. But second, there seemed to be an inner dynamic of which he himself was perhaps not fully aware. What began as a clear indictment of this most recent "new Vrindavan"—a place truly off the map of the historical landscape of new Vrindavans that he painted by virtue of its caring so little for its own past—had turned in the end to something else. There is no taking away Shrivatsa's disgust for the real estate explosion that infests Raman Reti these days and is fast absorbing the entire Braj country farther out to the west—precious retreats like Radhakund and Barsana and Mount Govardhan. Yet he confesses that he does not understand how even this excrescence must somehow be part of Krishna's lila.

Whatever the ultimate name of that lila game may be, Shrivatsa himself has a role to play. One of the things he does in the traditional gosvami fashion that his Chaitanyite community shares with the Vallabhites is to conduct tours called ban yatras (i.e., van yātrās—wilderness trips) in which devotees and interested others have a chance to make contact with the sites that have made Vrindavan and the surrounding Braj countryside sacred—places touched by the presence of some saint or another, or by Radha and Krishna themselves. We recall from Chapter 4 that many of these were identified by Narayan Bhatt in the sixteenth century, and Chaitanya is said to have put his finger on a number of others. Parallel accounts, though different, are offered in the Vallabh Sampraday. As usual, however, Shrivatsa has introduced an innovation in this practice. It is not just that he has restructured the ban yatra so that participants, some of whom are quite old, return to stay in Jaisingh Ghera's guestrooms each evening before heading out before dawn the following day to visit another set of sites. Nor is it just that these yatris travel in a fleet of SUVs, which takes away some of the doubtless character-building misery that David Haberman so memorably depicts in his book *Journey through the Twelve Forests*. This too is an aspect of "the new Vrindavan", you could say: physical discomfort is no longer understood to be the necessary price of insight. Indeed, one might observe that because these travelers are rested and free from pain they are far better able to attend to the witty, literarily and historically informed expositions that Shrivatsa offers at every stop along the way.

If a journey like this starts in Vrindavan, then it will be expected to conclude there as well, completing the circle that is an important part of the symbolism of the journey as a whole. This is a parikrama that encompasses not just Vrindavan but the whole Braj countryside—and by that token it venerates the territory it circumambulates. Shrivatsa's ban yātrā does that like all the others, but he concludes it at a specific place in Vrindavan, a place that is the culminating halt for no other such pilgrimage. This place is a little hillock that gently rises from the Yamuna not far from where many tourist buses park, disgorging their own yatris. A hulking temple is built on top of that hillock. Yes, it is the massive temple of Govindadev.

In some ways it is a discouraging sight. For one thing, it is under the protection of the Archaeological Survey of India and only functions in a minor way as a place of worship. Few locals go there and, as Shrivatsa points out, it has become a veritable picnic ground for the monkeys in town: they swing around the high balconies and sometimes make their way among the tourists on the ground floor. There is something eerie and threatening about it all. Not only that, Shrivatsa emphasizes, stones from the first temple of Govindadev—the one where Rupa Gosvami held sway in the middle of the sixteenth century, later demolished so that Mansingh's second Govindadev temple could be built on the site—have been allowed to be cannibalized and used as the foundation for another building. These stones now lie

Figure 6.4.   Shrivatsa speaking about the history of the Govindadev temple on the final day of his ban yātrā, November 10, 2016.

beneath the concrete building that houses the Radhagovind Public School, and the story of how they got there contributes to the general sense of disorder. Then too, the second Govindadev temple lacks its spire: How inspiring can such a place be?

Yet what Shrivatsa has to say when he leads his followers to this once central but now rather neglected place makes it something inspiring indeed (Fig. 6.4). Step by step he dismantles the usual account of how the temple's spire was removed, the one that is recounted by the local pandas. Disarmingly, Shrivatsa begins by seeming to cast his lot precisely with this received history. All the evidence is not all in, he concedes, but nonetheless it does seem clear to him that it was indeed the Mughal emperor Aurangzeb (r. 1658–1707) who was responsible for lopping off the temple's great spire. So far so good: he is playing with the home team. Aurangzeb is the Muslim Hindus love to hate. But here's the catch. According to Shrivatsa, Aurangzeb did what he did not out of religious bigotry, not out of any anti-Hindu sentiment that might have followed from the fact of his being a staunch Muslim, but for strictly political reasons. In the course of the late seventeenth century the Kachvaha kings of Amer and later Jaipur, successors to Raja Mansingh, sided with and hid from imperial view the Maharashtrian rebel Shivaji, who had escaped from Aurangzeb's control. With the help of Rajput sympathizers such as these, Shivaji managed to elude the emperor by taking refuge in three places—Banaras, Mathura, and Vrindavan. In an effort to make clear to such Rajputs that he was not going to stand by while the empire was dismembered by Shivaji, Aurangzeb destroyed the great temples for which each of these sacred cities was celebrated: the Vishvanath temple in Kashi, the Keshavdev temple in Mathura, and Govindadev here in Vrindavan.

But the last of these, actually, he partially spared. A substantial segment of the temple—the portion (aside from the erstwhile sanctum) that lay at the base of the shikhara—still remains, and Shrivatsa faces it as he gives his talk. The reason for this act of calculated mercy, he says, is that Aurangzeb wanted to continue to benefit from the services of the Kachvaha Rajputs, who had been so crucial to Mughal success since the time of his grandfather Akbar. Indeed, as we have learned, this temple was constructed by the greatest of Kachvaha generals working in the service of Akbar, Raja Mansingh. So there was a mixed message.

Shrivatsa goes on to remind his hearers that later, when Aurangzeb faced the last and most difficult battle of his rule, far to the south in the Deccan, he suspended that crucial confrontation with the Marathas and took nine months off to go to Chitrakut, where another threatened ruler, Ram, had bivouacked in the course of his own exile. There Aurangzeb constructed a temple for Ram, providing both the land and the funds. What kind of rabid Muslim fanatic would do that? If he was not personally a worshipper of Ram, he was at least his patron and someone who venerated Ram's role as righteous warrior in a long battle that took him far to the south. As Shrivatsa spins out this revisionist history, he rehabilitates the most hated of Mughal emperors with two bold strokes. He re-envisions his famous actions against three great Hindu temples as political, not religious, and he shows how Aurangzeb had a special respect for Ram.[14]

There are several other aspects to the history lesson that Shrivatsa gives his devotees as they sit in the shade and gaze at the Govindadev temple. Let's go back to beginning, he says: Why did Mansingh build it in the first place? As an act of defiance of Muslim rule on the part of a great Hindu king, as the pandas say? Hardly. The reason Mansingh built this edifice was that he was fulfilling a vow he had made at this very site in the presence of his Chaitanyite guru Raghunath Bhatt, who had a close relationship to the first iteration of the Govindadev temple. Mansingh had come here to ask Raghunath Bhatt to bless him in a battle that was looming on the western front of the Mughal Empire. If he were granted success in his Gujarat campaign on behalf of Akbar, he promised, he would return to build a great temple as an act of thanksgiving. Raghunath Bhatt did indeed bless Mansingh's efforts—"Let victory be yours"—and after the crucial battle was won, Mansingh returned to build the temple. In fact, when he returned from the battlefield at Haldighati in far-off Mewar, he came directly to this place rather than reporting first to Akbar, who was at that point in Delhi. These were the first terms of his battle engagement, it seems. And there is one crucial detail—hardly a detail—that people often forget: the king he vanquished in that battle was Rana Pratap, a "fellow" Hindu.

Thus on both sides—Aurangzeb's and Mansingh's—the "Panda Purana" is wrong. This temple is not about any kind of irreconcilable conflict between Hindus and Muslims, it is about a delicate form of dialogue between religion and politics and between Hindus and Muslims. Indeed, Shrivatsa goes on to say, the entire history of Vrindavan, properly understood, is about just this—samvād, that is, dialogue.[15] In a previous chapter we saw the irony of claiming the Chandrodaya Mandir to be the icon of an entirely new Vrindavan. Now we see that the very structure that makes this so—the sixteenth-century "skyscraper temple" before which Shrivatsa and his devotees stood—also has to be reinterpreted. Only a disinterested, diligent study of history can make that happen. If the Chandrodaya temple is truly to belong to this history, its promoters will have to abandon any rhetoric about looking down on the Taj Mahal. Rather, and rather unfortunately, what the Chandrodaya Mandir looks down on is Vrindavan itself.

That is Shrivatsa's true objection to this massive new structure. It is really not part of Vrindavan, but rather designed to be a world unto itself. Because its builders envision a structure in which all of

Vrindavan is encompassed on-site—the confrontations with the demons, the twelve forests of Braj that give plot structure to the ban yatra, the Yamuna itself, and even heavenly Golok Vrindavan—the Chandrodaya Mandir renders the old Vrindavan irrelevant. It fails to make a real connection to the history it claims. Rather, it tries to swallow it. Here, as Shrivatsa puts it, "heritage Vrindavan has become irrelevant for the new Vrindavan".[16] Thereby it implicitly excludes itself from what that conference in 1994 had called "the continuous creation of Braj". It obscures the fact that the VCM too is part of the centuries-long saga of building a new Vrindavan, a saga that goes back to the advent of Krishna himself and that took a powerful turn in the sixteenth and seventeenth centuries. Some aspects of that turn have been plain for a long time, but it all came much clearer thanks to a revolutionary development in the history of scholarship. Again Shrivatsa was on the scene.

Back in the 1970s the great Bengali historian Tarapada Mukherjee was teaching on the faculty of the School of Oriental and African Studies in London. At that point he learned, thanks to his colleague Ramdas Gupta, that the library of Jiva Gosvami had been transferred out of private hands and had become a part of the collection Gupta was in the process of assembling at the Vrindavan Research Institute, which he founded in 1968. Mukherjee came to Vrindavan and became deeply involved as a cataloguer for Bengali manuscripts in the institute. Working mainly from London, he developed an intimate knowledge of some of the most important documents in the collection from a historical, as against theological, point of view. We have already seen what havoc could be wrought on received wisdom by the theological side of Jiva's corpus in the controversy that developed between ISKCON and Satyanarayan Das in the early 1990s. History was about to repeat itself, so speak, and in a more strictly historical domain.

What Mukherjee discovered was a whole set of land deeds that had come into the hands of Jiva when he was general custodian for the growing Chaitanyite archive. Jiva later willed this library to his successor, and eventually these documents found their way to the Vrindavan Research Institute. Most of them involved local transactions, but on some occasions the hand of the Mughal state could also be felt. The result was to make it clear just how closely the gosvamis of Vrindavan were working with a state that was clearly Muslim. Mukherjee saw immediately that he was looking at history in the making—that is, a revision of history in the making—and that this was going to happen in a big way. He resolved to contact the undisputed doyen of Mughal historians, Irfan Habib, a friend and colleague, and he chose Shrivatsa to be his messenger. Shrivatsa traveled to London to receive from Mukherjee a packet of photocopies of these manuscripts. These he carefully shepherded to Delhi, and upon landing he took them to Habib—straight from the airport, no stops.

Irfan Habib, still active in his late eighties today, was then and is now the most Marxist of Marxist historians. The special focus of his work in Mughal history had been with peasants, who are, from a Marxist point of view, as the proletariat the true and proper subjects of history. But the records revealing their lives, with all their hardships, were kept by others well up the administrative food-chain. Irfan Habib knew this whole landscape better than anyone else in the world, and had been reading Persian documents in great detail for years. At the time Shrivatsa was commissioned to make contact with him, his work was very celebrated. Though based at Aligarh Muslim University, where he had attracted and groomed an impressive band of young Marxist historians, he had also been made the chairman of the Indian Council of Historical Research, with offices in Delhi. It was there that Shrivatsa went with his special parcel from London.

Shrivatsa remembers the moment with great relish and not a little wonder. When he made his way into Habib's office he found him sitting behind a very large desk, befitting his stature. Shrivatsa explained his mission and placed his parcel before Habib on the desk. With two elegant fingers, Habib pushed it right back in Shrivatsa's direction. "Mr. Goswami, religion is not a part of history", he explained. From a Marxist point of view, it wasn't. Shrivatsa dutifully took the packet back, restoring it to its place in the simple cloth shoulder bag in which he had brought it. He had effectively been dismissed and was getting ready to go, but then something came over him. "I thought I had been sent to speak with a historian", he said. Habib gestured that he should put the packet back on the desk. At that point Shrivatsa made his way out. The next morning, however, he received a telephone call from Professor Habib. "I have not slept one minute since I opened that package", he said.

His reflections on what he read, together with those of Professor Mukherjee, became the subject of Irfan Habib's presidential address before the annual meeting of the Indian History Congress in Goa. Two subsequent articles co-authored with Mukherjee filled out the story. Sadly, Mukherjee died as a victim of cancer before he could see the full outworking of the drama he had unleashed. The Jiva Gosvami papers revealed, for example, that in 1598 Akbar had sent his principal advisor, Abu'l Fazl, to recruit four leading Chaitanyite gosvamis to consult on the status of temples in the entire Braj area. Akbar recognized them and the temples they represented as the arbiters of the whole group, and he conferred on Vrindavan the status of an independent administrative entity that would be a tax-free zone. Effectively, the records showed, the emperor himself became fully the patron of Vrindavan, and there were many other state-related interactions at lower levels.

This historiographical breakthrough—this record of a remarkable interaction—has powered much of Shrivatsa's thinking ever since. It makes plain sense of what was going on with the Govindadev temple in the time of Akbar and Mansingh, showing it to be an implicit Hindu-Muslim "dialogue in stone", as Shrivatsa has dubbed it. And we know his views about what happened in the era of Aurangzeb— tensions and battles, for sure, but the half-broken, half-preserved fate of the great temple itself shows that the concordat was never entirely abandoned. There was more to come even after that—more in the way of new Vrindavans. Just after the death of Aurangzeb in 1707, a new period of instability ensued, and one of Shrivatsa's own personal patrons, Jaisingh II, whose name we have often heard, was already on the Kachvaha throne as a boy. As well as being a gifted strategist and administrator, he developed into a deeply religious man and a true Vaishnava, and as he matured he both validated the Mughal– Kachvaha concordat and in some ways moved beyond it. The kingdom he envisioned for himself, of which the new city of Jaipur was to be the capital, was designed in such a way as to be thoroughly Hindu in its governance—a pan-sectarian governance he saw as being Vedic. But at the same time the new capital city was to have ample quarters reserved for members of other faith communities, especially Jains and Muslims.[17] To such a Jaipur Shrivatsa has naturally been attracted over the years, and once again his father paved the way.

Back in 1972 Purushottam Goswami had a dream in which Govindadev appeared and addressed him. Govindadev, we recall, had to be spirited out of Vrindavan in 1669 so as to be spared the destruction that attended the Jat rebellion against the Mughals in that period—another aspect of the saga of the Maratha ruler Shivaji. It was especially the Kachvaha Raja Ramsingh who provided Govindadev with safe passage from Vrindavan at that point, and his grandson Jaisingh II later built a temple for him halfway between his palace at Amer and the city he was about to construct on the plains below—Jaipur. This he followed with a new temple for Govindadev—a new Vrindavan, in its way. It lay just opposite the new palace he was constructing for himself, and the deity has resided there ever since. It was a chapel royal, but at the same time open to the citizenry at large.

Over the years, unfortunately, this temple had been allowed to decline. Some twenty people, a pittance, would receive the darshan of Govindadev and his companion Radha in the course of a typical day. Therefore Govindadev called out to Purushottam Goswami in a dream to help set things right—or so Purushottam perceived it. Upon waking he vowed to perform the seven-day Bhagavat Katha each year at Jaipur for the deity's enjoyment, and he became deeply involved in efforts to restore the temple to its former glory, and not only it but the temple of Vinodilal, which sits just opposite the walled palace grounds near one of the city's major intersections. Shrivatsa's brother Venugopal, as we have heard, was to assume responsibility for the annual Bhagavat Saptah at the temple of Govindadev. But there was much else to do, and Shrivatsa became deeply involved, so much so that after 1999 he too would give regular Bhagavat Saptahs in Jaipur, often in the temple of Vinodilal.

Of course, he also travels elsewhere. Recently he inaugurated an annual journey that takes devotees to the south. They started in Tamil Nadu in January 2016, proceeded to Karnataka a year later, and plan to continue to Maharashtra and Gujarat before bringing the results of their learning and experience back to Vrindavan. Thus they are recapitulating the route that a hypostasized version of Bhakti says she herself took in the Bhagavata Mahatmya, a text in praise of the Bhagavata Purana that is typically regarded as a prelude to the main text. Shrivatsa also travels to many places—Pilibhit in UP, for example—to give the seven-day explorations of the Bhagavata for which he has become well known, and a series of talks he gave on the Bhagavad Gita in Kolkata in June 2014 proved so successful that he has been returning monthly to work slowly through the text with a group of some sixty people ever since. He's a busy man.

He's also been busy back in Vrindavan, and this is an invitation to loop into a more recent phase of the town's past. Once again we find ourselves in the messy self-serving domain called politics, but this time it is not the politics of the sixteenth or seventeenth century, but the twentieth. In this chapter of Vrindavan's history there was a real villain, Shrivatsa feels, not just the play of relative forces, and her name is Indira Gandhi. At two stages in her career as Prime Minister, he contends, Mrs. Gandhi had a significant effect on Vrindavan. The first is the less heinous of the two. In an effort to shore up her authority in the initial years of her first term (1966–77), she made it a practice to bus in huge numbers of rural people to cheer for her at public rallies in Delhi—either that or she brought them in by train. The chance to see Delhi was one reason they were willing to come, but an even more important factor was that they were promised they could visit Vrindavan while coming or going. This regular flood of visitors was the first major assault on the seasonal rhythms that had character-ized Vrindavan's role as host to pilgrims from outside of Braj well into Shrivatsa's early adulthood. Looking back, with Vrindavan being connected so vividly to Delhi, it seems this onslaught of a new kind of visitor marked the beginning of the year-round weekend culture that now dominates the town. These were huge numbers of people, and they might come at any time.

The second aspect of Indira Gandhi's connection to Vrindavan is similarly indirect, but more baleful. It has to do with the strenuous support she gave to the building of an oil refinery on the western outskirts of Mathura, not far down NH-2 from the "new" side of Vrindavan. The siting of such a massive—and massively polluting—facility in Mathura seems to Shrivatsa senseless. To feed the new refinery crude oil would have to be carried to Mathura by pipe all the way from Bombay High on the country's west coast, or from other locations even farther offshore. The motive cannot have been economic. It was purely political. Mrs. Gandhi was in search of some-thing big, splashy, and seemingly in the cause of development that would earn her popularity in a populous state whose votes she very much needed—UP. Apparently she succeeded.

It was almost a decade before the refinery itself began to be built—the early 1980s—but when that happened the effects were not just polluting in the physical sense but also, even more crucially, in the cultural and moral domain. Massive numbers of Russian construction workers were brought in to do the job, and with them came plenty of liquor. A major trade in prostitution grew up along the national highway. All of this was poison to Vrindavan, particularly its western gateway along the Chatikara Road. Over time, Shrivatsa feels, this refinery-building culture contributed importantly to the boozy aspects one sometimes finds nowadays in the new Vrindavan. Today at a Vrindavan wedding, he says, a Maruti car often runs parallel to the groom's barāt procession as it makes its way to the wedding venue. It's nothing but a moving bar, and it is apt to be present even when the groom or bride comes from a respectable gosvāmī family. Seeing the decline of public morals after the refinery began to be built, Shrivatsa joined with several other concerned citizens to appeal to Mrs. Gandhi to locate the project elsewhere. They made the trip to Delhi to deliver this message in person. Nothing happened. Oh well, sighed Shrivatsa, this was just another "part of the system called time".[18] But this time it was harder to see it as an expression of Krishna's lila.

One might be tempted to evaluate Shrivatsa's bitter resentment of Indira Gandhi by noting that his family has been wary of the Congress Party and sympathetic toward its BJP opponents for many years. This is also true for Vrindavan as a whole. It has been a BJP stronghold since the party's birth in 1980—and before that its residents tended to support its antecedent, the Bharatiya Jan Sangh Party. But before accusing Shrivatsa of partisanship one must remember that he is at least as critical of the failure of nerve and general corruption that have characterized the local government of Vrindavan—often enough BJP—since his father-in-law Magan Sharma stepped down. Local politicians have time and again stood in the way of any real progress in restoring the town to the administrative health it enjoyed when Magan Sharma was mayor. Shrivatsa remembers those days vividly. When he came back after his first long stay in Banaras as a student at BHU, he recalls, "the lanes in Vrindavan seemed smaller than they had been before

I went away". He had left his youth behind. But more than that, he simultaneously developed a sense of pride in the town for all the ways it seemed to contrast to Banaras. Vrindavan had good government, so the streets were clean, the temples were respected and protected, and people knew they could take their problems to the local authorities.

All that has long since changed. Way back in 1980, sensing the dangers that were sure to assault Vrindavan and seeing that the municipality had no plans for meeting this threat, Shrivatsa worked with the locally legendary environmental activist Seva Sharan, one of the town's sadhus, to frame a document that would serve as a charter for a better Vrindavan—a sewage disposal system, a green zone, the works. In their efforts, he and Seva Sharan were joined by R.C. Sharma, at that time the director of the Mathura Museum, with its fine collection of antiquities. They planned a public meeting in the vegetable market after its morning business hours, right in the center of town. They worked hard on their speeches, hoping to persuade all sorts of townspeople to join the cause. They canvassed all the local political leaders to make sure they would lend their support. And the result? Three people came—themselves. They delivered their speeches to each other. No one else was willing to rock the boat of corruption, or at least no one else was willing to be seen wanting to do so.

Thus by no means can the major share of blame for the decline of Vrindavan be hung around the neck of Indira Gandhi. Things were much more deeply rooted and various. Marwaris were forced out of Kolkata by the rise of a new kind of politics; in consequence some of them sought refuge in Vrindavan. Pilgrimage by bus blossomed in the 1980s, bringing another, more major spike in visitors, and the blocking of pilgrimage to the Himalayas in the 1990s and early 2000s owing to natural disasters exacerbated the trend. Thus there have been several agents of rapid change. But what tops the list is probably the moment in 1983 when a small, inexpensive Indian car named Maruti was first produced by the Suzuki Corporation. This, followed by the liberalization and consequent dramatic growth of the economy in the early 1990s, had a drastic effect. And along with this, ever so steadily, there was a doubling of the general population. People rarely talk of that as a major cause for Vrindavan's woes, not even Shrivatsa, but clearly it has been at least as fundamental as any. The effects of all this have so far been impossible to reverse. They're rolled into the steamroller called development.

What is Shrivatsa doing about all this? All one can say—and we've seen the evidence—is that he's trying to do something all the time, whether as an environmental activist, as a religious and cultural performer, or simply as someone who says his prayers. He laments that so few people realize that the heritage part of old Vrindavan is the life-giving Kamadhenu—the wishing cow—on which the town has always depended for its health. If that goes, so does it. Who's going to care about heritage parks if the heritage itself is gone?

An End, a New Beginning

The morning of February 21, 2017, was the beginning of a sober day. Shrivatsa went into his father's room on the ground floor of the big house where their extended family lives, just as he always did, and found that Purushottam had died. His long-revered eyes were still open, his body was still warm, and the two boys who cared for him day and night were still sleeping at his side, undisturbed by his evidently silent passing. At first Shrivatsa wondered whether he might still be alive. Purushottam had often been able to display remarkable composure: was this an expression of that same capacity? But indeed, he was gone. He had departed for the nitya lila, the eternal and ever-present lila that is Krishna's own, forever.

The senior Maharajji (Shrivatsa began to share the title many years ago) was 94. His remarkable stamina had been visible to the end (Fig. 6.5). It had been discovered about a week before he died that he had a deep abscess in one of his ankles. Somehow it had escaped the attention of the boys who bathed him and generally looked after his well-being, but it was a serious thing. Purushottam had evidently not felt it because for some years he had lost sensation below his waist; he was confined to a wheelchair.

"Confined", so they say. Maharajji's response to this new reality had been to adopt the practice of performing one or even two circumambulations of Mount Govardhan every day—by car, of course. His helpers would prepare him for the trip, tip his wheelchair back, and roll him down the ramp that had been built outside the front door of the house. Rather at top speed, I always thought, especially since

Figure 6.5. Purushottam Goswami in his nineties, at his family's Divali celebrations, October 30, 2016. His great-granddaughter Vishnupriya is in the foreground; Shrivatsa, in profile, is to the right.

there was a right-angle turn halfway down the ramp. But it didn't phase Purushottam; nothing ever had. It took a little while to load him into the little white car and perhaps lay a blanket across his lap for warmth. Those were often moments that would catch me walking in or out of the Ghera. It was a good time to stop and bow at his feet, as I had done for many years. He paid it a bit less mind in the last years of his life, but he always acknowledged me, even if silently. What more could I expect? He was on his way to Govardhan. Anil Ambani, the younger of the two fabulously wealthy brothers who had founded Reliance Industries, the communications and insurance giant, had recently made it a practice to fly in from Mumbai to Govardhan in his helicopter and jog through his circumambulation before getting back in the plane. This was Maharajji's way of doing the same—just as heroic and far more regular.

That last week, though, he had to go to the doctors in Mathura. Specialists were coming into the clinic from Delhi, so the timing was good. Aside from the wound everything seemed fine. His blood pressure was 120/70, as ever, which always stopped the doctors cold. Had they gotten it right? Sometimes they would go get another measuring device to make sure. Yes, he still had the vital signs of a young man, and he was proud of it. There were blood tests for biopsies, and it was a wearying visit, or so one would have thought. The wound had to be unbandaged, cleaned, and rebandaged; it took some time. When everyone was back home they urged Maharajji to get some rest. "Rest?" he asked. He was ready to go out to Mount Govardhan—and that is exactly what he did. At another point he was heard to claim that he was 19, not 90. But it can't have been easy when the doctors prescribed blood-thinners so that the circulation to his legs would increase and the wound could heal. That would have brought a higher level of pain. On one occasion, very uncharacteristically, I heard him shout.

On the day he died, a Tuesday, I happened to be in Delhi. Shrivatsa sent a text message: "Maharajji left for Nityalila this morning. Cremation Wednesday a.m". I prepared to head back to Vrindavan later in the afternoon, asking whether that would be appropriate. "No dear", he responded. "You carry on. U had his blessings. Radhe! Radhe!" It was true, I had always felt I did have his blessings. Somewhere back in the 1980s he surprised everyone (to put it mildly) by saying he thought I was going to be President of the United States. We all laughed, of course, but a special bond had existed between us ever since. I guess you could say it was a most unusual form of initiation. The other thing Maharajji said to me that I will never forget was conveyed, uncharacteristically, in English. I had said something regretfully and guiltily about not showing up for darshan often enough in Radharamanji's temple. Purushottam brushed it aside, quoting a phase he must have heard long ago, perhaps in school: "Work is worship". I was deeply grateful for this absolution, but it was also,

I realized, a charge. Work *should* be worship. One ought to make it so. On the day of his death I defied his sentiments, as implicitly conveyed by his son, and cancelled the lecture I was supposed to give in Delhi so that I could return to Vrindavan.

The next morning at nine the ceremonies did indeed start, but the mood was neither mournful in the way you might expect if you came from my Christian background nor anything like the death-defying shout of "rām nām satya hai" (The name of Ram is truth) that I had heard so often when I lived in Banaras many years ago. No, as these elegant Bengali musicians with their drums and hand-cymbals and dancing steps made plain, this was a different way of chanting the name of Ram—along with that of Krishna. It was the way Chaitanya had taught. It was the mahamantra that they sang—"Hare Krishna Hare Krishna Krishna Krishna Hare Hare"—just as daily and eternal (nitya) as the abode to which Purushottam had departed. The leader of this troupe of twelve or fifteen was the same man who sang the mahamantra daily in the Sansthan. A few women were present for this moment of departure, but it was mostly a men's affair: the women of the family watched from the door.

Once Shrivatsa and his brother and sons and the other family males had carried Purushottam's body out of the house and bound it to the pallet, and once the procession made its way out into the streets, the mahamantra resolved into a different chant. The name of Radharaman was intoned, followed by that of Gopal Bhatt, the fount of the Radharaman lineage of gosvamis, and then it was śrī vrindāvan nitya vihār, śrī vrindāvan nitya vihār, śrī vrindāvan nitya vihār" over and over again: "Blessed Vrindavan, eternal home". That last word, vihār, is hard to translate. Buddhists and Jains chose this term to designate the structures that served as places for monks to gather, since these ascetics were really wanderers, even if they lived together for a long period of time. Wandering is another basic meaning of vihār. But it also means pleasure, recreation, play, and we recall that the name of the town's most popular deity is Bihariji, built on the same word.[19] And let's not forget that Buddhist meaning, resting place. The chant that the mourners projected through the lanes of Vrindavan affirmed that Vrindavan is all of that, and that the bodyless Purushottam Goswami would never abandon Vrindavan. It would always be with him, and he with it: nitya vihār.

The musicians led the procession, then Purushottam and his bearers, then came the rest of us, tossing forward toward the pallet the rose petals we had been given from big plastic bags. One of the young men who had been Purushottam's helpers appeared from out of the crowd and jogged along beside me for a while, but my special friend was the art curator Navneet Raman, who had driven through the night from Banaras. With his curly hair and easy, smiling manner, he had made me feel at home in an everyday way as we waited for people to emerge from the house so that the funeral procession could begin. We spoke of our dear mutual friend Robyn Beeche, the London fashion photographer who later became an initiate of Maharajji's and Jaisingh Ghera's principal documentarian. We had lost her to cancer the previous year, and Navneet followed her to Australia to be with her to the end. He also quietly recalled his own first encounter with Purushottam. It was in the temple of Radharaman and Purushottam was standing next to Navneet as the music of the mahamantra kirtan began. He turned to him, looked down at his feet and said, "Dance!" That is, without having to say it all, "You're young and able-bodied: dance!"

Well into his final last decades, Purushottam never seemed too old. Figuratively speaking, as the procession moved along, we all danced our way behind him, solemnly and joyfully at the same time. Construction workers stopped to look, women came out of their houses, shopkeepers pressed their hands into the gesture of respect, and one sadhu turned to another and asked, "Who is it?" The answer was quickly offered. This was a great man on his last sankirtan yatra, his last musical journey through the streets—with the words of Chaitanya in his ears and his eyes on Krishna as the goal. Dance!

Shrivatsa had many duties to perform. As one of the chief pall-bearers, he always walked at the front, shoeless as they all were. We stopped at the temple of Gokulanand, where the memorial stones of so many important Gaudiyas from centuries past are found. There one could find a dark-barked tamāl tree planted in Robyn's name, too, and another, as we know, for T.N. Madan's wife Uma. Then we stopped at the place called Gyan Gudari or Yamuna Pulin, which marks the spot the Yamuna reaches when its floodwaters are at their highest. There the bier was lowered to the ground and Shrivatsa followed the family priest in mantras that accompanied a ritual act in which two little balls of barley flour, signifying the first seed of creation, which had been placed in Maharajji's palms, were replaced by two others in preparation for the fact that the corpse would shift its position. Initially Purushottam had been carried head first, so that he would be looking in the auspicious northward direction back toward the life from which he had come. Now his feet would go first as the procession made its way further southward; he would be facing the land of the dead, the directional quadrant ruled by Death himself, Yama. Shrivatsa would walk behind now—symbolically first among those still living.

It was a solemn moment, and those of us who accompanied the bier scooped up a little of the dust from the lane and sprinkled it on Purushottam's body. Then it was off through the long set of lanes that led further southward, out of town, and onto the open plane of the cremation ghat. A few of the fragrant deep-red roses were still being thrown onto the corpse, swathed in bright yellow, but most of the flowers were now gone. We passed through a set of arches meant to separate the town from the ghat—life protected from death. They projected a gentle sense of grandeur, as if we were about to enter a Greek amphitheater. Up ahead, across the vast expanse of sandy soil, was the Yamuna. It was completing the great U that it makes as it folds the town into the crook of its embrace. And then, in the distance, it disappears in the direction of Mathura—but not just Mathura: Agra, Allahabad, Banaras, Patna, so much of Bengal, and then at last the sea.

There, on the riverbank, the body was set down. A bright orange cloth had been stretched over four poles nearby to serve as its cover, but first it was laid on the sand so that we could pay our respects. Again we bent down to gather a little dust between our fingers, like seasoning—pinches of salt. Dust to dust: what religious tradition does not know this to be true, even those who burn their bodies rather than burying them? A few steps beyond the canopy beneath which Purushottam was then laid, the men began to prepare his fire—cowdung for fuel and wood of different kinds, including whole bushes of the sacred tulsi plant that had been allowed to dry beforehand. Here there were specialists in charge—the low-caste officiants of the ghats. I wondered who had known how to contact them and what had been said: substantial preparations had been made. The pyre would be large, the fire hot. One of their number wielded a big stick broom that kept the area around the bier immaculate. Farther away there were declivities that seemed to hold the remains of earlier funerals—cans empty of their ghee, pieces of wood, and the earthen pots that symbolize our hollow bodily frames.

I had never come to the cremation ghat before. You don't unless there is a reason. Across the river I could see other processions arriving, much more modest, and another body had just been burned a little distance away. It is all so flat, so inevitably flat out there on the Yamuna's floodplain. A dog trots around, skinny, her nipples flapping back and forth, hoping to get at a bit of the ghee that's used to make the blaze burn hot. A large tent has been raised some distance away so that mourners can sit under it on plastic chairs.

As the chief mourner, Shrivatsa creates his own arena. The people who surround him are all men. His older son Abhinav is there with a friend—he so often has a friend with him. Suvarna, though, the younger son, has positioned himself at Purushottam's head; he sits attentively under the flap of the informal canopy that has been stretched overhead. It is time for Shrivatsa to be shaved. But for the tuft that Brahmin men are expected to wear, his head will be totally bare. The barber, Manoj Thakur, has a shop just opposite what used to be the stand where horses were kept near Vrindavan's main bazaar. The horses and their carts are gone, but the shop remains, and this sinewy young man with a beautiful head of hair continues the family business. He and his forebears have been barbers to the men of Jaisingh Ghera for a long time. I remember Manoj's observing, when I last went in for a haircut myself, that when he cuts Shrivatsa's hair, his patron is on his cell phone the whole time. No wonder, I thought. He has a remarkable circle of devotees and many other connections; 7000 names are stored in the phone's address book. If that list were lost, his world would collapse—and plenty of other people's too—so he makes frequent back-ups. But when he is in Manoj's hands, he is not really on the phone: a cascade of cuttings from above would make conversations difficult. No, he's just monitoring emails and the news, and using the phone as a camera to keep track of Manoj's progress.

None of that is happening this time. There on the banks of the Yamuna Shrivatsa has no phone, so he and his barber just talk a little as Manoj goes about his work. In a way, they seem to be having a good time, as old friends do, something so usual in the midst of something so extraordinary. Manoj is an old friend to the ghats, too—he would have to be. This occasion and others like it always require his presence. Later on, when the pyre has been lit and the body has been consumed by the fire, he will still be there with Shrivatsa, helping to douse the fire by placing on top of it a small pile of wet sand. He is energetic in all he does.

Once shorn, Shrivatsa's next step is to bathe. The pollution of the cut hair must all be removed, and any other pollution that may be present. He must be, as it were, newborn. This requires the water of the Yamuna, or would have done in earlier, purer times. Shrivatsa is a fine swimmer, but he is not going to bathe in that river. Rather, Abhinav's friend, a strapping guy, brings in a huge bottle of water the size of a cylinder of natural gas, the kind you turn upside down when the office water-cooler has run dry. I can see him breathing hard with the effort—who knows how far he has had to carry it? Then, when the time comes, he peels away the seal from the top and goes down to the edge of the river to get a little Yamuna water to purify the rest—that is, in the same moment, to pollute it. But ritually speaking, it is to purify: that little bit of Yamuna water permeates the rest.

Shrivatsa strips to his underwear and bathes. Then he begins to gather around himself the endless lengths of white cloth that will comprise his dhoti (Fig. 6.6). I wonder how long it has been since he has done this in public. Usually this act of personal wrapping has long been performed before he appears: he sweeps into a room with the grace that only such a garment can provide. Now, though, he is backstage—backstage in front of everyone. Are we all imagining, the men among us, what it is to be so alone in this role? Or remembering, perhaps? And we are thinking about what it is to be in Purushottam's role, too. I think what a privilege it would have been to be able to perform this role for my own father, as the eldest son—or at least I think it would have been.

As the crowd of men shuffles around, Shrivasta seats himself before a small fire that has been prepared on the sand, a Vedic fire. He makes offerings of ghee and pieces of sandalwood chanting "svāhā svāhā" as the affectionate family priest says the requisite words. Meanwhile his brother Venugopal pours ghee on the pyre itself. Then

Figure 6.6.   Shrivatsa wrapping his dhotī around his waist after bathing. Background: Manoj Thakur. Funeral ceremonies for Purushottam Goswami, February 22, 2017.

Shrivatsa makes his way to the pyre. The canopy is removed from above Purushottam's body. Suvarna rises to participate in the action of lifting the body onto the pyre. Shrivatsa is given a long piece of wood that has been lit at one end. He circumambulates his father one last time and lights the fire, asking his younger brother join him, though it is not ritually prescribed to do so. The fire leaps up. We all have to retreat before the sudden heat (Fig. 6.7). It will take a long time before it has burned its way to nothingness, but in another way now it is done. Even such a man as Purushottam Goswami is a man in the end, and with this act as the seal, Shrivatsa is forever his son.

As the fire burns down, it needs to be stoked occasionally with ghee and camphor; that is done. The music resumes, ever the music. At first it is only the mahamantra, in that lilting Bengali style. It seems

Figure 6.7.   Lighting the funeral fire. Shrivatsa, in dark glasses, turns from the heat.

to breathe—first thin, then suddenly full—in a way that contrasts broadly to ISKCON's better-known public declamation. Here the mahamantra is a bellows for the fire. Shrivatsa sits nearby. And then, ever so gently, the musicians segue into songs of Holi. It is already the month of Phalgun, and when Phalgun reaches its full-moon night Holi with all its love and irreverent joy will be upon us. It too has its fire. "Ho ho ho ho holi!" the musicians half sing, half shout. After a while Suvarna comes over to say a friendly word. I go over to say one to Abhinav.

The pyre is still burning. A moment of ritual significance and personal poignancy comes when the fire has made deep inroads into every part of the body except the skull, which houses the hardest bone structure of all. At this point Shrivatsa must lift a long pole and make a hole in the skull so that the heat can escape from within. He pours ghee and camphor into the aperture; his father's soul escapes in the other direction. He has now said a final goodbye to his body. Guests are expected to stay until this moment, but now they are free to leave.

In fact, the convention is that they should come specifically for the ceremonies that have now been completed and depart directly rather than lingering for any other purpose; death requires this focused precision. But out of special respect for Purushottam, quite a number stay—some beneath the sun on the river's open plain, some beneath the tent that's been pitched for them. Many will wait for the fire to burn through the pyre in its entirety. The priest tells Shrivatsa he can go over and talk with them before it is time for them to leave. Sure enough, he does, holding court in a way that he has never quite done before. Forming a little circle of six or eight souls around himself—all seated on those serviceable plastic chairs, our measly industrial version of eternity—Shrivatsa beckons me over to meet one or two of his guests, some of whom are local dignitaries. I can tell that his mind is elsewhere, but it is also here. This is the beginning of the long journey back.

Afterward

I had to rush off to Delhi again—I'd canceled one day's lecture but not the next, and there was a train to catch. When I returned to Vrindavan a day later I found that much had changed. A few steps into the family house revealed that Purushottam was everywhere—three very large banners of different lengths with a dozen or so generously sized pictures of Maharajji printed upon them. He was almost always smiling, in his habitual extroverted way. The largest of these banners was sufficiently long that it could be hung from the third-floor balcony and reach all the way past the second: Purushottam, Purushottam, Purushottam all the way down. The whole atrium was thereby bathed in the yellow color he always wore—sometimes it verged over into saffron or orange—in imitation of Krishna's own yellow-colored dhoti. It was all consistent and all so much like him; Shrivatsa wears this color too, which had made the white dhoti he wore as the officiant at his father's last rites stand out all the more. In the courtyard everything looked beautiful, these unfurled images from different stages of Maharajji's life, so full of independent life and energy, so different from the unadorned cloth that had served as canopies and battens against the wind on the cremation ghat. It emerged that Robyn Beeche had sent these images of her guru from Australia. Somehow she had managed to complete this task in the last months of her life, an eloquent goodbye. Mysteriously they took half a year to arrive, but as it happened, they arrived just in time.

A little shrine with Maharajji's picture had been placed at the bottom of the great atrium, decorated with flowers, and from his room you could hear the sounds of the Bhagavata Purana being chanted by his own milky tenor voice. Someone had thought to record this long ago. The family sat around talking, remembering. Suvarna had been away in Pune when the news came. Before he heard it—a telephone call from his mother—he and his wife Aastha had been having a little meal while their daughter Karnika, almost two, slept beside them. Often she had been asleep in the family house, taking a nap, when her great-grandfather departed for his daily trip around Mount Govardhan, but he always called her name on the way out even so. Sometimes, of course, she heard, and her name for him was Kaka. She put these syllables to no other use. When Karnika, sleeping next to her parents in Pune, awoke from her nap, she uttered just those syllables—Kaka! It was the first time she had ever done this in his absence. Not long afterward Suvarna got the call that his grandfather he had left this world: come home.

The day after the cremation there was a beautiful ceremony of remembrance from 3:00 to 4:00 p.m. in the great hall of the Shri Chaitanya Prem Sansthan. Many people from around town had been invited—it looked like a veritable convention of the old Vrindavan. It was a silent service, a śraddhāñjali. People came in and seated themselves before an altar where a favorite picture from the 1980s had been placed, with a similarly sized image of Radharaman just above, all youth and beauty and energy eternally—nitya. All along the wall just behind these were Robyn's cloth-mounted pictures, removed from their positions on the banners she had sent and assembled to become a gallery, a museum built on the spot. Way down to the side of the hall on the ras lila dais was an image of Chaitanya, and just below sat the musicians—only three or four of them now, the very ones who sing the mahamantra for a two-hour stretch every morning and evening in that very hall; they sing it uninterruptedly throughout the twelve days of mourning. They sang the mahamantra here too, but in the softest of ways. People trickled in throughout the ceremony, until the hall was quite full. At the end Shrivatsa and his brother and sons stood in a row near the door so as to greet the guests with a wordless namaste as they left.

Shrivatsa was very pleased to have been able to honor his father in this simple, peaceful way at this simple, peaceful time. There would be other rituals. On the ninth day after Purushottam's death Shrivatsa would need to be shaved again, this time in the company of the other men of the immediate family. This is the first of three piṇḍapradāna ceremonies in which, through the offering of rice-balls, they encourage the spirit of the departed on the journey that makes it possible for him to take his place among those who have gone before. This transformation is enacted with substance, through food. Then, after the twelve days of ritual seclusion have been completed, the family holds a feast for thirty-one Brahmins, who come to the exact place where Purushottam died, his private room, and play the roles of different units of time adding up to a year. This makes it possible for the family to perform the ritual roles that will be required in the year ahead—a very important thing for a family such as this. And there are immediate consequences too. They can start eating on plates again, not sewn-together leaves, and their food can be spiced rather than being served plain. They are public persons again. They no longer carry the collective touch of death; they are released.

Yet in the way Shrivatsa approaches this thirteen-day-long parting from his father, it sometimes seems the reverse. He seems to treat these invisible ritual barriers not as fences that exile him from the world of the living but as markers of a zone of safety, a place where he can still be with his father and not have to depart. He wears a little red knit cap to keep his shaven head warm—or is it more a way to show respect, a signal that his head is covered with his father? Someone had quickly reached for it after his tonsure, and he has worn it all through the mourning period. Shrivatsa is unusually quiet and grave. He looks you straight in the eye but a bit blankly, it seems, without a smile or any hint of that special sense of connectivity he otherwise so lavishly displays. It is as if he is standing behind glass. The spices have been removed from all that he tastes. He executes the rituals he must, he performs his social persona, he plans what must be planned; but inside a part of him has died.

One time I stepped into the house to drop off a little gift. Sandhya welcomed me, and on hearing my voice, I think, Shrivatsa came out of his father's room. As the door swung open you could hear the constant chanting of the Bhagavata, recorded in his father's voice. Shrivatsa was as grave as he had always been in this period of mourning, but this time there was a difference: his eyes were pools of light. I wondered if he might have been crying. He wonders whether it might just have been the sight of a friend.

Eventually Shrivatsa did emerge from his seclusion, and the emergence had to be quite sudden. The Holi season, anticipating the spring harvest and celebrating purest play, was about to begin. This is one of two times in the course of a year (the other is during the monsoon) when Shrivatsa's family sponsors a set of ras lilas, a joyful and elaborate public affair. Devotees would descend. The ashram would throb with life. And Shrivatsa would certainly miss his father, who built the Shri Chaitanya Prem Sansthan on exactly the spot where Jaisingh had first brought the ras lilas out from temples like that of Radharaman into a more secular space. Purushottam always gave a stirring public sermon at "half time" in each of these performances, that is, once the circle rās dance had been ritually re-enacted and before the play (līlā) of the day began. Here were enacted, day by day, episodes from Krishna's boyhood and Radha's life as a girl in Braj—they were and are deeply in love. It is the eternal, archetypal childhood of us all. Here death plays no part.

Holi, the great spring festival, only accentuates this mood of eternal youthfulness. Everything is fun and joy. On the night before the final ras lila of the Holi sequence—the one in which the game of Holi itself is represented—there had been a scene of utter abandon in the Radharaman temple just down the lane. The deity himself was involved. He had come out from his sanctum chamber to watch the show—to move a step closer to the liveliness of the moment among his devotees. On one side of Radharaman's great silver throne, priests of the younger generation of gosvamis had a wonderful time throwing colored powder and handfuls of the dust of Braj out into the crowd gathered just below. Meanwhile, on the other side, another cadre of young gosvamis took out the great long squirt-guns called pichkārīs and drenched the worshipers with fragrant colored water. At the back of the temple, where the musicians sit, one of their number brought out the great daph drum that marks the Holi season (Fig. 6.8). It is a huge version of a tambourine but struck rhythmically like a drum,

Figure 6.8 One gopī plays the daph drum while another dances with the flute-playing Krishna at Holi time. Detail from an illustration for "maī mero man rācatu he bihārilāl sū", a poem attributed to Surdas; painting attributed to Manohar, Mewar ca. 1650. Kanoria Collection, Patna, VKK 117. Photo © Asian Art Archives, University of Michigan: ACSAA 4326.

not shaken. And the crowd are actors too. Many came in—men and women alike—colored with the remnants of fun-loving battles they had had in the streets or in more protected settings. At one point a whole group of young men erupted into shouts of "Hari bol" (Say "Krishna"!) and jumped up and down, hands raised above their heads. The whole scene was energy personified. How is a man in his sixties who has just performed the last rites for his revered father to join in the spirit of such a scene?

Shrivatsa did so with his customary dignity. As he came to the center of the ras lila stage in Jaisingh Ghera, however, he was uncharacteristically holding his iPhone. By that means he was able to consult the occasional note—the musical text he was expounding. It sounded like a song addressed by Krishna to Radha or the other way around: "daph kī har thāp meṅ āp kī āvāj sunāī detī hai" (With every beat of the drum, the sound of your voice resounds)—but actually it had been composed by one of his father' devotees and addressed to Purushottam himself. Shrivatsa now had it on his phone, and he didn't have time to put the phone away. Besides, he needed it for the lyrics. This mobile phone became part of the play—a prop that was more than a prop. Faced with an audience of people armed to the teeth with phones and looking forward to nothing more than record-ing a bit of the magic they were about to see, Shrivatsa urged them to put these appurtenances away—he demonstrated with the one in his own hand. If they wanted to take pictures, they should please move to the back so that others might savor whatever particularly significant instant the present might have in store for them—the instant when, in the immediacy of the moment, the Lord might grant a vision of himself. You never know when such a flash of time might come, he said. But whenever it does, your own eyes will prepare you for it far better than any external eye could do. Just be ready with open eyes. The lila will do the rest.

That was his principal message: all of us were about to have the chance to enter the eternal lila, to taste it for just a moment. But any-one who knew what Shrivatsa had just gone through himself would have sensed a special depth when he said that five years from now we might not be here. You never know when your time might come. And what would these machines be for us then? No, the picture has to be snapped with the inner eye—then it can be long-lasting. If you are fumbling for your iPhone in the moment that vision appears, it may be over before you return. There was the sense that it definitely *would* be over before you could come into its presence once again. Go for a moment you can't delete! Go for a moment that gets saved not in your head but in your heart! Make your whole life into a festival—be open to all that is around you, which you are about to see epitomized. This is the real meaning of Holi.

How did Shrivatsa know to give this message? What was his inspiration? He didn't come out and give the answer directly, but it was hidden not far behind the screen. Instead of telling his personal story, he took a page from an ancient contrast between Ram and Krishna, describing them as "best of persons". Ram is remembered as the best of persons from the point of view of propriety, moral action (maryādā). Krishna, by contrast, is the best of persons with respect to playfulness and drama (līlā)—the very form in which the audience was about to be engaged. To this familiar roster of two, Shrivatsa added another "best of persons"—the teacher, the guru, the one who shows the way. In doing so he also made reference to that ultimate "best of persons" who is God himself, manifest in each of the three he had listed. The word that lay at the center of this meditation was the word Purushottam, the name that had been given to his father as his own personal name: Best of Persons.

As Shrivatsa spoke his name in this context, his voice broke, inner tears threatening to undo outer speech. He recovered, and no one who did not know would have recognized the source. But for those who did, the scene took on a new and deeper meaning. The portrait of Purushottam Goswami that had been placed at the center of the ras lila hall throughout the twelve days of mourning had now been placed right up front—just next to where Fateh Krishna, the leader of this ras lila troupe, was sitting. Shrivatsa's father had been given the best box seat for the lila that was about to begin again—sign, symbol, and theater of the eternal game that is stitched together by our lives. No wonder there were inner tears as Shrivatsa faced into a public identity he would now have to enact without his father's living, loving gaze. As the lila began and the music started again, Shrivatsa picked up the daph drum and began to play.

7

The Sign of Our Times

At the heart of religion is the question of what's real, and the idea of Vrindavan has always raised this very question. O women of this world—and the woman in all of us: Is your husband, king of the mountain of dharma, your real husband, or are you drawn to another who champions a world unconstrained by ordinary dharma, the world of love, the forest, and the ras lila? Which is more real? And when this miraculous realer-than-real lover disappears, his footprints barely visible on the forest floor, what do you do? Do you not imitate his presence as the gopis did (rās līlā anukaraṇ), performing him in his absence so as to claim that reality as the greater reality, even so? From this urge, it is said, all the arts of Vrindavan emerge— paradigmatically the ras lila but also temple floristry, dances before the deity, evoking Krishna's presence in song, and a whole arsenal of food prepared specially to be offered to the divine murti so that it can be transfigured by the divine touch and return to ordinary life as prasad. That moment of metamorphosis infects ordinary reality with a reality that's deeper.[1]

Is Virtual Reality Real?

If this set of symbols is not your own, then substitute what is. It may be the revelations heard by Muhammad, which made him seem a man above all men, realer than the rest. Or it could be Jesus, who represents the intrusion of another reality, the Lord's, into human flesh. Or perhaps it's the special relation of covenant upon which Christian beliefs about Jesus rest: the Jewish conviction that Israel is somehow a nation unlike all others. Or perhaps the sense of true alignment and elevation that comes with the practice of yoga, the discovery of a compass more reliable than anything available in a life that doesn't make room for concentration. Or Buddhist meditation and compassion, where the assumed self is discovered to be something deeply unreal and the inner non-self makes peace with that fact. This is what religion's about—grappling with the unreality of so much that seems patently real. In Vrindavan's case this grappling is also escaping—escaping to a place of greater grace. It's discovering somewhere closer to the soul and simultaneously closer to the soil—the soil untilled; the pastoral before the agricultural; the forest, jungle, wilderness. This is the "van" at the end of the word Vrindavan. Wilderness asks if settled life is real, and the idea of wilderness is always constructed in relation to it. This is so precisely if we understand wilderness to be natural and unconstructed, anything but virtual itself.

Not all wildernesses are the same. Vrindavan's van is a long way from the wilderness that so long drove the American dream—the wilderness beckoning from the west, abundant enough to absorb the hordes of "pioneers" who would go there and turn it into tillable Christian land. Today Seattle and Silicon Valley, each hugging America's west coast, take up the slack of a lost frontier by generating a new one—virtual, of course, but still very American in tone and aim.[2] Vrindavan's wilderness is a different sort. It's untrammeled inner space set at the center of an ancient civilization. In that way the archetypal Vrindavan is a garden—bordered and protected, but still dedicated to its own natural base.

Some of Vrindavan's religious communities regard the motif of the nikunj, the forest bower and love hideaway, as the space most accurately representative of the real and true Vrindavan—they will not sing songs of anything else. But the Vrindavan that began to be built in the sixteenth century owed at least as much to the Mughal love of palace gardens, an idea with distinctly Persian associations.[3] The emperor Akbar was in charge, Mansingh Kachvaha was his principal general and architect, and Vrindavan sprang up as a garden that would lie between Akbar's two greatest capitals, Agra and Delhi. It bordered his favorite hunting grounds. This sixteenth-century Vrindavan was radically new (those remarkable unembellished temples!) and at the same time radically old (the memory of Krishna's childhood). It preserved an ancient idea of wilderness and simultaneously created a new one. With Vrindavan the old and the new were always in dialogue.

In the sixteenth century Vrindavan was curled in the arms of the same river that passed through both Delhi and Agra. In fact, it praised that river—the Yamuna, its chosen deity; it gave her in a new way her due. She was no longer just the water that passed by ancient Mathura, making that city into a holy bathing spot, a tīrtha; she was interactive with the land through Krishna's lilas. The built Vrindavan celebrated that fact. It was a different kind of capital from Agra and Delhi. It lined the river with ghats, not forts. Old Man River, then—perennial and even-flowing? Not quite, and irrespective of the gender disparity. The Yamuna rises and falls with each passing year, responsive to the monsoons and melting snows, yet it does communicate something constant and ancient—a view of life measured not in years but eons, the entanglements of age-old karma. It's into such a river that Krishna jumps when he jumps from the kadamba tree. That's where he plays with his girlfriends.

Now that cleansing, timeless river has been choked off. It threatens to disappear, and the wilderness-garden that borders it, as well.[4] In the early chapters of this book, we witnessed this process. We began with the battle for the archetypal ghat, the place where Vrindavan's wilderness most dramatically intersects with the river (Chapter 2). Not only is the link in danger of being permanently severed, as we saw, but the river itself is no longer "river" in the full sense—too polluted to be drunk or even entered; in fact, too polluted for Yamuna's ancient vehicle, the turtle, to live there anymore. As for that severing, it went under the heading of "beautification" and "waterfront development". These paradigms, imported from elsewhere, would render the river itself virtual—even the water that coursed there would not be the Yamuna's alone but that of the Ganga. These new paradigms and

Figure 7.1.   Looking across the Yamuna toward the lightly forested opposite bank. January 25, 2019. A boat awaits passengers at Pandavala Ghat as someone passes on a circumambulation path created by the newly sunk pipes.

the hybrid technologies they imply force us to ask whether Vrindavan has always actually been a theme park, a thing of human desiring that only pretends to be real in some primordial sense. It's a fair question; Vrindavan cannot be less virtual than religion itself. And yet there's that view from the ghats across the river—to the smooth sandy soil on the opposite bank and the low trees that embroider it in the distance (Fig. 7.1). If this is not real, what is? If this becomes a massive parking lot and a jungle of condominiums, what indeed will remain? The loss will be irreparable.

Chapter 2 followed the theme further. There we made our way into the radically new Vrindavan that lines the Chatikara Road. It is taking shape with a swiftness and a unified logic of external compulsion that far surpasses even the suddenness with which the old

Vrindavan appeared in the second half of the sixteenth century. This new Vrindavan, displaying so many of the features of a mall—a strip mall largely speaking but with impressive anchor "stores"—stands apart from the Vrindavan where it says it's based. This new Vrindavan made the rest "the old Vrindavan", and despite the metaphor of mall, it's hardly insular. It mimics similar strips and malls found elsewhere—in Delhi and Bangalore, in Doha and Dubai, whether themed in terms of religion or not, whether finished or still under construction. This new Vrindavan marches to a capitalist drum, a rhythm with no intrinsic national boundaries. Its properties are bought as investments—land values have risen dramatically because Vrindavan is effectively the frontier of the Delhi megalopolis—and they also serve as weekend retreats, the sort expected in that same internationally branded orbit. As for the stakeholders, they too aspire to be a global lot. They include not only Non-Resident Indians who live principally abroad but others who expect their children may do so. Vrindavan is their anchor to windward in this rapidly changing world. And then there are the devotees of intrinsically international spiritual leaders, whether themselves foreign by birth or Indian, whether ISKCON or something beyond. The *I* in ISKCON stands for "international".

In Chapter 4 we studied the institution that currently serves as the epitome of this new Vrindavan: the Vrindavan Chandrodaya Mandir situated near the outer extreme of the "mall of Vrindavan". It concentrates many of the forces that have brought the rest of this simultaneously spiritual and not-so-spiritual mall into being. Here the scale of real estate development is vastly increased—we are talking about a seventy-story tower—and we see in almost pure form the determination to make the new Vrindavan a Vrindavan of its own making. The VCM will be higher than the rest of Vrindavan by vast measures, and it establishes without embarrassment its own virtual world—theme parks and internal "heritage" replicas.[5] The VCM's ISKCON-of-Bangalore developers understand its patrons and spectators to be positioned worldwide. It's the beating heart of a spiritual investment operation that exists not only on the ground in Vrindavan but in field offices located in Gurgaon and Bangalore and very significantly in a different field altogether—the land of WhatsApp, Facebook, Google+, and YouTube.

The temple's under-construction virtuality enables it for the moment to be both flexible and ideal—religion, one might argue, in a pure sense—but challenges are sure to arise as a physical mandir begins to emerge from this virtual cloud of messages, belongings, and shared purpose. So far, the humanitarian organization Akshay Patra has largely played the role of grounding the VCM in the world of the "real" Vrindavan, yet never with a sense that its scope was confined to Vrindavan's boundaries. There too we have the familiar slippage: Akshay Patra is actually a Bangalore-based national organization, a "chain" with local franchises if we continue to pursue the economic metaphor. As to local realities, one wonders what will happen as the stakeholders of this dream-tower come and actually live there, or at least come and go. Then the safety zone created by religion's idealistic virtuality may begin to fray and show its strains. How long can the VCM portray itself as being ahead of its time—great wedge of the religion of the future—when it is inhabited by real-time people? Utopias have always faced this challenge, but it takes a particular shape in the new Vrindavan. The sense of specialness that the VCM projects is sure to be diminished as other aspects of megalopolitan Delhi rise to embrace it and render it normal. A huge new airport, fourth largest in the world, is projected to be built within a decade, and it will be closer to Vrindavan than to the center of Delhi. New forms of private and public transport will extend throughout the National Capital Region, there will be yet more population growth, and natural resources such as pure water and pure air will be even scarcer than they are today. The VCM will still be an epitome, but of what? Of religion scrambling to seem the beacon for all of this?

In Chapter 5 we explored another aspect of the new Vrindavan—not sanitation, population, or infrastructure, but the way in which new actors have responded to a very old image of the place: Vrindavan as a haven (or is it a prison?) for widows. We saw how senior figures from the Congress Party and the BJP, implacable rivals since the birth of the nation, have found themselves equally pulled into this particular side of the life of Vrindavan: what it means for women. Mohini Giri, a much-venerated Congress matriarch, founded Ma Dham as a new way to face up to the scandal of destitute widowhood—a model for addressing the cruelties of patriarchy. Her Ma Dham ashram is explicit about fighting this curse, and its ideals and practices resonate to much else in international feminist activism. Meanwhile, from the opposite side of the political spectrum, Sadhvi Ritambhara chartered out the vast campus of Vatsalya Gram. Her institution acknowledges the scandal of Vrindavan's widows only obliquely. Instead, it makes an effort to create new families exclusively headed by women. Such heads-of-household may in fact be widows, but Vatsalya Gram makes no mention of that fact. In Vatsalya Dham's vocabulary the word "widow" does not exist. No one points a finger at the cruelties of patriarchal Hinduism. Rather, Didi Ma (note the familial term of reference) overrides them. Her newly fashioned women-led families are intended to absorb children who have been abandoned by young mothers in the Vrindavan area, many of them probably unmarried. Most of these children are girls.

In both communities, which lie appropriately enough on opposite sides of town, we see efforts to refashion Vrindavan in a way that will make it truly a refuge for women—religious institutions that express realities long claimed in myth but rarely seen in real life. Ma Dham interprets the story of Radha's and Krishna's love as having no Hindu boundaries; its family is the family of humanity. Vatsalya Gram is just the opposite: a carefully cultivated Hindu commonwealth, with its martyrs and its specific anti-Muslim history and a guesthouse that introduces devotees to the feel of this new, forward-looking family. It's people from India's great cities who stay here mostly, and Didi Ma's parent organization, Param Shakti Peeth, has outposts in the global Hindu diaspora as well. This sets it parallel to Mohini Giri's Guild For Service, but the two international women's constituencies are quite different from one another. Ma Dham and Vatsalya Gram both house schools and foreground the education of girls, but their goals in doing so again diverge—it's education for self-sufficiency in one case, education for the nation in the other. Yet for all their contrasts, both these institutions model a sense of normalcy intended to surpass what happens at Bhajan Ashram, the singing community so directly tied to the image of the gopis.

Finally there's Shrivatsa Goswami, my old friend and the subject of Chapter 6, who has all along addressed himself simultaneously to the new Vrindavan and the old. For him, much that is claimed for the new Vrindavan has far deeper roots—roots that burrow into his own extended Radharaman family history, which nourished the innovations his father achieved. But Shrivatsa more than anyone has been frightened by the excesses of his own generation—the way Vrindavan's identity as a place of refuge has been cancerously attacked. Are Vrindavan's new and creative virtualities sufficient to enable him and his co-workers to salvage truths belonging to a Vrindavan that once seemed real and self-evident—the way it nestles on the riverbank, the vision that inspired its beautiful old temples and palaces, the striking combination of culture and rusticity that animates the ras lilas? All that remains to be seen. Shrivatsa's friends and devotees find him to be an unusually sensitive bellwether of our times, comprehending the forces of rapid change but not inundated by them. His opponents find him the troublesome bulwark of a hopelessly outdated past. Doesn't he see that he too will benefit from the new Vrindavan? His response: Don't they see that if more fundamental acts of preservation aren't enacted, there will be no Vrindavan to be made new? If religion is so virtual that it can be captured in a theme park, he asks, who needs any physical Vrindavan at all?

It's the Protestant question, I suppose. If the meaning of reality lies in our apprehension of it—our sense of the guiding principle rather than its actual physical expression—then what to make of our bodies in any case? What have we to do with these needless husks? Yet the guiding myth of Vrindavan insists that bodily attraction is crucial to the pursuit of truth. Love as we physically know it is the door to so much else. Sunk into our material beings is a principle that transforms them. This fact is exemplary of what is called achintyabhedābheda in the theological tradition to which Shrivatsa is heir—inconceivable difference and non-difference. This principle affirms that in an exquisite, almost embarrassing way, reality and virtuality need one another. To think along these lines is to recognize that virtual reality is not reality, however much religion may have tried to make it so, and similarly that reality is not plainly visible to the naked eye. It takes a sense of relationship—ultimately the relation between the virtual and the real—to know the truth, and humbling as it is, it's our own bodies that first teach us this lesson. It's dialectical materialism in a radically new, radically old way.[6]

Can that way of thinking save us from the world in which we live, this world of our own construction? As present-day Vrindavan clearly shows, we are eating up the ground on which we stand—the physical ground and probably the religious ground too. It's a new Vrindavan for sure—so bold, so imaginative, so hopeful. And so willfully unaware, it seems.

Rejuvenating Bhakti in Vrindavan

There is a wonderful, well-known story that embeds Vrindavan's myth in history, brokering its intrinsic virtuality with an aura of the real. This is the tale of how bhakti itself was born and grew to have a life of its own in Indian history. In this account bhakti is pictured as female—the Sanskrit word bhakti is a feminine noun. She is said to have been born in the Dravida country, matured and developed as she travelled north through the lands that border the Arabian Sea, and grown old and feeble in Gujarat. But that was just a prelude to the next step. She traveled further north to Vrindavan, and there she was restored to her youthful beauty. This tale, reported in the Bhagavata Mahatmya, first emerges in manuscripts dating to the early eighteenth century, and it seems indubitable that the Vrindavan of which it speaks is not only the site of Krishna's eternal, mythic boyhood but the Vrindavan so brilliantly constructed on the banks of the Yamuna in Mughal times. This Vrindavan was itself an effort to return to the beauties of Krishna's childhood; now, in the Bhagavata Mahatmya, it is figured as a phase in the history of Bhakti herself— her restoration.[7]

According to the Mahatmya, the ultimate goal of Bhakti's journey is actually not Vrindavan but Haridvar, where a weeklong performance of the Bhagavata Purana restores her sons Renunciation (vairāgya) and Wisdom (jñāna) to life. She travels on from Vrindavan to experience this moment of completion. In most people's retellings, however, this aspect of the narrative gets forgotten. It is as if the story has already achieved its denouement in Vrindavan, so people are apt to omit the rest. This is not a stupid error, for if we leave aside the matter of her sons, it is Vrindavan, not Haridvar, that serves as high point of Bhakti's journey. Here, it seems, is the fulfillment of the bhakti movement, and it's in Vrindavan that you'll hear the greatest concentration of Bhagavat Saptahs being performed. An example is the one we heard from Didi Ma, and billboards around town trumpet many others.

Yet this very same Vrindavan, the spirit of bhakti's rejuvenation, is itself in danger of succumbing to old age and ill health. In the Bhagavata Mahatmya the sage Narada glimpses Bhakti resting beside a picture-perfect river, but look at the scene today—the plastic bags, the sewage, the monkeys, the loudspeakers, the poor widows. Perhaps you see it differently, averting your eyes from these woeful desperations, focusing instead on the newest expression of this south-to-north bhakti thrust, namely, ISKCON-Bangalore's vision for the Vrindavan Chandrodaya Mandir. But the Bangalore gurus themselves are aware that they're averting their eyes from a great deal. Sometimes they try to do something to remedy the sorry state of the old Vrindavan—Akshay Patra stands out—but the VCM's main purpose is to overshadow the decrepit old town. What could be done to make the bhakti movement culminate in a more comprehensive Vrindavan? What could be done to make the whole of Vrindavan into the sort of place where Bhakti could be young and beautiful once again?

ISKCON-Bangalore, while claiming a specific skyscraper charge from Prabhupad, takes its actual operating models from international real-estate consortia and the likes of Universal Studios. A great deal gets left out of this picture—the entirety of the old Vrindavan, except as glimpsed through telescopes mounted in the new Golok Vrindavan way up on the seventieth floor. How can we return to the ground itself? What model can serve to guide Vrindavan's rejuvenation there?

As we have seen, people have been waiting for years for something to emerge from the Mathura Vrindavan Development Authority (MVDA), the arm of the UP government formally charged with this responsibility. Year after year no master plan is unveiled in any detail, and the reason, people suspect, is that if it were, the public could measure developments on the ground against the yardstick of what the plans say. Few think that will ever happen. Politicians of many parties agree only in this: they loathe transparency. So people are inured to looking away from it all—unless, of course, they pocket a few rupees themselves. People like me are guilty of cognate sins by making use of some of the things this corruption has produced. In my case, it's a quicker ride to the new Vrindavan than would be possible if I went through the town's main bazaar. Instead I jump into an e-rickshaw that skirts the heart of town by bumping along the road that sits atop some of the landfill that's been dumped along the Yamuna in recent years. This is the new Parikrama Marg that we've been talking about so much—the pavement that replaces the soft and dusty old footpath. Do I want this new road to disappear?

Because of the MVDA's inaction or lack of a publicly visible plan, other approaches to generating infrastructural improvements periodically surface. One such effort was undertaken in 2011 when the Save the Yamuna campaign mounted its great march from Allahabad through Vrindavan and onward to the center of national power in Delhi. Unfortunately, as we saw in Chapter 2, this produced no lasting response. Already in the prior year the government of Delhi had completely banned plastic bags, in part to prevent their showing up in the Yamuna. There was to be "no leniency" in the enforcement of this new regulation, and it would have had a substantial effect on Vrindavan. What were the results? Nothing.[8]

Still, there were efforts from other quarters. There soon emerged a possibility that the World Bank might fund efforts to rebuild Vrindavan through one of its Pro-poor Tourism Development Projects, this one coordinated with the government of Uttar Pradesh. The size of the grant would have been something on the order of 200 million dollars, and serious effort was devoted to envisioning what it could make possible. On April 1–3, 2015 representatives of the World Bank's working group on Urban, Rural, and Social Development undertook a site survey in Vrindavan and Mathura before framing the grant's final recommendations.[9] This effort was led by Priya Chopra, an accomplished singer with a special devotion to Mirabai who had performed before Radharamanji and had understandably strong interests in Vrindavan's Mirabai temple as well. Chopra and her team interviewed not only leaders of these two temples, Shrivatsa Goswami included, but the head priest of the temple of Banke Bihari and a member of its governing board. They also talked with the head of the Panda Sabha, the local organization of pilgrim priest-guides, and several others. At every point their purpose was to solicit ideas for a comprehensive plan of improvement, and to compare these local leaders' ideas with those based on the World Bank's experience elsewhere around the globe. A detailed plan did indeed emerge, addressing a whole set of issues systematically—the ways pilgrims arrived, Vrindavan's throng of shops, the lack of proper lodging, the unhygienic conditions in which much of Vrindavan's food is prepared, the garbage, the great shortage of public toilets, the elastic riverfront, and of course, the monkey menace. The severe congestion around the Banke Bihari temple generated a category all its own and was to have been the first problem the project addressed; more general recommendations about improving traffic flow followed from it. Last but not least, there was a section on corruption.[10]

For a time there was hope, but before long that initiative also ran afoul of politics. The state government, then in the hands of Akhilesh Yadav's Samajwadi Party, was eager to proceed, but the BJP-controlled federal government denied them the chance. Clearance could not be obtained at the national level.

Now, however, we have a full alignment of local, regional, and national power under the BJP, thanks to the elections of May 2017. Yet this new channeling of political clout has been no more beneficial for Vrindavan than the canals built to harness the Yamuna's energies have been for the river as a whole. Much is promised at the highest levels of government—the federal government in Delhi—but nothing seems to happen apart from a succession of master plans that peter out, leaving little trace of what has been spent or where the money has gone.[11] One example is the HRIDAY program inaugurated by the Ministry of Housing and Urban Affairs in January 2015. *Hriday* means "heart" in Sanskrit and Hindi. As an acronym it refers to the Heritage City Development and Augmentation Yojana (apparently the first two syllables of "Heritage" supply the H, R, and I), and Mathura is one of the cities named as a beneficiary. It was understood that a portion of the central government funds earmarked for Mathura would go to Vrindavan. Three years later the District Magistrate of Mathura was wondering why nothing had happened, and asked the Braj Foundation, which had prepared the plan for action in Vrindavan, to explain.[12] Evidently it had proposed to fund a new footpath alongside the paved Parikrama Marg and to pave—yet more paving—the informal parking lot that has appeared along the Parikrama Marg as it passes behind the temple of Banke Bihari. We have seen how fraught with objection such a plan would be, since it occupies alluvial land and closely neighbors the temple of Madan Mohan, which is under the protection of the Archaeological Survey of India.

So the story continues, and along the way it is fair to observe that projects undertaken by the Braj Foundation in the past have failed to address basic infrastructural issues. The Braj Foundation has indeed directed attention to the importance of wells and water sources in Vrindavan and elsewhere in Braj. It has rightly pointed out that these were among the main features of the town's ecological landscape in prior centuries and has drawn attention to how neglected they have become over the years. But this is in part because the water table has sunk so low that they no longer provide access to water that could actually be used for drinking or washing. Their restoration—a worthy task, no doubt—would therefore be an aesthetic victory more than anything else. Indeed, that is the case for the Braj Foundation's main achievement to date, the restoration of Brahma Kund, which it completed in 2009. Plenty of clean-up was involved, a laudable result, and there was beautification too, along with a significant element of theatricality: a nightly sound and light show.[13]

In this active history of peripheral dalliance and fundamental inaction one obvious resource has been ignored, even though it has been tapped elsewhere in India. This is the World Heritage Fund managed by UNESCO—an instrument of prestige as well as support, and one that would require attention to the basics as part of a well-coordinated plan for the protection of Vrindavan's interlocking architectural and performance heritages. Clearly Vrindavan has the potential to qualify as a beneficiary of these UNESCO monies and the committed expertise that stands beside them, but so far local leaders have failed to rally to the challenge. If Vrindavan became a World Heritage Site (WHS) it would join the ranks of the Taj Mahal, Bodh Gaya, Vijayanagara, and at current count thirty-four other Indian locales. Vrindavan doesn't exactly parallel any of these, but there is little question that the architectural distinction of its temples, palaces, and ghats, and the way they form a coordinated set make Vrindavan an excellent candidate for UNESCO recognition. A case could easily be made that these are things of "outstanding universal value", as the guidelines specify, and the crowds of pilgrim-tourists who flood the town testify to their meaning in the present day. Historically too there is a strong case: Vrindavan was the product of a remarkable Hindu-Muslim concordat, as we have stressed, though the Mughal-Muslim component is obscured in the consciousness of many Vrindavan residents and guides. Aspects of Vrindavan touch on all three kinds of heritage that shaped UNESCO thinking as it developed—tangible, natural, and intangible, the third of these referring to tradition and its living carriers. Vrindavan nicely illustrates how closely these three can sometimes be intertwined.[14]

Then too, there is the need. The old Vrindavan, at least, is in danger of falling prey to evils that are precisely envisioned in UNESCO guidelines: "large-scale public or private projects of rapid urban or tourist development projects; destruction caused by changes in the use or ownership of the land; ... changes in water level, floods and tidal waves".[15] Vrindavan is threatened by each of these perils and more. Some of the town's temples are already under the protection of the Archaeological Survey of India—Madan Mohan, Yugal Kishor, and Govindadev—but these monuments are not integrated into any broader plan. Instead they have become outliers to the religious and even tourist life of the town as a whole; they have not been seen either as magnets to enhance it or as landmarks to give it shape. The temples of Madan Mohan and Govindadev lie at the peripheries of Vrindavan's historic settlement, one upriver and one down, and Yugal Kishor, just behind Keshi Ghat, is right at the center. Yet Vrindavan's city fathers have never adopted a publicly stated, coordinated plan to protect this area, its ghats, and the river plain on which the entire built complex stands. To the contrary, it seems, the local land mafia has done everything possible to stand in its way. Might the prospect of a UNESCO endorsement—an even greater flow of visitors from around India and the world, and the infrastructure to support such an increase—serve as sufficient inducement to break that logjam?

It didn't work before. At the end of 2009 the UNESCO director for South Asia visited Vrindavan for a meeting with leading local citizens who represented different constituencies and points of view. The motivating concern was the Mayawati government's "Bridge to Nowhere". Signatures were then solicited for a common appeal, and the UNESCO director responded by saying that "Vrindavan is indeed a very important place in the religious cultural map of India. We would be glad to support, in the remit of our mandate and possibilities, the preservation and heritage-based development of Brajmandal and Vrindavan". Further steps were outlined, but the official request for UNESCO involvement had to come from the municipality, state, and central governments, and such a request never came.[16] I think this effort deserves another try.

Of course, it cannot be a panacea. Implicit in such a project is a clean-up operation—many of the features the World Bank's plan sought to achieve—and cleaning up means removing detritus. But detritus, like garbage, is a loaded word: detritus from whose point of view? At least some concerned citizens are quick to admit that it has to include plastic bags and sewage, though the public at large is far more apathetic. And what about the houses and shops that have accumulated along the parikrama path over the last quarter-century— structures resting on public lands governed by the Ministry of Water Resources?[17] These are the very "encroachments" I mentioned above—encroachments from the point of view of civic planners, but signifying home and livelihood to those who inhabit them. At other World Heritage Sites the displacement of relatively poor people living in such places has become a major issue, and it would be in Vrindavan too.[18] Other dwelling sites would have to be built to accommodate them. And what about the road itself and the whole "beautification" project that threatens to widen the current road by vast measures? "They're building a proper ghat", as people say (pakkā ghāṭ banegā). It sounds constructive, not the reverse.

All these things are deeply contentious, and then there's the issue of the spirit—what Americans would see as the value of freedom and private enterprise. No one wants to rob Vrindavan of the vibrancy of its street life. That's a lot of what people come for, and to which they contribute. No one wants to cut off that remarkable spirit of jerry-built invention in the name of something purer, older, better. Yet this wonderful country-fair feeling, testament to the ever-new life of the old Vrindavan, has to have its fairground, after all. The parking lots that cater to Bihariji's motorized devotees as well as the cow-shelters, temples, and teashops that now line the recently paved Parikrama Marg and separate the beautiful old ghats further and further from the river—these are not requisite components of the spirit of Vrindavan. It will take grit and a sense of shared purpose to clear them away— them and the haphazardly built road they now border.

Compromises will almost certainly have to be made. In the end, though, one has to turn the model of a different sort of urban vibrancy—what we see in the huge success of the Delhi Metro. There everyone can see the value of everyone else's restraint. Littering there is a punishable offense, and no one does. There's plenty of life left over after that. I am thinking of the Delhi Metro as a model for the entirety of a WHS project for Vrindavan, but it's also a model in a more specific sense. Now is the time to build in a light-rail plan that will connect future visitors to the NCR's public transport grid that is radiating out from that very same Metro. We can't pretend Vrindavan is the wilderness it once was; the present has overtaken it. To maintain its "wilderness" properties requires resituating it on an interurban grid—a new enactment of the sort of interurban template that set the conditions for the building of Mughal-Rajput Vrindavan in the first place.[19]

Certain features would have to be built into a WHS appeal on the part of Vrindavan, starting with a comprehensive plan to thread sewers through the old town and build new sewage treatment plants for the refuse they would channel. The appeal would also include a covenant to pay street-cleaners a far more favorable wage than at present and to provide them with uniforms and protective gloves if they wish, after the pattern established by Friends of Vrindavan way back in 1996. Plastic regulations would be next, part of the same picture—and not just because discarded plastic bags threaten to choke cows, as indeed they do.

There would also be regulations for one-way traffic and a prioritizing of non-carbon vehicles—the latter, a trend that has already begun. The Vespas that scream around town, especially at night, are life-threatening and would have to be controlled by speed limits stated and enforced. Pedestrian-only areas are required, where the only allowable motorized traffic will serve the disabled. In the spirit of the Mughal-Rajput concordat that got the town established in the first place, there should be openly stated accommodations for non-Hindu religious buildings, though not at the expense of existing structures in the older part of town. Noise regulations are crucial, as certain citizen groups have begun to argue, and volume levels will have to be imposed on any new sound-and-light shows that may emerge. Luckily the main life of the old Vrindavan will always be its temples and gardens; there public regulations should intrude no more than necessary.

Here is a tough one: the monkeys. Sensitively and creatively mimicking their human cousins, Vrindavan's monkeys have become not just playful actors on the scene—wandering the walls as in so many miniature paintings—but outright predators. Local practice includes monkey-to-monkey instruction in the art of grabbing glasses and smartphones, making Vrindavan hell for humans dependent on those devices. The scene does have its exciting aspects. People who happen to be in the market, say, at the moment when a monkey darts down from the rafters and snatches a woman's glasses off her face suddenly find themselves united in their determination to recover the lost object. But it gets old quick, and it's never any fun for the victim. There have been many injuries. People get resigned to the constant battle even as it grows, often recognizing the monkey in themselves, but the menace worsens year by year. What's needed is a thorough and doubtless expensive campaign to remove the problem, capturing these monkeys down to the last ones in the area comprising the old town and transporting them somewhere else. Otherwise the scourge will never cease as glasses- and phone-grabbing techniques get perpetuated down the generations. Famously, monkey see, monkey do. For the moment the new Vrindavan seems safe—it could probably be policed by langurs, who represent the competition—but it won't be long before the bandar gang rules there too. Forestry officials who work on a nationwide basis would need to be involved, determining locales to which these bandars could be humanely relocated, where their presence would no longer be a threat to humankind. It would be a huge task requiring unprecedented cooperation, but so far there seems no other way out.[20]

As a number of observers have made clear, making Vrindavan a World Heritage Site will not solve every problem. Other agencies will have to be involved, for example, to increase the flow of Yamuna water and make it purer as it approaches the town, but a WHS status would greatly strengthen efforts to mobilize such action.[21] Yet there are worries. Some people fear that, as at other such sites, "heritage" controls around landmarked sites might turn the older parts of Vrindavan into a museum and place unwarranted limitations on its thriving, ever-changing, acutely present-day religious life.[22] At Bodh Gaya, for example, plans to recreate the "serene, verdant ambience" believed to have served as the background for the Buddha's enlightenment experience, a presumed draw for international visitors, threatened the livelihood of local street vendors and shopkeepers and caused the eviction of people whose dwellings were judged to be encroachments.[23]

The authorities also introduced modifications in patterns of worship within the Mahabodhi Temple itself by limiting the use of oil lamps, which were said to be harmful to the structure and create a mess.[24] Luckily Vrindavan's dominant moods are different and more diverse, and the garden areas that had to be carved out at Bodhgaya before they could exist have long been a valued part of Vrindavan; they formed an integral part of its planning in earlier centuries. Some of those "forests" and gardens may now be infested with monkeys, but they do exist; no structure has to be demolished to create them. The threat of the creation of new "Disneylands" presents a different challenge, however, arising from a conflation of WHS objectives and the tourism goals held dear by national, regional, and local governments and by a phalanx of eager entrepreneurs.[25]

Forebodings about external control are understandable in any case, and I appreciate the fact that for some people an international body will seem exactly the wrong place to look for a solution to Vrindavan's problems. No one wants Indians to become second-class citizens in their own country once again. Specifically Indian solutions might well be preferable, but so far we lack a successful model, apart from the Delhi Metro. Prime Minister Modi's Swacch Ganga campaign is a fine idea, but doesn't yet seem to be yielding much in the way of benefit to the river itself. For a time there had been stiff local opposition to his plan to create an open corridor between the Kashi Vishvanath Temple and the ghats below on the Ganga, which enacts his own ideal template—a new way to envision the city's sacredness.[26] But this was quieted by government buyouts that recompensed property-holders at utterly unheard of levels. Thankfully, once again, Vrindavan's position is different. No venerable structures would be threatened by a WHS plan for preservation. To the contrary, the point would be to offer them better maintenance and make sure they are secure against their own disintegration and any plans for radical change that would eliminate or substantially alter them in the name of beautification. In this cause, funds from outside India could be very helpful. Indeed, they would help circumscribe the effects of foreign funding that can already be seen in the newer parts of town. The most important "foreign" investors driving India's current real estate juggernaut may indeed be persons of Indian origin, but they have been trained in international capitalism by living in places like New York, London, and Dubai.[27]

Some argue that to engineer Vrindavan's future is to tamper with the natural momentum that the bhakti movement has always provided—India's own story of how Vrindavan matters. It was here that bhakti gained a new lease on life, as the story goes, with a logic of history that mere humans may not understand. Yet there never was a primordial past to which Vrindavan simply, unquestionably belonged. The view of history that came to be articulated in the tale of the bhakti movement always had its ties to worldly power. In its full-blown form, the idea of the bhakti movement was tinged with the importance of what the state called "national integration". The state in question was the nation that was coming into existence to replace what the British had wrought, and the period I have in mind extended from the 1920s to the 1970s. Nor were these political associations absent in earlier centuries, when several of the main motifs that fed into the "mature" idea of the bhakti movement appeared. The motif of the four sampradays is one such major strand—religious communities said to have tied an older south to a newer north. That idea seems to have emerged just as the Mughal state was taking hold across north India, and answered to it implicitly with a fully subcontinental Indian view of Indian history. Later, in the time of Raja Jaisingh II of Amer, it took an explicitly political form. The four-sampraday model was supposed to structure a religion supervised and supported by the state, and there was even a direct tie to Vrindavan. Govindadev, Vrindavan's best-known image, was installed at the heart of the polity Jaisingh was building—just opposite the new palace he built for himself in the new planned city of Jaipur—while the king himself continued to have a home in Vrindavan. So to cry "Hands off Vrindavan!" in the name of its key role in the bhakti movement—something we see at the heart of the Bhagavata Mahatmya's telling—is to forget that politics have always played an important role in projecting and absorbing that very story. The point is not to keep all hands off but to make sure that the hands that do get involved are good ones. They may, in part, be foreign hands.

The bhakti movement's story no longer belongs to India alone. It has grown to international proportions. Bengalis living in London, Biharis in the Caribbean, and Tamilians shot through the Silicon Valley all play a role in this story, but no actor has been more important than ISKCON. The Hare Krishna movement has reshaped the town where Prabhupad lived, and made it a major node in the network of global religion. To think of that network in less than global terms is to try to reset the clock; it can't happen. Rather, one must realize that in every period of its history and for all its sense of local specialness, Vrindavan has always made sense in terms that reach beyond itself.[28] Vrindavan is not the world as such but a mirror of that world, whether Rajput-Mughal, colonial-Bengali, or international in current senses of the word. People from around the world have found themselves reflected in Vrindavan, and if anyone is simultaneously local and global, it's Krishna. If we lose his mirror—the "van" built into Vrindavan—that will be a loss we can't repair.

Anthropocene Obscene

The celebrated entomologist Edward O. Wilson has thought long and hard about the complex and delicate relationship between human beings and other forms of life that festoon the planet. He has worried more than most—both as specialist scholar and as public figure—about the fact that his own species is responsible for the rapid disappearance of a great deal of the unfathomable miracle of global biodiversity, a colossal act of collective hubris. Anthropocene obscene, we might call it.[29]

Yet there are times when human beings unknowingly reenact a deeply encoded sense of the balance between our own species-specific order and the conditions that made it possible for us to emerge so successfully on the inter-species playing field. Wilson points to just such moments in the course of his book *The Creation: An Appeal to Save Life on Earth*, in which he addresses a fictitious Christian pastor aggregated from his own Southern Baptist past in an attempt to establish common ground between science and religion. He speaks of a series of "quirks of human nature" that can helpfully be thought about as being consistent with (though hardly proving) the widely held hypothesis that *Homo sapiens* emerged as an independent species in the savanna regions of Africa:

> Researchers have found that when people of different cultures, including those of North America, Europe, Asia, and Africa, are given freedom to select the setting of their homes and work places, they

prefer an environment that combines three features. They wish to live on a height looking down and out, to scan a parkland with scattered trees and copses spread before them, closer in appearance to a savanna than to either a grassland or a closed forest, and to be near a body of water, such as a lake, river, or sea. Even if all these elements are purely aesthetic and not functional, as in vacation homes, people who have the means will pay a very high price to obtain them. ... Subjects in choice tests prefer their habitation to be a retreat, with a wall, cliff, or something else solid to the rear. They want a view of fruitful terrain in front of the retreat. They like large animals scattered thereabout, either wild or domestic. Finally, they favor trees with low horizontal branches and divided leaves.[30]

All of the features of these highly valued landscapes—"retreats", he sometimes calls them—correspond to conditions that would have been present in the African savanna at the time when *Homo sapiens* made its first great leap forward. This is the forest primeval, though it doesn't look quite like what Longfellow had in mind when he famously uttered that phrase.[31] Rather, our species-specific forest of origins turns out to look more like a savanna. And that in turn looks a lot like Vrindavan. The gentle height is there—the bluff overlooking the Yamuna; the body of water is out and beyond; and the "parkland with scattered trees and copses" aptly describes the "van" that used to exist before the new Vrindavan wiped it away. The trees are far more like shrubs than Longfellow's "murmuring pines", and the fragrant, medicinal, low-to-the-ground tulsi tree—the vrindā in Vrindavan—corresponds nicely to what one might expect to see in a savanna landscape. There are even large animals moving about freely in our conception of the Vrindavan that once was—Krishna's cows, first and foremost. This is a wilderness worth preserving. No wonder it connoted the essence of retreat for those who imagined Krishna's amours—and for Chaitanya's followers and many others when they left their more "civilized" homes to come live here.

Vrindavan is exquisitely positioned to connote the moment when human beings first emerged from the pre-human or more-than-human "wilderness" to which they natively belonged. We have spoken about the implicit contrast with city life that Vrindavan has always conveyed—the way it shares with that larger and specifically human landscape without actually replicating it—yet here we sense a more archaic resonance. Its particular setting harks back poignantly to what for our species is the primal scene—or did so until almost yesterday. Of course, the built Vrindavan was never pure wilderness. How could it be, since it was built? But it enshrined an idea of wildness that was fundamental and kept its meaning alive. Vrindavan always knew it was the opposite of Mathura, that ancient and archetypal city, even if Mathura was just a short way down the road. Mathura symbolizes city; Vrindavan symbolizes forest.[32]

Vrindavan stands for wilderness, yet by token of that very fact, it stands for home as well. Vrindavan is both van and dham—very different but closely interdependent concepts baked into a single self-conception. This is why Vrindavan's wilderness is conceived to lie at the center of inhabited space rather than at the edge, the periphery. The theologians of Vrindavan have long claimed that its dham—its sense of "homeness"—lies at the hub of India, that is, effectively, the known world.[33] The remaining four dhams, by contrast, mark the cardinal points of direction—they are at the edge. We see echoes of this conception in the story of the bhakti movement that the Bhagavata Mahatmya provides. There Bhakti starts her journey from the south, gradually moving to the heart of the known world—to Vrindavan, which lies at the heart of India's largest expanse of riverine plain. Eventually she proceeds further north, but her rejuvenation happens at the center: this primordial, savanna-style home.[34]

Today Vrindavan is in danger of being submerged in a sea of general "world-class-ness" that takes away its independent reason for being.[35] The new Vrindavan mocks the old Vrindavan's longstanding sense of wilderness-as-home by covering it over with an ideology of moneyed leisure. This new ideology may be sold under the slogan "live blessed!" as if it were specific to Vrindavan, but the conditions that allow it to arise endanger the very blessedness that slogan evokes. The phrase itself is imported from abroad: there's an American Christian TV channel of that name. We can see the uncoupling of the new Vrindavan from the old in other ways, too. The purveyor of the "live blessed!" slogan is Krishna Bhūmi (diacritics and all), the VCM's special real estate partner, and it bills what it has to sell as "A World Class Temple Township in the heart of Vrindavan. Only 90 minutes from Delhi NCR (Via Yamuna Expressway)".[36] This is false, actually. The Chandrodaya Mandir and the buildings that will surround it are not in the heart of Vrindavan but at its edge. If they're at the heart of anything, it's "the world"—the world in which you must participate to have the money to live there.

What we see in Vrindavan today is a new tectonic plate crashing into the old. Vrindavan stands at a special juncture, with Uttar Pradesh on one side and Delhi on the other. Uttar Pradesh—India's poorest, most populous region—shows what happens when an ancient fertile plain can no longer support the life that once thrived there; Delhi exhibits the horrors of galloping global urbanization. It's a recipe for disaster on both sides, and when they converge, even more so. India's population is expected to surpass China's by 2025, yet no one in the Indian government ventures to discuss birth control. The state of national emergency that Indira Gandhi declared in the 1970s, with its measure to enforce birth control, was so hated that officials simply don't dare to raise the issue now. Vrindavan's vanished wilderness shows what's in store as a consequence.[37]

Nature is fighting back. The wells no longer yield water: the rapidly receding water-table lies farther and farther beneath the new and the old Vrindavan. The Yamuna is acrid and mostly refuses to touch the town. All this sounds "biblical" in its proportions, but rather, we might say, it's puranic. It's Kaliya and Keshi all over again, reflexes of a planet that's been frontally assaulted. These affronts are not just the emissaries of a determined asura king. The Bhagavata Purana calls them all asuras—Kamsa's agents—in such fashion that they seem to be reflexes of a human world turned despotic, but the older view, put forward in the Bhagavata's own sources, sees these as much more generic intruders, intrinsic to the landscape itself. This generic push-back is what we seem to be seeing in response to Vrindavan's careening development.

There is a haunting story in the old Harivaṃśa, our earliest surviving source for the life of Krishna, to the effect that Krishna once released a pack of wolves on his fellow cowherds, exuding them from his own body. It was tough love: there was no other way to persuade them to pasture elsewhere once present sources of nourishment had been exhausted. This vignette evidently seemed so offensive to the author of the cultured, elegant Bhagavata Purana that he dropped it from his own telling of the Krishna story. So did everyone else. It was inconceivable that Krishna could do such a thing. The author of the

Bhagavata faithfully carried forward other parts of the myth, adorning and beautifying them as he did so, but the story of the wolves was apparently beyond the pale.[38]

Now, though, we see why this story was there. Vrindavan's wilderness-home has rough edges, no matter how centrally located in the cosmos it may be. Indeed, if we think of Vrindavan as representing the planet as a whole, there's no place left to go. In the Harivaṃśa there were many places to roam, and the story of the wolves was merely a prelude to the discovery of that best of all wildernesses, Vrindavan itself, the one that lies on the banks of the Yamuna amid so many kadamba trees. But coded into the story of its discovery is the realization of how horrible a wilderness can become when it is defiled by overuse. The healing, fecund wilderness always threatens to become its own desiccated opposite, and there's no longer anyplace else to roam.

"Live blessed"? To do so, one has to contend with a sense of being vulnerable at the very core. One of the great challenges of designing Vrindavan as a World Heritage Site would be to keep that sense of vulnerability front and center. UNESCO has a special category of World Heritages Sites devoted to keeping a wilderness "wild". Since so much of the wilderness that even recently surrounded the old town of Vrindavan has succumbed to the bulldozer, it will be key for the WHS plan to have jurisdiction over lands on the opposite bank of the Yamuna, which should never be more developed than they are now. There's no other way for the town to keep recalling the primal scene Wilson described. Bihariji's primordially youthful song will fall silent at the source, no matter the attempts to amplify it by artificial means. The place will no longer be, in the UNESCO sense that corrects what we see in the new Vrindavan, "world class".[39]

A Theology of World Heritage

In the nineteenth century there was a panic about Krishna. To the British and to quite a number of indigenous Indian reformers his dalliances with the gopis seemed too much—a moral blight on the country.[40] In 1886 Bankim Chandra Chattopadhyay wrote a treatise to set the record right.[41] For him, as we have seen, Krishna was rational, intellectual, historical, martial, and fully practical—not a ladies' man, but a man's. The Vrindavan so loudly trumpeted in the Bengali

Vaishnavism that surrounded him stood on the wrong side of all this—the wrong side of history, as it then seemed. Nowadays, though, it's the very flexing of these masculinist muscles that seems all wrong. The great desire to build up, up, up has sunk the foundations upon which the edifice rests. Vrindavan's precious wilderness-home is in danger of extinction.

I worry about some of the theology that has helped propel this process. I think it will not do to imagine Krishna as someone whose very essence is to attract attention to himself, as in a major strand of ISKCON-Bangalore's theology. It makes him too much a symbol of our narcissist species. Rather, I think, his attraction radiates from the fact that he reflects the world he naturally inhabits, just as the peacock spreads its gorgeous feathers in response to the monsoon mating season. The image of that Krishna's reflective power is Vrindavan—the old Vrindavan very much more than the new. The traditional ras lilas of Braj radiate from that peacock moment.

Other images of Krishna—or Vishnu, to be more precise—envision him in a much more openly universal manner. Kashmiri sculptors and theologians of the late first millennium especially loved to depict him as a heavenly presence, lord of Vaikuntha (Fig. 7.2). There we see the earth, represented as Prakrti (nature) and understood as female, between his legs. His Vaikuntha heaven straddles the earth, keeping her/it safe as she adoringly looks up, while his four faces, two of them theriomorphic, parry dangers that might approach from any direction. This is a more hierarchical and cosmic image than Vrindavan's, but it shares with it a sense of comprehensive relationality.

Another image of Vishnu probes at the meaning of this evidently hierarchical order, where the male principle stands atop the female. It as if someone was paying close attention to the motif so often heard in Vrindavan's ras lilas, to the effect that the sentiments of lordship and mastery (aiśvarya) are secondary to those in which relationality is a more intimate, evenly balanced thing (mādhurya). In this anti-hierarchical but still cosmic image of Vishnu, we first meet him in the guise of a dwarf—a diminutive Brahmin who knocks at the door of a great king. This is the asura king Mahabali, a very righteous ruler indeed and powerful for that reason, as his name implies. The king asks the dwarf what he would like, ready to give, and the dwarf begs modestly for just one boon—ground enough to walk on with

Figure 7.2.   Vaikuṇṭha Vishnu, Kashmir, late eighth century. Metropolitan Museum of Art 1991.301, gift of Florence and Herbert Irving.

three steps. With the first of these he encompasses the entire earth. (He is Vishnu, after all.) With the second he vaults the heavens as well, and from his toe emerges the Ganges, standing in for all the world's rivers and for the cosmic system of water-recycling of which they are a crucial part. All that is left for the erstwhile dwarf to do with his third step is to mount the king's own back, an act that blesses the monarch with his touch and simultaneously makes Vishnu the lord of the underworld: the pressure of his third step makes Mahabali, now his devotee, ruler of these nether realms. In just three steps, thus, Vishnu has ballooned to such a size that he encompasses the universe. Each step marks a victory, and the lord is called collectively by all three: Trivikrama, he of the three victories. There's a Vishnu to comprehend each register of known space—the underworld, the earth, the sky. Just give him a little ground to stand on and he'll take it all. So his enormous upraised leg proclaims (Fig. 7.3).

Figure 7.3.   Trivikrama Vishnu, here shown as Krishna, standing atop King Mahabali and with the Ganges flowing down from his lifted foot. Panel from an illustration of the poem "mahārāj terī līṣī na pare ho", partially inscribed. The complete version bears the signature of Surdas (no. 104 in the Nāgarī Pracāriṇī Sabhā *Sūrsāgar*). Mewar ca. 1720. Government Museum, Udaipur, 1097 26/303.

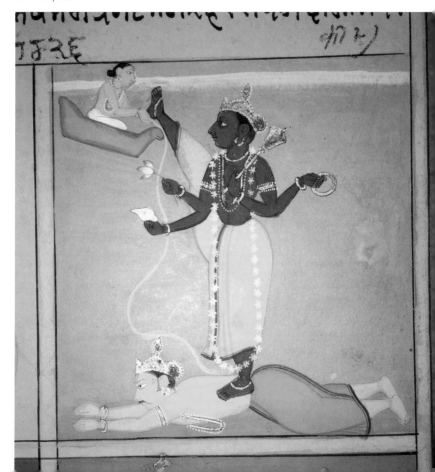

Both the Vaikuntha and Trivikrama images broadcast mastery and wonder—Vishnu as the all-seeing ruler, the lord of every height. But they don't prepare us for what we see in the rest of Vrindavan. There we meet the child in whose mouth we see the world. Vrindavan's Krishna, wily as he is, is really just a little boy with a voracious appetite for butter—or later a magnificent young man with an appetite for the girls (Fig. 1.1). Those appetites, in fact, connect, and he lives in an ecosystem where they can flourish. They encompass him, and he them.

Yes, he is still a hero. He kills Keshi and all the other murderous forces, but he doesn't have to be big to accomplish the feat (Fig. 2.2). Rather, his energy emanates from within, as in the case of any good dancer—Shiva and Krishna himself included. Significantly, in the long history of human attempts to understand the Krishna who lives in Vrindavan, two other heroic deeds have emerged as paradigmatic: the lila he performs with Govardhan, the mountain, and the one he visits on Kaliya, the snake. In the visual record—in sculptures that survive from the beginning to 1500 CE—these episodes appear far more frequently than any other others. People thought they mattered, and I believe it was for a reason. Both have their vertical dimension—the hierarchical axis of power, you might think—but in both cases hierarchy outside the box is questioned. What is validated is the relational order within. Both lilas proclaim Krishna as truly belonging to Vrindavan.[42]

In the first of these vignettes Krishna defends his Braj companions and their cattle against the unruly assault of Indra, king of the gods (Fig. 7.4). Indra, who rules the heavens, storms without cease for a whole week, but Krishna lifts Mount Govardhan as an umbrella for them all. We've seen this pictured at the Jvala Mukhi Ashram (Figs. 3.4–3.5) and it shows up at Prem Mandir and at many other places around town. You might think the rain-god represents non-human actors like disastrous monsoons and hurricanes, actors in the drama of climate change, and I don't want to dismiss that thought. But the story itself takes a different turn. Indra's assaults are those of an offended, extraneous deity, someone not implied in Krishna's own ecosystem. The challenge to which he reacts is the challenge to hierarchy itself: Krishna displaces the old hierarchy of gods. He lifts the mountain, which epitomizes Braj, in the cause of protecting that

Figure 7.4.   Krishna lifting Mount Govardhan, with some help from two cowherd friends. Indra, defeated, bows in reverence below. Detail from an illustration for "bādar kī bar āī deṣo", attributed to Surdas, who is shown elsewhere in the painting. Mewar ca. 1720. Government Museum, Udaipur, 1097 26/16.

very thing. To do so he acts from within. He lifts his hand or just his finger and all is well. Indra eventually stops and bows.

As for the second lila, it too is paradigmatic (Fig. 7.5). We also saw this on the grounds of Prem Mandir, and it's remembered at more than one place along the parikrama path. In the story itself, Krishna attacks Kaliya because he has poisoned the Yamuna by coming too far upstream. He has intruded from the sub-surface world into Vrindavan's beautiful, productive harmony. Cows cannot drink from

Figure 7.5. Krishna subduing Kāliya, who is surrounded by his serpent wives, illustration to the Bhāgavata Purāṇa, Garhwal, ca. 1785. Metropolitan Museum of Art, New York, accession number 27.37.

the river and birds flying overhead drop from the sky. The serpent's heat is unbearable, just as Vrindavan's heat and the world's heat, stoked by the release of masses of carbon from beneath the earth's surface, become more unbearable year by year. What does Krishna do with Kaliya? He doesn't kill him; he merely dives into the river and appears as a dancer on his several heads. He banishes the snake once again to the periphery of the ecosystem he inhabits, rather than striking him dead. Thus Krishna acts on behalf of humanity in distress, but he does so without compromising his place in the wider world, a world that displays the interplay between humans and the rest. All creatures play a part in the known world, and they interact in fair proportions as they do so.[43]

Nowadays, such proportions have been lost. The known world has exploded. What we have come to understand, though, is that our beautiful little planet is peripheral in itself—it circulates in a vast unchartable space (Fig. 7.6). We cannot ultimately know the extent of whatever logic (if any, ultimately) propels this complex ecosystem, since we ourselves are within it, and that should cause us to be

Figure 7.6.   Planet Earth as seen from DSCOVR (Deep Space Climate Observatory) on July 16, 2016. Note the frown, the expression of pain.

humble. All we can see is that our actions have consequences, and they are often not the consequences we wish. It won't help to strut about with the bravado of a Donald Trump or to expect that artificial intelligences we ourselves are capable of generating can act as our salvation. Once I worried aloud when the check-out person in a supermarket put what I'd bought into yet another plastic bag. What would happen, I wondered, when the continent-sized mass of plastic we've already consigned to the Pacific Ocean grows to a size too big to circumvent. "They'll think of something", she replied. I marveled at her belief in science and the force of American ingenuity.[44]

Something simpler has to be involved—a vision of truth that stands humble before the conditions of our species' own emergence. We have to learn to see our limits, and it is hard. Americans have to know that severely constrained Vrindavan is the sign of our common planetary future, not the likes of ever-expanding Las Vegas or Los Angeles. It may seem you can have a "world class" Vrindavan that mimics the West, but the conditions and consequences make you look again—not just in India but everywhere. Vrindavan's vision of wilderness and home as a single field helps us face this fact, but look at Vrindavan today and you see how hard it is to keep this ideal alive. Everything depends on seeing Vrindavan as the image of the world, yet we see how fragile the real Vrindavan is.

When Amitav Ghosh comes to the end of his deeply pessimistic book about global climate change, *The Great Derangement*, he appeals to religion for help—to people like Pope Francis and those who, for religious reasons, are able to come to "an acceptance of limits and limitations" because they have "an idea of the sacred, however one may wish to conceive of it".[45] You may smile at the cautious disclaimer expressed in that last phrase, thinking it sounds too much like Dwight Eisenhower when he so famously said, "our form of government has no sense unless it is founded in a deeply felt religious faith, and I don't care what it is".[46] Eisenhower had his reasons for not caring. For him it was the feeling of shared equality that mattered—humility in the face of whatever differences of status we seem to have. Such things are only illusions, Eisenhower felt, and Ghosh is dedicated to stressing the same point. We're all in this together, and a sense of the sacred helps us see how. But what if it's all illusion, our species-specific instinct for the sacred? What if religion is just a virtual thing? Vrindavan teaches us it's always been so, and knowing that helps us take stock.

In the end we share this virtual-real world. We share our wilderness-home. If Eden burns, it scalds us all. Religion's great gift is to make us aware of how tenuous our claims to authority are, and organized religion, as Ghosh appreciates, can indeed be a force for good. But we poison religion's gift by wielding it so often as a weapon, saying *we* have seen the light and *you* have not. Vrindavan, built on love, hopes to save us from such delusions, but Vrindavan too is built on religion.

Has Vrindavan really been plowed under? Are efforts to redeem it simply for naught? If so, that's likely true for the planet. Vrindavan is the sign of our times.

Notes

Chapter 1   Paradise—Lost?

1. Slight changes in the wording have been introduced in more recent "singings", but this is the version that was familiar to me as I was growing up. The words are those of Jane L. Borthwick (1813–1897), the musical setting ("Ora Labora") by T. Tertius Noble (1897–1953), as in *Pilgrim Hymnal* (Boston: Beacon Press, 1965 [1st ed. 1931]), 293.
2. Max Weber, *The Protestant Ethic and the Spirit of Capitalism*, tr. Talcott Parsons (London: Allen & Unwin, 1930) from *Gesammelte Aufsätze zur Religionssoziologie*, 1920–1.
3. "In Wildness Is the Preservation of the World". Henry David Thoreau, "Walking", in *Excursions* (Boston: Ticknor and Fields, 1864), 185; delivered orally in Concord, 1862. Surveying a terrain in which the notion of pilgrimage is very much present—the Holy Land!—Thoreau makes reference to Europe, Asia, Africa, and especially America, sometimes rhapsodizing along the way: "I believe in the forest, and in the meadow, and in the night in which the corn grows" (185); "Give me the ocean, the desert or the wilderness!" (189–90). A short retrospective is Douglas Brinkley, "Thoreau and the Legacy of Wildness", *New York Times Book Review*, July 9, 2017.

4. Kenneth E. Bryant and J.S. Hawley, *Sur's Ocean: Poems from the Early Tradition* (Cambridge: Harvard University Press, 2015), 292–5. For an exposition of the full logic of this poem, see Hawley, *Into Sur's Ocean: Poetry, Context, Commentary* (Cambridge: Harvard University Press, 2016), 439–41.

5. R. Parthasarathy, *The Tale of an Anklet, An Epic of South India: The Cilappatikāram of Iḷaṅkō Aṭikaḷ* (New York: Columbia University Press, 1993), canto 17, 170–8.

6. This echo can also be heard in reverse. The life story of the fourteenth-century Sanskrit poet Vedāntadeśika, told in Tamil, says that he made a pilgrimage to various classic locations including the "northern Madurai" (vaṭa maturai), that is, Mathura. Steven P. Hopkins, *The Flight of Love: A Messenger Poem of Medieval South India by Veṅkaṭanātha* (New York: Oxford University Press, 2016), 3–4.

7. Archana Venkatesan, *The Secret Garland: Āṇṭaḷ's Tiruppāvai and Nācciyār Tirumoḻi* (New York: Oxford University Press, 2010), 186–8. More broadly, Dennis Hudson, "Vraja among the Tamils", *Journal of Vaishnava Studies* 3:1 (1994), 113–40.

8. Valerie Stoker, *Polemics and Patronage in the City of Victory: Vyāsatīrtha, Hindu Sectarianism, and the Sixteenth-Century Vijayanagara Court* (Berkeley: University of California Press, 2016), 37, 159–60.

9. Barbara Stoler Miller, *Love Song of the Dark Lord: Jayadeva's Gītagovinda* (New York: Columbia University Press, 1977), 77, 135 (part 1, song 4, verse 45).

10. Rodney Sebastian, "Cultural Fusion in a Religious Dance Drama: Building the Sacred Body in the Manipuri *Rāslīlās*" (PhD Dissertation, University of Florida, 2019), and "Constructing the Manipuri *Rāslīlās*: Agency, Power, and Consensus", paper delivered to the American Academy of Religion, Denver, 18 November 2018.

11. T. Richard Blurton, *Krishna in the Garden of Assam: The History and Context of a Much-Travelled Textile* (London: The British Museum, 2016).

12. Pika Ghosh, *Temple to Love: Architecture and Devotion in Seventeenth-Century Bengal* (Bloomington: Indiana University Press, 2005), 187–99.

13. Sukanya Sarbadhikary, *The Place of Devotion: Siting and Experiencing Divinity in Bengal-Vaishnavism* (Berkeley: University of California Press, 2015); Varuni Bhatia, *Unforgetting Chaitanya: Vaishnavism and Cultures of Devotion in Colonial Bengal* (New York: Oxford University Press, 2017), 161–99; Bhatia, "Finding a Birthplace", *Journal of Vaishnava Studies* 23:1 (2014), 157–88; and Jason D. Fuller, "Bengali Vaishnava Homelands", *Journal of Vaishnava Studies* 18:1 (2009), 39–52.

14. Bhakti Puruṣottama Swami, *Śrī Navadvīpa Parikramā* (Mayapur: Mayapur Media, 2010), 25.

15. A pictorial introduction to the site in West Virginia is Varsana Swami, *Appreciating New Vrindaban-Dhama: Her Beauty and Glory, Message and Grace* (n.p.: Moontower Publications, 2018); as to vexed aspects of its history, see John Hubner, *Monkey on a Stick: Murder, Madness, and the Hare Krishnas* (San Diego: Harcourt Brace Jovanovich, 1988). On the Mumbai initiatives of Radhanath Swami, see http://www.radhanathswami.com and Claire C. Robison, "A Return to a Place One Has Not Been: ISKCON and the Rhetoric of *Bhakti* Revivalism in Mumbai", unpublished paper, November, 2018.

16. E. Allen Richardson, *Seeing Krishna in America: The Hindu Bhakti Tradition of Vallabhacharya in India and its Movement to the West* (Jefferson, NC: McFarland and Co., 2014).

17. Patterns of invention and replication such as those just described are not unique to Vrindavan, yet Vrindavan charts out a particular pattern of relationships between archetype and replica. For contrasting patterns within a broadly Indian orbit see, e.g., Diana L. Eck, *Banaras: City of Light* (New York: Alfred A. Knopf, 1982), 283–8; Toni Hubner, *The Holy Land Reborn: Pilgrimage and the Tibetan Reinvention of Buddhist India* (Chicago: University of Chicago Press, 2008); and, in a more theatrical vein, Satyasundar Barik, "Krishna and Kansa Come Alive for 11 Days Every Year in This Odisha Village", *The Hindu*, January 19, 2019; www.thehindu.com/entertainment/art/krishna-and-kansa-come-alive-for-11-days-every-year-in-this-odisha-village/article26036571.ece.

Chapter 2   The Battle of Keshi Ghat

1. Jan "Jagat" Brzezinski thinks the dramatic growth of the area in which monkeys steal glasses in the last ten or fifteen years may be explained by the fact that when young males come of age, they are expelled from their immediate clan by the ruling alpha male. When this happens, they take along with them a knowledge the clan's "expert technology" to other areas where they are able to unseat a different alpha male (Brzezinski, interview, Jiva Institute, December 2, 2016). It is the "technology" that is new to Vrindavan; moneys are not. Peter Mundy, traveling there in the 1630s, noted their great number, which he attributed to the fact that they were fed as acts of piety, and in an illustrated manuscript of Bihārīlāl's *Rasikapriyā* produced at just about that time in Mewar, the monkeys' playfulness formed a notable aspect of the ideal Vrindavan "scene". See

Alan W. Entwistle, *Braj, Centre of Krishna Pilgrimage* (Groningen: Egbert Forsten, 1987), 209, and Mirjam Westra, "Kṛṣṇa Approaches Rādhā and Her Confidante in a Garden with Trees, Playful Monkeys, and Glorious Blue Peacocks (1620–1640)", *Aziatische Kunst* 48:1 (2018), 94–101. The danger posed by today's vast monkey population, however, even outside Vrindavan, is made evident in a series of incidents recently experienced in Agra ("Monkey Enters House, Snatches Infant from Mom, Mauls Him to Death in Agra", *Times of India*, November 14, 2018). A follow-up article on the shortage of anti-rabies vaccine in a local hospital carried the headline "Monkey Bites Up by 50% in Last 3 Months" (*Times of India*, November 17, 2018).

2. Generally on this subject, see Samrat Schmiem Kumar, "Sacred Modernity and Its Fragments: Space, Environment, and Life-worlds in the Indian Temple Town Vrindavan" (PhD dissertation, University of Oslo, 2014), and *Vrindavan's Encounter with Modernity: Changing Environment and Life-worlds in an Indian Temple Town* (Berlin: LIT Verlag, 2019); also Samrat Schmiem Kumar and Elida Jacobsen, "Heritage and Environment: Visions of Past and Future in the Indian Temple Town of Vrindavan", *Peaceworks* 7:1 (2017), 116–30. On real estate and black money, Ravi Agrawal, *India Connected: How the Smartphone Is Transforming the World's Largest Democracy* (New York and Delhi: Oxford University Press, 2018), 173–4, 185.

3. An image of this projected gondola can be seen in Hawley, "Vrindavan and the Drama of Keshi Ghat", in A. Srivasthan, Annapurna Garimella, and Shriya Shridharan, eds., *The Contemporary Hindu Temple: Fragments for a History* (Mumbai: Marg Publications, 2019), 67, fig. 12. Other photographs relevant to this chapter also appear there.

4. The inspiration comes, in part, from a gondola currently being built from the road beneath Radha's natal town, Barsana, to the top of the hill on which it sits. Barsana lies some 25 miles from Vrindavan; serious tourists often visit both.

5. On the phenomenon of the cell phone in India broadly, see Agrawal, *India Connected*.

6. Compare Bruce M. Sullivan, "Theology and Ecology in the Birthplace of Kṛṣṇa", in Lance E. Nelson, ed., *Purifying the Earthly Body of God: Religion and Ecology in Hindu India* (Albany: State University of New York Press, 1998), 255–6.

7. Chandrakant Gupta, interviews, July 14, 2018 and January 23, 2019.

8. For general context on difficulties faced by local governments—financial, administrative, and historical—see Assa Doron and Robin Jeffrey, *Waste of a Nation: Garbage and Growth in India* (Cambridge: Harvard

University Press, 2018), 162–87; on prospects for and obstacles to change in that context, 183–7; on challenges posed to a flush-toilet system by a shortage of water resources, 85–8. More generally on caste in relation to human waste, see Diane Coffey and Dean Spears, *Where India Goes: Abandoned Toilets, Stunted Development, and the Costs of Caste* (Noida: HarperCollins, 2017).

9. There is debate about how much the current course of the Yamuna, largely bypassing the historic ghats, should be attributed to natural changes and how much to self-conscious efforts on part of the local "land mafia" to push the river back and make way for new buildings, new parking lots, and eventually such efforts as those the Futurists champion. In regard to the existence of such a "mafia" and the use of the term, see, e.g., "Saints' Lives in Danger as Land Mafias Eye Ashrams" and "Land Use Scams Involving District Officers Comes [*sic*] to Light", *Vrindavan Today*, June 6, 2018; compare Nicholas Martin and Lucia Michelutti, "Protection Rackets and Party Machines: Comparative Ethnographies of 'Mafia Raj' in North India", *Asian Journal of Social Science* 45:5 (2017), 692–722. There have also apparently been changes in the plotting of the Parikrama Marg over time. It would likely have been less extensive than it is today at the time when the town was established in the sixteenth century, since the settlement itself was smaller (Sushant Bharati, private communication, Delhi, February 12, 2019).

10. At this writing, this video is a DVD not yet uploaded to the internet. Paramadvaiti Swami, *Healthy Sacred Water: Yamuna & Ganga* (Vrindavan: Vrindavan Act Now, 2010); compare Braj Vrindavan Act Now, vrindavanactnow.org. The DVD also contains a video in which K.P.S. Gill (on whom, see later) discusses his views.

11. "Massive March for Yamuna River Reaches Delhi," *New York Times*, March 11, 2013, https://india.blogs.nytimes.com/2013/03/11/massive-march-for-yamuna-river-nears-delhi/.

12. "New Mathura Plan Geared for Tourism; No Mention of Sewage, Waste Management", *Vrindavan Today*, June 9, 2017; compare "Hema Malini Working on Braj's Water Issues, Creating Funparks", *Vrindavan Today*, May 13, 2018. The theme park is under construction in the Jawaharbagh area of Mathura. Hema Malini's principal residence is in Mumbai—this is quite possible in the Indian political system—but she is building a residence in the Omaxe complex in Vrindavan that will count as a second home.

13. Current developments ought to be searchable on the website of the Mathura Vrindavan Development Association, http://mvda.in. As accessed on September 9, 2018 under "Nodel [*sic*] Agency" with reference to the UP government's Braj Tīrtha Vikās Pariṣad, a newly established

agency to coordinate planning for all of the state's pilgrimage (tīrtha) sites, one reads that some 1893 lakhs of rupees have been sanctioned for the beautification and firming up (saundaryakaraṇ evam sudṛḍhīkaraṇ) of the Parikrama Marg. Further details were not given. Subsequently, see https://www.upbtvp.in/projects.php.

14. Anthony Acciavatti, *Ganges Water Machine: Designing India's Ancient River* (San Francisco: Applied Research and Design, 2015), 109–210.

15. "Pipeline to Bring Ganga Water to the Yamuna Declared Successful", *Vrindavan Today,* January 25, 2018: the "successes" relate to the absence of water pressure loss in the very limited district so far affected; farmers of Mant continue to oppose the project because of the low land valuations they say the government assigns to lands of theirs that would be appropriated for the laying of the Gangajal Project pipes. Compare Shruti Jain, "Twelve Years after Gangajal Project, Agra Still Waits for Clean Drinking Water", *The Wire,* June 24, 2017.

16. Compare Peter van der Veer, *The Value of Comparison,* chapter 6: "Who Cares? Care Arrangements and Sanitation for the Poor in India and Elsewhere" (Durham: Duke University Press, 2016), 130–46, 168–70.

17. Item no. 10, court no. 2, under the jurisdiction of Justice Raghuvendra S. Rathore, Judicial Member, and Dr. Satyawan Singh Garbyal, Expert Member. The NGT's decision falls short of openly embracing the "precautionary principle" appropriate to legal and civic engagements with the relationship between rivers and cities in an age of advancing environmental devastation, but it falls in line with such objectives. See Awadhendra Sharan, "A River and the Riverfront: Delhi's Yamuna as an In-Between Space", *City, Culture and Society* 7 (2016), 267–73.

18. Margaret H. Case, *Seeing Krishna: The Religious World of a Brahman Family in Vrindaban* (New York: Oxford University Press, 2000), 16–21.

19. Frederic Salmon Growse, *Mathurá: A District Memoir,* 3rd ed. (Allahabad: North-Western Provinces and Oudh Government Press, 1883), 264.

20. "Mathurā–Vṛndāvan meṅ Yamunā Kināre 200 Mīṭar tak Nirmāṇ par Rok: Galat Halaphnāmā Dene ke Māmle meṅ Jalnigam ke Pariyojanā Prabandhak par Girī Gāj", *Amar Ujālā,* reported from Allahabad bureau, December 23, 2017. Also "High Court Declares Yamuna Plain as 'No Construction Zone,'" *Vrindavan Today,* December 24, 2017.

21. Vijay Kumar of Hathras, an employee of Ajay Contruction Co., Meerut (Vrindavan, December 23, 2017).

22. Notification No. 1799/9-7-17-8 (Seema Vistar)/2016, Government of Uttar Pradesh, Nagar Vikās Anubhāg-7, Lucknow, May 12, 2017.

23. In the regulations that were in force under Vrindavan's own Nagar Palika Parishad, a building's maximum height was determined according to a

formula called the Floor Surface Index (FSI), which maintained a relatively high ratio for lands within the orbit of roughly the Parikrama Marg
and adopted a lower, more liberal one for construction farther from the
center of the old town. Up until 2007 building regulations for structures
in the oldest parts of town were even more restrictive.

24. For details, see the Namami Gange ("I honor the Ganga") posting by Nitin
Gadkari on Facebook: https://www.facebook.com/238734830200028/
posts/415762349163941. The omission of the Kosi Nala is crucial.
Awadhendra Sharan has emphasized the point that "pollution, as we
understand it today, was not a product of the traditional arrangement
of things but of the centralized water and sewerage works that were
inaugurated by the colonial regime itself". The Kosi Nala forms a part
of this vast system. See Awadendhra Sharan, "The Ganges as an Urban
Sink: Urban Waste and River Flow in Colonial India in the Nineteenth
Century", in Martin Knoll, Uwe Lübken, and Dieter Schott, eds., *Rivers Lost,
Rivers Regained: Rethinking City-River Relations* (Pittsburgh: University of
Pittsburgh Press, 2017), 214.

25. Shrivatsa Goswami, when discussing these things, contrasts Vrindavan's
situation to that of Banaras where, whatever other trials the city may be
enduring, sewage has never been allowed to cross the barrage of ghats
that lines the river (interview, Vrindavan, January 25, 2019).

26. The *Hindustan Times* reports as a matter of public concern that India
draws more ground water out of the earth than any other country in the
world and that "the rate of depletion has increased by 23% between 2000
and 2010" (Editorial page, March 21, 2019).

27. Chowpatty Beach arrived elsewhere in town with the recent building of
a flashy restaurant called Chowpatty, that is, Chaupāṭī—the signage is
all in Hindi. It sits directly across from Prem Mandir and extends its
happy-go-lucky mood. Chaupāṭī has an entirely open-air format—street
food is its staple—and it sports a dramatic roof that hovers two or three
stories above. Numerous bulbs studding the roof make the night bright.
The mood is intended to evoke Mumbai, but the owners themselves are
locals, and they have ensconced a gregarious local milkman right in the
center of the restaurant's open space as if to make the point. Sometimes
dressed in a saffron-orange kurta-pajama, and an equally orange turban,
he ladles out warm milk from an enormous wok. The color seems simply celebratory, but it also matches what Kripaluji, the founder of Prem
Mandir, always wore. Not a beat is missed.

28. The head of this project, Vijay Singh of Shivom Constructions, did not
actually mention the national elections when he told me that the MVDA
had contracted for the work to be done by the end of April 2019, but as

with the prior UP state elections it was not hard to see the connection (conversation, Vrindavan, March 24, 2019).

29. J.S. Hawley and Shrivatsa Goswami, *At Play with Krishna: Pilgrimage Dramas from Brindavan* (Princeton: Princeton University Press, 1981), 40.

30. Such āratīs have become a business of late. A local merchant by the name of Gangavale runs a boisterous āratī there every afternoon. He posts the number of his mobile phone on a sign painted next to some of the Pandavala Ghat's steps so that you can contact him to avail yourself of his services. Or you can come directly if you wish. He posts the summer and winter timings.

Chapter 3   Mall of Vrindavan

1. I am indebted to Samrat Schmiem Kumar for much of what I have just written here (personal communication, October 7, 2016). Compare Hawley and Goswami, *At Play with Krishna,* 22, 24, 29.

2. Amar Nath Pandey, interview, Vrindavan, March 24, 2017.

3. Anne Feldhaus, *Water and Womanhood: Religious Meanings of Rivers in Maharashtra* (New York: Oxford University Press, 1995); Diana L. Eck, *India: A Sacred Geography* (New York: Harmony Books, 2012), 131–88.

4. A comprehensive view of the Yamuna's pollution is provided by David L. Haberman, *River of Love in an Age of Pollution: The Yamuna River of Northern India* (Berkeley: University of California Press, 2006), 74–94, 141–95. Other resources include documentary films such as Krisztina Danka's *The Stolen River* (Karuna Productions, 2017), which builds upon her earlier, more extensive "Rescuing the Sacred River" (2015). In regard to the Ganga, sister to the Yamuna, see Kelly D. Alley, *On the Banks of the Gaṅgā: When Wastewater Meets a Sacred River* (Ann Arbor: University of Michigan Press, 2002), and "Separate Domains: Hinduism, Politics, and Environmental Pollution", in Christopher Key Chapple and Mary Evelyn Tucker, eds., *Hinduism and Ecology: The Intersection of Earth, Sky, and Water* (Cambridge: Center for the Study of World Religions, Harvard Divinity School, 2000), 355–87. Citizens' efforts to clean their water sources are recounted in Ann Grodzins Gold, *Shiptown: Between Rural and Urban North India* (Philadelphia: University of Pennsylvania Press, 2017), 196–207, and Drew Thomases, *Guest Is God: Pilgrimage, Tourism, and Making Paradise in India* (New York: Oxford University Press, 2019), 52–77; "Making Pushkar Paradise: Hindu Ritualization and the Environment", *International Journal of Hindu Studies* 21:2 (2017), 187–210.

5. An account of what it was like in the old days appears in Klaus Klostermaier, *In the Paradise of Krishna: Hindu and Christian Seekers*, tr. Antonia Fonseca (Philadelphia: Westminster, 1969), 14–26. The German original is *Christ und Hindu in Vrindaban* (Köln: Jakob Hegner, 1968).

6. When I asked the man sharing a battery-powered rickshaw about this couplet on March 24, 2017, the actual verse he quoted was: "chitrakūṭ kā rām raj, vrindāvan kā dhūl; yah raj mastak lage, pāp hoeṅ sab dūr". I have made slight emendations for metrical reasons. Chitrakut is a forest locale where Ram tarried in the course of his fourteen-year exile from Ayodhya.

7. Interview, Vrindavan, December 29, 2016. See also his "Bhaktivedanta Marg and the Three Vrindavans", *Vrindavan Today*, March 2, 2016, https:// vrindavantoday.com/bhaktivedanta-marg-and-the-three-vrindavans/. Worthy of comparison, and with a similar irony lurking in the wings, are these sentences from the mouth of a well-known Puṣṭimārgīya gosvāmī: "Śrījī has long since left Nathdwara and returned to Braj. An icon may remain, but Śrīnāthjī himself has gone". See Emilia Bachrach, "In the Seat of Authority: Debating Temple Spaces and Community Identity in a Vaiṣṇava Sampradāy of Contemporary Gujarat", *Journal of Hindu Studies* 10:1 (2017), 27. Citing this passage, Rupert Snell quips, "Perhaps Braj was not to prove such a safe refuge after all" (email communication, March 11, 2019).

8. Samrat Kumar, *Vrindavan's Encounter with Modernity*, 61.

9. Vaishno Devi's eminence extends far beyond the Punjab. On the evening of July 5, 2018, I was waiting for a somewhat belated Taj Express at the Mathura Railway Station when another train pulled in on the same track. As the label on all bogeys proclaimed, it was the Shri Mata Vaishno Devi Katra Express. This title had been grafted onto the erstwhile Andaman Express, whose name also appeared on the first car, since the train's terminal stop is the town of Katra, located at the base of the Himalayas not far from Vaishno Devi's mountain home. This transformation reflects Vaishno Devi's new importance in the world of pilgrimage tourism. When the Taj Express arrived, I discovered that it too had been hybridized. It was now labeled the Shan-e Punjab Taj Express, since the train now terminates not in New Delhi but in Amritsar.

10. The Devanagari spelling—with the long *a* at the end—is technically incorrect: this lengthened or "heavy" (guru) vowel ought to indicate a feminine ending rather than a masculine one. Normally the name Krishnā would refer to Draupadī, the wife of the five Pāṇḍava brothers, yet the being to whom reference is made here is none other than Krishna himself. His name is properly spelled with a short *a* at the end, a schwa,

not the more emphatic *ā*. When I asked about this at the ashram's desk, however, there was absolutely no sense that anything had gone awry. "The *ā* is for chanting", said the cheerful young man with whom I spoke, and he treated me immediately to a nice set of mantras, starting with the familiar "Hare Krishna" one (not insignificantly, considering the influence of ISKCON and perhaps his perception of me) and moving on from there to a repeated chanting of only the name Krishna itself. One needs this *ā* for space between the consonants, he explained—for sonority. He insisted that the issue had to do with pronunciation, and he dropped that English word into his Hindi sentences to make his point. The English-language association proved not to be accidental. Often when foreigners' English pronunciation is given a Hindi transliteration, this extra *a* is added, as happened some years ago with the Ashoka Hotel in Delhi, a well-known instance in the field. What started as English speakers' respect for the final shwa vowel—as if one were pronouncing Sanskrit rather than Hindi, where it is dropped (Ashok, not Ashoka)—was then carried over into Hindi when the name of that iconic hotel was written in Devanagari script. The same thing had happened here—a silent genuflection to the prestige of the international language (English this time, not Sanskrit)—and with it, implicitly, the hope that this hotel too would be perceived as international in its appeal and clientele. My interlocutor acknowledged all of this with a smile (interview, Deepak Goel, Vrindavan, July 7, 2018). The English-inflected *ā* also appears in the name of the charitable trust responsible for constructing the building, and one can see it in several other places on this side of Vrindavan where there is a gesture to the West, for instance, the apartment complex Shri Krishna (that is, Krishnā) Greens and that classic concept Ayurveda, now spelled Āyurvedā on various signs to be seen in the vicinity of the Chatikara Road.

11. Gurū Granth page 470, rāg āsā 3:2.5–6. In a number of ways what Nanak says here contrasts with standard accounts. The figure Krishna is said to have abducted ought to be his wife-to-be Rukmiṇī, not Chandrāvalī, and the theft of the Pārijāta tree is associated with Satyabhāmā, not a gopī. As for the question of exactly what Nanak means by "rangu kīyā", which I have translated "enjoyed himself", there can certainly be differences of opinion. The word "rang" or "rangu" calls up everything from color per se to erotic love.

12. Gurū Granth pages 464–5, āsā dī vār 32.4–5. I follow the interpretation of Norvin Hein, *The Miracle Plays of Mathurā* (New Haven: Yale University Press, 1972, 116–17), where a translation also appears.

13. Interview, Nanak Tila Gurdwara, December 28, 2016.

14. On the analogy—and indeed connection—between economy and religion in broad terms, compare the recent work of Nile Green, *Terrains
of Exchange: Religious Economies of Global Islam* (New York: Oxford
University Press, 2014). For a more specific usage of my own, see *Krishna,
the Butter Thief* (Princeton: Princeton University Press, 1983), 261–87,
and, of course, we have Weber's *The Protestant Ethic and the Spirit of
Capitalism*. Finally, we must take account of the distinctive architectural
sensibilities being displayed along the Chatikara Road, for which a
classic study of Las Vegas serves as essential background reading, even
if it focuses on much that is quite different from Vrindavan: Robert
Venturi, Denise Scott Brown, and Steven Izenour, *Learning from Las
Vegas: The Forgotten Symbolism of Architectural Form* (Cambridge: MIT
Press, 1977).

15. On the four sampradāys in their classical form, see Hawley, *A Storm of
Songs*, 99–147.

16. Kripalu Ji Maharaj [attributed], *Prem Mandir: A Tribute to Divine Love*
(New Delhi: Radha Govind Samiti, 2013), 18–19. The cover bears a somewhat different title than the title page: *Prem Mandir: A Transcendental
Gift of Divine Love by Jagadguru Shri Kripalu Ji Maharaj to Shri Vrindavan
Dham*. This is one of two glossy introductions to the site available for
purchase at the Prem Mandir bookstore in late 2106. The other, in Hindi,
differs from its English cousin by containing a substantial set of felicita-
tions by important religious and political figures, especially BJP ones,
at the beginning and reproducing the complete text of Kripalu's poetic
compositions inscribed on the inner walls of the temple itself (Anon.,
Prem Mandir Śrī Vṛndāvan Dhām, n.d. [2012], 34–67).

17. D.S. Pandey, interview, Prem Mandir, March 21, 2017.

18. Kripalu Ji Maharaj [attributed], *Prem Mandir* [in English], 55.

19. Philip Lutgendorf, "My Hanuman Is Bigger than Yours", *History of
Religions* 33:3 (1994), 211–45. To the point that such sacred displays are
hardly out of place in what was assumed to be an ever-secularizing "secu-
lar city", see, e.g., Meera Nanda, *The God Market: How Globalization Is
Making India More Hindu* (New York: Monthly Review Press, 2009), Kajri
Jain, *Gods in the Bazaar: The Economies of Indian Calendar Art* (Durham:
Duke University Press, 2007), and Tulasi Srinivas, *The Cow in the Elevator:
An Anthropology of Wonder* (Durham: Duke University Press, 2018). The
point of comparison is Harvey Cox, *The Secular City: Secularization and
Urbanization in Theological Perspective* (New York: Collier Books, 1965).

20. That Vrindavan has become an important wedding destination is indicated by the fact that, when *The Guardian* posted an article on changing
marital mores in Hindu India, it chose as an accompanying illustration

a photograph of a recent wedding in Vrindavan. Amrit Dhillon, "Out with the Old: App-wise Indians Reject Caste and Dowry Traditions", *The Guardian*, July 10, 2018.

21. Amit Rajpoot, interview, November 8, 2016; Shailendra Dixit, interview, February 24, 2019.

22. Rajdeep Singh, interview, December 28, 2016.

23. The ISKCON group of which I am speaking belongs to the Russian community resident in the Nikunj Samadhi Mandir just off Parikrama Marg not far away. It has an interesting American-Russian history that underscores the internationalism of the order. ISKCON devotees living there do not dance in front of Prem Mandir every day—perhaps once every ten or fifteen.

24. That is, prasād, in Hindi. The Sanskrit accusative -*am* ending is one of the endearing flourishes adopted from Prabhupad's missionizing argot. It has become linguistic truth within ISKCON, as has the pronunciation of the much-used "devotee" with the accent on the middle syllable, not the last.

25. William H. Deadwyler, "Cleaning House and Cleaning Hearts: Reform and Renewal in ISKCON", in Edwin F. Bryant and Maria L. Ekstrand, eds., *The Hare Krishna Movement: The Postcharismatic Fate of a Religious Transplant* (New York: Columbia University Press, 2004), 161.

26. Satyanarayan Das, interview, Vrindavan, February 11, 2017.

27. Satya Nārāyaṇa Dāsa and Kuṇḍalī Dāsa, *In Vaikuṇṭha Not Even the Leaves Fall: A Treatise on the Bondage of the Jīva* (Vrindavan: Jiva Institute of Vaisnava Studies, 1994), xiv.

28. Satyanarayan Das, interview, Vrindavan, February 11, 2017.

29. On the Bishop Michael designation, as understood within the Bhakti Marga community, see Robert Lindsey, "Divine Encounter, Miracles, and Christianity: Religious Experience in Paramahamsa Vishwananda's *Bhakti Marga* Movement", 14–15. Unpublished paper, Columbia University, 2016.

30. Swami Vishwarevatikaantananda, interview, Vrindavan, December 2, 2016.

31. Satyanarayan Das, interview, Vrindavan, February 11, 2017.

32. I am grateful to Robert Lindsey, who documented the dancing moment on December 3, 2016 and suggested the question about the future.

33. Editing Team of Bhakti Marga Publications, *Giridhari, the Uplifter of Hearts: A Selection of 108 Insights from Paramahamsa Vishwananda* (Springen, Germany: BhaktiMarga Publications, 2016), 8.

34. Swami Vishwarevatikaantananda, interview, Springen, June 28, 2018.

35. Swamini Vishwamohini, interview, Vrindavan, July 13, 2018.

36. In the Vallabh Sampradāy too such a pairing is made, but in that context Krishna is not actually shown as the Mountain-Lifter, though that is an important facet of his personality in the community as a whole (Srinathji). David Haberman makes the point that stones from Mt. Govardhan are invariably found in temples dedicated to the Yamuna on Vishram Ghat in Mathura, but again this is not the same as what we see here (Haberman, *River of Love in an Age of Pollution*, 101–2).

37. J.S. Hawley, *Three Bhakti Voices: Mirabai, Surdas, and Kabir in Their Time and Ours* (Delhi: Oxford University Press, 2005), 103–5.

38. David L. Haberman, "Bhakti as Relationship: Drawing Form and Personality from the Formless", in J.S. Hawley, Christian Lee Novetzke, and Swapna Sharma, eds., *Bhakti and Power: Debating India's Religion of the Heart* (Seattle: University of Washington Press and Hyderabad: Orient BlackSwan, 2019), 134–41. See also Haberman, *Loving Stones: Making the Impossible Possible in the Worship of Mount Govardhan* (New York: Oxford University Press, 2020).

39. Sitārāmśaraṇ Bhagavān Prasād "Rūpkalā", ed. *Śrī Bhaktamāl* with the *Bhaktirasabodhinī* commentary of Priyādās (Lucknow: Tejkumār Press, 1969 [1910]), 721. The story is sometimes told with Jiva's uncle Rupa Gosvami as Mirabai's adversary. See J.S. Hawley and Mark Juergensmeyer, *Songs of the Saints of India* (Delhi: Oxford University Press, 2004 [1988]), 126, 203.

40. Swami Vishwarevatikaantananda, interview, Vrindavan, December 4, 2016. On the touch of gurus more broadly, but with absolutely no implication that sexual improprieties are involved, see Amanda Lucia, "Guru Sex: Charisma, Proxemic Desire, and the Haptic Logics of the Guru-Disciple Relationship", *Journal of the American Academy of Religion* 86:4 (2018), 953–88.

41. Interview, Vrindavan, December 4, 2016.

42. Lindsey, "Divine Encounter, Miracles, and Christianity", 27–8, Appendix IX; Swami Revatikaantananda, interview, Springen, June 28, 2018.

43. Swami Vishwananda, interview, Munger Raj Mandir, Vrindavan, December 1, 2016.

44. *Giridhari, the Uplifter of Hearts*, 50.

45. Emile Durkheim, *The Elementary Forms of the Religious Life*, tr. Joseph Ward Swain (New York: Free Press, 1965 [1915]), 258; compare 255–61, 466, 469, 474–5. On liminality, see Victor Turner, "The Center Out There: Pilgrim's Goal", *History of Religions* 12:3 (1973), 191–230, and *The Ritual Process: Structure and Anti-Structure* (Chicago: Aldine, 1969), 14, 94–165. On New Year's Day in quite a different Hindu context, see J.S. Hawley and Vasudha Narayanan, eds., *The Life of Hinduism* (Berkeley: University

of California Press, 2006), 1–4. As to the vibrancy of pilgrimage in other parts of the world, including the element of self-imposed hardship, see, e.g., Kirk Semple, "Virgin of Guadalupe Is 'No. 1 Mother' in Mexico, a Binding Force across Divides", *New York Times*, December 15, 2018.

Chapter 4   *The Skyscraper Temple*

1. Rakesh Pathak, interview, Vrindavan, December 21, 2017.
2. Especially powerful for Gauḍīya memory is the Sanskrit drama *Chaitanyachandrodaya* composed by one of Chaitanya's most gifted followers, Kavikarṇapūra, in 1572. Further, see Rembert Lutjeharms, *A Vaiṣṇava Poet in Early Modern Bengal: Kavikarṇapura's "Splendor of Speech"* (Oxford: Oxford University Press, 2018), 42, 62–3.
3. This was not the first time that a plan for a massive new structure had emerged in ISKCON circles. Bhaktisiddhanta Dasa, a native of New York residing in Vrindavan, published *Vrindavana, the Crest Jewel of India* (Vrindavan: Prabhupada Institute of Culture, [1990]), describing "The Vrindavan Vedic City: The Transcendental Land of Lord Krishna— the Supreme Personality of Godhead". He envisioned a futuristic "The Glory of India Museum", a temple, a Vrindavan University, a "multi-media Haribol stadium", and "two large 5-star hotels" in addition to "a deer running park, elephant park and a large Goshala" (11). The project was a self-conscious response to "the tremendous vacuum created right after [Prabhupad's] disappearance", that is, death (11). So far as I know, none of these plans came to fruition in the form they were envisioned.
4. Sarvanand Gaurang Das, interview, Gurgaon, November 25, 2016. But size itself—and particularly height—is also key, as the comparison of these structures reveals, with the VCM being clearly the tallest. A recent entry into this game, world-wide, is the People's Salvation Cathedral scheduled to be completed in Bucharest in 2024. It will be "the tallest Orthodox church in the world", as described by the *New York Times* (Kit Gillet, "Big Debate in Romania over a Big Cathedral and Its Big Price Tag", December 4, 2018.)
5. Kavita Singh, "Temple of Eternal Return: The Swāminārāyan Akshardhām Complex in Delhi", *Artibus Asiae* 70:1 (2010), 50. Otherwise on monumentality in contemporary South Asia, see, e.g., Bruce McCoy Owens, "Monumentality, Identity, and the State: Local Practice, World Heritage, and Heterotopia at Swayambhu, Nepal", *Anthropological Quarterly* 75:2 (2002), 269–316, and Melia Belli, "Monumental Pride: Mayawati's Memorials in Lucknow", *Ars Orientalis* 44 (2014), 85–109.

6. Kajri Jain, "Post-Reform India's Automotive-Iconic-Cement Assemblages:
    Uneven Globality, Territorial Spectacle, and Iconic Exhibition Value",
    Identities: Global Studies in Culture and Power, May 8, 2015, especially 8–9,
    13–16; and "Gods in the Time of Automobility", *Current Anthropology* 58:
    supplement 15 (2017), accessed November 28, 2016. It would be wrong
    to conclude, however, that premodern Hindu temples lacked something
    that could be called "exhibition value" in a number of regards. True, it may
    be the case that one's physical proximity to an image results in an experi-
    ence of greater intensity than otherwise—and can often be measured by
    one's greater, more immediate access to prasād in its various forms, but
    at the same time distance (as in the distance created by the mediating
    figure of a priest or of an area that only such priests can enter) is also a
    feature that has value: to see an image (vigraha, mūrti) or emblem (linga)
    at a distance is to experience its radiating power, whether in the form of
    a single long visual prospect or as a feature of a performance space that
    contributes to the field of force that is felt to emanate from the deity.
    Kajri Jain has commented on the fact that, in the course of elaborat-
    ing the contrast Walter Benjamin observed between ritual and political
    valences of images before and after the age of mechanical reproduction,
    he underestimated or failed to notice aspects of display (for example,
    processions that transpired within a church building) that contributed
    to the felt power of the image itself ("When the Gods Emerge from the
    Temples: Iconic Exhibition Value and Democratic Publicness in India",
    lecture delivered under the auspices of the Institute for Religion and
    Culture in Public Life, Columbia University, October 9, 2018. Compare
    Benjamin, "The Work of Art in the Age of Mechanical Reproduction",
    Illuminations, ed. Hannah Arendt, tr. Harry Zohn (New York: Schocken
    Books, 2007 [orig. Frankfurt: Suhrkamf Verlag, 1955]), 220–5); similarly,
    Phyllis Granoff, "Halāyudha's Prism: The Experience of Religion in
    Medieval Hymns and Stories", in Vishakha N. Desai and Darielle Mason,
    eds., *Gods, Guardians, and Lovers: Temple Sculptures from North India,
    A.D. 700–1200* (New York: The Asia Society Galleries and Ahmedabad:
    Mapin Publishing, 1993), 66–93. A matter for further reflection is the
    status of decoration in relation to an image: is it sufficiently intrinsic to
    the presence of the image that it counts, in Benjamin's terms, as "aura"
    or not? A strong claim as to the distinction between mūrti and ābhūṣaṇ
    would be the view that ornamentation is applied so as to modify and
    control a presence that would otherwise be too strong for the limitations
    of human viewers/devotees: Cynthia Packert, *The Art of Loving Krishna:
    Ornamentation and Devotion* (Bloomington: Indiana University Press,
    2010), 87. The reports of others and prescriptions contained in texts

governing ritual practice suggest, however, that such a view is in the nature of a pious fiction, one dedicated to annunciating the limitless beauty of a divine person. To the contrary in the realm of poetry, see Richard David Williams, "A Theology of Feeling: The Radhavallabhi Monsoon in the Eighteenth Century", in Imke Rajamani, Magrit Pernau, and Katherine Butler Schofield, eds., *Monsoon Feelings: A History of the Emotions in the Rain* (New Delhi: Niyogi Books, 2018), 84–5.

7. On the global success of Disney's own theme-park business, even in comparison with other aspects of Disney's enterprises, see Brook Barnes, "Disney Theme Parks Prepare for Liftoff", *New York Times*, November 17, 2018, B1, B4–5.

8. Madhu Pandit Dasa, Chanchapathi Dasa, Bhaktilata Devi Dasi, and Prashanth Kadkol, *Reaching to the Sky* (Bangalore: International Society for Krishna Consciousness, 2015), 85.

9. Rimpesh Sharma, interview, Gurgaon, March 27, 2017; joined by Jagminder Jit Singh, January 16, 2019.

10. Sarvanand Das, interview, Gurgaon, November 25, 2017.

11. A worshipful account of the Akshay Patra initiative, narrative in format, is presented in Rashmi Bansal's *God's Own Kitchen: The Inspiring Story of Akshaya Patra—a Social Enterprise Run by Monks and CEOs* (Chennai: Westland, 2017). The practice of offering free food to the needy is widespread among South Asian religious communities—Hindu, Sikh, and Muslim. It became a specially featured ISKCON practice under the heading of pure vegetarian prasādam early in the history of the movement.

12. Modi's keynote address can be viewed, for instance, at www.ndtv.com/india-news/pm-modi-in-vrindavan-to-serve-3-billionth-akshay-patra-meal-today-live-updates-1991591. More extensive, official coverage was posted at www.narendramodi.in/pm-modi-attends-third-billionth-meal-of-akshaya-patra-mid-day-meal-programme-in-vrindavan-543479. At one point Modi made reference to an article in *The New York Times* about the Kumbh Mela, then underway in Allahabad. For the first time, he said, the *Times* reported not on the naked sadhus who usually attract so much attention in the national and international press, but on the government's efforts to create cleanliness at this massive gathering. What he did not say was that the main thrust of the *Times* article was actually to show how the BJP government had tried to turn the Kumbh into a veritable advertisement for Narendra Modi and Yogi Adityanath, posting images of them everywhere. See Jeffrey Gettleman and Hari Kumar, "Millions of Indians Trek to the Ganges, and Modi Chases Their Votes", *New York Times*, February 10, 2019.

13. Chanchalapati Das, interview, Bangalore, January 30, 2019.

14. Narendra Modi, keynote address.
15. Yudhishthira Krishna Das, interview, Vrindavan, January 1, 2017. On the implicit and sometimes explicit selectivity of the term "heritage" in dialogue with the notion of "culture", see Romila Thapar, *Indian Cultures as Heritage: Contemporary Pasts* (Delhi: Aleph Books, 2018), xxii–xxvi, xxxvii–xl, 20–37, 102–33. 179–205.
16. "Pitch" is a perfectly normal part of the VCM team's self-description.
17. Nalini Thakur, interview, Delhi, December 26, 2016. Compare Thakur, "The Indian Cultural Landscape: Protecting and Managing the Physical to the Metaphysical Values", in Ken Taylor and Jane L. Lennon, eds., *Managing Culture Landscapes* (London and New York: Routledge, 2012), 164–72. The heritage concept has been specifically deployed in contexts that pertain closely to the VCM. See Christiane Brosius, "The Cultural Politics of Transnational Heritage Ritual: Akshardham Cultural Complex in New Delhi", in C. Brosius and Karin M. Polit, eds., *Ritual, Heritage, and Identity: The Politics of Culture and Performance in a Globalized World* (New Delhi: Routledge, 2011), 97–125, especially plate 5.1 on page 103.
18. Sarvanand Das, interview, Gurgaon, November 25, 2016.
19. The classic study of the term dhām as it occurs in Vedic literature is Jan Gonda, *The Meaning of the Sanskrit Term Dhāman* (Amsterdam: N.V. Noord-Hollandsche Uitgevers Maatshappu, 1967), but the range of meanings discussed there is far greater than usages pertinent to what is envisioned for the VCM, where "Vedic" has been strictly Vaishnavized. As context for such a move, especially as regards the Bhāgavata Purāṇa, the Bṛhadbrahma Saṃhitā, and the theological writings of Rupa and Jiva Gosvami, see Barbara A. Holdrege, *Bhakti and Embodiment: Fashioning Divine Bodies and Devotional Bodies in Kṛṣṇa Bhakti* (New York: Routledge, 2015), 199–270; Holdrege, "*Vraja-Dhāman* as a Meditation Maṇḍala", *Journal of Vaishnava Studies* 27:1 (2018), 69–95; and Holdrege, "*Vraja-Dhāman*", in Ravi M. Gupta and Kenneth R. Valpey, eds., *The Bhāgavata Purāṇa: Sacred Text and Living Tradition* (New York: Columbia University Press, 2013), 91–116. For contemporary usage in Braj, see David L. Haberman, *Journey through the Twelve Forests: An Encounter with Krishna* (New York: Oxford University Press, 1994), 72–3, and Jan K. Brzezinski, "Globalized Braj Dham: Pilgrimage and Residence", *Journal of Vaishnava Studies* 27:1 (2018), 53–67.
20. On conceptions of Golok that appear in Sanskrit texts, see Gopal Narayan Bahura, "Śrī Govinda Gāthā: Service Rendered to Govinda by the Rulers of Āmera and Jayapura", in Margaret H. Case, ed., *Govindadeva, A Dialogue in Stone* (New Delhi: Indira Gandhi International Centre for the Arts, 1996), 195–9. On the model as a whole, in relation to the template

provided by the Bhāgavata Purāṇa as filtered through the theological system of Jiva Gosvami, see Holdrege, "Vraja-*Dhāman*", 99–106.

21. One can sense the importance of the chār dhām idea in contemporary religious politics by noting that in 2011 the long-standing chief minister of Sikkim inaugurated in Namchi a "Char Dham pilgrimage cum cultural complex", this time focusing not on Vishnu or Krishna but on Shiva. Again, vertical monumentality was involved—a 108-foot-tall image of Shiva (Jain, "Post-Reform India's Automotive-iconic-cement Assemblages", 10).

22. Staff writer, *Vrindavan Today*, January 22, 2014.

23. Compare the impetus to "materialize the Bible" that one sees at the Ark Encounter theme park in northern Kentucky and a whole set of related sites. See James S. Bielo, *Ark Encounter: The Making of a Creationist Theme Park* (New York: New York University Press, 2018), 32–58. For locative Hinduism as represented in the multi-story Bharat Mata Mandir in Haridvar, see Lise McKean, *Divine Enterprise: Gurus and the Hindu Nationalist Movement* (Chicago: University of Chicago Press, 1996), 144–63.

24. Bhāgavata Purāṇa 10.28.11–17. On Jiva Gosvami's exposition, see Holdrege, "Vraja-*Dhāman*", 110–14.

25. Bhāgavata Purāṇa 10:39.38–57.

26. The Jai Gurudev movement has a Radhasoami connection too, so the model provided by the Soamibagh temple is not incidental. See Daniel Gold, *Provincial Hinduism: Religion and Community in Gwalior City* (New York: Oxford University Press, 2015), 212–18.

27. On a visit to Prem Mandir on July 13, 2018, for instance, I was told by an official in the book shop that 200,000 people visit the temple on festival days and in such popular seasons as the month of Kārttik and the lunar intercalary month celebrated once every three years. "Normal" out-of-prime-season days bring in 50,000–60,000. If you do the math, you quickly see that the numbers claimed for Prem Mandir, perhaps 25–30 million visitors annually, vastly overshadow the Taj Mahal's 7–8 million. The national and ethnic backgrounds of visitors to the two sites are, of course, vastly different.

28. I do not know the extent to which "out-Tajing the Taj" ideas may have circulated in ISKCON circles—not Bangalore ones—in earlier days, but one finds it very clearly in *Vrindavana, the Crest Jewel of India*. "No longer will the Taj Mahal be the spot which has all the importance. Through the VVC [Vrindavana Vedic City] Project, Vrindavana will reveals itself AS IT IS—the real wonder of the world, reality the beautiful" (20).

29. Chanchalapati Das, interview, Bangalore, January 30, 2019.

30. Madhu Pandit Dasa et al., *Reaching to the Sky*, 12. There is also an oblique variant in Prabhupad's having once sighted a "large water tower" on the way from the Delhi airport to Vrindavan and saying "We should built one like that in Vrindavan". See Gurudas (i.e., Roger Siegel), *By His Example: The Wit and Wisdom of His Divine Grace A.C. Bhaktivedanta Prabhupada*, 2nd ed. (Vrindavan: ISKCON Library Society, 2013), appendix 1, 255. This idea may have served as a precursor for the 115-foot "tower of water" that features in Bhaktisiddhanta Dasa's projection of a "Manasa Mandir" (*Vrindavana, the Crest Jewel of India*, 21–2). Chanchalapati Das also seemed to be referring to it when he claimed a third instance of Prabhupad's authorizing a tower in Vrindavan. He referred to the Gurudas source explicitly (interview, Bangalore, January 31, 2019).

31. Courtney Bender, "Religious Horizons in New York's 1920s", unpublished paper, 2017, especially 11–22, and "Studying Up: A Brief History of the Religion of the Future", presentation to the Columbia University Department of Religion, February 20, 2018.

32. Chanchalapati received some of this education at St. Joseph's Indian High School, Bangalore, but it is possible that a more direct connection can be found in Steve Esomba, *The Book of Life, Knowledge, and Self-Confidence* (Lulu.com, June 6, 2012), 167, where the phrase also appears.

33. Yudhishthira Das, interview, Vrindavan, January 1, 2017. On questions of the historicity of Krishna see, e.g., Bimanbihari Majumdar, *Kṛṣṇa in History and Legend* (Calcutta: University of Calcutta, 1969). As to the general framework for such questions, see Edwin F. Bryant, *The Quest for the Origins of Vedic Culture: The Indo-Aryan Migration Debate* (New York: Oxford University Press, 2001).

34. Sarvanand Das, interview, Gurgaon, November 25, 2016.

35. Bankim Chandra Chatterjee, *Krishna-Charitra: Translated from the Bengali and with an Introduction by Pradip Bhattacharya* (Calcutta: M.P. Birla Foundation, 1991); Sudipta Kaviraj, *The Unhappy Consciousness: Bankim Chandattopadhyaya and the Formation of Nationalist Discourse in India* (Delhi: Oxford University Press, 1998), 72–106.

36. Sarvanand Das, interview, Gurgaon, November 25, 2016.

37. Shrivatsa Goswami, standing in an old Gaudīya line of succession—one that also has a connection to the Shrirangam temple through its founder Gopāl Bhaṭṭ—greatly admires this aspect of the Bangalore circle, and of Madhu Pandit Das in particular. He is keenly aware that figures like Ramanuja and Madhva were not just theologians but ritually knowledgeable temple officiants and administrators (interview, Mumbai, February 6, 2017).

38. Sarvanand Das, interview, Gurgaon, November 25, 2016.
39. Sarvanand Das, interview, Gurgaon, July 15, 2018, referring to Bhagavad Gītā 3.21. Sarvanand also had in mind the fact that Krishna divulges this supreme teaching to Arjuna, who was hardly a commoner.
40. On written documents his name comes across more sanskritically—as Pañca Gauḍa Dāsa—which follows the ISKCON convention we encounter in almost all branches of the movement. For a note on Panch Gaur Das's background I am grateful to Steven Rosen, email communication, February 5, 2018.
41. Compare Krishnakant Desai, Sunil Awatramami (Adridharan Das), and Madhu Pandit Das, "The No Change in ISKCON Paradigm", in Edwin F. Bryant and Maria L. Ekstrand, eds., *The Hare Krishna Movement: The Charismatic Fate of a Religious Transplant* (New York: Columbia University Press, 2004), 194–213.
42. It may not be accidental that the one legal challenge to the building of the VCM came in the form of a petition to the National Green Tribunal that was mounted by one of the Americans long associated with the Krishna Balaram Temple. The charge, made in the summer of 2018, was that the VCM's Yamuna Creek would divert water from the river itself. This was not true, as the VCM explained—the "creek" would not be connected to the Yamuna—and the NGT dismissed the case. To remove any possible confusion, however, and be as sensitive as possible to others' concerns, the VCM's planners decided to drop the name Yamuna Creek (Chanchalapati Das, interview, Bangalore, January 30, 2019).
43. Urmila Mohan, "The 'Temple of the Vedic Planetarium' as Mission, Monument, and Memorial", *Jugaad: A Material Religions Project*, September 30, 2014, https://jugaad.pub/the-temple-of-the-vedic-planetarium-as-mission-monument-and-memorial.
44. See Temple of the Vedic Planetarium, https://tovp.org/vedic-science/vedic-planetarium. As understood by devotees, see John Fahy, "The Constructive Ambiguities of Vedic Culture in ISKCON Mayapur", *Journal of Hindu Studies* 11:3 (2018), 234–59.
45. This four-dhām scheme is only one of a number of numerical classifications that converge upon the idea of Navadvip in the thinking of those who established the ISKCON presence in Mayapur. In addition to the significance of the nine islands that account for the name of the town itself (nava + dvīp) Navadvip is said to encompass the seven holy cities, the twelve forests of Vrindavan, the four yugs that constitute cosmic time, and versions of India's sixteen sacred rivers (Bhakti Purushottama Swami, *Śri Navadvīpa Parikramā*, 30–4).

46. These measurements, proposed by Shrivatsa Goswami as 120 by 90 meters, are necessarily approximate, since the spire or śikhara has now been destroyed and even aspects of the structure that can be observed at ground level are incomplete with respect to the original building. See Nalini Thakur, "The Building of Govindadeva" with photographs by Robyn Beeche, in Margaret H. Case, ed., *Govindadeva: A Dialogue in Stone*, 11–68; George Michell, *Late Temple Architecture of India 15th to 19th Centuries: Continuities, Revivals, Appropriations, and Innovations* (Delhi: Oxford University Press, 2015), 139; Irfan Habib, "Braj Bhūm in Mughal Times", in Habib, ed., *Proceedings of the Indian Historical Congress, Seventeenth Session* (Aligarh: Aligarh Historians Society, 2010–11), 297–301; and J.S. Hawley, "The Ideal Real Vrindavan of Jaisingh's Dining Room", in Rembert Lutjeharms and Kiyokazu Okita, eds., *The Building of Vṛndāvana* (Leiden: Brill, forthcoming).

47. On Mathura as a prototype for Madurai, see D. Dennis Hudson, *Krishna's Mandala: Bhagavata Religion and Beyond*, ed. J.S. Hawley (Delhi: Oxford University Press, 2010), 12, 70–4.

48. Entwistle, *Braj, Centre of Krishna Pilgrimage*, 253.

49. George Michell, "The Missing Sanctuary", in Case, ed., *Govindadeva*, 121–2; compare Heidi Pauwels and Emilia Bachrach, "Aurangzeb as Iconoclast: Vaishnava Accounts of the Krishna Images' Exodus from Braj", *Journal of the Royal Asiatic Society* 28:3 (2018), 485–508, especially 499–501.

50. Irfan Habib, "Dealing with Multiplicity: Mughal Administration in Braj Bhum under Aurangzeb (1659–1707)", *Studies in People's History* 3:2 (2016), 153–5.

51. Once extrapolated, the current figure tallies with those given by Tathagata Chatterji, *Citadels of Glass* (Chennai: Westland, 2015), 20, and I am grateful for a personal communication from Awadhendra Sharan (January 30, 2019).

52. Chatterji, *Citadels of Glass*, 76.

53. Philip Lutgendorf, "Imagining Ayodhya: Utopia and Its Shadows in a Hindu Landscape", *International Journal of Hindu Studies* 1:1 (1997), 19–54. Compare A. Whitney Sanford, "Shifting the Center: Yakṣas on the Margins of Contemporary Practice", *Journal of the American Academy of Religion* 73:1 (2005), 89–110, where the focus is on how certain earlier, more deeply "natural" aspects of the sacred cosmology of Braj failed to be fully integrated into this urbanely informed "pastoralization" project.

54. Staff reporter, *India Daily Times*, March 28, 2016. The title has also been awarded to Banaras and Bodh Gaya, but Vrindavan's proximity to Delhi

gives this designation a special edge. Not accidentally, ISKCON Bangalore has used the phrase in connection with the VCM project: www.iskcon-bangalore.org/vrindavana-spiritual-capital, accessed November 24, 2018.

55. The National Capital Region, for its part, is connected in various ways to a set of mega-urban private-public enterprises that span all of Asia. See Gavin Shatkin, "Planning Privatopolis: Representation and Contestation in the Development of Urban Integrated Mega-Projects", in Ananya Roy and Aihwa Ong, eds., *Worlding Cities: Asian Experiments and the Art of Being Global* (Chichester, West Sussex: Wiley-Blackwell, 2011), 77–97.

56. Shrivatsa Goswami, interview, Mumbai, February 5, 2017.

57. J.S. Hawley, "The *Bhāgavata-Māhātmya* in Context", in Heidi R.M. Pauwels, ed., *Patronage and Popularization, Pilgrimage and Procession: Channels of Transcultural Translation and Transmission in Early Modern South Asia. Papers in Honor of Monika Horstmann* (Wiesbaden: Harrassowitz, 2009), 87–8. The phrase "spatial transposition" was first employed by Diana Eck in *Banaras: City of Light* (New York: Alfred A. Knopf, 1982), 283–4; on Gokarn in Banaras, see 145, 354–5.

58. A favorite of mine is a school in Mathura that has named itself Growing Soul Kidz Gurukul, but directly across the highway from Spaze IT Park we have a residential development called Eldeco MansionZ.

59. An indispensable trio of recent books on Gurgaon, each quite different from the other, is Sanjay Srivastava, *Entangled Urbanism: Slum, Gated community, and Shopping Mall in Delhi and Gurgaon* (Delhi: Oxford University Press, 2015); Llerena Guiu Searle, *Landscapes of Accumulation: Real Estate and the Neoliberal Imagination in Contemporary India* (Chicago: University of Chicago Press, 2016; Delhi: Primus Books, 2017); and Veena Talwar Oldenburg, *Gurgaon: From Mythic Village to Millennium City* (Noida: HarperCollins, 2018). The broader literature on contemporary cities, even specifically in Asia, is too vast to cite. Representative works that bear in different ways on Vrindavan's position in relation to greater Delhi and the NCR region are Shail Mayaram, ed., *The Other Global City* (New York and London: Routledge, 2008); Rashmi Varma, *The Postcolonial City and its Subjects: London, Nairobi, Bombay* (New York and London: Routledge, 2012); and Anne Rademacher and K. Shivaramakrishnan, eds., *Ecologies of Urbanism in India: Metropolitan Civility and Sustainability* (Hong Kong: Hong Kong Scholarship Online, 2014 [print 2013]).

60. Here, as throughout this section, I rely on an interview with Rimpesh Sharma in Gurgaon on January 2, 2017, preceded by others on December 26, 2016 and January 1, 2017.

61. Contrariwise, the VCM claims the fifteenth century for this event. See www.vcm.org.in/sri-radha-raman-mandir-in-gurugram, accessed July 12, 2018.

62. Rakesh Shetty, interview, Vrindavan, July 11, 2018.

63. Rimpesh Sharma, interview, Gurgaon, March 27, 2017.

64. Compare Richard H. Davis, "Henry David Thoreau, Yogi", *Common Knowledge* 24: 1, 56–89, https://doi.org/10.1215/0961754X-4253822.

65. Sarvanand Das, interview, Gurgaon, March 18, 2017.

66. Rimpesh Sharma, interview, Gurgaon, March 27, 2017.

67. Sarvanand Das, interview, Gurgaon, July 15, 2018. I rely on this interview also for the paragraphs that follow.

68. Consonant with this is a billboard located close to Vrindavan's entrance to the Yamuna Expressway that urges you to "Come Again" and announces "Holydays: First Spiritual Timeshare Product", accompanied by a picture of the Vrindavan Chandrodaya Mandir and a number to call if you are interested (February 11, 2019).

69. Sarvanand Das, interview, Gurgaon, July 15, 2018. See *Bhaktirasāmṛtasindhu* 2.89, 2.235–8, and 2.43 in David L. Haberman, *The Bhaktirasāmṛtasindhu of Rūpa Gosvāmin* (New Delhi: Indira Gandhi National Centre for the Arts, 2003), 38–9, 70–3. In the last two of these sequences it is clear that Vrindavan is also meant. Rupa's authorship of the *Mathurā Māhātmya*, a text praising the glories of Mathura, is a somewhat more difficult matter (Hawley, *A Storm of Songs*, 155, 360). Relevant passages appear in Bhūmipati Dāsa, *Śrī Mathurā Māhātmya: The Glories of Mathurā Maṇḍala* (Vrindavan: Rasbihari and Sons, n.d.), especially 1.45, 1.53–6.

70. Rimpesh Sharma, interview, Gurgaon, January 16, 2019; modified by Chanchalapati Das, interview, Bangalore, January 30, 2019. Chanchalapati envisions three tiers of residence towers on VCM land near the temple—premium, budget (the intermediary level), and economy.

71. Chanchalapati Das, interview, Bangalore, January 30, 2019.

72. Rimpesh Sharma, interview, Gurgaon, January 16, 2019.

73. For Chanchalapati, the biography presented in Krishnadas Kaviraj's *Chaitanyacharitāmṛta* was evidently to be taken as simple fact. He was sure he knew Chaitanya's exact words and views, by contrast to scholars who have doubted this perfect match. See especially Tony K. Stewart, *The Final Word: The Caitanya Caritāmṛta and the Grammar of Religious Tradition* (New York: Oxford University Press, 2010), whose perspectives I have embraced in *A Storm of Songs*, 165–79.

74. This was also described to me by Naveen Neerad Das, Head of Strategic Communication & Projects, on November 10, 2018 in New York.

75. Chanchalapati Das took the Bhāgavata Purāṇa and the Garga Saṃhitā as his sources, and I wondered as well about the impact of many years of seeing the air-brushed "neo-Vedic" art forms that ISKCON has perfected. See, e.g., Priyasakhi Barchi, "Neo-Vedic Krishna: Fusion of Tradition and Innovation" (unpublished paper, Barnard College, Columbia University, December, 2017) and Richard H. Davis, "Krishna Enters the Age of Mechanical Reproduction", *Journal of Vaishnava Studies* 21:2 (2013), 31–42. On the panopticon, Michel Foucault, *Discipline and Punish: The Birth of the Prison* (New York: Vintage, 1995; and, moving in the reverse direction, Michel de Certeau, "Walking in the City", in Certeau, *The Practice of Everyday Life* (Berkeley: University of California Press, 1984), 91–110, 218–21.

76. The rās līlās are eloquent in making this point. See Hawley and Goswami, *At Play with Krishna*, 49–51.

77. Sarvanand Das, interview, Gurgaon, January 16, 2019.

78. An alternately poignant and wondrous sense of time emerges in Tulasi Srinivas's portrait of life in heavily technologized Bangalore itself (*The Cow in the Elevator*, chapter 5, "Timeless Imperatives, Obsolescence, and Salvage", 172–205).

Chapter 5   A Different Refuge for Women

1. Pavan K. Varma, "Widows of Vrindavan", dated 2002, as quoted by Khushwant Singh in "Surviving Yet Another Cold War", *The Tribune*, February 1, 2003: www.tribuneindia.com/2003/20030201/windows/ above.htm. Lamentations in other media include Pankaj Butalia, *Moksha* (English: *Salvation*, film, 1993); Kusum Ansal, *The Widow of Vrindavan*, translated from the Hindi *Tapasī* by Masooma Ali (New Delhi: HarperCollins, 2004); Fazal Sheikh, *Moksha* (Göttingen: Steidl, 2005); and Leena Yadav, *Parched*, produced by Ajay Devgan (Mumbai: Ajay Devgn Ffilms, 2015), released September 23, 2016).

2. Hawley and Goswami, *At Play with Krishna*, 44–8.

3. Svāmī Apūrvānand, *Śrīsāradādevī: Saṃkṣipt Jīvanī tathā Upadeś* (Nagpur: Ramakrishna Math, 1984), 37–43; Swami Chetanananda, "Holy Mother's Pilgrimage (August 1886-August 1887)", in Swami Animeshananda, ed., *Bodhan Souvenir 2012 ... Ma Sarada Kutir* (Vrindavan: Ramakrishna Math and Ramakrishna Mission Sevashrama, 2012), 10–17; Swami Nikhilananda, *Holy Mother: Being the Life of Sri Sarada Devi, Wife of Sri Ramakrishna and Helpmate in his Mission* (London: Allen & Unwin, 1962), 95–9.

4. I am grateful to T.N. Madan for email communications on January 14–15, 2019. In the couplet quoted, the title "rahīm" surely refers to the great Mughal courtier and Brajbhāṣā poet Abdul Rahīm Khān-i-Khānā, but it also echoes the word "rahimān" in the couplet's first line, with which it shares three consonants. Both are in the first instance names of Allah and only secondarily those of human beings. Nārāyaṇ is a standard designation for Vishnu.

5. Martha Alter Chen, *Perpetual Mourning: Widowhood in Rural India* (Delhi: Oxford University Press, 2000), 262–4; V.N. Datta, *Sati: A Historical, Social, and Philosophical Enquiry into the Hindu Rite of Widow Burning* (Delhi: Manohar, 1988), 195–7; Manisha Roy, *Bengali Women* (Chicago: University of Chicago Press, 1972), 146–7. More broadly, see Susan S. Wadley, "No Longer a Wife: Widows in Rural North India", in Lindsey Harlan and Paul B. Courtright, eds., *From the Margins of Hindu Marriage; Essays on Gender, Religion, and Culture* (New York: Oxford University Press, 1995), 92–118; Uma Chakravarti, *Everyday Lives, Everyday Histories: Beyond the Kings and Brahmanas of 'Ancient' India* (New Delhi: Tulika Books, 2006), chapter 8, "Gender, Caste, and Labour: Ideological and Material Structure of Widowhood", 156–78; and the vast literature on satī.

6. V. Mohini Giri, interview, Delhi, July 16, 2018. Mohini Giri is the author of a number of books, all published in English, including *Deprived Devis: Women's Unequal Status in Society* (2006) and the edited volumes *Living Death: Trauma of Widowhood in India* (2002), and *Status of Elderly Women in India* (2013), all published in New Delhi by Gyan Publishing House.

7. "Oprah in India", on "Oprah's Next Chapter", www.youtube.com/watch?v=Y814cP3IB1s, and www.youtube.com/watch?v=aBhpng2NzVc, accessed July 28, 2018. On Oprah herself from a Religious Studies point of view, see Kathryn Lofton, *Oprah: The Gospel of an Icon* (Berkeley: University of California Press, 2011).

8. V. Mohini Giri, interview, Delhi, July 10, 2018.

9. V. Mohini Giri, interview, Delhi, July 7, 2018.

10. Ramsiya Bajpeyi, interview, Vrindavan, December 24, 2017.

11. V. Mohini Giri, interview, Delhi, July 7, 2018.

12. Pavan Varma has also written a poem about this incident. It begins, "In life we are flesh/clad in white/embalmed in ashrams/to mark us out/as someone else's right ..." It is said to have been published in a book called *Widows of Vrindavan* and is numbered 11th in the collection, but I have been unable to trace the full printed source (V. Mohini Giri, photocopy, January 29, 2019). This poem became the basis for a Bharat Nāṭyam dance by Pratibha Prahlad in 2003.

13. "The Divinity Speaks", *Vatsalya Gram (A Village of Maternal Love)* (Delhi: Param Shakti Peeth, n.d. [acquired 2017]), 1.

14. Vatsalya Gram representatives mentioned, for example, the Ramanlal Shorawala International School in Mathura and the Bhonsala Military School in Nagpur, Maharashtra (Vrindavan, January 20, 2019). See also Tarun Nangia, "Sadhvi Ritambhara Makes Her Own World", *Indian Express*, June 19, 2011.

15. An institution affecting the lives of far more girls in the Vrindavan area is the Sandipani Muni School established preponderantly for girls by Rupa Raghunath Das, an ISKCON devotee of Italian parentage. The school, which has been in existence since 2002, currently educates some 1200 girls of very modest means thanks to private donations, from the lowest levels through the twelfth grade. The school's network reaches out to nearby villages: www.vina.cc/2010/09/25/third-sandipani-muni-school-opens-in-vrindavan.

16. V. Mohini Giri, interview, Delhi, February 1, 2019.

17. Vatsalya Gram's short English-language informational and fund-raising video "Gokulam" speaks of ancient ashrams as "the ancient Indian system of social security", where any person in need would be "accepted as family". In this context the term "Vedic" is not specifically used. Elsewhere we have the very phrase to which Mohini Giri often appeals—vasudhaiva kutumbh—but in a substantially different context, www.youtube.com/watch?v=vFqQb_UzuTA, accessed October 7, 2018.

18. *Vatsalya Gram (A Village of Maternal Love)*, 4.

19. The relationship between Sadhvi Ritambhara and Svami Paramanand Giri is featured regularly in Ma Dham's publications. A series of articles on that subject, for example, served as the point of departure for an issue of the monthly house publication *Vātsalya Nirjhar* (October, 2017) that bore the subtitle *Mere Gurudev* (My Honored Guru).

20. Sadhvi Ritambhara, *Yaśodā Bhāv: Vātsalya Grām kī Mūl Preraṇā* (New Delhi: Vātsalya Prakāśan, 2013), 1 and cover.

21. "Sainik kī Ātmā meṅ Basā Bhārat", *Vātsalya Nirjhar*, October 2016. *Vātsalya Nirjhar*, the monthly magazine, contains features called "svādhīntā sangrām ke śahīdoṅ ko raktāṅjali", that is, a blood-offering of martyrs in the struggle for independence, or "naman śahīdoṅ ko" (in honor of martyrs). In the October 2016 issue, for example, Pundit Chandrashekhar Azad was featured (30–1); in the June 2017 issue, it was Bahadur Shah Zafar, the last Mughal emperor (30)—a Muslim, be it noted. Death dates are given for both (1931, 1861).

22. Ravi Agrawal reports that the current ratio of girl and boy babies stands at 919:1000 (*India Connected*, 204).

23. David L. Haberman, "On Trial: The Love of the Sixteen Thousand Gopees", *History of Religions* 33:1 (1993), 44–70; J. Barton Scott, *Spiritual Despots: Modern Hinduism and the Genealogies of Self-Rule* (Chicago: University of Chicago Press, 2016), 119–49, 241–7; Karsandas Mulji, *History of the Sect of Maharajas, or Vallabhacharyas, in Western India* (London: Trubner, 1865); Amrita Shodhan, *A Question of Community: Religious Groups and Colonial Law* (Kolkata: Samya, 2001), 117–200; Kaviraj, *The Unhappy Consciousness*, 72–106.

24. Usha Garg, interview, Vrindavan, December 28, 2017.

25. "Supreme Court Sets up Committee on Rehabilitation of Vrindavan's Widows", *Vrindavan Today*, August 12, 2017; with a request for "additional indicators on widows" some months later (*Vrindavan Today*, February 7, 2018). Both Sulabh International and the Guild for Service are represented on the six-member action committee that was formed at the Supreme Court's bidding.

26. Swamini Vishwamohini, interview, Vrindavan, July 13, 2018.

27. Nirala, "Toḍtī Patthar", written in 1935, published in the collection *Anāmikā* in 1938 (Allahabad: Bhāratī Bhaṇḍār, 1963), 81; translated as "Breaking Stones" by David Rubin, *A Season on the Earth* (New York: Columbia University Press, 1976), 40–1.

28. This is not true universally. The Manipuri expression of the rās līlā is an exception.

29. Aastha Goswami, "Songs for Krishna in Autumn: Devotional Music from North India", interview and performance, New York, October 5, 2018.

30. Haribol Paṇḍāl, Vrindavan, November 8, 2016. Generally on this subject see McComas Taylor, *Seven Days of Nectar: Contemporary Oral Performance of the Bhāgavatapurāṇa* (New York: Oxford University Press, 2016), 204, and Hawley, "Bhāgavata Across Boundaries", *Journal of Hindu Studies* 11:1 (2018), 4–20. On non-Brahmin Bhāgavats historically, see Hawley, *A Storm of Songs*, 70–2.

31. Vishnupriya Goswami, interview, Vrindavan, December 29, 2017; update, Vrindavan, March 5, 2019.

32. J.L. Masson, "The Childhood of Kṛṣṇa: Some Psychoanalytic Observations", *Journal of the American Oriental Society* 94:4 (1974), 454–9; Sudhir Kakar, *The Inner World: A Psycho-analytic Study of Childhood and Society in India*, 2nd ed. (Delhi: Oxford University Press, 1981), 147–53; Sudhir Kakar and John M. Ross, *Tales of Love, Sex, and Danger* (Delhi: Oxford University Press, 1986), 88, 98–100; and J.S. Hawley, "Krishna and the Gender of Longing", in *Three Bhakti Voices* (Delhi: Oxford University Press, 2005), 165–78. A very different sort of perspective emerges in a recent volume edited by two Indian women, namely, Malashri Lal and Namita Gokhale, eds., *Finding Radha: The Quest for Love* (Gurgaon: Penguin, 2018).

33. Compare Ruth Vanita, *Love's Rite: Same-Sex Marriage in India and the West* (Delhi: Penguin, 2005), 166–7.

34. Bhāgavata Purāṇa 10:30.17–44.

Chapter 6 Being Shrivatsa

1. Shrivatsa Goswami, interview, Mumbai, February 3, 2017. Subsequent quotations in this section are also drawn from five two-hour interviews that Shrivatsa granted me between February 3 and 8, 2017. I cite specific moments only occasionally.

2. Interview, Mumbai, February 4, 2017.

3. Interview, Mumbai, February 8, 2017.

4. Interview, Mumbai, February 6, 2017.

5. Sundarānand Dās Vidyāvinod, *Vaiṣṇava-Siddhānte Śrīgurusvarūpa* (Calcutta: Śrī Karuṇā Dās, 1965), chapter 10 (*guru tyāga*), 209–34. A short and somewhat sanitized version of the controversy appears as a footnote in Bhakti Vilāsa Swami's three-volume biography of Bhakti Siddhant Sarasvati entitled *Śrī Bhaktisiddhānta Vaibhava* (Surat: Bhakti Vikas Trust, 2009), vol. 2, 345.

6. Charles R. Brooks, *The Hare Krishnas in India* (Princeton: Princeton University Press, 1989), 155–70.

7. Kumar, "Sacred Modernity and its Fragments", 100–1.

8. Shrivatsa Goswami, interview, Mumbai, February 4, 2017.

9. Peter Manuel, "Syncretism and Adaptation in Rasiya, A Braj Folksong Genre", *Journal of Vaishnava Studies* 3:1 (1994), 33–60.

10. Case, *Seeing Krishna*, 111–50.

11. Shrivatsa Goswami, "Gopal Bhatt: Carrier of *Bhakti* to the North", in Tyler Williams, Anshu Malhotra, and J.S. Hawley, eds., *Text and Tradition in Early Modern North India* (Delhi: Oxford University Press, 2018), 335–53.

12. All quotations in this and the next two paragraphs are from an interview with Shrivatsa Goswami in Mumbai on February 5, 2017.

13. Shrivatsa Goswami, Mumbai, February 5, 2017. He expressed the same sentiments in an interview with Judith Jansen, Vrindavan, February 18, 2017.

14. In this, Shrivatsa follows the evidence put forward by Richard Eaton in, for example, "Temple Desecration and Indo-Muslim States", *Journal of Islamic Studies* 11:3 (2000), 283–319. A subsequent summary appears in Audrey Truschke, *Aurangzeb: The Man and the Myth* (Gurgaon: Viking, 2017), 107–13.

15. Shrivatsa Goswami, "Govinda Darśana: The Lotus in Stone", in Case, ed., *Govindadeva*, 269–77.

16. Interview, Mumbai, February 5, 2017.

17. Vibhuti Sachdev, *Building Jaipur: The Making of an Indian City* (Delhi and New York: Oxford University Press, 2002); Monika Horstmann, *Visions of Kingship in the Twilight of Mughal Rule* (Amsterdam: Royal Netherlands Academy of Arts and Sciences, 2006).

18. Shrivatsa Goswami, interview, Mumbai, February 5, 2017.

19. Compare Richard David Williams, "A Theology of Feeling: The Radhavallabhi Monsoon in the Eighteenth Century", in Imke Rajamani, Margrit Pernau, and Katherine Butler Schofield, eds., *Monsoon Feelings: A History of the Emotions in the Rain* (New Delhi: Niyogi Books, 2018), 71–96, especially 94.

Chapter 7   The Sign of Our Times

1. Generally and eloquently on the broader theme, see David Shulman, *More Than Real: A History of the Imagination in South India* (Cambridge: Harvard University Press, 2012). Specifically in relation to the rās līlā as a form, see David V. Mason, *Theatre and Religion on Krishna's Stage* (New York: Palgrave Macmillan, 2009). A very successful TV series, also available online, opened with exactly this set of questions, transporting the rās līlā to a new medium and attracting ever more pilgrim-tourists to Vrindavan. This is Star Bharat's daily serial "Radha Krishna", starring Sumedh Mudgalkar and Mallika Singh, produced in Hindi and also available in Tamil, which premiered on October 1, 2018: www.hotstar.com/tv/radhakrishn/s-1695.

2. On standard American conceptions of wilderness, where the wild must always be at the periphery, see Willliam Cronon, "The Trouble with Wilderness: Or, Getting Back to the Wrong Nature", *Environmental History* 1:1 (1996), 13; Roderick Frazier Nash, *Wilderness and the American Mind*, 5th ed. (New Haven: Yale University Press, 2014 [1967]), especially 238–71, 342–85: and Frederick Jackson Turner with commentary by John Mack Faragher, *Rereading Frederick Jackson Turner: "The Significance of the Frontier in American History", and Other Essays* (New Haven: Yale University Press, 1998).

3. Further on this, and with respect to urban and sometimes specifically royal canons of taste governing the conception and design of Vrindavan as a "garden city", see Philip Lutgendorf, "Imagining Ayodhyā: Utopia and Its Shadows in a Hindu Landscape", *International Journal of Hindu Studies* 1:1 (1997), 37–40. Lutgendorf's term is "city in a garden" (urbs in horto), 19–21, 37. On the idea of the nikuñj, see Rupert Snell, "The Nikuñja as Sacred Space in Poetry of the Rādhāvallabhī Tradition", *Journal of Vaishnava Studies* 7:1 (1998), 63–84; as a specific emphasis in the design of eighteenth-century Vrindavan, Sugata Ray, *Climate Change and*

the Art of Devotion: Geoaesthetics in the Land of Krishna, 1550–1850 (Seattle: University of Washington Press, 2019), 119–29; as used interchangeably with the idea of van, Entwistle, *Braj: Centre of Krishna Pilgrimage*, 301.

4. The online (and now print) publication *Vrindavan Today* is a substantial resource for information on various aspects of environmental degradation in Vrindavan and events related to it. A general thematic contribution is Ranchor Prime, "Restoring the Forests of Braj", *Vrindavan Today,* July 22, 2014. For a long view on developments upriver, see Awadhendra Sharan, *In the City, Out of Place: Nuisance, Pollution, and Dwelling in Delhi ca. 1850–2000* (Delhi: Oxford University Press, 2014), 22–69 (on water) passim.

5. An influential early statement on the interpenetration of virtuality and a great many aspects of experiential knowledge in a "heritage" environment is Barbara Kirschenblatt-Gimblett's *Destination Culture: Tourism, Museums, and Heritage* (Berkeley: University of California Press, 1998), e.g., 189–200. More recently, with specific regard to India, see Thapar, *Indian Cultures as Heritage*.

6. For a variety of perspectives on embodiment and what it entails in contexts such as these, see Barbara A. Holdrege and Karen Pechilis, eds., *Refiguring the Body: Embodiment in South Asian Religions* (Albany: State University of New York Press, 2016); specifically in relation to Rupa and Jiva Gosvami, see Holdrege, *Bhakti and Embodiment*. The primary interest here, as in the theological writings of these gosvāmīs, is to transmute ordinary senses of embodiment into more subtle forms, or rather to detect those subtler forms as lying behind the ordinary. This means that down-to-earth realities characterized by terms such as śarīra, deha (both "body"), and rūpa (more broadly "form" but also "bodily form") tend to be submerged in their perfective (sādhakarūpa) or perfected (siddharūpa) forms rather than directly exposited as such. The dialectal quality of their relationship therefore sometimes fails to be made fully explicit—significantly, rūpa becomes the pivotal term and not the other two—although these relationships are fundamental to the enterprise. See Holdrege, *Bhakti and Embodiment*, 97–101, especially 98. For a short primer on achintyabhedābheda see Edward C. Dimock, Jr., *The Place of the Hidden Moon: Erotic Mysticism in the Vaiṣṇava-Sahajiyā Cult of Bengal* (Chicago: University of Chicago Press, 1966), 129–34.

7. Generally on themes that appear in this paragraph, see J.S. Hawley, *A Storm of Songs*, and on the *Bhāgavata Māhātmya* in particular, chapter 2, 59–98; also Hawley, "The *Bhāgavata Māhātmya* in Context".

8. Victor Mallet, *River of Life, River of Death: The Ganges and India's Future* (Delhi: Oxford University Press, 2017), 248.

9. The project was supervised by Stefania Abakerli, with the India expertise coming especially from Priya Chopra, to whom I am grateful for an interview at the World Bank in Washington, June 12, 2017.

10. Priya Chopra et al., "Uttar Pradesh Pro-poor Tourism Development Project (P146936): Site Visit to Vrindavan (April 1–3, 2015)", April 10, 2015.

11. For an assessment focused on the Ganga but including the Yamuna as well, see Mallet, *River of Life, River of Death*, 242–52. There was a time, apparently, when it was possible to document the spending of more than 100 million rupees for "restoration and research" through a contract made between the MVDA and the Braj Foundation, but in its current form the MVDA website no longer reflects that. See Kumar and Jacobsen, "Heritage and Environment", 121, 125, 128, and www.mvda.in.

12. "HRIDAY Scheme Development Assessed", *Vrindavan Today*, January 14, 2018.

13. See "Projects", the Braj Foundation, www.brajfoundation.org/projects. php?brajfoundation=55, accessed September 14, 2018.

14. Compare Barbara Kirshenblatt-Gimblett, "Intangible Heritage as Metacultural Production", *Museum International* 56:1–2 (2004), 52–65.

15. Jacob N. Kinnard, *Places in Motion: The Fluid Identities of Temples, Images, and Pilgrims* (New York: Oxford University Press, 2014), 120.

16. Armoogum Parasuramen, head of the UNESCO office in Delhi, letter to Shrivatsa Goswami, convener of the Vrindavan group, entitled "UNESCO-Vrindavan Cooperation", February 1, 2010. A follow-up meeting was suggested for April, but owing in part to a downward turn in Mr. Parasuramen's health it never transpired. More to the point, state and local governments declined to become involved.

17. The full name of this arm of the central government is Ministry of Water Resources, River Development, and Ganga Rejuvenation, as formed by the BJP government in 2014. For the history involved, see http://mowr. gov.in/about-us/history.

18. On Penang's George Town jetties, see Laignee Barron, "Unesco-cide: Does World Heritage Status Do Cities More Harm Than Good", *The Guardian*, August 30, 2017. On Bodh Gaya and Porto, see Kinnard, *Places in Motion*, 141–2, and compare David Geary, *The Rebirth of Bodh Gaya: Buddhism and the Making of a World Heritage Site* (Seattle: University of Washington Press, 2017), 137–46, 168–79. More broadly within Asia, Natalia Bloch, "Evicting Heritage: Spatial Cleansing and Cultural Legacy at the Hampi UNESCO Site in India", *Critical Asian Studies* 48: 4 (2016), 556–78; Denis Byrne, "Western Hegemony in Archaeological Heritage Management", *History and Anthropology* 5:2 (1991), 269–76; and Byrne,

Counterheritage: Critical Perspectives on Heritage Conservation in Asia (London: Routledge, 2014).

19. Briefly on this subject, see Hawley, *A Storm of Songs*, 150–7.

20. I have witnessed a parallel campaign involving a very different species and considerably less physical confrontation that seems to have succeeded. It concerns merganser ducks whose interaction with snails living on the bottom of the lake where I learned to swim in the state of Michigan caused thousands of cases of swimmers' itch that extended over many years, keeping children especially out of the water but affecting many adults as well. In a comprehensive and well-planned campaign, the ducks were eventually captured and relocated to habitats where the snails do not exist, breaking the chain that caused the problem. From all reports the mergansers are thriving in their new homes. As to Vrindavan itself, though from 1997, see Ekwal Imam, H.S.A. Yahya, and Iqbal Malik, "A Successful Mass Translocation of Commensal Rhesus Monkeys *Macaca mulatta* in Vrindaban, India", *Oryx* 36:1 (2002), 87–93.

21. Over the long haul, see Haberman, *River of Love in an Age of Pollution*, 169; Mallet, *River of Life, River of Death*, 244.

22. Kinnard, *Places in Motion*, 119. Compare Richard Handler, "The 'Ritualization of Ritual' in the Construction of Heritage", in Christiane Brosius and Karin M. Polit, eds., *Ritual, Heritage, and Identity* (London: Routledge, 2011), 33–4, and more broadly Mary E. Hancock, *The Politics of Heritage from Madras to Chennai* (Bloomington: Indiana University Press, 2008). In regard to comparable "ambivalences" in quite a different region—Mayan Mexico—see Lisa Beglia, *Monumental Ambivalence: The Politics of Heritage* (Austin: University of Texas Press, 2006).

23. Geary, *The Rebirth of Bodh Gaya*, 159, 169–73, 188–91.

24. Kinnard, *Places in Motion*, 123–4.

25. This is a threat of which repeated mention is made in the literature on "heritage", e.g., Kinnard, *Places in Motion*, 142; Geary, *The Rebirth of Bodh Gaya*, 176.

26. In regard to the Kashi Vishwanath Mandir Vistarikaran-Saundaryakaran Yojana and its opponents, see Faisal Fareed, "In Varanasi, a Plan to Build Corridor from Kashi Vishwanath Temple to River Ganges Sparks Anger", *Scroll.in*, February 10, 2018; Sanjay Singh, "Kashi Vishwanah Pathway: Over 100 Houses To Be Demolished, Rehabilitation in Ramnagar", *Economic Times*, May 14, 2018; A. Srivathsan, "Varanasi, by Design: Vishwanath Dham and the Politics of Change", *The Hindu*, March 23–24, 2019; and Joanna Slater, "How Narendra Modi Is Remaking Hinduism's Holiest City—and India in the Process", *Washington Post*, May 27, 2019. For Prime Minister Modi's views, see his

Twitter posting of March 9, 2019: https://twitter.com/narendramodi/
status/1104398525050376194; there are notable resemblances to the
"waterfront" video that circulated in Vrindavan in late 2019. For general
ecological context, Doron and Jeffrey, *Waste of a Nation*, 95–7, 267–71,
and Raghu Dayal, "Dirty Flows the Ganga: Why Plans to Clean the River
Have Come a Cropper", *Economic and Political Weekly* 51:25, June 18,
2016, 55–65.

27. Searle, *Landscapes of Accumulation*, 1–46.

28. Hence, for example, the sixteenth-century Gauḍīya aesthete Kavikarṇapura
wrote a play called *Ānanda-Vṛndāvana* ("The Vrindavan of Bliss", as
Rembert Lutjeharms translates it) to evoke the paradigmatic, intrinsically
luminous Vrindavan that mysteriously inhabits its physical antetype—or
the other way around. In doing so, he establishes a brilliant medium of
double entendre that floats between prose and poetry by means of the
champū genre (Lutjeharms, *Splendor of Speech*, 244–77).

29. On the concept "Anthropocene" and its history, see Helmuth Trischler,
"The Anthropocene: A Challenge for the History of Science, Technology,
and the Environment", *N.T.M.*, 24 (2016), 309–35.

30. E.O. Wilson, *The Creation: An Appeal to Save Life on Earth* (New York:
W.W. Norton, 2006), 66. Among the researchers to whom he refers,
Wilson singles out George H. Orians and Judith H. Heerwagen for
their article "Evolved Responses to Landscapes", in Jerome H. Barkow,
Leda Cosmides, and John Tooby, eds., *The Adapted Mind: Evolutionary
Psychology and the Generation of Culture* (New York: Oxford University
Press, 1992), 555–79.

31. Henry Wadsworth Longfellow, *Longfellow's Evangeline* (Boston: Houghton,
Mifflin & Co., 1883 [originally 1847]).

32. The landscape of the African savanna corresponds more closely to
the Indian "jungle" (Sanskrit *jangala*) than we usually realize; it too is
understood as a semi-arid expanse, not the dark and dense jungle that
comes to mind for English speakers. See Francis Zimmermann, *The
Jungle and the Aroma of Meat: An Ecological Theme in Hindu Medicine*
(Berkeley: University of California Press, 1987), 1–19; Michael R.
Dove, "The Dialectical History of 'Jungle' in Pakistan", *Journal of
Anthropological Research* 48 (1992), 231–47; Philip Lutgendorf, "City,
Forest, and Cosmos: Ecological Perspectives from the Sanskrit Epics",
in Chapple and Tucker, eds., *Hinduism and Ecology*, 269–87. The
founder of ISKCON is on record as explicitly denying this sort of view
as it might relate to Vrindavan: "The word *vāna* [sic] means 'forest.'
Actually it is not a forest as we ordinarily consider a forest because it
is very thick with green vegetation". Lecture, Mayapur, April 9, 1975,

as recorded in A.C. Bhaktivedanta Swami Prabhupāda, *Śrī Vṛndāvana Dhāma As It Is* (Vrindavan: Bhaktivedanta Book Trust, 2005), 53; in Hindi, *Śrī Vṛndāvan Dhām Yathārūp*, 54.

33. On religion and the concept of "home", see Thomas A. Tweed, *Crossing and Dwelling: A Theory of Religion* (Cambridge: Harvard University Press, 2006), 103–22; rather differently, Jonathan Z. Smith, *To Take Place: Toward Theory in Ritual* (Chicago: University of Chicago Press, 1987), 24–32, 44–6. On dhām for Chaitanyites, see Stewart, *The Final Word*, 57, 124–8, *passim;* Holdrege, *Bhakti and Embodiment*, 199–270. In regard to recent scholarly conceptions of "place" as it relates to religion, see Luke Whitmore, *Mountain, Water, Rock, God: Understanding Kedarnath in the Twenty-First Century* (Berkeley: University of California Press, 2018), 21–7, 201–6.

34. Vrindavan is the fifth dhām in the way the Bhāvagata Purāṇa is proclaimed to be the fifth Veda—the overarching essence that serves as summation and rationale for all the rest. The RSS has recently turned this logic on its head by proposing that Angkor Wat be acclaimed Hinduism's fifth dhām, acquiring vast tracts of land on site to be used to build a temple intended to proclaim that status. See, e.g., Parul Pandya Dhar, "Why the Sangh Parivar's Idea of Building a 'Hindu Dham' in Cambodia Is Wrong", *The Wire*, June 16, 2018.

35. On what Ananya Roy calls "the hegemonic icon of the world-class city" (267) and the tensions attending its enactment, with a special focus on Kolkata, see Roy, "The Blockade of the World-Class City", in Ananya Roy and Aihwa Ong, eds., *Worlding Cities*, 259–78. The entire volume is pertinent to the subject at hand, including the concept "zones of spectacle" in Aihwa Ong, "Hyperbuilding: Spectacle, Speculation, and the Hyperspace of Sovereignty", 208.

36. Email attachment from Naman Ahuja (August 11, 2018) reflecting a printed advertisement he saw in the course of 2017. The "world class" branding and the "Live blessed!" slogan are ubiquitous in Śrī Krishna Bhūmi's advertising campaign, across media.

37. The issue's many aspects were the subject of an essay written by Abantika Ghosh for "The Big Picture" of the Sunday issue of *The Indian Express,* July 8, 2018, but the general silence is deafening. For UN projections of India's population, estimating a peak of 1.65 billion by 2060, see https://population.un.org/wpp/Graphs/Probabilistic/POP/TOT/; Agrawal, *India Connected*, 203–4.

38. *Harivaṃśa* 52.8–53.9 in Parashuram Lakshman Vaidya, ed., vol. 1, 350–5 (Pune: Bhandarkar Oriental Research Institute, 1969). On the succession of puranic narratives of Krishna's childhood, see Daniel H.H. Ingalls,

"The *Harivaṃśa* as a *Mahākāvya*", *Mélanges d'indianisme à la mémoire de Louis Renou* (Paris: Éditions de Boccard, 1968), 381–94.

39. On "world class" branding in a UNESCO context, see Geary, *The Rebirth of Bodh Gaya*, 165–9. As to the eastern bank of the Yamuna, there is reason to believe that this is a special target of Vrindavan's land mafia. There is only so much land in peninsular Vrindavan. The opposite bank of the river is the obvious target for further expansion, just as happened with the building of Noida east of Delhi. No wonder there is speculation on the land.

40. See Chapter 5, note 23.

41. On the complexity of what Bankim achieved in his *Kṛṣṇacaritra*, see Sudipta Kaviraj, *The Unhappy Consciousness*, 72–106, 176–83. The chapter in question is provocatively entitled "The Myth of Praxis".

42. J.S. Hawley, "Krishna's Cosmic Victories", *Journal of the American Academy of Religion* 47:2 (1979), 201–21.

43. This motif has been a favorite in various efforts to elaborate a theology of "Krishna the environmentalist", as Ranchor Prime has called him. See Prime [a.k.a. Ranchor Dasa], "Reviving the Forests of Vṛndāvana", *Back to Godhead* 26 (1992), 24–39, specifically 31.

44. Compare Christina Caron, "Floating Boom Sent to Pacific Garbage Patch to Start Trapping 87,000 Tons of Plastic", *New York Times*, September 10, 2018, A12. Along another gradient, Kurt Andersen, *Fantasyland: How America Went Haywire, A 500-Year History* (New York: Random House, 2017).

45. Ghosh, *The Great Derangement: Climate Change and the Unthinkable* (Gurgaon: Penguin Books, 2016), 182. More broadly, see "*JAS* Round Table on Amitav Ghosh, *The Great Derangement: Climate Change and the Unthinkable*", involving Julia Adeney Thomas, Prasannan Parthasarathi, Rob Linrothe, Fa-Ti Fan, Kenneth Pomeranz, and Ghosh himself, *The Journal of Asian Studies* 75:4 (2016), 929–55.

46. Patrick Henry, "'And I Don't Care What It Is': The Tradition-History of a Civil Religion Proof-Text", *Journal of the American Academy of Religion* 49:1 (1981), 35–47.

Bibliography

Acciavatti, Anthony. *Ganges Water Machine: Designing India's Ancient River.* San Francisco: Applied Research and Design, 2015.

Agrawal, Ravi. *India Connected: How the Smartphone Is Transforming the World's Largest Democracy.* New York and Delhi: Oxford University Press, 2018.

Alley, Kelly D. "Separate Domains: Hinduism, Politics, and Environmental Pollution". In *Hinduism and Ecology: The Intersection of Earth, Sky, and Water,* edited by Christopher Key Chapple and Mary Evelyn Tucker, 355–87. Cambridge: Center for the Study of World Religions, Harvard Divinity School, 2000.

————.*On the Banks of the Gaṅgā: When Wastewater Meets a Sacred River.* Ann Arbor: University of Michigan Press, 2002.

Andersen, Kurt. *Fantasyland: How America Went Haywire, A 500-Year History.* New York: Random House, 2017.

Anonymous. *Prem Mandir Śrī Vṛindāvan Dhām.* Vrindavan: Prem Mandir, n.d. [2012].

Ansal, Kusum. *The Widow of Vrindavan,* translated from the Hindi *Tapasī* by Masooma Ali. New Delhi: HarperCollins, 2004.

Apūrvānand, Svāmī. *ŚrīsāradādevI: Sankshipt Jīvanī tathā Upadeś.* Nagpur: Ramakrishna Math, 1984.

Bachrach, Emilia. "In the Seat of Authority: Debating Temple Spaces and Community Identity in a Vaiṣṇava Sampradāy of Contemporary Gujarat". *Journal of Hindu Studies* 10:1 (2017), 18–46.

Bahura, Gopal Narayan. "Śrī Govinda Gāthā: Service Rendered to Govinda by the Rulers of Āmera and Jayapura". In *Govindadeva, A Dialogue in Stone*, edited by Margaret H. Case, 195–9. New Delhi: Indira Gandhi International Centre for the Arts, 1996.

Bansal, Naresh Chandra. *Caitanya-Sampradāy: Siddhānt aur Sāhitya*. Agra: Vinod Pustak Mandir, 1980.

Bansal, Rashmi. *God's Own Kitchen: The Inspiring Story of Akshaya Patra—a Social Enterprise Run by Monks and CEOs*. Chennai: Westland, 2017.

Barchi, Priyasakhi. "Neo-Vedic Krishna: Fusion of Tradition and Innovation". Unpublished paper, Barnard College, Columbia University, December 2017.

Barik, Satyasundar. "Krishna and Kansa Come Alive for 11 Days Every Year in This Odisha Village". *The Hindu*, January 19, 2019. Available at www.thehindu.com/entertainment/art/krishna-and-kansa-come-alive-for-11-days-every-year-in-this-odisha-village/article26036571.ece.

Barnes, Brook. "Disney Theme Parks Prepare for Liftoff". *New York Times*, November 17, 2018, B1, B4–5.

Barron, Laignee. "Unesco-cide: Does World Heritage Status Do Cities More Harm than Good". *The Guardian*, August 30, 2017.

Belli, Melia. "Monumental Pride: Mayawati's Memorials in Lucknow". *Ars Orientalis* 44 (2014), 85109.

Bender, Courtney. "Religious Horizons in New York's 1920s". Unpublished paper, 2017.

———. "Studying Up: A Brief History of the Religion of the Future". Paper presented to the Department of Religion, Columbia University, February 20, 2018.

Benjamin, Walter. "The Work of Art in the Age of Mechanical Reproduction". In *Illuminations*, edited by Hannah Arendt, translated by Harry Zohn, 217–51. New York: Schocken Books, 2007 [Frankfurt: Suhrkamf Verlag, 1955].

Bhakti Puruṣottama Swami. *Śrī Navadvīpa Parikramā*. Mayapur: Mayapur Media, 2010.

Bhaktisiddhanta Dasa. *Vrindavana, the Crest Jewel of India*. Vrindavan: Prabhupada Institute of Culture, ca. 1990.

Bhakti Vilāsa Swami. *Śrī Bhaktisiddhānta Vaibhava*, 3 vols. Surat: Bhakti Vikas Trust, 2009.

Bhaktivedanta Swami, A.C. "Prabhupāda". *Śrī Vṛndāvana Dhāma as It Is* (Hindi translation: *Śrī Vṛndāvan Dhām Yathārūp*). Vrindavan: Bhaktivedanta Book Trust, 2005.

Bhatia, Varuni. "Finding a Birthplace". *Journal of Vaishnava Studies* 23:1 (2014), 157–88.

———. *Unforgetting Chaitanya: Vaishnavism and Cultures of Devotion in Colonial Bengal*. New York: Oxford University Press, 2017.

Bhūmipati Dāsa. *Śrī Mathurā Māhātmya: The Glories of Mathurā Maṇḍala*. Vrindavan: Rasbihari and Sons, n.d.

Bielo, James S. *Ark Encounter: The Making of a Creationist Theme Park*. New York: New York University Press, 2018.

Bloch, Natalia. "Evicting Heritage: Spatial Cleansing and Cultural Legacy at the Hampi UNESCO Site in India". *Critical Asian Studies* 48:4 (2016), 556–78.

Blurton, T. Richard. *Krishna in the Garden of Assam: The History and Context of a Much-Travelled Textile*. London: The British Museum, 2016.

Borthwick, Jane L. "Come, Labor On". *Pilgrim Hymnal*. Boston: Beacon Press, 1965 [1931].

Brinkley, Douglas. "Thoreau and the Legacy of Wildness". *New York Times Book Review*, July 9, 2017.

Brooks, Charles R. *The Hare Krishnas in India*. Princeton: Princeton University Press, 1989.

Brosius, Christiane. "The Cultural Politics of Transnational Heritage Ritual: Akshardham Cultural Complex in New Delhi". In *Ritual, Heritage, and Identity: The Politics of Culture and Performance in a Globalized World*, edited by Christiane Brosius and Karin M. Polit, 97–125. New Delhi: Routledge, 2011.

Bryant, Edwin F. *The Quest for the Origins of Vedic Culture: The Indo-Aryan Migration Debate*. New York: Oxford University Press, 2001.

Bryant, Kenneth E. and John Stratton Hawley. *Sur's Ocean: Poems from the Early Tradition*. Cambridge: Harvard University Press, 2015.

Brzezinski, Jan K. "Jagat". "Globalized Braj Dham: Pilgrimage and Residence". *Journal of Vaishnava Studies* 27:1 (2018), 53–67.

———. "Bhaktivedanta Marg and the Three Vrindavans". *Vrindavan Today*, March 2, 2016.

Butalia, Pankaj. *Moksha* (English: *Salvation*). London: Vital Films for Channel Four Television, 1993.

Byrne, Denis. "Western Hegemony in Archaeological Heritage Management". *History and Anthropology* 5:2 (1991), 269–76.

———. *Counterheritage: Critical Perspectives on Heritage Conservation in Asia*. London: Routledge, 2014.

Caron, Christina. "Floating Boom Sent to Pacific Garbage Patch to Start Trapping 87,000 Tons of Plastic". *New York Times*, September 10, 2018, A12.

Case, Margaret H. *Seeing Krishna: The Religious World of a Brahman Family in Vrindaban*. New York: Oxford University Press, 2000.

Certeau, Michel de. "Walking in the City". In Certeau, *The Practice of Everyday Life*, 91–110, 218–21. Berkeley: University of California Press, 1984.

Chakravarti, Uma. *Everyday Lives, Everyday Histories: Beyond the Kings and Brahmanas of "Ancient" India*. New Delhi: Tulika Books, 2006.

Chatterjee (Chattopadhyaya), Bankim Chandra. *Krishna-Charitra: Translated from the Bengali and with an Introduction by Pradip Bhattacharya*. Calcutta: M.P. Birla Foundation, 1991.

Chatterji, Tathagata. *Citadels of Glass*. Chennai: Westland, 2015.

Chen, Martha Alter. *Perpetual Mourning: Widowhood in Rural India*. Delhi: Oxford University Press, 2000.

Chetananda, Swami. "Holy Mother's Pilgrimage (August 1886–August 1887)". In *Bodhan Souvenir 2012 … Ma Sarada Kutir*, edited by Swami Animeshananda, 10–17. Vrindavan: Ramakrishna Math and Ramakrishna Mission Sevashrama, 2012.

Chopra, Priya, et al. "Uttar Pradesh Pro-poor Tourism Development Project (P146936): Site Visit to Vrindavan (April 1–3, 2015)". Unpublished paper, The World Bank, April 10, 2015.

Coffey, Diane, and Dean Spears. *Where India Goes: Abandoned Toilets, Stunted Development, and the Costs of Caste*. Noida: HarperCollins, 2017.

Corcoran, Maura. *Vṛndāvana in Vaiṣṇava Literature*. Vrindavan: Vrindavan Research Institute and New Delhi: D.K. Printworld, 1995.

Cox, Harvey. *The Secular City: Secularization and Urbanization in Theological Perspective*. New York: Collier Books, 1965.

Cronon, Willliam. "The Trouble with Wilderness: Or, Getting Back to the Wrong Nature". *Environmental History* 1:1 (1996), 7–28.

Daivīśakti Deveī Dāsī. *Vṛndāvana Parikramā*. Vrindavan: Bhaktivedanta Book Trust, 2017.

Danka, Krisztina. *Rescuing the Sacred River*. New York: Karuna Productions, 2015.

———. *The Stolen River*. New York: Karuna Productions, 2017.

Datta, V.N. *Sati: A Historical, Social, and Philosophical Enquiry into the Hindu Rite of Widow Burning*. Delhi: Manohar, 1988.

Davis, Richard H. "Krishna Enters the Age of Mechanical Reproduction". *Journal of Vaisnava Studies* 21:2 (2013), 31–42.

———. "Henry David Thoreau, Yogi". *Common Knowledge* 24:1 (2018), 56–89. Available at https://doi.org/10.1215/0961754X-4253822.

Deadwyler, William H. "Cleaning House and Cleaning Hearts: Reform and Renewal in ISKCON". In *The Hare Krishna Movement: The Postcharismatic Fate of a Religious Transplant*, edited by Edwin F. Bryant and Maria L. Ekstrand, 149–69. New York: Columbia University Press, 2004.

Deane-Drummond, Celia, Sigurd Bergmann, and Markus Vogt, eds. *Religion in the Anthropocene*. Eugene: Cascade Books, 2017.

Desai, Krishnakant, Sunil Awatramami (Adridharan Das), and Madhu Pandit Das. "The No Change in ISKCON Paradigm". In *The Hare Krishna Movement: The Charismatic Fate of a Religious Transplant*, edited by Edwin F. Bryant and Maria L. Ekstrand, 194–213. New York: Columbia University Press, 2004.

Dhar, Parul Pandya. "Why the Sangh Parivar's Idea of Building a 'Hindu Dham' in Cambodia Is Wrong". *The Wire*, June 16, 2018.

Dhillon, Amrit. "Out with the Old: App-wise Indians Reject Caste and Dowry Traditions". *The Guardian*, July 10, 2018.

Dimock, Jr., Edward C. *The Place of the Hidden Moon: Erotic Mysticism in the Vaiṣṇava-Sahajiyā Cult of Bengal*. Chicago: University of Chicago Press, 1966.

Doron, Assa, and Robin Jeffrey. *Waste of a Nation: Garbage and Growth in India*. Cambridge: Harvard University Press, 2018.

Dove, Michael R. "The Dialectical History of 'Jungle' in Pakistan". *Journal of Anthropological Research* 48 (1992), 231–47.

Durkheim, Émile. *The Elementary Forms of the Religious Life*, translated by Joseph Ward Swain. New York: Free Press, 1965 [1915].

Eaton, Richard. "Temple Desecration and Indo-Muslim States". *Journal of Islamic Studies* 11:3 (2000), 283–319.

Eck, Diana L. *Banaras: City of Light*. New York: Alfred A. Knopf, 1982.

———. *India: A Sacred Geography*. New York: Harmony Books, 2012.

Elison, William. *The Neighborhood of Gods: The Sacred and the Visible at the Margins of Mumbai*. Chicago: University of Chicago Press, 2018.

Entwistle, Alan W. *Braj, Centre of Krishna Pilgrimage*. Groningen: Egbert Forsten, 1987.

———. "The Cult of Krishna-Gopal as a Version of the Pastoral". In *Devotion Divine: Bhakti Traditions from the Regions of India: Studies in Honor of Charlotte Vaudeville*, edited by Diana L. Eck and Françoise Mallison, 73–90. Groningen: Egbert Forsten, 1991.

Esomba, Steve. *The Book of Life, Knowledge, and Self-Confidence*. Lulu.com, June 6, 2012.

Fahy, John. "The Constructive Ambiguities of Vedic Culture in ISKCON Mayapur". *Journal of Hindu Studies* 11:3 (2018), 234–59.

Fareed, Faisal. "In Varanasi, a Plan to Build Corridor from Kashi Vishwanath Temple to River Ganges Sparks Anger". *Scroll.in*, February 10, 2018.

Feldhaus, Anne. *Water and Womanhood: Religious Meanings of Rivers in Maharashtra*. New York: Oxford University Press, 1995.

Foucault, Michel. *Discipline and Punish: The Birth of the Prison*. New York: Vintage, 1995.

Fuller, Jason D. "Bengali Vaishnava Homelands". *Journal of Vaishnava Studies* 18:1 (2009), 39–52.

Geary, David. *The Rebirth of Bodh Gaya: Buddhism and the Making of a World Heritage Site*. Seattle: University of Washington Press, 2017.

Gettleman, Jeffrey, and Hari Kumar. "Millions of Indians Trek to the Ganges, and Modi Chases Their Votes". *New York Times*, February 10, 2019.

Ghosh, Abantika. "The Big Picture". *Indian Express*, July 8, 2018.

Ghosh, Amitav. *The Great Derangement: Climate Change and the Unthinkable*. Gurgaon: Penguin Books, 2016.

Ghosh, Pika. *Temple to Love: Architecture and Devotion in Seventeenth-Century Bengal*. Bloomington: Indiana University Press, 2005.

Gillet, Kit. "Big Debate in Romania Over a Big Cathedral and Its Big Price Tag". *New York Times*, December 4, 2018.

Giri, V. Mohini. *Living Death: Trauma of Widowhood in India*. New Delhi: Gyan Publishing House, 2002.

———. *Deprived Devis: Women's Unequal Status in Society*. New Delhi: Gyan Publishing House, 2006.

———. *Status of Elderly Women in India*. New Delhi: Gyan Publishing House, 2013.

Gold, Ann Grodzins. *Shiptown: Between Rural and Urban North India*. Philadelphia: University of Pennsylvania Press, 2017.

Gold, Daniel. *Provincial Hinduism: Religion and Community in Gwalior City*. New York: Oxford University Press, 2015.

Gonda, Jan. *The Meaning of the Sanskrit Term Dhāman*. Amsterdam: N.V. Noord-Hollandsche Uitgevers Maatshappu, 1967.

Goswami, Aastha. "Songs for Krishna in Autumn: Devotional Music from North India". Interview and performance, Barnard College, Columbia University. New York, October 5, 2018.

Goswami, Shrivatsa. "Gopal Bhatt: Carrier of *Bhakti* to the North". In *Text and Tradition in Early Modern North India*, edited by Tyler Williams, Anshu Malhotra, and John Stratton Hawley, 335–53. Delhi: Oxford University Press, 2018.

Goswami, Shrivatsa, and Robyn Beeche. *Celebrating Krishna*. Vrindavan: Sri Caitanya Prema Samsthana, 2001.

Granoff, Phyllis. "Halāyudha's Prism: The Experience of Religion in Medieval Hymns and Stories". In *Gods, Guardians, and Lovers: Temple Sculptures from North India, A.D. 700–1200*, edited by Vishakha N. Desai and Darielle Mason, 66–93. New York: The Asia Society Galleries and Ahmedabad: Mapin Publishing, 1993.

Green, Nile. *Terrains of Exchange: Religious Economies of Global Islam*. New York: Oxford University Press, 2014.

Growse, Frederic Salmon. *Mathurá: A District Memoir*, 3rd ed. Allahabad: North-Western Provinces and Oudh Government Press, 1883.

Gupta, Moti Lal. *Braj: The Centrum of Indian Culture*. Delhi: Agam Kala Prakashan, 1982.

Gurudas (Roger Siegel). *By His Example: The Wit and Wisdom of His Divine Grace A.C. Bhaktivedanta Prabhupada*, 2nd ed. Vrindavan: ISKCON Library Society, 2013.

Haberman, David L. "On Trial: The Love of the Sixteen Thousand Gopees". *History of Religions* 33:1 (1993), 44–70.

———. *Journey through the Twelve Forests: An Encounter with Krishna*. New York: Oxford University Press, 1994.

———. *The Bhaktirasāmṛtasindhu of Rūpa Gosvāmin*. New Delhi: Indira Gandhi National Centre for the Arts, 2003.

———. *River of Love in an Age of Pollution: The Yamuna River of Northern India*. Berkeley: University of California Press, 2006.

———. "Bhakti as Relationship: Drawing Form and Personality from the Formless". In *Bhakti and Power: Debating India's Religion of the Heart*, edited by John Stratton Hawley, Christian Lee Novetzke, and Swapna Sharma, 134–41. Seattle: University of Washington Press, 2019.

———. *Loving Stones: Making the Impossible Possible in the Worship of Mount Govardhan*. New York: Oxford University Press, 2020.

Habib, Irfan. "Braj Bhūm in Mughal Times". In *Proceedings of the Indian Historical Congress, Seventeenth Session*, edited by Irfan Habib, 297–301. Aligarh: Aligarh Historians Society, 2010–1.

———. "From Arith to Rādhākund: The History of a Braj Village in Mughal Times". *Indian Historical Review* 38 (2011), 211–24.

———. "Dealing with Multiplicity: Mughal Administration in Braj Bhum under Aurangzeb (1659–1707)". *Studies in People's History* 3:2 (2016), 151–64.

Hancock, Mary E. *The Politics of Heritage from Madras to Chennai*. Bloomington: Indiana University Press, 2008.

Handler, Richard. "The 'Ritualization of Ritual' in the Construction of Heritage". In *Ritual, Heritage, and Identity*, edited by Christiane Brosius and Karin M. Polit, 39–54. London: Routledge, 2011.

Hawley, John Stratton. "Krishna's Cosmic Victories". *Journal of the American Academy of Religion* 47:2 (1979), 201–21.

———, in association with Shrivatsa Goswami. *At Play with Krishna: Pilgrimage Dramas from Brindavan*. Princeton: Princeton University Press, 1981.

———. *Krishna, the Butter Thief*. Princeton: Princeton University Press, 1983.

————. *Three Bhakti Voices: Mirabai, Surdas, and Kabir in Their Time and Ours.* Delhi: Oxford University Press, 2005.

————. "The *Bhāgavata-Māhātmya* in Context". In *Patronage and Popularization, Pilgrimage and Procession: Channels of Transcultural Translation and Transmission in Early Modern South Asia. Papers in Honor of Monika Horstmann,* edited by Heidi R.M. Pauwels, 81–100. Wiesbaden: Harrassowitz, 2009.

————. *A Storm of Songs: India and the Idea of the Bhakti Movement.* Cambridge: Harvard University Press, 2015.

————. *Into Sur's Ocean: Poetry, Context, Commentary.* Cambridge: Harvard University Press, 2016.

————. "Bhāgavata Across Boundaries". *Journal of Hindu Studies* 11:1 (2018), 4–20.

————. "Vrindavan and the Drama of Keshi Ghat". In *The Contemporary Hindu Temple: Fragments for a History,* edited by A. Srivasthan, Annapurna Garimella, and Shriya Shridharan, 60–73. Mumbai: Marg Publications, 2019.

————. "The Ideal Real Vrindavan of Jaisingh's Dining Room". In *The Building of Vṛndāvana,* edited by Rembert Lutjeharms and Kiyokazu Okita. Leiden: Brill, forthcoming.

Hawley, John Stratton, and Mark Juergensmeyer. *Songs of the Saints of India.* Delhi: Oxford University Press, 2004 [1988].

Hawley, John Stratton, and Vasudha Narayanan, eds. *The Life of Hinduism.* Berkeley: University of California Press, 2006; Delhi: Aleph Books, 2017.

Hein, Norvin. *The Miracle Plays of Mathurā.* New Haven: Yale University Press, 1972.

"Hema Malini Working on Braj's Water Issues, Creating Funparks". *Vrindavan Today,* Vrindavan, May 13, 2018.

Henry, Patrick. "'And I Don't Care What It Is': The Tradition-History of a Civil Religion Proof-Text". *Journal of the American Academy of Religion* 49:1 (1981), 35–47.

"High Court Declares Yamuna Plain as 'No Construction Zone'". *Vrindavan Today,* Vrindavan, December 24, 2017.

Holdrege, Barbara A. *Bhakti and Embodiment: Fashioning Divine Bodies and Devotional Bodies in Kṛṣṇa Bhakti.* New York: Routledge, 2015.

————. "*Vraja-Dhāman*". In *The Bhāgavata Purāṇa: Sacred Text and Living Tradition,* edited by Ravi M. Gupta and Kenneth R. Valpey, 91–116. New York: Columbia University Press, 2013.

————. "*Vraja-Dhāman* as a Meditation Maṇḍala: Perspectives from the Vṛndāvana-Māhātmya". *Journal of Vaishnava Studies* 27:1 (2018), 69–95.

Horstmann, Monika. *Visions of Kingship in the Twilight of Mughal Rule.* Amsterdam: Royal Netherlands Academy of Arts and Sciences, 2006.

Holdrege, Barbara A., and Karen Pechilis, eds. *Refiguring the Body: Embodiment in South Asian Religions.* Albany: State University of New York Press, 2016.

Hopkins, Steven P. *The Flight of Love: A Messenger Poem of Medieval South India by Veṅkaṭanātha.* New York: Oxford University Press, 2016.

Hoque, Ashraf, and Lucia Michelutti. "Brushing with Organized Crime and Democracy: The Art of Making Do in South Asia". *The Journal of Asian Studies* 77:4 (2018), 991–1011.

Howley, John (Jada Bharata Dasa). *Vrindavana and Braja Mandala: A Practical Guide.* Vrindavan: Bhaktivedanta Book Trust, 1997.

"HRIDAY Scheme Development Assessed". *Vrindavan Today,* Vrindavan, January 14, 2018.

Huber, Toni. *The Holy Land Reborn: Pilgrimage and the Tibetan Reinvention of Buddhist India.* Chicago: University of Chicago Press, 2008.

Hubner, John. *Monkey on a Stick: Murder, Madness, and the Hare Krishnas.* San Diego: Harcourt Brace Jovanovich, 1988.

Hudson, D. Dennis. "Vraja among the Tamils". *Journal of Vaishnava Studies* 3:1 (1994), 113–40.

———. *Krishna's Mandala: Bhagavata Religion and Beyond,* edited by John Stratton Hawley. Delhi: Oxford University Press, 2010.

Imam, Ekwal, H.S.A. Yahya, and Iqbal Malik. "A Successful Mass Translocation of Commensal Rhesus Monkeys *Macaca mulatta* in Vrindaban, India". *Oryx* 36:1 (2002), 87–93.

Ingalls, Daniel H.H. "The *Harivaṃśa* as a *Mahākāvya*". In *Mélanges d'indianisme à la mémoire de Louis Renou,* 381–94. Paris: Éditions de Boccard, 1968.

Jain, Kajri. *Gods in the Bazaar: The Economies of Indian Calendar Art.* Durham: Duke University Press, 2007.

———. "Post-Reform India's Automotive-Iconic-Cement Assemblages: Uneven Globality, Territorial Spectacle, and Iconic Exhibition Value". *Identities: Global Studies in Culture and Power,* May 8, 2015, 1–18.

———. "Gods in the Time of Automobility". *Current Anthropology* 58: supplement 15 (2017), accessed November 28, 2016.

———. "When the Gods Emerge from the Temples: Iconic Exhibition Value and Democratic Publicness in India". Lecture, Institute for Religion and Culture in in Public Life, Columbia University, October 9, 2018.

Jain, Shruti. "Twelve Years after Gangajal Project, Agra Still Waits for Clean Drinking Water". *The Wire,* June 24, 2017.

Kakar, Sudhir. *The Inner World: A Psycho-analytic Study of Childhood and Society in India,* 2nd ed. Delhi: Oxford University Press, 1981.

Kakar, Sudhir, and John M. Ross. *Tales of Love, Sex, and Danger*. Delhi: Oxford University Press, 1986.

Kaviraj, Sudipta. *The Unhappy Consciousness: Bankim Chandattopadhyaya and the Formation of Nationalist Discourse in India*. Delhi: Oxford University Press, 1998.

Kinnard, Jacob N. *Places in Motion: The Fluid Identities of Temples, Images, and Pilgrims*. New York: Oxford University Press, 2014.

Kirshenblatt-Gimblett, Barbara. *Destination Culture: Tourism, Museums, and Heritage*. Berkeley: University of California Press, 1998.

———. "Intangible Heritage as Metacultural Production". *Museum International* 56:1–2 (2004), 52–65.

Klostermaier, Klaus. *In the Paradise of Krishna: Hindu and Christian Seekers*, translated by Antonia Fonseca from *Christ und Hindu in Vrindaban*. Köln: Jakob Hegner, 1968. Philadelphia: Westminster, 1969.

Kripalu Ji Maharaj [attributed]. *Prem Mandir: A Tribute to Divine Love*. New Delhi: Radha Govind Samiti, 2013.

Kumar, Hari. "Massive March for Yamuna River Nears Delhi". *New York Times*, March 11, 2013.

Kumar, Samrat Schmiem. "Sacred Modernity and Its Fragments: Space, Environment, and Life-worlds in the Indian Temple Town Vrindavan". PhD dissertation, University of Oslo, 2014.

———. *Vrindavan's Encounter with Modernity: Changing Environment and Life-worlds in an Indian Temple Town*. Berlin: LIT Verlag, 2019.

Kumar, Samrat Schmiem, and Elida Jacobsen. "Heritage and Environment: Visions of Past and Future in the Indian Temple Town of Vrindavan". *Peaceworks* 7:1 (2017), 116–30.

Lal, Malashri, and Namita Gokhale, eds. *Finding Radha: The Quest for Love*. Gurgaon: Penguin, 2018.

"Land Use Scams Involving District Officers Comes [sic] to Light". *Vrindavan Today*, Vrindavan, June 6, 2018.

Lindsey, Robert. "Divine Encounter, Miracles, and Christianity: Religious Experience in Paramahamsa Vishwananda's *Bhakti Marga* Movement". Unpublished paper, Columbia University, 2016.

Lofton, Kathryn. *Oprah: The Gospel of an Icon*. Berkeley: University of California Press, 2011.

Longfellow, Henry Wadsworth. *Longfellow's Evangeline*. Boston: Houghton, Mifflin & Co., 1883 [1847].

Lucia, Amanda. "Guru Sex: Charisma, Proxemic Desire, and the Haptic Logics of the Guru–Disciple Relationship". *Journal of the American Academy of Religion* 86:4 (2018), 953–88.

Lutgendorf, Philip. "My Hanuman Is Bigger Than Yours". *History of Religions* 33:3 (1994), 211–45.

————. "Imagining Ayodhyā: Utopia and Its Shadows in a Hindu Landscape". *International Journal of Hindu Studies* 1:1 (1997), 19–54.

————. "City, Forest, and Cosmos: Ecological Perspectives from the Sanskrit Epics". In *Hinduism and Ecology: The Intersection of Earth, Sky, and Water*, edited by Christopher Key Chapple and Mary Evelyn Tucker, 269–87. Cambridge: Center for the Study of World Religions, Harvard Divinity School, 2000.

Lutjeharms, Rembert. *A Vaiṣṇava Poet in Early Modern Bengal: Kavikarṇapura's "Splendor of Speech"*. Oxford: Oxford University Press, 2018.

Madhu Pandit Dasa, Chanchapathi Dasa, Bhaktilata Devi Dasi, and Prashanth Kadkol. *Reaching to the Sky*. Bangalore: International Society for Krishna Consciousness, 2015.

Majumdar, Bimanbihari. *Kṛṣṇa in History and Legend*. Calcutta: University of Calcutta, 1969.

Mallet, Victor. *River of Life, River of Death: The Ganges and India's Future*. Delhi: Oxford University Press, 2017.

Manuel, Peter. "Syncretism and Adaptation in Rasiya, a Braj Folksong Genre". *Journal of Vaishnava Studies* 3:1 (1994), 33–60.

Martin, Nicholas, and Lucia Michelutti. "Protection Rackets and Party Machines: Comparative Ethnographies of 'Mafia Raj' in North India". *Asian Journal of Social Science* 45:5 (2017), 692–722.

Mason, David V. *Theatre and Religion on Krishna's Stage*. New York: Palgrave Macmillan, 2009.

Masson, J.L. "The Childhood of Kṛṣṇa: Some Psychoanalytic Observations". *Journal of the American Oriental Society* 94:4 (1974), 454–9.

"Mathurā-Vṛndāvan meṅ Yamunā Kināre 200 Mīṭar tak Nirmāṇ par Rok: Galat Halaphnāmā Dene ke Māmle meṅ Jalnigam ke Pariyojanā Prabandhak par Girī Gāj". *Amar Ujālā*, Allahabad, December 23, 2017.

Mayaram, Shail, ed. *The Other Global City*. New York and London: Routledge, 2008.

McDowall, Anna, and Arvind Sharma, eds. *Vignettes of Vrindavan*. New Delhi: Books & Books, 1987.

McKean, Lise. *Divine Enterprise: Gurus and the Hindu Nationalist Movement*. Chicago: University of Chicago Press, 1996.

Michell, George. "The Missing Sanctuary". In *Govindadeva: A Dialogue in Stone*, edited by Margaret H. Case, 115–22. New Delhi: Indira Gandhi National Centre for the Arts, 1996.

————. *Late Temple Architecture of India 15th to 19th Centuries: Continuities, Revivals, Appropriations, and Innovations*. Delhi: Oxford University Press, 2015.

Miller, Barbara Stoler. *Love Song of the Dark Lord: Jayadeva's Gītagovinda*. New York: Columbia University Press, 1977.

Mītal, Prabhudayāl. *Braj kā Sāṅskṛtik Itihās*, parts 1–2. Delhi: Rājkamal Prakāśan, 1966.

———. *Braj ke Dharma-Sampradāyoṅ kā Itihās*. Delhi: National Publications House, 1968.

Mohan, Urmila. "The 'Temple of the Vedic Planetarium' as Mission, Monument, and Memorial". *Jugaad: A Material Religions Project*, September 30, 2014.

"Monkey Bites Up by 50% in Last 3 Months". *Times of India*, Agra, November 17, 2018.

"Monkey Enters House, Snatches Infant from Mom, Mauls Him to Death in Agra". *Times of India*, Agra, November 14, 2018.

Moodie, Deonnie. *The Making of a Modern Temple and a Hindu City: Kālīghāṭ and Kolkata*. New York: Oxford University Press, 2018.

Mukherjee, Tarapada, and Irfan Habib. "Akbar and the Temples of Mathura and Its Environs". In *Proceedings of the Indian History Congress*, 48th Session, 234–50. Panaji: Goa University, 1988.

———. "The Mughal Administration and the Temples of Vrindavan during the Reigns of Jahangir and Shahjahan". In *Proceedings of the Indian History Congress*, 49th Session, 287–300. Dharwad: Karnataka University, 1989.

———. "Land Rights in the Reign of Akbar: The Evidence of the Sale-Deeds of Vrindaban and Aritha". In *Proceedings of the Indian History Congress*, 236–55. Gorakhpur: Gorakhpur University, 1990.

Mulji, Karsandas. *History of the Sect of Maharajas, or Vallabhacharyas, in Western India*. London: Trubner, 1865.

Nanda, Meera. *The God Market: How Globalization Is Making India More Hindu*. New York: Monthly Review Press, 2009.

Nangia, Tarun. "Sadhvi Ritambhara Makes Her Own World". *Indian Express*, June 19, 2011.

Nash, Roderick Frazier. *Wilderness and the American Mind*, 5th ed. New Haven: Yale University Press, 2014 [1967].

"New Mathura Plan Geared for Tourism; No Mention of Sewage, Waste Management". *Vrindavan Today*, Vrindavan, June 9, 2017.

Nikhilananda, Swami. *Holy Mother: Being the Life of Sri Sarada Devi, Wife of Sri Ramakrishna and Helpmate in His Mission*. London: Allen & Unwin, 1962.

"Nirala", Suryakant Tripati. *Anāmikā*. Allahabad: Bhāratī Bhaṇḍār, 1963.

Oldenberg, Veena Talwar. *Gurgaon: From Mythic Village to Millennium City*. Noida: HarperCollins, 2018.

Ong, Aihwa. "Hyperbuilding: Spectacle, Speculation, and the Hyperspace of Sovereignty". In *Worlding Cities*, edited by Ananya Roy and Aihwa Ong, 205–26. Chichester: WileyBlackwell, 2011.

Orians, George H., and Judith H. Heerwagen. "Evolved Responses to Landscapes". In *The Adapted Mind: Evolutionary Psychology and the Generation of Culture*, edited by Jerome H. Barkow, Leda Cosmides, and John Tooby, 555–79. New York: Oxford University Press, 1992.

Owens, Bruce McCoy. "Monumentality, Identity, and the State: Local Practice, World Heritage, and Heterotopia at Swayambhu, Nepal". *Anthropological Quarterly* 75:2 (2002), 269–316.

Packert, Cynthia. *The Art of Loving Krishna: Ornamentation and Devotion*. Bloomington: Indiana University Press, 2010.

Padmalochan Das. *Cintamani-Dhama (A Guide to Vrindavan)*. Juhu: Bhaktivdeanta Book Trust, n.d.

Paramadvaiti Swami. *Healthy Sacred Water: Yamuna & Ganga*. Vrindavan: Vrindavan Act Now (VAN), 2010.

Parthasarathy, R. *The Tale of an Anklet, an Epic of South India: The Cilappatikāram of Iḷaṅkō Aṭikaḷ*. New York: Columbia University Press, 1993.

Pauwels, Heidi R.M. "Imagining Religious Communities in the Sixteenth Century: Harirām Vyās and the Haritrayī". *International Journal of Hindu Studies* 13 (2009), 143–161.

———. "Hagiography and Community Formation: The Case of a Lost Community of Sixteenth-Century Vrindāvan". *Journal of Hindu Studies* 3:1 (2010), 53–90.

Pauwels, Heidi, and Emilia Bachrach. "Aurangzeb as Iconoclast: Vaishnava Accounts of the Krishna Images' Exodus from Braj". *Journal of the Royal Asiatic Society* 28:3 (2018), 485–508.

Pinch, William R. *Warrior Ascetics and Indian Empires*. Cambridge: Cambridge University Press, 2006.

"Pipeline to Bring Ganga Water to the Yamuna Declared Successful". *Vrindavan Today*, Vrindavan, January 25, 2018.

Prime, Ranchor. "Reviving the Forests of Vṛndāvana". *Back to Godhead* 26 (1992), 24–39.

———. "Restoring the Forests of Braj". *Vrindavan Today*, Vrindavan, July 22, 2014.

Rademacher, Anne, and K. Shivaramakrishnan, eds. *Ecologies of Urbanism in India: Metropolitan Civility and Sustainability*. Hong Kong: Hong Kong Scholarship Online, 2014 [print 2013].

Ray, Sugata. *Climate Change and the Art of Devotion: Geoaesthetics in the Land of Krishna, 1550–1850*. Seattle: University of Washington Press, 2019.

Richardson, E. Allen. *Seeing Krishna in America: The Hindu Bhakti Tradition of Vallabhacharya in India and Its Movement to the West*. Jefferson, NC: McFarland and Co., 2014.

Ritambhara, Sadhvi [attributed]. *Vatsalya Gram (A Village of Maternal Love)*. Delhi: Param Shakti Peeth, n.d.

———. *Yaśodā Bhāv: Vātsalya Grām kī Mūl Preraṇā*. New Delhi: Vātsalya Prakāśan, 2013.

Robison, Claire C. "A Return to a Place One Has Not Been: ISKCON and the Rhetoric of *Bhakti* Revivalism in Mumbai". Unpublished paper, November, 2018.

Roy, Ananya. "The Blockade of the World-Class City". In *Worlding Cities*, edited by Ananya Roy and Aihwa Ong, 259–78. Chichester: WileyBlackwell, 2011.

Roy, Manisha. *Bengali Women*. Chicago: University of Chicago Press, 1972.

Rubin, David. *A Season on the Earth*. New York: Columbia University Press, 1976.

"Rūpkalā", Sitārāmśaraṇ Bhagavān Prasād, ed. *Śrī Bhaktamāl* with the *Bhaktirasabodhinī* commentary of Priyādās. Lucknow: Tejkumār Press, 1969 [1910].

Sachdev, Vibhuti. *Building Jaipur: The Making of an Indian City*. Delhi and New York: Oxford University Press, 2002.

"Saints' Lives in Danger as Land Mafias Eye Ashrams". *Vrindavan Today*, Vrindavan, June 6, 2018.

Sanford, A. Whitney. "Shifting the Center: Yakṣas on the Margins of Contemporary Practice". *Journal of the American Academy of Religion* 73:1 (2005), 89–110.

Sarbadhikary, Sukanya. *The Place of Devotion: Siting and Experiencing Divinity in Bengal-Vaishnavism*. Berkeley: University of California Press, 2015.

Satya Nārāyaṇa Dāsa and Kuṇḍalī Dāsa. *In Vaikuṇṭha Not Even the Leaves Fall: A Treatise on the Bondage of the Jīva*. Vrindavan: Jiva Institute of Vaisnava Studies, 1994.

Schultz, Kai. "A Sanctuary for India's Abused and Exiled Widows." *New York Times*, August 27, 2019, A10, https://www.nytimes.com/2019/08/27/world/asia/india-women-widows.html.

Scott, J. Barton. *Spiritual Despots: Modern Hinduism and the Genealogies of Self-Rule*. Chicago: University of Chicago Press, 2016.

Searle, Llerena Guiu. *Landscapes of Accumulation: Real Estate and the Neoliberal Imagination in Contemporary India*. Chicago: University of Chicago Press, 2016; Delhi: Primus Books, 2017.

Sebastian, Rodney. "Constructing the Manipuri *Rāslīlās*: Agency, Power, and Consensus". Paper delivered to the American Academy of Religion, Denver, November 18, 2018.

"Cultural Fusion in a Religious Dance Drama: Building the Sacred Body in the Manipuri *Rāslīlās*". PhD dissertation, University of Florida, 2019.

Semple, Kirk. "Virgin of Guadalupe Is 'No. 1 Mother' in Mexico, a Binding Force across Divides". *New York Times*, December 15, 2018.

Sharan, Awadhendra. *In the City, Out of Place: Nuisance, Pollution, and Dwelling in Delhi c. 1850–2000*. Delhi: Oxford University Press, 2014.

———. "A River and the Riverfront: Delhi's Yamuna as an In-Between Space". *City, Culture and Society* 7 (2016), 267–73.

———. "The Ganges as an Urban Sink: Urban Waste and River Flow in Colonial India in the Nineteenth Century". In *Rivers Lost, Rivers Regained: Rethinking City-River Relations*, edited by Martin Knoll, Uwe Lübken, and Dieter Schott, 200–215, 374–9. Pittsburgh: University of Pittsburgh Press, 2017.

Shatkin, Gavin. "Planning Privatopolis: Representation and Contestation in the Development of Urban Integrated Mega-Projects". In *Worlding Cities: Asian Experiments and the Art of Being Global*, edited by Ananya Roy and Aihwa Ong, 77–97. Chichester: WileyBlackwell, 2011.

Sheikh, Fazal. *Moksha*. Göttingen: Steidl, 2005.

Shodhan, Amrita. *A Question of Community: Religious Groups and Colonial Law*. Kolkata: Samya, 2001.

Shulman, David. *More than Real: A History of the Imagination in South India*. Cambridge: Harvard University Press, 2012.

Singh, Kavita. "Temple of Eternal Return: The Swāminārāyan Akshardhām Complex in Delhi". *Artibus Asiae* 70:1 (2010), 47–75.

Singh, Sanjay. "Kashi Vishwanah Pathway: Over 100 Houses to Be Demolished, Rehabilitation in Ramnagar". *Economic Times*, May 14, 2018.

Slater, Joanna. "How Narendra Modi Is Remaking Hinduism's Holiest City—and India in the Process". *Washington Post*, May 27, 2019.

Smith, Jonathan Z. *To Take Place: Toward Theory in Ritual*. Chicago: University of Chicago Press, 1987.

Snell, Rupert. "The Nikuñja as Sacred Space in Poetry of the Rādhāvallabhī Tradition". *Journal of Vaishnava Studies* 7:1 (1998), 63–84.

Srinivas, Tulasi. *The Cow in the Elevator: An Anthropology of Wonder*. Durham: Duke University Press, 2018.

Srivastava, Sanjay. *Entangled Urbanism: Slum, Gated Community, and Shopping Mall in Delhi and Gurgaon*. Delhi: Oxford University Press, 2015.

Srivathsan, A. "Varanasi, by Design: Vishwananath Dham and the Politics of Change". *The Hindu*, March 23–4, 2019.

Stewart, Tony K. *The Final Word: The Caitanya Caritāmṛta and the Grammar of Religious Tradition*. New York: Oxford University Press, 2010.

Stoker, Valerie. *Polemics and Patronage in the City of Victory: Vyāsatīrtha, Hindu Sectarianusm, and the Sixteenth-Century Vijayanagara Court*. Berkeley: University of California Press, 2016.

Sullivan, Bruce M. "Theology and Ecology in the Birthplace of Kṛṣṇa". In *Purifying the Earthly Body of God: Religion and Ecology in Hindu India*, edited by Lance E. Nelson. Albany: State University of New York Press, 1998.

Taneja, Anand Vivek. *Jinnealogy: Time, Islam, and Ecological Thought in the Medieval Ruins of Delhi*. Stanford: Stanford University Press, 2018.

Taylor, McComas. *Seven Days of Nectar: Contemporary Oral Performance of the Bhāgavatapurāṇa*. New York: Oxford University Press, 2016.

Thakur, Nalini. "The Building of Govindadeva" with photographs by Robyn Beeche. In *Govindadeva: A Dialogue in Stone*, edited by Margaret H. Case, 11–68. New Delhi: Indira Gandhi National Centre for the Arts, 1996.

Thakur, Nalini. "The Indian Cultural Landscape: Protecting and Managing the Physical to the Metaphysical Values". In *Managing Culture Landscapes*, edited by Ken Taylor and Jane L. Lennon, 164–72. London and New York: Routledge, 2012.

———, with photographs by Robyn Beeche. "The Building of Govindadeva". In *Govindadeva: A Dialogue in Stone*, edited by Margaret H. Case, 11–68. New Delhi: Indira Gandhi National Centre for the Arts, 1996.

Thapar, Romila. *Indian Cultures as Heritage: Contemporary Pasts*. Delhi: Aleph Books, 2018.

Thomas, Julia Adeney, Prasannan Parthasarathi, Rob Linrothe, Fa-Ti Fan, Kenneth Pomeranz, and Amitav Ghosh. "*JAS* Round Table on Amitav Ghosh, *The Great Derangement: Climate Change and the Unthinkable*". The *Journal of Asian Studies* 75:4 (2016), 929–55.

Thomases, Drew. "Making Pushkar Paradise: Hindu Ritualization and the Environment". *International Journal of Hindu Studies Making Pushkar* 21:2 (2017), 187–210.

———. *Guest Is God: Pilgrimage, Tourism, and Making Paradise in India*. New York: Oxford University Press, 2019.

Thoreau, Henry David. *Excursions*. Boston: Ticknor and Fields, 1864.

Trischler, Helmuth. "The Anthropocene: A Challenge for the History of Science, Technology, and the Environment". *N.T.M.* 24 (2016), 309–35.

Truschke, Audrey. *Aurangzeb: The Man and the Myth*. Gurgaon: Viking, 2017.

Turner, Frederick Jackson, with commentary by John Mack Faragher. *Rereading Frederick Jackson Turner: "The Significance of the Frontier in American History", and Other Essays*. New Haven: Yale University Press, 1998.

Turner, Victor. *The Ritual Process: Structure and Anti-Structure*. Chicago: Aldine, 1969.

———. "The Center Out There: Pilgrim's Goal". *History of Religions* 12:3 (1973), 191–230.

Tweed, Thomas A. *Crossing and Dwelling: A Theory of Religion*. Cambridge: Harvard University Press, 2006.

Vaidya, Parashuram Lakshman, ed. *Harivaṃśa*, vol. 1. Pune: Bhandarkar Oriental Research Institute, 1969.

Vajpeyi, Ananya. "Our House of Love". Available at http://indianculturalforum. in/2017/06/22.

Van der Kooij, Arjen, and Ramon Dekkers. *Doorway to Eternity: Celebrating the Land of Krishna*. San Rafael: Mandala Publishing, 2003.

van der Veer, Peter. *The Value of Comparison*. Durham: Duke University Press, 2016.

Vanita, Ruth. *Love's Rite: Same-Sex Marriage in India and the West*. Delhi: Penguin, 2005.

Varma, Rashmi. *The Postcolonial City and Its Subjects: London, Nairobi, Bombay*. New York and London: Routledge, 2012.

Varsana Swami, *Appreciating New Vrindaban-Dhama: Her Beauty and Glory, Message and Grace*. N.p.: Moontower Publications, 2018.

Vātsalya Nirjhar. October 2016 and June 2017.

Vaudeville, Charlotte. "Braj, Lost and Found". *Indo-Iranian Journal* 18:3–4 (1976), 195–213.

Venkatesan, Archana. *The Secret Garland: Āṇṭāḷ's Tiruppāvai and Nācciyār Tirumoḻi*. New York: Oxford University Press, 2010.

Venturi, Robert, Denise Scott Brown, and Steven Izenour. *Learning from Las Vegas: The Forgotten Symbolism of Architectural Form*. Cambridge: MIT Press, 1977.

Vishwananda, Paramahamsa [attributed]. *Giridhari, the Uplifter of Hearts: A Selection of 108 Insights from Paramahamsa Vishwananda*. Springen: BhaktiMarga Publications, 2016.

Wadley, Susan S. "No Longer a Wife: Widows in Rural North India". In *From the Margins of Hindu Marriage; Essays on Gender, Religion, and Culture*, edited by Lindsey Harlan and Paul B. Courtright. New York: Oxford University Press, 1995.

Weber, Max. *The Protestant Ethic and the Spirit of Capitalism*, translated by Talcott Parsons from *Gesammelte Aufsätze zur Religionssoziologie*, 1920–1. London: Allen & Unwin, 1930.

Westra, Mirjam. "Kṛṣṇa Approaches Rādhā and Her Confidante in a Garden with Trees, Playful Monkeys, and Glorious Blue Peacocks (1620–1640)". *Aziatische Kunst* 48:1 (2018), 94–101.

Whitmore, Luke. *Mountain, Water, Rock, God: Understanding Kedarnath in the Twenty-First Century*. Berkeley: University of California Press, 2018.

Williams, Richard David. "Krishna's Neglected Responsibilities: Religious Devotion and Social Critique in Eighteenth-Century North India". *Modern Asian Studies* 50:5 (2016), 1403–40.

————. "A Theology of Feeling: The Radhavallabhi Monsoon in the Eighteenth Century". In *Monsoon Feelings: A History of the Emotions in the Rain*, edited by Imke Rajamani, Magrit Pernau, and Katherine Butler Schofield, 71–96. New Delhi: Niyogi Books, 2018.

Wilson, E.O. *The Creation: An Appeal to Save Life on Earth*. New York: W.W. Norton, 2006.

Winfrey, Oprah. "Oprah in India". In "Oprah's Next Chapter". Available at www.youtube.com/watch?v=Y814cP3IB1s, www.youtube.com/watch?v=aBhpng2NzVc. Accessed July 28, 2018.

Yadav, Leena. *Parched*, produced by Ajay Devgn. Mumbai: Ajay Devgn Ffilms, 2015; released September 23, 2016.

Zimmermann, Francis. *The Jungle and the Aroma of Meat: An Ecological Theme in Hindu Medicine*. Berkeley: University of California Press, 1987.

Index

About the Author

As a boy Jack Hawley loved to study the encyclopedia, but maps, wherever they emerged, were even better. Back in the 1940s and 1950s there was a great deal of pink on world maps—sign of the British Empire—but soon the pink began to shrink. Citizens of India played a major role in making that happen.

If maps were great, the globe was better—three dimensions, round, and you could twirl the sphere at will. At 9 or 10 Jack began to wonder what it would have been like if he'd been born on the other side of the globe. How would the world have looked from that perspective? Surely very different from his own. He put one finger on Chicago, near his home at the time, and tried to place another finger, from another hand, on exactly the opposite spot on the globe—way down under, somewhere near the base, and totally invisible to Illinois. There his invisible twin must be hiding. Was it Thailand? China? His finger tended to slip. Maybe, in the end, it was India.

Thirty years later Jack went to take a look, and he's been coming back to India ever since. What could be better than talking with the driver of a three-wheeler in Delhi or Vrindavan? Best of all, sharing a joke in Hindi. Meanwhile, after the US immigration laws changed, many Indians headed the opposite direction, and some of their children—or they themselves—wandering into Jack's classes in New York. Thus the globe keeps turning.

Jack's wife, Laura Shapiro, is a food historian—the author, among other books, of *What She Ate: Six Remarkable Women and the Food That Tells Their Stories* (2017). Their daughter, Nell Shapiro Hawley, is a Sanskritist and student of world literature. She and Sohini Pillai have edited *Many Mahabharatas* (2020), a volume nearly as epic as its name.